Endgame 1758

A. J. B. JOHNSTON

Endgame
1758

The Promise,
the Glory, and
the Despair of
Louisbourg's
Last Decade

Cape Breton University Press
Sydney, Nova Scotia

Cape Breton University Press recog-
nizes the support of the Province of
Nova Scotia, through the Department
of Tourism, Culture and Heritage.
We are pleased to work in partnership
with the Culture Division to develop
and promote our cultural
resources for
Nova Scotians.

We acknowledge the support of the
Canada Council for the Arts for our
publishing program.

Library and Archives Canada
Cataloguing in Publication

Johnston, A. J. B.

Endgame 1758 : the promise, the glory,
and the despair of Louisbourg's last
decade / A.J.B. Johnston.

Includes bibliographical references and
index.

ISBN 978-1-897009-20-8

1. Louisbourg (N.S.)—History—Siege,
1758. 2. Canada—History—1713–1763
(New France).   I. Title.

FC2349.L6J62 2008   971.6'955
C2007-904266-x

For Colin, Michael, and Mark

Contents

List of Illustrations | *viii*
List of Maps | *viii*
Acknowledgments | *ix*
Terminology and Dates | *x*

PROLOGUE: The Book Ahead | *1*
CHAPTER 1. Opening Moves, 1749 | *23*
CHAPTER 2. Middle Game, 1750–1755 | *46*
CHAPTER 3. The Match Heightens, 1756–1757 | *88*
CHAPTER 4. Beginning of the End, Early 1758 | *148*
CHAPTER 5. This Time for Real, June 1–7, 1758 | *184*
CHAPTER 6. Attack and Defend, June 8–July 27, 1758 | *207*
CHAPTER 7. Winner Take All | *273*

APPENDIX 1: French Ships to Louisbourg, 1758 | *291*
APPENDIX 2: British Ships at Louisbourg, 1758 | *292*
APPENDIX 3: French Land Forces at Louisbourg, 1758 | *294*
APPENDIX 4: British Land Forces at Louisbourg, 1758 | *295*

Notes | *297*
Bibliography | *337*
Index | *351*

Illustrations

1. Île Royale (Cape Breton Island) | *xi*
2. French Stronghold | *xii*
3. British Rival | *34*
4. Vaudreuil's Map, 1755 | *93*
5. Preparations Ashore, 1757 | *129*
6. Naval Standoff, 1757 | *133*
7. Lay of the Land | *205*
8. The Assault Landing | *208*
9. Coastline and Camps | *231*
10. British at Lighthouse Point, June 1758 | *234*
11. Town under Siege | *239*
12. The Besiegers' Perspective | *247*
13. *Prudent* Ablaze, *Bienfaisant* Captured, July 26 | *263*

List of Maps

1. Military Presence, ca. 1753 | *54*
2. Acadian Settlements before 1755 | *56*
3. Louisbourg, 1758 | *203*

Acknowledgments

I would like to thank the following individuals for their assistance in the preparation of this book: B. A. Balcom, Charles Burke, René Chartrand, Elisabeth Demers, Kenneth Donovan, Bruce Fry, Heather Gillis, Mike Hunter, Eric Krause, Yvon LeBlanc, Earle Lockerby, Heather Lundine, William Newbigging, Bill O'Shea, Lewis Parker, John Rhodehamel, Judith-Marie Romard, Bernadette Samson, Miriam Walls, Barbara Wojhoski, and Joeth Zucco, as well as the anonymous referees for the book at the manuscript stage.

Several institutions provided access to information and/or illustrations, as will be noted in the illustration captions. Thanks go to the Huntington Library, Art Collections and Botanical Gardens, in San Marino, California, for allowing me to look at, and later to cite extracts from, Jeffery Amherst's speech to the troops while they were floating off Louisbourg in June 1758. I am equally appreciative of the William L. Clements Library at the University of Michigan for allowing me to reproduce two crucial maps from the British campaign of 1758. The Bibliothèque nationale de Paris and the Archives de la Marine in France authorized the reproduction of two plans relating to the 1757 campaign; and the National Archives of Canada, the Library of Congress in Washington DC, and the Royal Artillery Institution in England gave permission to reproduce one illustration each. The Fortress of Louisbourg National Historic Site kindly allowed me to reproduce five illustrations in their holdings.

Terminology, Dates, and Translations

The reader will encounter both Mi'kmaq and Mi'kmaw in this text. Mi'kmaq is the spelling used when the people as a whole are being described. Mi'kmaw refers to a single person, and it is the adjectival form.

All dates are presented according to the Gregorian calendar, which is the system in use today. Prior to 1752 Great Britain and its colonies followed the Julian calendar. By the eighteenth century there was an eleven-day difference between the two systems of recording time. This meant that the same day had different dates in the records of French or British citizens. For example, what was July 1 in London was July 12 in Paris. The British finally switched to the Gregorian calendar in 1752.

Unless otherwise noted, all translations from the French are mine.

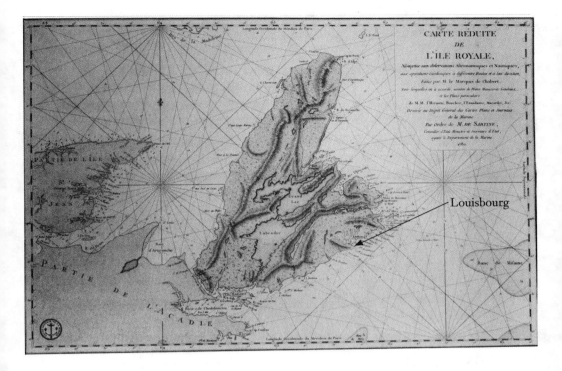

Louisbourg

FIGURE 1. **Île Royale (Cape Breton Island)**

Though the map was produced in 1780, it shows the geographical setting of Île Royale (Cape Breton Island), the major French colony in Atlantic Canada during the period 1749–58. The concentration of placenames on the eastern coast of the island illustrates which areas were of greatest interest to French fishers, colonists, and military officers. As can be seen, Louisbourg was located at the approximate midpoint of the various settled harbors. What the cartographer identified as "Partie de l'Acadie" was in British eyes mainland Nova Scotia; "Île St. Jean" is today Prince Edward Island. *Courtesy of Parks Canada, Fortress of Louisbourg, National Historic Site of Canada, Photo Number: 2000 R 01 09.*

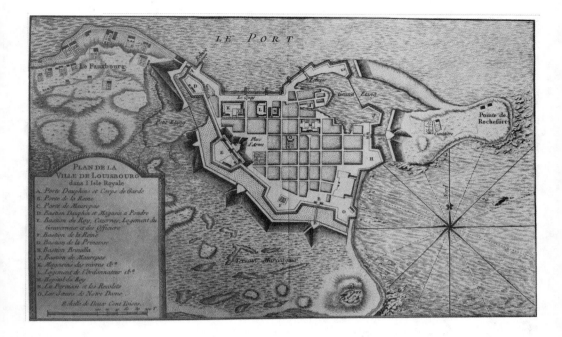

FIGURE 2. **French Stronghold**

Originally settled in 1713, Louisbourg became a fully enclosed fortified town in the early 1740s. The plan above depicts the town and its interior streets and blocks as they appeared before the French stronghold fell to an army of New Englanders in 1745. Neither plan reveals the many private houses, warehouses, fences, and gardens. The plan at right dates from after 1758 and shows the fortifications as they stood at the time. Two new defenses added during the 1750s are the demi-lune beside the Princess Demi-Bastion and the De Salvert battery on Rochefort Point. *Courtesy of Parks Canada, Fortress of Louisbourg, National Historic Site of Canada, Photo Numbers: 2000 R 02 02 and 2000 R 02 01.*

PLAN DE LOUISBOURG.

Echelle.

150 Toises.

Ouvrage executé pendant le siège.

RENVOIS
DU PLAN DE LOUISBOURG,
dans L'Isle Royale, au Canada.

1. *Ouvrages projettés.*
2. *Porte de la Reine.*
3. *Place d'Armes.*
4. *Porte Dauphine.*
5. *Porte de Maurepas.*
6. *Pointe de Rochefort.*
7. *Cap Noir.*
8. *Lac, qui sert de Port en hiver.*

Tentative inutile des Anglois sur Louisbourg, le 7. Sept.bre 1757.
Le 26. Juillet, en 1768. Louisbourg se rend, aux Anglois.

Endgame 1758

Prologue

The Book Ahead

I did not realize it when I began to write this book, but it has turned out to be the closing chapter of my multivolume biography of eighteenth-century Louisbourg. It may sound odd to speak of a constantly evolving settlement of thousands of people over the span of four decades in terms of a biography. Nonetheless, that is how I now see this account of the events of the second and final French occupation of Louisbourg.

The story of what happened at Louisbourg between 1749 and 1758 is one of the great dramas in the history of Canada, indeed, of North America. It is a tale with many twists and turns, which brings in the end roughly forty thousand men, women, and children on shore and afloat at Louisbourg in June and July 1758. The resulting clash was monumental by anyone's standards. One of the largest British military forces ever to campaign in North America—roughly twenty-seven thousand soldiers and sailors—went up against approximately eighty-five hundred French soldiers and sailors. The exact number of French civilians within the walls of Louisbourg is unknown, but the total was likely around four thousand. By itself the overall forty thousand figure reveals not only the massive scale of the undertaking but also the importance the two imperial powers placed on Louisbourg, the one to defend it and the other to capture it.

The participants fully recognized the magnitude of the struggle in which they were involved as they were living through it. So did the people residing in the nearby French and British colonies because they too had a stake in the outcome. And, obviously, so did their superiors in the mother countries, as they were the ones who authorized the massive land and sea forces that crossed the ocean to collide at Louisbourg. What unfolded at the French stronghold on Cape Breton Island in the summer of 1758 was to have a far-reaching influence on the outcome of the long Anglo-French contest for supremacy in North America. It was nothing less than the first major British victory in the most recent war, following a string of setbacks and disappointments. Had Louisbourg *not* fallen in 1758, as it had avoided doing in 1757, when a large fleet of French warships within Louisbourg harbor and a storm at sea thwarted a massive British expedition, then who knows how differently the Seven Years' War might have ended? Would yet another reverse—following those of Braddock's defeat in 1755, the loss of Oswego in 1756, the surrender of Fort William Henry in 1757, and the French victory at Fort Carillon/Ticonderoga in 1758—have been enough to undo the administration in London led by William Pitt? We will never know because the British did achieve victory at Louisbourg. And with it, the tide in the Seven Years' War turned dramatically in their favor. The campaign at Louisbourg was celebrated long and loud in Britain and its colonies, suggesting that there was as much relief as joy when people learned the news.

Fame, of course, is fleeting. So it was with the capture of Louisbourg in 1758. That siege and the decade that preceded it in Atlantic Canada are not well remembered, except by a relatively small number of historians.[1] By the twenty-first century the simultaneous French tragedy and British glory represented by "Louisbourg 1758" had receded into the dim background of the continent's collective consciousness. Historians with an interest in the Seven Years' War tended to focus instead on the siege of Quebec in 1759, with its drama of a decisive few moments on the Plains of Abraham, with the unrivaled symmetry of the deaths of both commanders, Wolfe and Montcalm. Those who think of the Louisbourg campaign of the preceding year, if they think of it at all, regard it as a prelude to the main event. Historians have long followed a tradition in which the campaign at Louisbourg was boiled down to a few paragraphs or at best a few pages.[2]

Through such a lens the ending of the colony of Île Royale (as Cape Breton Island was known to the French between 1713 and 1758) and the removal of its population become small details in the advance of one empire and the decline of another. Also, most narratives look at the Louisbourg sidebar from an exclusive military history perspective, one in which the British victors tend to receive far more ink than the losing French side. That approach misses the fascination and poignancy of the final decade of Louisbourg's existence, for what happened at Louisbourg in 1758 is as much a tale of dashed French hopes and plans as it is of a British victory.

While the long shadow cast by the 1759 siege of Quebec was one factor that kept Louisbourg's own siege from being better known, another influence was at work. For many years the historical profession underestimated the significance of Louisbourg as a seaport and settlement. Despite the in-depth book published in 1918 by J. S. McLennan, which demonstrated the scale and scope of the French colony, Île Royale long occupied a marginal position in the dominant narratives on New France.[3] That began to change in the 1970s and 1980s, when a new round of studies on Louisbourg's society and economy began to appear.[4] For those who read such works, the French colonization of Cape Breton Island ceased to be the simple story of a fort "guarding" the entrance to the part of New France that existed along the shores of the Saint Lawrence River. Rather, Louisbourg and Île Royale came to be seen as an important and sizable colonizing initiative in its own right, with its own distinct economy.[5] Stronghold, yes, argued the authors of those studies, but not merely an advance post for Quebec and Montreal. That, after all, was a role Louisbourg could perform only when a fleet of French warships was based there, which did not happen very often. And without a squadron riding at anchor, Louisbourg's guns and garrison could do nothing to prevent an attack on the Saint Lawrence settlements.

In France few historians were interested at all in the long-lost colony of Île Royale in any context. One of the few was François Caron, who put forward an interpretation in 1983 that Louisbourg was for the French in North America what Gibraltar was for the British on the Mediterranean. "To protect Louisbourg," writes Caron, "is to defend the whole colony." To be sure, the military historian's perspective reflects the importance that the Cape Breton stronghold had for officials at Versailles in the years leading up to 1758, yet that was a fairly recent development. In the beginning, which for Louisbourg occurred in 1713, the settlement was established not to be a "guardian" of the Gulf of Saint Lawrence but as an economic engine or base. Year after year throughout the 1720s–1750s, France's Ministry of the Marine, which was responsible for the navy and overseas colonies, allocated an important portion of its budget to develop and defend Louisbourg because Île Royale was valued in and of itself, for its maritime economy of fishery and commerce.[6]

The numbers speak louder than words. That Louisbourg represented much more than a well-fortified frontier post is clearly reflected in the following figures summarizing the community that would be wiped out in 1758. In the span of four decades of life and growth, the parish at Louisbourg witnessed over 2,200 baptisms, 565 marriages, and nearly 1,200 recorded burials.[7] There would be no more such events in the town after the British victory, at least not involving French settlers. As soon as the British could after their conquest, they sent to France virtually every soldier, sailor, and civilian—perhaps as many as twelve thousand people in the latter half of 1758. The term "deportation" is not usually applied to that forced removal, but the relocation took place at the same time as the much better known Acadian deportations of 1755–62.

As the subject of a biography, Louisbourg offers three main sides to its personality: fortress, seaport, and community. All three are examined in this book in varying degrees. Looked at collectively, the French colony had a short lifespan. The bookend dates are 1713 and 1758, and it should be noted that from the midpoint in 1745 until the midpoint in 1749 Louisburg was in British hands and spelled without a second *o*. Forty-five years is not long by any standard. Most people in today's North America and Europe live far longer, and so did many of their predecessors in the eighteenth century. Brief or not, the era in which Louisbourg was a French base on Île Royale was one of the turning points in the history of North America. Innumerable colonial actions and reactions brought countless changes to people on both sides of the Atlantic. Wars, territory-changing treaties, and massive population declines and movements are the most obvious. The short- and long-term impacts of eighteenth-century colonialism on the peoples of the Americas, Europe, and Africa are incalculable and still with us in the twenty-first century.

Louisbourg is only one case among many, yet from my vantage point it is among the more riveting. During its four and a half decades, Louisbourg evolved from an unsettled harbor into a bustling fishing and trading port and a populous walled town. It became the virtual capital for the French in Atlantic Canada, enduring two protracted sieges. Each time, in 1745 and 1758, the sieges ended in defeat and removal for the French defenders and colonists. After the second loss, which is the focus of this study, British sappers systematically destroyed the once-vaunted fortifications. Louisbourg became something of a modern Carthage.

Put briefly, Louisbourg and the colony of Île Royale packed a lot into a brief lifespan. And no part of that history is more intriguing than the ten-year period that began in 1749. *Endgame 1758* focuses squarely on those final ten years. It was a decade dominated by war or, more accurately, by thoughts of, worries about, and preparations for war. For the first nine years people dealt with the aftermath of the preceding conflict, the War of the Austrian Succession (King George's War), and with the work judged necessary in anticipation of the next attack. The preparations involved measures on shore and afloat, for British blockades of the French colony became a part of life beginning in the mid-1750s. The tenth year, 1758, turned out to be Louisbourg's last, at least as a French bastion. The promise Louisbourg had once held for the French evaporated when British arms found glory.

The emphasis in *Endgame 1758* is on two parallel stories. One is the French side of the imperial equation, with the focus on events at Louisbourg. The other story is the British side, where events involving Halifax, Louisbourg's counterbalance, are of primary interest. Though these are the twin foci of the book, all incidents and episodes of the 1749–58 period are not treated equally. Some are included because they provide insights into the nature and character of life at Louisbourg and on Île Royale. Put differently, they flesh out the biography. Others contribute directly to the military saga that culminated in the siege of 1758. The first half of the book essentially sets the stage for an in-depth depiction of what happened in the two final years, 1757 and 1758.

By the end of the book the reader should see that the imperial power that prevailed at Louisbourg was the one that brought and effectively used more resources: warships, artillery, and ground troops. The latter part of the formulation, about effective use, must be added. One thing military history makes clear is that battles and campaigns are not determined by numbers alone. If that was all there was to it, the British would have won easily at Fort Carillon/Ticonderoga in 1758, when in fact they were soundly defeated by a much smaller force of French defenders. At Louisbourg the events of 1757 demonstrated that the British could not just show up off the coast with a large fleet and expect the French to lower their flag. To force the French leadership at Louisbourg to surrender, an enemy had to accomplish three main goals: implement an effective naval blockade, get large numbers of troops ashore, and advance against the fortified town sufficiently to make capitulation inevitable. That undertaking is a lot easier stated in the twenty-first century, from the comfortable position of knowing how things turned out, than it was achieved in the eighteenth century by the people who actually had to make it happen.

Anyone who has read the short summaries on Louisbourg that have appeared in countless books over the years knows already that the 1758 siege lasted about seven weeks and the British prevailed. However, there is much more that could and should be said about the fateful campaign against Louisbourg. The details of how and why the French colony ended the way it did, not just in June and July 1758 but over the decade that preceded the siege, are a little-known and compelling story. It is also high human drama. No one on either side knew how things were going to end—none of us ever does. In the pages that follow I present Louisbourg's final years with the sense of uncertainty that must have colored people's lives at the time.

The Game of Empire

Viewed through the time lapse of centuries, far from the tragedy of actual lives lost, the territorial competition waged by Great Britain and France in the eastern half of North America might be characterized as a long, drawn-out chess match. At the highest levels of the two European-based empires, gains and losses were sometimes treated as a game, albeit a deadly one. Ashore and afloat, the French and the British took turns being the aggressor. For a century and a half an advance by one side was frequently met by a countermove from the other. Alliances and broad strategic interests meant that conquests were sometimes exchanged. A classic example is the way in which France and England (and after 1707, Great Britain) handed Acadia back and forth repeatedly up until the Treaty of Utrecht in 1713. Another is the British return of Cape Breton Island to the French by the terms of a 1748 European treaty, to the annoyance of the New Englanders who had captured the stronghold at Louisbourg three years earlier.

At times the moves of European monarchs, or more accurately the administrations that acted in their name, puzzled or enraged people in North America. Kings and their advisers found it relatively easy to think of territories on a map as far-flung "holdings" to be kept or handed away, but the people actually living in those areas could not form such a detached perspective.[8] The burned buildings, devastated landscapes, captured vessels, and lost lives were all too real to the indigenous peoples and European colonists.

On an existential level, therefore, a chess analogy is an artificial and unsatisfactory construct. It does not capture the pain and suffering inflicted by the various wars. Moreover, it does an injustice to the complexity of the conflicts in North America before 1763. There were many more than two players struggling for sovereignty or simple existence. The mix included dozens of Aboriginal tribes, whose warriors often greatly outnumbered the European combatants. In seventeenth-century New France, for example, the Canadiens battled the Five Nations far more often than they did their English or New England rivals. A similar situation existed in the Anglo-American colonies, where seventeenth-century wars were predominantly with Native warriors, not French soldiers.

Another problem with the chess metaphor is that the "board" on which the imperial wars were waged was not well defined. In the early 1600s the French, the English, the Scottish, the Dutch, and the Swedish all made tentative settlements at several spots along the Atlantic seaboard; the rest of the continent remained in the control of the indigenous peoples. Slowly but steadily the Europeans spread inland as the decades went by, aided by the germs as well as the arms they had brought from overseas. By the period treated in this book, the imperial arena in North America stretched across perhaps a third of the continent. The North American "board," of course, was only one zone where European imperial ambitions were clashing. A good part of the planet was by then in play, with Spain, Portugal, and Holland major players along with Britain and France. There were flashpoints in India and Africa as well as the Americas. The more territory the empires covered, or aspired to cover, the more important became control over sea lanes. In that area the British eventually emerged with the upper hand, though their ascendancy was not always apparent nor was it ever a foregone conclusion.[9]

In eastern North America, where competing Anglo-French imperial dreams clashed head on for a century and a half, the indigenous peoples were drawn into and affected by the struggle. The Aboriginal tribes were no monolith. There were enormous differences—including, on occasion, longstanding enmity—among the different groups. A common strategy was for a given tribe to ally itself with one European power in the hope that it could stem the advance of another. Samuel Johnson perceptively observed from London that the British and the French had "parted the northern continent of America between them, and [were then] disputing about their boundaries." Each sought "the destruction of the other by the help of the Indians, whose interest it [was] that both should be destroyed."[10]

Despite its weaknesses as a concept for the broader war, the chess metaphor is nonetheless a useful shorthand for the particular history of Louisbourg. It captures the essence of that late-starting French colonial initiative. The place began from scratch in 1713 as a deliberate stroke of imperial design by Louis XIV and the comte de Pontchartrain, the minister of the marine, who held the responsibility for the navy and overseas colonies. Louisbourg's subsequent growth—demographically, economically, and militarily—under Louis XV resulted in large part from policies pursued by subsequent ministers of the marine, especially the comte de Maurepas. And its defeats—not once but twice—occurred because France's great imperial rival, Britain, in concert with its Anglo-American colonies, was determined to remove the Cape Breton stronghold from the geopolitical map. Admittedly, Native warriors were involved on both sides in the two conflicts at Louisbourg, yet not in large numbers, and they did not play determining roles. This was because the campaigns waged at Louisbourg in 1745 and 1758 were fundamentally European-style sieges, though some irregular forces and light infantry were needed.

Aboriginal combatants were valued and present, yet they formed part of the supporting, not the leading, cast. In contrast to many other conflicts in eighteenth-century North America, where chiefs and warriors sometimes played a key military role, the two struggles at Louisbourg were primarily matches between the two longtime European rivals.[11]

The chess analogy also suits Louisbourg because it conveys the generally detached perspective of the kings, ministers, and advisers in London and Versailles who ultimately determined the fate of the place. That does not mean that those officials did not have strong feelings about the value of Louisbourg and the colony of Île Royale, because they did. Yet the importance assigned in Versailles or London to the fortified town and port on Cape Breton Island—either to retain it or to eliminate it—was determined by the utility envisioned for it in the larger context of the French or the British Empire. There was little or no attachment to the colony as an entity unto itself. In that utilitarian outlook the European colonists and indigenous peoples who actually lived in the territories were regarded as pieces in a global match, not players who should be encouraged to make their own moves.

Louisbourg and Atlantic Canada

This book focuses not on the global imperial contest but on the corner of North America known today as Atlantic Canada. Readers who think of the area as either a summer vacation destination or an economically disadvantaged region may be surprised to learn that the zone once figured prominently in the military, economic, and strategic thinking of France and Great Britain. Imperial interest peaked in the decade 1749–58. Those years witnessed the end of a long Anglo-French struggle for dominance along the Atlantic seaboard, with tragic ramifications for the French, the Acadians, and the Mi'kmaq. The British and the Anglo-Americans, on the other hand, benefited from the misfortunes of the others.[12] When the period is extended a few more years to include the fall of Quebec in 1759 and of Montreal in 1760, the era of the Seven Years' War (or if one prefers, the French and Indian War) was one of *the* pivotal periods in North American history.[13]

Two conditions put Louisbourg and other key parts of Atlantic Canada in the spotlight between 1749 and 1758. The first was an increased determination on the part of the leadership in Great Britain to win a *complete* victory over the French in North America. Previously, limited or regional gains had been enough. Beginning in 1749, however, the British showed a previously unseen determination concerning the North American colonies. That resolve waxed and waned over the decade like a stock market graph, yet the overall trend was unmistakable. An influential and growing number of officials in Britain wanted to see all French pieces swept off the colonial chess board. The most dramatic strokes were the founding of Halifax in 1749; an aggressive sea campaign that began a few years later; eight years of deportations of thousands of Acadians; and the sending of unprecedented numbers of soldiers and warships to the North American theater in the late 1750s.[14]

The second condition that put a spotlight on Atlantic Canada between 1749 and 1758 was the French response to the British initiatives. Put bluntly, they had to keep up or give up. In response to British militancy a succession of French administrations made concerted efforts to hang on to their nation's economic and strategic interests in the Atlantic region. The single most important stronghold in the zone, from the perspective of the different ministers of the marine, was Louisbourg. Beginning in 1749 and accelerating in 1755, the marine ministry committed more soldiers and ships to Louisbourg than it had ever done before. That strengthening of the capital of Île Royale by the French in turn hardened British resolve to capture the place. The various imperial moves of the early 1750s represented a sort of arms race, though of course the term had not yet been coined.

Looking at the larger North American context, the French altered and refined their vision of what they wanted to achieve in *Amérique septentrionale* as the decades passed. By the mid-eighteenth century the imbalance in the colonial populations made it clear that there was no hope of completely eliminating the British from North America. In round numbers there were more than ten times as many Anglo-American colonists as there were French ones: over a million to fewer than one hundred thousand. Indeed, Massachusetts alone had roughly three times the population of New France.[15] Consequently, the best hope for the French lay in consolidating their strengths in three main ways. One was to reinforce garrisons at primary fortresses such as Louisbourg and Quebec. That was done, and I shall have more to say on that topic later. A second approach was to send additional warships to the theater. Everyone acknowledged that the Royal Navy had a dominant edge by the mid-eighteenth century, but no one assumed the French were going to lose every naval encounter, nor did they. On the contrary, as events would demonstrate in the 1750s, the French were able to send formidable squadrons to nullify or at least reduce the British advantage. On this subject, too, there will be much more later.

The third way in which the France of Louis XV sought to enhance its North American empire was to establish a line of posts and a network of Native alliances on the interior of the continent to arrest the growth of the Anglo-American territories. Those efforts lie mostly beyond the scope of this book and have been dealt with by many historians. It is nonetheless worth noting that the many French forts probably looked impressive on maps reviewed at Versailles; they certainly do today when identified on maps in modern texts.[16] Yet tiny garrisons in scattered outposts across a frontier that stretched several thousand miles were unable to exercise effective control much beyond the range of the soldiers' muskets. The key to the French having influence in the territories along and close to the Mississippi, Ohio, and other rivers lay in having support from and alliances with the dozens of Aboriginal nations for whom the areas were homelands. For the most part the French were adept at using traditional Aboriginal diplomatic forms to develop relationships with the indigenous peoples, allowing those who acted on behalf of Louis XV to have more influence than they would have otherwise. Such alliances served French military interests well for a long time, including in Atlantic Canada, where the Mi'kmaq generally shared a common fear or distrust of the British and/or the Anglo-Americans.[17] Lest some think the French were universally loved by Aboriginal nations, let me make clear that they were not. The Iroquois, the Chickasaws, and the Fox, among others, fought long and bloody campaigns against the men of Louis XIV and Louis XV. In Atlantic Canada, however, there were no such French conflicts with the Native peoples, though there were times of tension and resentment, particularly when some bands began to sign treaties with the British (which happened in 1725–26 and 1752). The breadth of the French sphere of influence across a good part of the map of North America was impressive yet not solidly planted except in a few areas. Historian Ian Steele expresses the vulnerability poetically when he writes that the "reach of

New France was swift and light, but fragile, like the birch-bark canoes they adopted from the Algonquin and Huron."[18]

As the 1750s unfolded many showdowns occurred throughout northeastern North America. Louisbourg loomed large in the thinking of the imperial powers, close to the top of both the French and the British list. To the one empire Louisbourg was a vitally important place to defend; to the other it was a primary target to remove. In chess parlance the final phase of the match is the endgame. Louisbourg's own endgame came before that of the continent-wide war, yet the 1758 result on Île Royale helped shape the larger outcome.

This narrative reflects, as far as the available sources allow, the perspectives of all participants. Those sources are long and deep for the main protagonists, the French and the British, yet sparse when it comes to the Mi'kmaq and other Native allies of the French. Although those warriors had only a small role in and impact on the events of 1758, it would have been desirable to know what their leadership thought of the conflict.

In keeping with the opening observation that this book is essentially a biography, the central character is Louisbourg itself. At the risk of repeating myself, the major fortified town and seaport on Île Royale was perceived as the key to Atlantic Canada. For French colonists, Acadian settlers, and Aboriginal allies such as the Mi'kmaq, the Wolastoqiyik (Maliseet), and the Abenaki, Louisbourg was a formidable bastion that people hoped would keep the British and the Anglo-Americans at bay. For the several thousand civilians who actually lived in or near the walled town on a year-round basis, Louisbourg was the community that sustained them. On the other side of the board, for the British and the Anglo-American colonists the fortress on Cape Breton Island was an economic and military threat, an obstacle to be overcome. This book strives to explain what happened to and at these three different Louisbourgs— stronghold, community, and threat—during the decade that ultimately settled the place's destiny.

A Recapitulation: Louisbourg 1713–1748

Within a few years of the French landing on the shores of Louisbourg harbor in 1713, it became evident that the fledgling seaport would play a crucial role in the contest for North America. Its predecessors in the Atlantic realm—Port-Royal (Annapolis Royal, Nova Scotia) and Plaisance (Placentia, Newfoundland)—had fallen to the British during the war just ended (War of the Spanish Succession, 1701–13). Once the French made the decision to concentrate their interests in the Atlantic region on the two major islands over which they still claimed sovereignty, Île Royale and Île Saint-Jean (Prince Edward Island), it was inevitable that the new stronghold at Louisbourg would be tested. The only questions were when and how. When would an assault take place, and how would the place hold up?

For three decades those questions went unanswered. Louisbourg grew much larger and far stronger than the settlements that had preceded it along the Atlantic shores. Past defeats, therefore, did not seal the fate of the current fortified town. It would take a massive army and navy, superior to any force the British and their Anglo-American colonists had yet mustered in the region, to accomplish that. No one could foresee in the 1720s and 1730s when such an initiative might be forthcoming.

Luckily for the people who came to Louisbourg in 1713 and afterward, there was no immediate war. For three decades the settlements on Île Royale, especially Louisbourg, enjoyed peace and relative prosperity. Of course, there were hard times and occasional severe shortages. Yet overall the first thirty years of Louisbourg's history were characterized by remarkable growth. The cod fishery employed hundreds and brought wealth to many individual proprietors. Using dried cod as the primary export, merchants in Louisbourg and elsewhere developed trading links throughout France's Atlantic realm. The capital of Île Royale emerged as a "junction" or transshipment center. Vessels sailing to and from France, the West Indies, Canada, and even potentially "enemy" destinations in New England and Nova Scotia (the former Acadie) dropped anchor at Louisbourg to off- or on-load various commodities. The establishment of the port as an active seaport gave "new structure" to France's Atlantic empire.[19]

The quest for commercial wealth was the primary force behind colonial development and territorial rivalry in the eighteenth century, as indeed it was in earlier and later periods. The individual most responsible for France's colonial policies at the time was Jean-Frédéric Phélypeaux, comte de Maurepas, minister of the marine until 1749. Maurepas artic-ulated the link between commercial and naval power as follows: "Com-merce creates the wealth and consequently the power of States; naval forces are absolutely necessary for the support of maritime commerce and for the defense of a State bounded by the sea." In Maurepas' vision, Louisbourg was an important colonial venture. To his way of thinking, Île Royale "assumed an economic role that could not be separated from its military role."[20] It remained to be seen, of course, whether France could provide the necessary military and naval forces to protect its in-terests on Île Royale and in its other colonies if and when Great Britain attacked the place.

Blessed with a buoyant maritime economy based on fishery and com-merce, Louisbourg largely achieved the objectives the minister of the ma-rine set for it. The Cape Breton port became one of the busiest harbors in colonial North America. Over one hundred vessels a year made their way in and out of its protected anchorage during the shipping season. When the harbor traffic slowed in late fall, wrote an eyewitness, the commu-nity presented a "portrait of sadness, much different from the spectacle that the gathering of navigators produced during the summer."[21] By the 1740s Louisbourg was a community of perhaps two thousand permanent civilian inhabitants. Immigration, especially from France, accounted for much of the growth, though natural increase did its part. In 1720 chil-dren represented 22.4 percent of Louisbourg's civilian population. Four years later the figure was 29.4 percent, and in 1737 children represented 45.4 percent (664 of 1,463) of the total for civilians.[22]

While Louisbourg was the undisputed center of the colony of Île Royale, there were about a dozen other settled harbors on the island and more again on nearby Île Saint-Jean. A few outports came to have populations of several hundred; almost all were dominated by adult fishermen or by fishing families. Attempts were made to develop agriculture and to di-versify the economy in other ways, but Île Royale did not have much ara-ble land on its eastern coast, where most of the settlements were located. Moreover, the climate was often cool and damp. Today the island aver-ages about fifteen hundred millimeters of precipitation a year, two-thirds of which falls as rain, and there are typically between 100 and 140 frost-free days.[23] Weather data do not exist for the eighteenth century, but the climate may have been even colder and wetter than it is today. Local officials in 1727 reported that the need for firewood was "equal to the need for bread." One of the British engineers at Louisbourg in the late 1740s wrote: "[Y]ou never Saw Such a Country. No Bright Sun, this month past, and what Sallade I have had is from ye Heat of ye Dung not of the Sun." In the 1750s a French observer decided that there were "so to speak, only two seasons, winter and autumn."[24] The climate, combined with the poor land generally found on Cape Breton's eastern shore, presented a disincentive for Acadians to relocate to Île Royale from mainland Nova Scotia. Most preferred to stay put, even though they found themselves living under the sovereignty of a British Protestant monarch after 1713, or to move somewhere they could practice their traditional agriculture by reclaiming tidal marshes from the sea. As a result relatively few Acadians chose to relocate out of Nova Scotia until the changed context of 1749 and the early 1750s forced many to take the option seriously.[25]

Meanwhile, at Louisbourg many homeowners dealt with the limited agricultural potential of the island by establishing kitchen gardens on their property. A plan from the 1730s reveals that more than half the developed lots inside the fortifications at Louisbourg were given over to cultivation of vegetables and herbs. Although definitely helpful, these gardens were insufficient to feed the population on a year-round basis.[26] As a result the colony always required a level of imported food supplies. One supply area, contrary to the mercantilist principles of the era, was New England.

Though not self-sufficient in food, Île Royale had an economy that generated surpluses in fishery and commerce. Louisbourg in particular benefited from its role as the administrative capital and strategic stronghold for France's Atlantic possessions. Across the span of its history, the town witnessed a large amount of government spending—to the tune of 4 million livres on fortifications and 16 million livres on other expenditures. (The livre was not the equivalent of the British pound, but closer in value to the shilling.) The outlay was enormous in the colonial context because France was then facing severe financial difficulties and attempting to reduce expenditures. The typical annual budget allocation for the entire marine ministry—which included the navy, galley ships on the

Mediterranean, salaries and pensions of marine troops and other personnel, and expenditures on overseas colonies—was 9 million livres. Of that total, 1.7 million livres were earmarked for all the French colonies. As historian Catherine Desbarats points out, the colonies "competed directly with France's fleet for shrinking naval funds." Though the navy received the lion's share of the marine allotment, it was not enough for it to keep pace with the increase in the number of Great Britain's warships.[27]

The French colonies that the minister of the marine and his officials had to oversee were located across a considerable tract of North America and in the West Indies, India, and Africa. Though Île Royale was only one small island, French officials nonetheless allocated a significant portion of the entire colonial budget to that possession. During the 1720s Île Royale's share was about 10 percent of total spending on colonies; in the 1730s and 1740s its share rose to around 20 percent and above.[28] The financial commitment speaks volumes about the importance the authorities attached to Louisbourg. The expectation was that the colony of which Louisbourg was the capital would provide a base for a bountiful fishery, intercolonial commerce, and a strategically placed land and naval base.

With the benefit of hindsight, some have interpreted the 20 million livres total of king's money spent on Louisbourg as excessive, even a sign of waste. Historian Fred Thorpe, however, notes that the annual expenditure on Louisbourg (typically about 150,000 livres a year) amounted to less than the cost of a six-month cruise by a single warship (200,000 livres and up). In such a comparison France did not fare badly for the money spent on Île Royale. For the first three decades of Louisbourg's existence, the investment paid handsome dividends. By itself the cod fishery returned three or four times the 20 million livres expenditure. Commercial trade passing through Louisbourg was equally lucrative.[29]

As for the military side of the equation, the capital of Île Royale came to have some of the most elaborate fortifications in colonial North America as well as a sizable military presence to go along with the bastions and batteries. By the 1740s between six hundred and seven hundred soldiers were garrisoned there. During the 1750s there would be up to five times that number of soldiers. The military side of Louisbourg influenced its urban development. With masonry fortifications surrounding the main town and streets laid out on a rectilinear grid that served military and commercial needs, the town presented a striking image. It was a planned European fortified town rising on the wooded shores of North America.[30]

Officials in the marine ministry in France were able to follow Louisbourg's evolution because administrators, engineers, and officers in the colony sent across the ocean hundreds of plans, thousands of pages of correspondence and reports, and dozens of censuses. The comte de Maurepas and his successors felt they were well informed. So important was the capital of Île Royale held to be in some circles that Voltaire described the place in one of his history books as "the key to their [French] possessions in North America."[31] A remark attributed to Louis XV, that he expected to see the towers of Louisbourg rise above the horizon because of the sums spent there, has never been found and appears to be apocryphal.

Many on the British side shared the French assessment that Louisbourg was a place of great significance, but their perspective was that it was a threat that needed to be destroyed. In part that was because French schooners and shallops based on Île Royale were competing with New Englanders in the harvest of cod on the offshore banks. The success Louisbourg enjoyed as a transshipment center for merchant trade was also a factor. As early as 1714 some on the British side predicted that Île Royale was likely to become the "most powerful colony the French [had] in America, and of the greatest danger and damage to all the British Colony's [*sic*] as well as the universal trade of Great Britain."[32] A half-century later the British view was that Louisbourg and the colony of Île Royale had lived up to their potential. "No Part of North America can boast of a more advantageous Situation for Commerce & Fishing," wrote the engineer Samuel Holland, "than the Island of Cape Britain. . . . The French were early sensible of this, & improved upon it. . . . [It became] a Mart for the Commodities of Old & New France . . . by returning immense Quantities of Fish, Peltry, Whalebone, Train Oil, &c, not only sufficient for Home, but Foreign Markets."[33]

An important aspect of the fishing and commerce linked to the existence of Louisbourg and Île Royale was the idea of a "nursery of seamen." The nursery concept requires a brief elaboration for readers unfamiliar with the eighteenth century. No European seafaring nation had enough sailors in its regular navy to man all its ships in time of war. Instead, it turned to the well-trained sailors from the private sector—fishery and commerce—to fill those roles when the time came. In the case of France historian Jean-François Brière estimates that perhaps as many as one-quarter of the forty thousand to sixty thousand sailors the country needed for naval service came out of the fishery that operated off Newfoundland, Cape Breton, and the Gulf of Saint Lawrence.[34] It did not take much imagination for Anglo-Americans to see that the elimination of Louisbourg would disrupt the overall French colonial system, in particular fishing, commerce, and the nursery of seamen. That would bring additional prosperity to the Anglo-American colonies, or so they reasoned. Besides the economic motivation for an attack, Louisbourg also posed a military and naval threat to New England. The fortified harbor was a base, actual and potential, for expeditions, warships, and privateers. For those who still needed convincing, there was the matter of the Roman Catholic faith adhered to in the French colony. To militant Protestants doctrinal differences provided sufficient justification for a crusade against Louisbourg.

The better the prize, the harder the victory. Louisbourg's enemies knew the place would not fall easily. Benjamin Franklin wrote to his brother, who was about to besiege the French stronghold in 1745, that the Cape Breton fortress would be a "tough nut to crack." A British officer declared that Louisbourg was "certainly the strongest fortified Harbour [he] ever saw." Another added that it was "much stronger than any place in England." The comments contained hyperbole typical of the era; something about crossing the ocean to a New World led Europeans to spin great tales. That certainly happened at Louisbourg, for the place often inspired superlatives. Some thought it the strongest place they had ever seen, which if they had not been to Europe, it probably was. Those who were contrary minded also tended to go to extremes. One described the Cape Breton stronghold as "a place shaped like an amphitheatre . . . which . . . [could] be raked with cannonballs and musketry so effectively that no one [was] safe there, either in the houses or in the streets." The end result of all the exaggerations was that Louisbourg took on, during its own lifetime, a renown of mythic proportions.[35]

Louisbourg was first put to the test of war in the spring of 1745. A European conflict (the War of Jenkins Ear) began in 1739–40 and then spread to become the War of the Austrian Succession. The hostilities finally reached North America in the spring of 1744, when George II and Louis XV declared war on each other. In the months that followed there were a number of military actions in the Atlantic region. Louisbourg-based privateers opened a war at sea by taking numerous prizes, while its soldiers launched expeditions against Canso and Annapolis Royal, the only two English settlements in Nova Scotia at the time. (Much more numerous were the Acadian villages of the region, typically located along the Bay of Fundy, which were also in what the British called Nova Scotia.) Canso fell to the French in late May; Annapolis Royal did not fall at all but withstood two separate assaults by Mi'kmaq, Wolastoqiyik, and French attackers. The following year, envisioned the French and their allies, success would be theirs. As soon as a sufficient force could be assembled, Annapolis Royal would be taken and Nova Scotia would become Acadie once more.[36]

The French campaigns in 1744 had an impact in New England circles, though not the one the French had in mind. New Englanders viewed Nova Scotia as an extension or "outpost" of their own colonies. Ever vigilant about French moves in the region, the Anglo-Americans worried that their hold on Nova Scotia was precarious. A resident of Louisbourg would later write: "[T]hey [the New Englanders] might never have troubled us had we not affronted them first." Over the course of the winter of 1744–45, the Anglo-Americans committed to eliminate the threat posed by Louisbourg. Governor William Shirley of Massachusetts took the lead when he proposed a preemptive strike. Shirley argued that nothing "would more effectually promote the interests of [Massachusetts] ... than a reduction of that place [Louisbourg]." The vote in the Massachusetts legislature was close—a one-vote victory after pressure was exerted by Boston merchants—and in the end a plan to attack Louisbourg was adopted. The adjacent colonies soon joined in, contributing either troops, ships, or money. It was a rare example of intercolonial cooperation, whose like would not be seen again until the colonists took up arms as revolutionaries against Great Britain a generation later.[37]

Four thousand New Englanders, with William Pepperrell of Maine in command, set sail in the spring of 1745 for the Cape Breton fortress.

A supporting fleet of over one hundred New England and British vessels, under the leadership of British Commodore Peter Warren, provided the necessary convoy. For nearly seven weeks they besieged and blockaded the stronghold of Île Royale. The French held out as long as they could, yet they were outgunned and did not have sufficient naval ships to disrupt the blockade. The end came on June 28, 1745. The British and the New Englanders marched in and took over a town that had suffered from much bombardment. An eyewitness recorded: "[M]ost of the Houses, which are two hundred and fifty, are demolished, or very much shattered, which makes lodging very uncomfortable. Here was a fine Church, which is intirely destroyed by the Shot."[38]

The victors removed several thousand French inhabitants from Île Royale soon after the capitulation, transporting them to France. The New England expeditionary force had accomplished what it set out to do. It had put an end to France's Atlantic bastion; Louisbourg became Louisburg. The commander of the British squadron throughout the siege, Commodore Peter Warren, was named British governor of Cape Breton Island. Warren soon urged that the major port be retained, its French-built careening facility improved, and a ten-ship British squadron assigned to the harbor as a defensive measure against the remaining French bases in North America. The naval officer also proposed an expedition to capture Canada and advocated a policy of removing the Acadians from Île Saint-Jean and Baie Verte and transporting them to France.[39]

The French, not surprisingly considering the investment they had made over roughly three decades, were not ready to give up on their Cape Breton colony, despite its loss in 1745. Île Royale had played an important role in the colonial trading network and was a valued part of the French economy. British victories at sea during the War of the Austrian Succession had a devastating effect on that commerce. At the end of 1745 losses among ships of the Compagnie des Indes were evaluated at 16 million livres. Roughly half of the six hundred ships in the colonial trade were lost. The commerce of Marseilles and the Levant fell off 120 million livres, and many French privateers had been captured by the Royal Navy. Something had to be done to regain the lost trade. Though only one part of a much larger equation, a strengthened Louisbourg was seen as part of the answer.[40]

In late 1745 and on into 1746, informants sent reports to officials at Quebec, then on to France, of British-occupied Louisbourg, especially the number of ships and troops stationed there. The reports encouraged the idea that Louisbourg could be reconquered. One informant was of the opinion "that if Louisbourg had been attacked during the winter by 300 Indians, it might have been taken."[41]

The authorities in France came up with a plan that was without parallel in North American history to that point. Despite financial difficulties, the highest officials controlling the navy and the army committed to send across the Atlantic a massive armada totaling sixty-four vessels and nearly eleven thousand men. Its objectives were to protect Canada; to drive the British from mainland Nova Scotia; and to wreak as much havoc as possible on British colonial shipping and settlements. Considering the superiority the British usually held at sea, the expedition might be seen as a bold stroke. Or a bad idea.

Organizational difficulties delayed the departure of the flotilla from France. When it finally put to sea, the situation worsened. Inexperienced leadership, storms at sea, and devastating diseases exacted a horrendous death toll. When the fleet finally reached Nova Scotia waters—specifically an anchorage that three years later would be settled by the British and renamed Halifax—it was no longer capable of mounting any kind of assault. The devastated fleet limped back to France as best it could. An estimated three thousand of its men had died, including its commander, the duc d'Enville.[42]

History is full of what-might-have-been. The 1746 d'Enville expedition is one of the more noteworthy to speculate about in the history of Atlantic Canada. Its utter failure was providential to British interests. So complete was the French catastrophe in 1746 that the Anglo-American conquerors of Louisbourg must have thought they had seen the last of a French presence on Cape Breton Island. They were soon disappointed. The peace that ended the overall war soon handed back to Louis XV what his soldiers and sailors had been unable to retain by force of arms.

The Treaty of Aix-la-Chapelle formally concluded the War of the Austrian Succession in October 1748. Throughout the treaty negotiations British strategists regarded the New England capture of Louisbourg and

Île Royale as a detail in a much larger conflict. In contrast to the Anglo-Americans, who took pride in their conquest, the British did not view the retention of Cape Breton Island as an end in itself. Britain's negotiators took other interests and aspirations into account. Without many victories in the European theater, the British were open to suggestions to hand back Île Royale if it meant achieving other objectives. In the end that is what happened. Louis XV's diplomats reacquired Louisbourg by giving up several conquered border towns in what is now Belgium. To the British it seemed like a fair trade-off because it reestablished the prewar balance of power on the European continent. Anglo-Americans took the exchange as a bitter disappointment.[43]

Thanks to the Treaty of Aix-la-Chapelle, France had a renewed opportunity to strengthen its presence in what is now Atlantic Canada. The first question was what would the minister of the marine decide to do with the opportunity? The immediate answer was obvious: Louisbourg and Île Royale would be reoccupied. There was a fishery to reestablish, commerce to renew, and a fortress to make strong again. But how would these goals be achieved? And were the French going to do anything differently in the light of the war just concluded? The answers to those questions would begin to be revealed in the summer of 1749.

Opening Moves, 1749

S ome dates loom larger than others, and in what is now Atlantic Canada, 1749 was a year of paramount importance. Two events that summer were to have a deep impact on all peoples in the region: Mi'kmaq, Wolastoqiyik (Maliseet), French, Acadians, and British. One event was the British founding of Halifax; the other was the French reoccupation of Louisbourg. It was no coincidence that the two initiatives occurred within days of each other. The unprecedented British settlement initiative in Nova Scotia was undertaken precisely because the French were reestablishing themselves at Louisbourg. Authorities in London were not willing to see an enemy *ville fortifiée* reemerge on Cape Breton Island without creating a rival stronghold of their own.

The twin actions of 1749 took place in an atmosphere of anticipated war. No one ever knows the future, yet there were few who regarded the treaty signed at Aix-la-Chapelle in 1748 as the start of an enduring peace. Most expected further hostilities, and sooner rather than later. In the case of the indigenous peoples in the region, they felt no commitment to the peace settlement signed overseas between the two European powers. The Mi'kmaq, the Wolastoqiyik, and the Abenaki had not been part of any stage of the negotiations, nor were they signatories to the final treaty. The particular grievances the Mi'kmaq had about the British founding of Halifax were summarized in a document composed in the

Mi'kmaw and French languages and sent on to the newly arrived governor Edward Cornwallis. The letter opened: "The place where you are, where you are building dwellings, where you are now building a fort, where you want, as it were, to enthrone yourself, this land of which you wish to make yourself now absolute master, this land belongs to me."[1] British officials who read or heard such declarations from the Mi'kmaq or other Aboriginal peoples were unmoved. It was a rare European who had sympathy for what the twentieth century would come to know as the rights of indigenous peoples.

For their part the French encouraged and aided allies such as the Mi'kmaq in their gripes and struggles against the British. Much of the French success in North America lay in their ability to develop alliances with indigenous nations, first against rival Aboriginal tribes, "then against the English colonists, and eventually against the British army."[2] That did not mean, however, that the French recognized the sovereign rights of the indigenous peoples any more than did the British. If they had, they might have invited the Mi'kmaq and others to provide input into the treaties the French monarch made with his British counterpart, when territories were being signed away or acquired. To eighteenth-century Europeans, indeed to nineteenth-century Europeans, such participation was inconceivable.

From the perspective of the imperial governments in Great Britain and France, the founding of Halifax and the refounding of Louisbourg were strategic acts that allowed each to retain its respective sphere of influence in the Atlantic region. If things went as both hoped—which was impossible because their visions overlapped and clashed—then the initiatives of 1749 might allow them to expand their spheres. The warlike edge of the two ventures was apparent to any onlooker. Each expedition contained a sizable military contingent along with civilian settlers. Each had large financial subsidies from its backing administration, which was exceptional in the generally parsimonious colonial era. The arrival in 1749 of massive flotillas, one French off the Cape Breton coast and one British off the eastern shore of Nova Scotia, was not about the peaceful settlement of the region. They were the opening gestures in what would turn out to be a decade of tension and warfare. A century and a half of simmering rivalry and warfare, begun in 1613 when an expedition of Virginians sailed north to destroy several French settlements in Acadie, was about to begin to boil.[3]

Preliminaries

The negotiation of the final version of the Treaty of Aix-la-Chapelle took months. By the time the preliminary agreements were reached at the end of April 1748, long before the peace was formally signed on October 18, 1748, the direction in which the treaty was heading was obvious to both the British and the French. With regard to Atlantic Canada, the clock was going to be turned back (*status quo ante bellum*) to before the siege of 1745. Cape Breton Island was again to become Île Royale, a French possession of economic and strategic significance. The protracted nature of the diplomatic process meant that officials representing each nation were able to take steps in anticipation of the final treaty.

On the French side, officials in the Ministry of the Marine expected right from the fall of Louisbourg in 1745 that the surrendered fishing, commercial, and military base would eventually be returned to their control. For four years they acted as if the restoration of the colony was a foregone conclusion. Dispatches and memoranda continued to be exchanged on the business of Louisbourg and Île Royale, admittedly on a reduced scale since there was no real colony to be administered, only a colony-in-waiting.[4] Some individuals retained their old roles and responsibilities, which included safeguarding the thousands of folio pages of the island's documentary records.[5] The property concessions, court cases, financial statements, parish registers, stores lists, and other categories of documentation would be needed when the colony started up again.

Trunks of paper records were of course much easier to control than thousands of displaced colonists. What of the family groups and individuals who were removed from Île Royale in 1745? Where did they live and what did they do during the four years Louisbourg was occupied by New Englanders and the British? The documentary record is far from complete, yet the deportees were clearly not dispersed and absorbed into the general population of France after they arrived in the mother country in the latter half of 1745. They remained in coastal areas in western France. Whether they did so willingly or were encouraged or forced to do so by the authorities is not clear. When word first came from Aix-la-Chapelle that Louisbourg was likely to be returned to Louis XV, the minister of the marine, the comte de Maurepas, directed officials in the different French ports to begin the process that would culminate in the resettlement of Île Royale. Arrangements were made for ships and provisions for the crossing, food for the settlers when they arrived, and a range of equipment so that the fishery could begin anew.[6]

The authorities knew just where to look for the former colonists of Île Royale. They also had a firm idea of how many people were involved, in terms of both the former colonists and those who would be joining them for the first time. Mention was made of lists. Such recordkeeping was not unusual. Île Royale had witnessed frequent census taking during the 1720s and 1730s, and it would again during the 1750s. The areas mentioned where there were concentrations of waiting settlers for Île Royale were Brittany (with Saint-Malo the port from which people were to sail), Rochefort, Bordeaux, and the southwest corner (where Bayonne and Saint-Jean-de-Luz were located).[7] Generally speaking, those regions along the west coast of France had been the principal places of origin for the majority of the colonists on Île Royale during its first period of occupation.[8] What is unknown is the degree to which French administrators may have used pressure or even force to keep the colonists "together" so that they would be able to find them when the time came.

Colonial officials recognized that it might not be a good thing to send back every single person who had been on Île Royale before its capture in 1745. The old, the infirm, and the indigent, for instance, would be a drain. The priority was to send those who had trades or who could otherwise help reestablish the fishery, trade, and other parts of the economy.[9] One potentially complicated issue was the matter of the land and buildings previously owned or occupied by colonists up to mid-1745. The minister decided that houses could be reclaimed by their returning owners, and that properties that were not occupied within one year would revert to the king. Another decision was that temporary living quarters would be provided for people whose houses had been destroyed in 1745 or afterward and also for people arriving in the colony for the first time. Meanwhile, the minister specified that the couple of dozen French subjects who had remained on the island during the four years of British occupation would be investigated and their fates determined once information had been gathered. If there were any disputes among returning colonists in the course of the resettlement of Île Royale, the minister wanted the incoming governor and financial administrator to use their judgment to make final decisions at the local level.[10]

At the same time as the civil population was being organized so too were the military personnel who would be sailing to Louisbourg. A contingent of Île Royale troops, veteran soldiers and new recruits, had been kept together since the garrison returned to France in 1745. They remained in service either at Rochefort or on the Île de Ré, off La Rochelle. Most were destined to make the transatlantic voyage in 1749. Not returning to Louisbourg were the foreign mercenaries of the Karrer Regiment. Marine officials blamed that 150-man unit for both the mutiny that took place in December 1744 and the subsequent loss of the colony in the spring of 1745. The other units that served in the colony up to 1745 were to return. They were the independent companies of marine soldiers and a small company of artillery specialists, the Canoniers-Bombardiers. In both cases there would be many more men in those units going to Louisbourg in 1749 than had served there up to 1745. The loss of Île Royale in 1745 had convinced the comte de Maurepas that Louisbourg needed a larger garrison. In 1745 there had been an allocation of 560 soldiers of the Compagnies franches de la Marine. By the end of 1749, however, nearly double that total—1,050 soldiers—would be assigned to the colony.[11]

In 1748, when the conclusion of the Aix-la-Chapelle peace process was imminent, a contingent of troops destined for Île Royale left France and sailed to Quebec, where they spent the winter of 1748–49. They were permitted to fly their own colors, dating from their earlier time in Louisbourg.[12] Governor General La Galissonière in Quebec dispatched a small detachment of soldiers to Île Saint-Jean to begin to prepare that island for its return to French jurisdiction.[13] The rest of the Île Royale troops did not cross the Atlantic until 1749, when they set sail as part of the convoy that brought the civil population as well. Once they arrived, most of the soldiers would remain at Louisbourg, though twenty to thirty men would be sent on to garrison Port-la-Joye on Île Saint-Jean and Port Toulouse on Île Royale. Before the massive convoy left France in 1749, Louis XV decided to replace the official who had been most responsible for the emergence of Louisbourg as a trading center and military stronghold.[14] After twenty-six years in charge of the marine portfolio, the comte de Maurepas no longer had the confidence of the king. A contributing factor in the decision to replace the minister, according to the rumor mill at Versailles, was the loss of Louisbourg in 1745. Maurepas was so closely associated with the expenditures on the colony that it was inevitable that he would share a portion of the blame for its defeat.[15] In truth Maurepas had annoyed Madame de Pompadour, the king's favorite mistress, and that likely played a larger role than the loss of Louisbourg in bringing about his dismissal.

Antoine-Louis Rouillé, comte de Jouy, took over as the new secretary of state for the navy and overseas colonies. Rouillé did not have prior experience with the twin responsibilities of the marine portfolio, yet in the assessment of the author of a recent study, he "proved a surprisingly good administrator." Over the next six years France would launch 34 ships of the line, which began to close the gap between it and Britain, though the latter still had by far the larger and more powerful navy. The achievement was less ambitious than what Maurepas had envisioned— he had projected building over a ten year period 110 ships of the line and 54 frigates—but there is no guarantee the outgoing minister would have found the funds for such an expansion of the French navy.[16] Certainly Rouillé ran into financial constraints; in 1752 he had to end an initiative he had ordered to replenish the naval supplies at France's three naval ports: Brest, Rochefort, and Toulon.[17] Rouillé was to administer the portfolio until 1754, when another top-level change occurred. There was yet another switch in 1757, then one more in 1758. Counting Maurepas, who served for a while in 1749, Louisbourg's final decade witnessed five secretaries of state, or ministers, of the marine. The revolving door in the portfolio, along with underfunding, was both the symptom and the cause of serious problems in the ministry.[18]

Across the channel from France, a debate was taking place in Britain regarding what to do with Cape Breton Island following its capture in 1745. In the minds of leading Anglo-Americans and numerous pamphleteers in Great Britain, Louisbourg had to be retained. Supporters of that position pictured the place becoming an important port and stronghold within the British Empire, as it had been for France. Officials in London who administered imperial budgets, however, did not see the acquisition in the same light. They saw immediate costs and unwanted future obligations. Moreover, they wanted the War of the Austrian Succession to end sooner, not later. To their way of thinking, Louisbourg was an attractive carrot to dangle in front of French negotiators. That perspective was reflected in a comment by the Earl of Chesterfield. In August 1745, upon hearing of the capture of Louisbourg, the soon-to-be secretary of state for the Northern Department wrote that Cape Breton had "become the darling object of the whole nation . . . ten times more popular than ever Gibraltar was." Nonetheless, Chesterfield foresaw "the impossibility of keeping it."[19] The man who succeeded Peter Warren as governor of Cape Breton, Commodore Charles Knowles, provided assessments of Louisbourg that were diametrically opposed to those of his predecessor. Knowles detested everything about the place, including its climate. Not shy about superlatives, the commodore wrote his superiors in the admiralty that Louisbourg was "the most miserable ruinous place" he had ever been.[20]

The rumor that the British government was willing to hand Louisbourg back to Louis XV gave the impression to some in New England that imperial decision makers were less concerned about protecting *their* interests than in sacrificing the hard-won conquest for European interests. The truth is that the government wanted peace, and their immediate priority was domestic issues. The 1745–46 uprising by Jacobite supporters of the Stuart claim to the British throne forced the authorities to focus more on their own shores than on those across the ocean. Though Louisbourg was seen as a bargaining chit with the French, the British were nonetheless determined to strengthen their grasp on mainland Nova Scotia. Up until 1749 that grasp was not at all firm. There were only two tiny English-settled areas in the region: a small garrison and a clutch of officials at Annapolis Royal and a fishing base at Canso that an expedition from Louisbourg had captured in 1744. The rest of the peninsula was either the domain of the Mi'kmaq or settled by a rapidly increasing population of French-speaking, Roman Catholic Acadians, who by 1755 numbered slightly more than fourteen thousand.[21] In British eyes neither group could be trusted.

Just as the British presence was relatively insignificant on land, so it had long been weak in the waters off Nova Scotia. Although the admiralty had committed a station ship to Newfoundland since 1677; to Massachusetts, New York, and Virginia from the mid-1680s; to South Carolina since the 1720s; and to Georgia from the 1730s, Nova Scotia before 1749 received only occasional visits from vessels normally stationed at one of the nearby northern colonies.[22]

The vulnerability to attacks of the territory the British called Nova Scotia—which the French usually continued to refer to as Acadie and which for the Mi'kmaq was part of their traditional homeland of Mi'kma'ki—was brought home to the British in the 1740s. In May 1744 a contingent from Louisbourg captured and destroyed Canso. Later that year there were two unsuccessful Mi'kmaw, Maliseet, and French assaults on Annapolis Royal. In 1745 and 1746 the French made fresh attacks on Annapolis, and the armada commanded by the duc d'Enville in 1746, had it not been decimated by diseases and storms, would have easily restored French rule in Nova Scotia/Acadie.[23] Then, in 1747 a French and Native expedition made a bold attack on Anglo-American troops installed in Acadian houses at Grand-Pré. That assault, in the middle of the night and in the midst of a snowstorm, resulted in the death of about eighty provincial soldiers, including the commander.[24]

Given the precariousness of the British presence in Nova Scotia, some imperial supporters in Great Britain wanted to see a bold and innovative step to correct the situation, and quickly. For the advantage gained in Europe—with the border towns in the Low Countries being relinquished by the French—did nothing to bolster the British position in Nova Scotia. The simplest remedy was thought to be an influx of settlers loyal to George II, who would counterbalance the Acadians and the Mi'kmaq. Different settlement schemes had been urged for years. One idea floated in 1748 was to send overseas some Scottish Highlanders about to be disbanded from British regiments.[25] The government considered the project too expensive, so a less costly idea gained support, that of transporting "foreign Protestants" to the colony. That made sense in an era in which religious adherence was considered a more important determinant of loyalty than ethnicity and language.[26] No one thought it essential to have settlers from the British Isles as long as the colonists were hostile to Roman Catholic France and their Roman Catholic allies, the Mi'kmaq. It was taken for granted that all Protestants, including foreign ones, had the potential to become good British subjects.[27] Nonetheless, the "foreign Protestants" would have to swear oaths of allegiance to confirm their loyalty, which the Acadians had resisted since 1713.[28]

The settlement of non-British Protestants in a British overseas colony had already been tried in North America. In 1710 about three thousand German Protestants from the Palatinate were sent to an area along the Hudson River in upstate New York. Similar approaches were proposed for Nova Scotia throughout the period from 1711 to the 1740s, yet none was carried out, for there were several complicating factors. The Mi'kmaq were expected to be hostile; the Acadians already occupied the best agricultural land; the British wanted two hundred thousand acres set aside as reserved timberland for the use of the Royal Navy; and the authorities were typically reluctant to commit large expenditures to colonizing ventures.[29] What made the peopling of Nova Scotia a matter of urgency in 1748–49 was the return of Louisbourg to the French through the Treaty of Aix-la-Chapelle. With the once and future enemy stronghold to be reestablished on Cape Breton, the British wanted an equivalent base in the region. Thus during the spring of 1749, contemporaneous with the preparations undertaken by the marine department on France's west coast, England witnessed its own flurry of colonizing activity. After decades of consideration, a government-sponsored British expedition to Nova Scotia was finally underway.

When French officials familiar with the situation in Atlantic Canada learned of the scale and scope of the British venture, they perceived it as a serious threat to their interests. François Bigot, financial administrator (*commissaire ordonnateur*) at Louisbourg from 1739 to 1745 and incoming intendant for all New France, wrote: "If that establishment proves successful, we can abandon Acadia."[30] The remark turned out to be prescient, though at the time it was penned, 1749, it was a call for action to disrupt and destabilize the British attempt to expand its sphere of influence. The most effective means the French could devise to achieve that end in the early 1750s was to encourage attacks on British positions by the Mi'kmaq.

Initial British plans called for settlements in five locations of Nova

Scotia. For 1749, however, the focus was on only one, the primary destination. It was the large harbor the Mi'kmaq had for centuries called Kjipuktuk, situated midway along the eastern, or ocean, coast of Nova Scotia. Early in the eighteenth century, before the 1713 Treaty of Utrecht, a French engineer projected fortifications for the haven he called Chibouquetou.[31] In the 1730s British Captain Thomas Durell authored a draft of the harbor, and in 1739 Captain Peter Warren proposed it as a site for British settlement.[32] Then in 1746 the anchorage was the rendezvous site for the duc d'Enville and his ill-fated armada. The French commander and hundreds of sailors came to a tragic end along its shores, but the potential of the big harbor was unmistakable. When the British established themselves there in 1749, they renamed it Halifax, after George Montague Dunk, Earl of Halifax. His lordship was president of the Board of Trade, which played the leading role in supporting the project of a settlement expedition to Nova Scotia.

The move the Board of Trade took in establishing Halifax in 1749 was not unique, though it was unusual in the overall British colonizing approach. Louis XIV had decided in the 1660s that it would henceforth be best to have direct royal control over colonies, but the British had not followed that path. Their preference was for colonization by companies, families, and individuals. Not until 1732–33, with the creation of Georgia out of South Carolina, did the British government initiate a large-scale, subsidized colonial venture. As was the case with Halifax, the initiative in Georgia was primarily strategic. In the case of the southern colony, Georgia was to serve a buffer between the Anglo-American colonies and French Louisiana and Spanish Florida. Nova Scotia, with Halifax and other new settlements, was to strengthen the British presence in a region that had Canada on one side and Île Royale and Île Saint-Jean on the other. If Georgia was a breakthrough, the founding of Halifax was an escalation of the policy. Of the two initiatives, according to a specialist on the British colonial administration, "the colonization of Nova Scotia, which was a measure of defence against the French in Cape Breton and Canada, was . . . [the] more expensive project." Between 1748 and 1752 the British Parliament voted sums "amounting to £336,707 for the enterprise, and the expenditure continued on only a slightly smaller scale for the next five years." Such appropriations were exceptional in the context of British colonial policy. Renowned Parliamentarian Edmund Burke protested the money spent in Nova Scotia. "Good God!" exclaimed Burke. "What sums the nursing of that ill-thriven, hard-visaged and ill-favored brat has cost to this wittol nation! Sir, this colony has stood us in a sum of not less than £700,000."[33]

The Founding of Halifax

The expedition that established Halifax began as an advertisement in the London *Gazette* on March 18, 1749; on the outdated Julian calendar the British were still following at the time, the notice appeared on March 7. The advertisement announced a "civil government" was to be established "for the better peopling and settling" of Nova Scotia. Land grants were available to qualified settlers, with the largest acreages reserved for military officers. Tools, materials, and rations were offered for a full year. The organizers hoped to attract former soldiers and sailors who would help defend the place against anticipated attacks by French and Mi'kmaq. Equally important, the venture required a range of trades people, first to build the settlement and later to make it prosper. Individuals and families interested in relocating to Nova Scotia had one month to think it over because the deadline for signing up was April 18. Would-be settlers were to be on board three days later, with the expedition to sail on May 1.[34] Given the risks and uncertainties involved in a journey to a faraway land inhabited by those known to be hostile to British settlers—there were profound fears of Aboriginal peoples in many parts of Europe—it was a short time frame for possible emigrants to make up their minds.[35]

The departure for Nova Scotia ended up being delayed, until May 25, when at last a flotilla of thirteen transports set sail, accompanied by the sloop of war the *Sphinx*, with 2,576 settlers, a large majority of whom were adult males. According to the person in charge of the expedition, however, "the number of industrious, active men proper to undertake and carry on a new settlement, [was] very small." Colonel Edward Cornwallis thought most of the settlers were idle and worthless. He commented that there were only about three hundred willing to do the work that was going to be necessary.[36]

In 1749 Edward Cornwallis (1713–76) was a thirty-six-year old career army officer who had seen active service in Flanders in 1744 and in Scotland in 1745–46, including at the battle of Culloden. His career path had

33

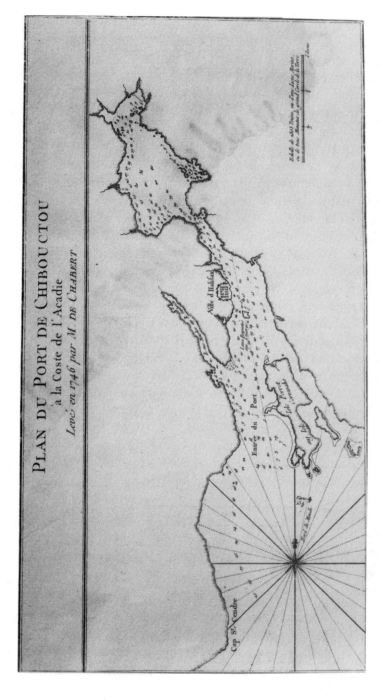

FIGURE 3. **British Rival**

This French map of the newly settled British base on mainland Nova Scotia—Halifax was established in 1749—reveals how closely the administration at Louisbourg followed developments at Halifax. "Chibouctou" is derived from the language of the Mi'kmaq and means "at the biggest harbor." *Courtesy of Parks Canada, Fortress of Louisbourg, National Historic Site of Canada, Photo Number: 2000 R 01 06.*

been helped by connections at court. A royal page at twelve, Cornwallis became a groom of the royal bedchamber in 1747. His promotion to colonel took place in March 1749, just as the plan to settle Nova Scotia was hastily implemented. His instructions reiterated the information in the London *Gazette*, namely, that the colony was being founded "for the better peopling of [the] said Province with British Subjects." Moreover, the initiative was for "improving and extending the valuable fishery thereof."[37] Cornwallis sailed to Nova Scotia aboard the *Sphinx* and became governor on arrival. The laws and governmental structure of the newly expanded colony were based on those of Virginia.[38] In an effort to attract people from the Anglo-American colonies to the south, settlers to Nova Scotia were given protection from debts incurred previously in another colony, a provision that might have sounded attractive to ne'er-do-wells.[39]

Edward Cornwallis and the other officials of the 1749 expedition had two main tasks before them. The first was to render the new settlement habitable before the onset of winter. They had several months to lay out lots and concessions and to erect houses and other forms of shelter. The location they selected for construction was roughly halfway along a peninsula that had Halifax harbor on one side and an inlet today called the Northwest Arm on the other. The second task was equally important: to make the fledgling town defensible. The spot selected as the town site was one where the land rose steeply from the water's edge—at the foot of a drumlin a glacier had left behind—which later generations would come to call Citadel Hill. In short order blockhouses stood at five locations encircling the settlement, initially linked by felled trees and logs and later by a palisade of pickets.

The British anticipated that the settlement could be attacked by land or sea or from both approaches at the same time. The enemy expected by land was the Mi'kmaq; the enemy feared from the sea, even though it was theoretically a time of peace, was the French. Two infantry regiments, Hopson's and Warburton's, arrived from Louisbourg after it was handed over to the French in July 1749 to give Halifax a force to defend itself. Also present to help out in the defense were sixty or so rangers led by Captain John Gorham. Some were Mohawks; others came from a mix of Native and European backgrounds. They were accustomed to the guerrilla warfare of the North American frontier, which typically meant sudden raids on vulnerable individuals and groups rather than formal maneuvers by lines of massed troops.[40] In addition to the land-based forces, a number of armed vessels kept communications and goods moving among the few scattered British posts in Nova Scotia.[41]

The challenges involved in creating a European-style community on the forested slopes of Halifax harbor were largely met. An eyewitness described the first few weeks in these terms:

> We have already cleared about 20 acres, and everyone has a hut by his tent. Our work goes on briskly, and the method of employing the people in ships' companies has a good effect, and as the Governor is preparing to lay out the lots of land, we shall soon have a very convenient and pleasant town built, which is to be called Halifax. There are already several wharves built, and one gentleman is erecting a saw mill; public store houses are also building, and grain of various sorts have been sown. We have received constant supplies of plank and timber for building, and fresh stock and rum in great quantities, 20 schooners frequently coming in one day. We have also a hundred cows and some sheep, brought down to us by land, by the French [Acadians] at Minas. . . . The French Deputies [Acadians] who came to make submission have promised to send us 50 men for the purpose, and to assist us as far as they are able; we have received the like promise, and friendship and assistance from the Indians, the Chief having been with the Governor for that purpose. In short, every thing is in a prosperous way.[42]

The optimism of the letter writer was premature. Substantial government expenditures had allowed Halifax to become an instant town, yet the place was to endure a number of crises and setbacks in its first few years. They included an excessive sale and consumption of alcohol and an epidemic of typhus that claimed nearly one thousand lives over the winter of 1749–50. Novelist cum historian Thomas Raddall wrote that the loss of life was actually "all . . . for the best" as "Halifax was purged of its worst human element": "the unclean, the drunken, the shiftless, the physical dregs of a populace," More recent historians observe that the initial losses were offset by an influx of settlers from New England, "mainly small businessmen and professionals, drawn north by the lure of government money."[43]

While disease was a definite worry, many settlers at Halifax had an equal dread of the Mi'kmaq. The thought of an attack by Native warriors filled most Europeans with terror.[44] Despite the optimism of the eyewitness quoted earlier, the chiefs or other leaders who met with Governor Cornwallis in 1749 were not in a position to guarantee peaceful relations since none were from the immediate area. They were Wolastoqiyik (from the Saint John River Valley, New Brunswick), Passamaquoddies (from the Maine–New Brunswick border area), and Mi'kmaq from the Chignecto isthmus (Nova Scotia–New Brunswick border). The Mi'kmaq from the heartland of peninsular Nova Scotia and from Île Royale, where an alliance with the French was strongest, did not welcome the British initiative. They were enraged by the venture.[45]

Mi'kmaw Reaction

As mentioned at the beginning of this chapter, when the Mi'kmaq of the Maritimes learned that a large British settlement party had arrived at Kjipuktuk to clear land and put up buildings, there was consternation. Relations between the two peoples had not been extensive over the preceding century, because the English (later British) presence had been limited. Nonetheless, there had been numerous incidents of hostility, especially at or near Canso. Historian Olive Dickason claims that Anglo-Mi'kmaq warfare was "the longest of all Amerindian conflicts in North America."[46] A treaty was made between some northeastern tribes and British officials in Boston in 1725, a version of which was ratified by some Nova Scotia Mi'kmaq at Annapolis Royal in 1726.[47] Yet the bands allied with the French—those in the eastern half of mainland Nova Scotia, on Île Royale, on Île Saint-Jean, and in what is now New Brunswick—were not signatories to the peace initiative.[48] For them the prospect of British settlers and soldiers establishing themselves at Kjipuktuk was cause for profound worry.

The anxieties of the Mi'kmaq undoubtedly deepened when they listened to French missionaries offer their perspectives. Abbés Pierre Maillard and Jean-Louis Le Loutre were the most influential of the missionaries. Maillard was based on Île Royale while Le Loutre was active on the mainland, first in the Shubenacadie region and later in the Chignecto isthmus.[49] British officials typically blamed the warlike actions of the Mi'kmaq on the influence of the French missionaries. Two and a half centuries later, reading some of the self-congratulatory comments of the Abbé Le Loutre, it is difficult not to conclude that the missionaries did have influence. Le Loutre wrote to the minister of the marine in France in July 1749: "I will do all that is possible to make it seem to the English that this design comes from the Indians and that I have nothing to do with it."[50]

No sooner were the British ashore at Halifax than Mi'kmaw elders and chiefs within the Maritime region met to discuss how to deal with the changed situation. The place they chose to hold their talks was on Île Royale, at or near today's St. Peter's, which the French called Port Toulouse and the Mi'kmaq referred to as Potlotek. The area was a traditional portage route and meeting place.[51] Chiefs, elders, and other leaders gathered there in September 1749, two months after the British landed in Halifax. Abbé Maillard, a fluent speaker of the Mi'kmaw language, took part in the discussions and likely had a hand in composing the letter of protest that resulted, which was written in French and Mi'kmaq. While Maillard may have helped the chiefs to articulate their concerns in French, he did not invent or impose the sense of anger the leadership expressed. The letter to the British governor at Halifax was finalized on September 24 ("five days before St. Michael's day"). The outrage and disappointment that the Mi'kmaq felt is apparent in these extracts.

> The place where you are, where you are building dwellings, where you are now building a fort, where you want, as it were, to enthrone yourself, this land of which you wish to make yourself now absolute master, <u>this land belongs to me</u>. I have come from it as certainly as the grass, it is the very place of my birth and of my dwelling, this land belongs to me, the Native person, yes I swear, it is God who has given it to be my country for ever . . . you drive me out; where do you want me to take refuge? You have taken almost all this land in all its extent. Your residence at Port Royal does not cause me great anger because you see that I have left you there at peace for a long time, but now you force me to speak out by the great theft you have perpetrated against me.[52]

The Mi'kmaw perspective was consistent with the sentiment expressed in writing nearly three decades earlier. In October 1720 a group of chiefs meeting at Les Mines (Minas) sent a letter to Governor Richard Philipps at Annapolis Royal, expressing their concerns. The letter was written entirely in French, presumably with the help of a French missionary. Translated, a portion of the document reads as follows:

> We believe that God gave us this land. . . . However, we see that you want to drive us from the places where you are living, and you threaten to reduce us to servitude, which is something you should not dream of. We are our own masters, not subordinate to anyone. . . . If we wanted to go to England to live there, what would they say to us, if not to make us leave. For the same reason, we do not want the English living in our land, the land we hold only from God. We will dispute that with all men who want to live here without our consent.[53]

Of course, not in 1720 nor in 1749 were the British receptive to the perspective of the Mi'kmaq. No letter or protest, no matter how eloquently written, was going to prompt a withdrawal. The establishment of Halifax as a counterbalance to Louisbourg was an imperial priority, a move that strengthened the British grasp on Nova Scotia. Its very raison d'être was to weaken the Mi'kmaw, Acadian, and French presence in the region.

It was not long before the British made more moves in Nova Scotia. There were soon additional posts in the Sackville area and in 1750 in Dartmouth, across the harbor from Halifax; they established Lunenburg as a major new "foreign Protestant" town in 1753; and they erected forts and posts right in the heart of various Acadian areas—in the Chignecto region, at Pisiquid, and at Grand-Pré—all in the early 1750s. Another initiative, pursued simultaneously, was to send rangers out to confront and attack the Mi'kmaq. For their part the Mi'kmaq sought to protect traditional territories. They launched attacks coincident with or soon after the delivery of their 1749 letter to Governor Cornwallis. British lives were lost or prisoners were taken wherever the warriors struck. At Chignecto the Mi'kmaq attacked two ships, while other warriors seized several vessels at Canso. In the vicinity of Halifax, beginning at a sawmill beyond the fortified enclosure, there were more deaths and more prisoners.[54] The Mi'kmaw warriors came from across the region, including Île Royale. Generally speaking, the assaults terrified the British settlers, soldiers, and those responsible for the administration of the colony.

The Halifax authorities responded to the attacks with measures designed to return terror with terror. Cornwallis refused to declare war on the Mi'kmaq because such a step would imply they were a sovereign people, which contemporary European thought did not envisage. Nonetheless, Cornwallis and the governing council of Nova Scotia authorized a campaign of full-scale warfare against their enemies. They directed British regulars and ranger companies to capture or kill any and all Mi'kmaq they encountered. Spared from the campaign were the Wolastoqiyik (Maliseets) and other signatories of the peace and friendship treaty signed at Halifax soon after its founding.

> For all these causes we, by and with the advice and consent of His Majesty's Council, do hereby authorize and command all Officers Civil and Military, and all His Majesty's Subjects or others, to annoy, distress, take or destroy the savages commonly called Mic-macks wherever they are found, and all such as are aiding and assisting them; and we further . . . do promise a reward of Ten Guineas for every Indian, Mic-mack, taken or killed to be paid upon producing such savage taken or his scalp (as is the custom in America) if killed, to the Officers commanding at Halifax, Annapolis Royal or Minas.[55]

Brutal though the measure was, scalping bounties were not unusual at the time.[56] One needs to recall as well that it was an era in which millions of Africans were enslaved and public executions in European countries and their colonies were routine. In the specific context of European-Aboriginal relations, the French, the British, and the Anglo-Americans all paid bounties for scalps on at least an occasional basis.[57] The money was a temptation some could not resist. On one occasion British soldiers shot twenty-five French and brought in their scalps, claiming they were Mi'kmaq so they could obtain the £250 bounty.[58]

Although the French and British were officially at peace, in the Nova Scotia of 1749 acts of violence in anticipation of war occurred across the region.

Louisbourg Reborn

The ships that were to reestablish the French presence on Île Royale arrived off the rocky coast of Louisbourg on June 29, 1749. At the same time, Edward Cornwallis and the British settlers were a few days sail away from Halifax. The Louisbourg-bound French flotilla consisted of two men-of-war, a convoy of transports with the civil population and a contingent of soldiers, and a frigate drawing up the rear. The ships remained outside the port while the incoming French governor dispatched a shore party to discuss with the British commander at Louisbourg the details of how and when the French would enter the harbor. Two officers went ashore as envoys, Michel de Gannes de Falaise and Jean-Chrysostome Loppinot. For both it was a homecoming of sorts. Both had been born in Port-Royal, though each had spent most of his life and military career at Louisbourg before the loss of the colony in 1745.[59]

The outgoing British commander was Colonel Peregrine Thomas Hopson, a career military officer. He had taken over as Louisbourg's governor from Charles Knowles in 1747. Three years into the future, in 1752, he would replace Edward Cornwallis as governor of Nova Scotia.[60] In late June 1749 his immediate preoccupation was overseeing the handover of Louisbourg and the relocation of the British forces to Halifax. In his initial discussions with Gannes and Loppinot, Hopson agreed that the French vessels could sail into Louisbourg harbor at noon the following day, June 30. Accordingly, when the moment arrived, the incoming French ships fired artillery salutes, to which the British-manned shore batteries responded with their own salvos. The combination was loud and impressive, the greatest display of gunpowder since the place had been bombarded into submission four years earlier. More ceremonial honors took place in the afternoon of June 30, when the French governor and his staff officers went ashore to meet with Hopson. Additional meetings took place over the next few weeks as the two sides worked out the details of transferring the colony from one side to the other. As the logistics of the formal handover were being finalized, there were pressing matters that could not wait. Four French settlers waiting at anchor died before the British withdrew. Each received a Roman Catholic burial service performed by the incoming Récollet priests and was interred in the town's parish cemetery.[61]

41

The new governor of Île Royale, and by extension of Île Saint-Jean (Prince Edward Island), was Charles Desherbiers de La Ralière (1700–1752). Desherbiers was already familiar with Louisbourg, or at least with its port facilities. His entire career had been in the marine service, and as a ship's officer he had made previous voyages to New France, including Louisbourg. This was his first posting on land, and he accepted it with reluctance. As was typical of many high-placed appointees for Île Royale, Desherbiers came to Louisbourg without his wife—she remained in France—but he was accompanied by a cook and seven other servants. It did not take him long to begin asking for a position back in France. His wish was granted in 1751. Though he spent only two years on Île Royale, Desherbiers dealt with the major challenges of reestablishing Louisbourg and the many smaller settlements on the island that were essential for the fishery. In addition Governor Desherbiers gave much thought to dealing with the new reality of a major British presence in the region, something that had not existed prior to the founding of Halifax. When Desherbiers returned to France, he could look back on having overseen a successful transitional phase in which Île Royale reemerged as a bastion of Louis XV's overseas empire.[62]

Accompanying Governor Desherbiers to Louisbourg in the summer of 1749 was a civil population of just under two thousand men, women, and children.[63] Most were familiar with the town because they had lived there prior to its capture in 1745. On their return to the colony they were perhaps surprised to learn that several dozen subjects of Louis XV had not crossed the sea to France in 1745. These were individuals who had opted to stay and live and work on the island despite the fact that it had fallen to the enemy. The incoming French officials ordered a census of that group. The total came to forty-five individuals, all of whom were objects of suspicion. The doubts were most pronounced about a man who had worked as a pilot for the British for the four years in question. The new Louisbourg authorities noted that he claimed "to have been forced by them."[64]

One small group had actually preceded the 1749 refounding expedition: a detachment of soldiers sent to the colony by the acting governor general of New France. When word of the preliminary peace settlement from Aix-la-Chapelle reached Quebec in the summer of 1748, the marquis de La Galissonière sent twenty-five to thirty soldiers to Île

Royale and a similar squad to Île Saint-Jean. The contingents were selected from the troops who had traveled from Rochefort to Quebec in 1748. La Galissonière obtained the permission or agreement of the British commanding officers on the two islands before sending the soldiers. The detachments were to carry out a range of tasks, with cutting firewood the most important. La Galissonière wanted the two former colonies to be as prepared as possible for the arrival of the approximately three thousand colonists and soldiers in mid-1749.[65]

Louisbourg in July 1749 was not exactly the place the French had sailed away from in 1745. The effects of the siege and of the subsequent occupation by Anglo-American and then British troops had brought changes. The British documented what they considered to be thirty-five noteworthy alterations they had made to the town and its fortifications.[66] Some houses and storehouses remained unrepaired from the bombardment of 1745; others were improved. There were several new buildings in town, the largest being a brewery and a barracks. The changes, for better or for worse, mattered immensely to individual owners whose property was affected. Yet in broad terms the fortified town of Louisbourg was certainly recognizable to those who had lived there until 1745. Four years of military occupation by the enemy were insufficient to change the fundamental shape and character of the fortified town as it had developed over the preceding three decades.

When the French had initially taken possession of Louisbourg in 1713, they had not marked the event with elaborate ceremonies. It was September, they had nowhere to live, and there was neither the time nor the inclination for pageantry. The people in charge of the 1749 reoccupation, however, felt it was imperative to reflect the high value the king placed on Île Royale. Thus they organized elaborate ceremonies. The fact the British were still present in town likely provided an added incentive. The actual transfer of possession took place on July 23, more than three weeks after the French arrival. When the big day arrived, the French organized a ceremony with assembled lines of troops, drumrolls, and booming artillery salutes. The union flag of Great Britain was lowered and the white flag of France raised on each flagstaff. In the culmination of the day's pageantry, Hopson handed the keys to Desherbiers. Louisbourg and Île Royale were officially back in French hands.[67]

Despite the formal handover, the British did not in fact sail away for another week, not until July 30. The overlap of thousands of people from two rival and suspicious sides, with much coming and going in the town and on the harbor, generated confusion. An English child, aged about three months, somehow got away from her parents. When no family member claimed the girl, she was accepted into the French community. The conditional baptism took place on July 27, when she was christened Angélique.[68]

Once the British withdrawal from Louisbourg was complete—it was hastened by the French offer to use a few of *their* transports to carry the British troops to Halifax—it was time for yet another celebration. On August 3, a *Te Deum*, the ancient Latin hymn of Thanksgiving, was sung. The entire French garrison, about one thousand marine troops, took part in the event. They stood outside on the ramparts and on the *place d'armes* of the King's Bastion, for there was insufficient room inside the relatively small Chapelle Saint-Louis, which served as the community's parish church. At the conclusion of the *Te Deum*, three rounds of musket fire and a twenty-one-gun salute marked the occasion.[69]

When the French vessels returned from transporting British troops to Halifax, they brought with them aboard *Le Grand St-Esprit* the remains of the duc d'Enville. The commander of the ill-fated 1746 expedition had perished at Halifax, where he was interred on the small snowshoe-shaped island the British came to call Georges Island.[70] Brought to Louisbourg on September 3, Enville's remains were reinterred, with artillery salutes from ships in the harbor and batteries on shore. There was a full funeral service, and the remains were buried beneath the floor of the Chapelle Saint-Louis. This marked the third major interment in that general area, as two previous commandants of Île Royale, Isaac-Louis de Forant and Jean-Baptiste-Louis Le Prévost Duquesnel, were already buried there. The expenditures for the duc d'Enville's arrival and interment at Louisbourg were even greater than what was spent on the formal ceremonies celebrating the reestablishment of the colony a month earlier. A total of 388 livres were spent on artillery salutes and another 546 livres and 454 livres for "diverse supplies" and interment, respectively.[71]

The various ceremonies held in the first few months of the return of the French to Louisbourg share an underlying quality. They were all official demonstrations that Île Royale was once more a French possession. As celebratory assertions their scale had never before been seen in Louisbourg, which suggests that officials wanted to drive away the cloud of loss and defeat that had hung over the colony since 1745. When the ceremonies were over, everyone could look ahead. Nearly two thousand civilians were back, and the fishery, trade, and other ventures were reestablished. Importantly, Louis XV had sent a garrison of soldiers numbering roughly twice that in 1745. The increase demonstrated a fresh resolve on the part of the king and the minister of the marine to hold on to Louisbourg and Île Royale. Around the same time additional troops were also sent to Louisiana and to Canada.[72] From the French perspective, therefore, there were definite reasons to be optimistic about the future.

2

Middle Game, 1750–1755

T he events of 1749 altered more than the physical surroundings at Halifax and Louisbourg. Because the two major initiatives elevated the hopes and fears of all implicated peoples—the Mi'kmaq, the Acadians, and the British and the French colonists—it became apparent to all that fresh clashes were likely if not inescapable. Like time-release chemicals, the founding and refounding expeditions of 1749 were destined to make even more volatile an already unstable situation.[1]

Louisbourg Reinvents Itself

Most of the nearly two thousand civilians who disembarked at Louisbourg in July 1749 had a sense of déjà vu as they sailed into the harbor. One imagines they studied the shoreline to see how the fortified town and port had changed since they left four years earlier. Those who looked for familiar landmarks found them in the dominant spires of the barracks and the hospital. For those whose gazes sought differences rather than similarities, they found some buildings altered and some entirely new construction. Returning property owners were soon to discover that the New England and British troops who had occupied Louisbourg for four years had moved or uprooted boundary markers, which caused confusion for more than a few neighbors.[2]

It is possible that many returnees came back to Louisbourg with the beginnings of a common identity beyond that of being French-speaking and Roman Catholic. The life-altering events and shared experiences of the past four years—siege, forced removal, exile, return—may have fostered a common identity of Louisbourgeois or Île Royalais or some other specific colonial tag. The documents are completely silent on this point, but then they were primarily produced by officials for the specific needs of the state. Nomenclature was not a topic on which they commented. All we can safely surmise is that most settlers coming back to the colony would have done so with a heightened sense of vulnerability, having learned firsthand what a lost siege could bring.

The weather proved especially unwelcoming for the resettlement contingent. The winter of 1749–50 was uncharacteristically bitter, or so said those who had lived in the colony before. Winds out of the north and the west persisted, large snowfalls slowed construction work, and there was what financial administrator Jacques Prévost described as "excessive cold." The combination also disrupted the winter cod fishery, one of two main fishing periods on Île Royale. Prévost reported to the minister of the marine that scurvy and the severe weather attacked those who were new to the island colony, and it outright killed "some of the idlers and laziest." The difficult winter made the colonists long for contact with the outside world. Prévost recorded that the first news from the Chignecto region—where lies today's border between Nova Scotia and New Brunswick—arrived around April 4. Twenty-three days later a ship from Saint-Jean-de-Luz sailed into Louisbourg harbor with the first news from France.[3]

Weather and isolation aside, life in the reestablished capital of Île Royale was not the same as it had been before 1745. For starters the French garrison was starting out 50 percent larger than before, and the number of soldiers would soon climb again. In 1755 the total would rise to about 2,100 enlisted men, triple the level of 1745. In 1758 it jumped once more, to approximately 3,500 soldiers. The increases pushed the military from being about one-quarter of the town's population in the 1740s to nearly one-half by the mid-1750s. In other words, men in uniform became even more conspicuous in streets, taverns, and other public areas than they had been during the first French occupation. More soldiers meant greater security, at least in times of war. In times of peace, though, more men-at-arms usually meant an increased likelihood for conflicts and strife between the civil and the military segments of the population.

In addition to a larger garrison, Louisbourg of the 1750s witnessed a higher concentration of civilians within its fortifications than before. In the 1720s, when the port was only beginning to take shape, roughly half of the civilians lived on fishing properties ringing the harbor. During the 1730s, because construction was increasingly taking place within the rising fortifications, the proportion outside the defenses declined to 34 percent. Following the devastation that occurred in 1745, the second period of French occupation would witness a further decrease in those willing to live beyond the defenses. A census in 1752 recorded only 21 percent of the civil population living *extra muros*. In absolute terms that meant there were 2,490 civilians at Louisbourg in 1752, with 1,969 within the fortified town and 521 outside. The numbers suggest that many inhabitants, consciously or unconsciously, feared a second assault.

Though Louisbourg's defensive readiness was the responsibility of military engineers, senior officers, and top royal officials, ordinary colonists would have had their own thoughts on the matter. Anyone with family, property, or other interests to protect had to worry that the new stronghold at Halifax was going to have a negative impact. One civilian who put his thoughts on paper was Jean-Pierre Roma. Roma was a merchant and fishing proprietor who spent about fifteen years in France's Atlantic colonies, mostly on Île Saint-Jean. During that time he was a frequent visitor to Louisbourg. When his establishment on Île Saint-Jean was destroyed by a force of New Englanders in 1745, Roma made his way to Quebec. In 1750 he penned a memoir of over sixty pages on the situation in the Atlantic region. His analysis emphasized that the founding of Halifax changed everything. The size of the establishment meant that the British were able to adopt a more aggressive attitude toward the Acadians and the Mi'kmaq. The new enemy stronghold, therefore, was a definite threat to Île Royale and Île Saint-Jean. Roma repeated the cliché that Île Royale was the rampart for Canada, to which he added that Louisbourg was the "key" to that role. In the evolving situation, he wrote, the French stronghold "asked not to be a little better fortified, but *much* better." Roma offered pages of suggestions on how to render the vulnerable "amphitheater" at Louisbourg more defensible.[4]

Roma's lengthy and detailed comments were unlikely to have had any impact on the minister of the marine at Versailles or on officials at Louisbourg. Neither tended to listen to civilian opinions. So it was probably only a coincidence that Roma got his wish when the authorities in France sent an experienced engineer to the colony in 1750, for the express purpose of making recommendations on how to improve defenses around the region. The engineer was Lieutenant Colonel Louis Franquet (1697–1768).[5]

Franquet, a fifty-three-year-old bachelor, reached Louisbourg in August 1750, at which time he was intending to remain on Île Royale only long enough to assess the situation. He ended up spending much of the next eight years in the colony, though there were trips to Canada, Île Saint-Jean, the Chignecto region, and France during that period. In 1751 he was promoted to colonel, and from 1754 onward, while based at Louisbourg, Franquet held the title of director of fortifications for all New France. The longer the engineer stayed at Louisbourg, many colonists may have thought, the more likely it was that the batteries and *enceinte* of their town were going to be strengthened. After all, that was the reason the engineer was sent to the colony. Yet were there not likely a few cynics who offered that studies and recommendations are just talk until money turns ideas into reality? Franquet's plans and drawings, no matter how well conceived, were not going to defend anyone.

The engineer's examination revealed that parts of the Louisbourg fortifications were still showing the effects of the recent siege. For instance, the New Englanders had reduced to rubble the main landward entrance, the Dauphin Gate on the west side of town, which compelled the victorious army to enter by the Queen's Gate on the eastern side of town in 1745. They did so with flags flying, drums beating, and trumpets, violins, and flutes playing.[6] The British undertook some fortification repairs during their four years of occupation—the place had to be defensible in the event of a French counterattack—yet Franquet saw there was much left to be done. Damage aside, the newly arrived engineer from France pointed out that the Louisbourg defenses were modest in comparison with some of the elaborate fortresses in Europe. The Louisbourg enceinte was simple, one that could be likened to a so-called first system of the great seventeenth-century engineer Sébastien Le Prestre de Vauban.[7] In North America, where earthworks and palisades were the usual form of defense, Louisbourg's masonry revetments made it a formidable stronghold. Or at least that was the impression some contemporaries took away when they gazed from a distance at stone bastions and curtain walls. Louis Franquet was under no such illusion. The reason he was in the colony was to recommend ways the defenses could be improved to avoid a repeat of 1745, when an amateur army of determined Anglo-Americans had proven that Louisbourg was far from invincible.

Franquet knew as well as the next military engineer that the great Vauban had written that with time and sufficient force, any fortress could be taken. In the particular case of Louisbourg, located on an island remote from any possible reinforcements from Canada or France, one of the keys to its defense was the presence of a strong naval squadron. Unfortunately for the French, the British were the dominant imperial power in that regard. And it was in an attempt to compensate for that relative weakness on the high seas that the French erected a few key land-based strongholds, of which Louisbourg was one.[8] Franquet's mission was to find ways to improve the walls and outer defenses of that particular bastion. In 1751 he produced plans for elaborate redoubts to be constructed on the landward side. The minister of the marine, Rouillé, however, said no; there was no money in his budget to fund the project. Consequently, Franquet's impressive outer works existed only on paper. The engineer would be able to add only a few new earthworks and modest batteries to the Louisbourg enceinte during the 1750s.[9] When a second assault on Louisbourg did come, the *ville fortifiée* would look much like it had in 1745.

Life Goes On

The state of the fortifications was not the only concern at Louisbourg in the 1750s; food was another worry. There were garden plots in the backyards of most houses, yet the vegetables and herbs they produced were never enough to feed everyone all year long. Imported food was a vital part of life. Moreover, the returning inhabitants had arrived too late in 1749 to plant much during what was left of the relatively short growing season on Île Royale. Thus January and February 1750 found officials in the marine ministry in France making plans for massive amounts of supplies to be sent to the colony. The quantities were so large that ships were engaged to carry provisions to the colony from a variety of French ports: Rochefort, Bayonne, Bordeaux, Saint-Malo, Nantes, and Le Havre.[10]

Despite the overarching worries about security and food, the inhabitants of Louisbourg went on with their lives. The cycle of life continued. Thanks to an increased civil population, the annual totals for baptisms, marriages, and burials were higher than ever before. Over the span of the decade that began in 1749, the Louisbourg parish registers would record 1,114 baptisms, 332 marriages, and 579 burials. That would make for more than two thousand occasions in ten years to come when families and friends had reason either to celebrate or to mourn. When compared with the figures from the first period of French occupation at Louisbourg—the twenty-three-year period from 1722 to 1745 for which parish records are available—the numbers from the 1750s are striking. Louisbourg's last decade witnessed 100 more marriages and about the same number of baptisms and burials as in the earlier twenty-three-year period.[11]

Central to each religious ceremony were the parish priests. The Récollets of Brittany continued to serve Louisbourg as they had since the town's founding in 1713. Once again most services were performed in the Chapelle Saint-Louis, in the King's Bastion barracks. Louisbourg still had no bona fide parish church, thanks to the profound parsimony of the town's inhabitants, so the garrison chapel filled that role for another decade. The two other religious communities that had come to Louisbourg during the first period of occupation, the Brothers of Charity of Saint John of God and the Sisters of the Congregation of Notre-Dame, also returned to the colony in 1749. The brothers operated the same one-hundred-bed King's Hospital they had run until 1745, while the sisters reopened their school for girls.[12]

Another routine aspect of life that reemerged at Louisbourg was wrongdoing. Crimes were again committed. Most years only a couple of processes made their way through the courts, but in both 1751 and 1756 there were seven. Thefts were the most common infraction; next came incidents involving alleged insults or assaults. The decade also witnessed three murders and a case of disallowed marriage. If crimes were the talk of the town when they occurred, so were the punishments when the processes concluded. They ranged from fines and public apologies at one end of the spectrum through instances of banishment to people being whipped, branded, sent to the Mediterranean galleys, or executed at the other end. There was nothing hidden about the way the criminal justice system operated. Trials were generally over quickly and sentences meted out soon afterward. When there were physical punishments, they took place in public settings in front of onlookers from the community.[13]

One far from typical event in the early 1750s was the year spent in the colony by an astronomer from France. When Louis Franquet sailed to Louisbourg in 1750, a fellow passenger aboard the *Mutine* was Joseph-Bernard Chabert de Cogolin. Not surprisingly, the engineer and the astronomer dined together at the captain's table throughout the crossing. Chabert de Cogolin had previously been in Atlantic waters in 1746 as part of the ill-fated d'Enville expedition, when he was a navigator. In 1750, now an astronomer, he came to Louisbourg to make observations to correct existing maps and charts and to advance the cause of determining the longitude of known points of land. Latitudinal measurements had long been mastered by mariners and scientists, but the puzzle of longitude was still unsolved in the 1750s.

Chabert de Cogolin selected Louisbourg as the base for his experiments because it was a prominent Atlantic port in the world of French commerce. He and his assistant stayed in the colony from August 1750 to September 1751, charting the coasts of Île Royale and mainland Nova Scotia. The two scientists also oversaw the construction of an observatory on the ramparts of the King's Bastion at Louisbourg. Through the roof they trained their telescopes on the sky. Within two years of his return to France, Chabert de Cogolin published his astronomical findings on Île Royale, an important step in what turned out to be a long career.[14]

The ships that brought Chabert de Cogolin to Louisbourg and around the region for his measurements were but a few of the many vessels that sailed in and out of Île Royale waters in 1750 and 1751. In December 1750, for instance, the staff of financial administrator Jacques Prévost tabulated several ships lists. They recorded that in the course of that single year, 21 boats and schooners were built on Île Royale and Île Saint-Jean, while 30 vessels—schooners, brigantines, and boats of a generally larger tonnage—were sold at Louisbourg by vendors from the Anglo-American colonies.[15] The link with New England maritime interests was strong once more, as it had been before the last war broke out. Excluding the 30 Anglo-American vessels sold at Louisbourg and 8 more that were sent away because they were "suspects," the local admiralty office recorded another 34 New England ships that came and went as trading vessels in the course of 1750. That number was exceeded only by the 42 vessels that reached Louisbourg from European, mostly French, ports of origin. Another 33 ships sailed to Louisbourg from islands in the West Indies, and 12 from Canada.[16] Adding the numbers together, without counting the ships either sold or turned away, 121 trading vessels sailed in and out of Louisbourg harbor in 1750. The figure confirmed that the capital of Île Royale had reemerged as a busy commercial and fishing port. Merchants who worried it might not make a comeback, given the outcome of the last war, slept a little better as the year came to a close.

Move and Countermove
The war that had descended on Île Royale in 1745 was still on everyone's mind in 1749–50, as was the possibility of another conflict. The twin thoughts—recent past and probable future—affected French settlement patterns island-wide. This was because the Anglo-American campaign had brought about not only the loss of Louisbourg but also the destruction of most of the outlying settlements in the colony. When the French returned in 1749, they reoccupied the fishing outports immediately to the north of Louisbourg—Scatarie, Lorembec, and Baleine—in smaller numbers than before 1745. There was a similar drop in the population of Saint-Esprit, to the south of Louisbourg. Meanwhile, Niganiche, once the most northerly French-settled outport on Île Royale, attracted not a single French colonist in the second French period. Yet before 1745 it had been home to more than 600 inhabitants. The only part of Île Royale, besides Louisbourg, to have a population increase during the 1750s was the southeastern corner. After 1749 Petit-de-Grat became the second largest community in the colony after Louisbourg, with Port Toulouse third. A census taken in 1750 recorded that in the southeast corner of the island there were 127 families and a total population of 867.[17] That was approximately twice as many settlers in that overall area as had been there before 1745.

53

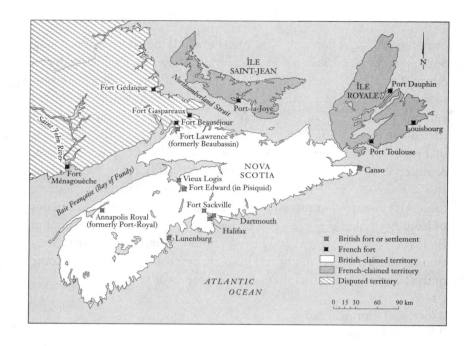

Map labels (within image):

ÎLE SAINT-JEAN

Fort Gédaïque

Northumberland Strait

Fort Gaspareaux

Fort Beauséjour

Port-la-Joye

Fort Lawrence (formerly Beaubassin)

ÎLE ROYALE

Port Dauphin

Louisbourg

Port Toulouse

Saint John River

Fort Ménagouèche

Baie Française (Bay of Fundy)

Vieux Logis

Fort Edward (in Pisiquid)

NOVA SCOTIA

Canso

Fort Sackville

Annapolis Royal (formerly Port-Royal)

Dartmouth

Halifax

Lunenburg

ATLANTIC OCEAN

N

Legend:
- British fort or settlement
- French fort
- British-claimed territory
- French-claimed territory
- Disputed territory

0 15 30   60   90 km

MAP 1. **Military Presence, ca. 1753**

In the middle of the eighteenth century the region known today as mainland Nova Scotia, Cape Breton Island (Île Royale), Prince Edward Island (Île Saint-Jean), and southeastern New Brunswick (marked as disputed territory) was a zone coveted by both France and Great Britain. This map shows the locations where the French and the British had posts or forts; it does not indicate the areas of Acadian villages or the reality that the entire region was the homeland of the Mi'kmaq and, along the Saint John River, of the Wolastoqiyik (Maliseet).

Though French colonists encountered numerous difficulties reestablishing themselves on Île Royale, their situations were nowhere near as confusing or unsettling as those faced by the Acadians and the Mi'kmaq in mainland Nova Scotia. The scale and scope of the issues and predicaments arising beyond Île Royale are best illustrated by the developments that occurred on the Chignecto isthmus.

The confused, and ultimately deadly, situation in the Chignecto area arose out of the failure of both the Treaty of Utrecht in 1713 and the Treaty of Aix-la-Chapelle in 1748 to provide precise boundaries for French and British territories. The 1713 treaty had simply made the vague reference that France was ceding to Great Britain what was Acadie according to its "ancient limits". France was to claim later that meant only a small portion of mainland Nova Scotia, whereas the British held the view that they had obtained sovereignty over all of mainland Nova Scotia and a good part of what is today's New Brunswick. As the years went by, the issue over which imperial power had jurisdiction over the Chignecto zone—neither power imagined that the indigenous people, the Mi'kmaq, might want to have a say—became far more than a debate over abstract principles. The Acadian population in the overall Chignecto area, especially at Beaubassin, was growing steadily. Were they British subjects, as the administration at distant Annapolis Royal maintained, or were they French, as claimed by even more distant officials at Louisbourg and Quebec? The boundary matter came up during the discussions at Aix-la-Chapelle in 1748, but the delegates decided to refer the topic to a specially appointed commission rather than hold up the peace process. French and British commissioners were duly named, and they would meet after the treaty was signed, but neither side showed any inclination toward compromise. France's foreign minister during the Seven Years' War, the duc de Choiseul, would later blame his predecessor for not having settled the Chignecto boundary question, because the issue had contributed to setting the stage for the next war.[18]

Legal arguments aside, the Chignecto region was critically important for strategic reasons. In the words of historian Guy Frégault: "To command the isthmus of Chignecto, linking the peninsula to the continent, was to hold Nova Scotia by the throat." Governor Edward Cornwallis shared that perspective. Writing in December 1749, only six months

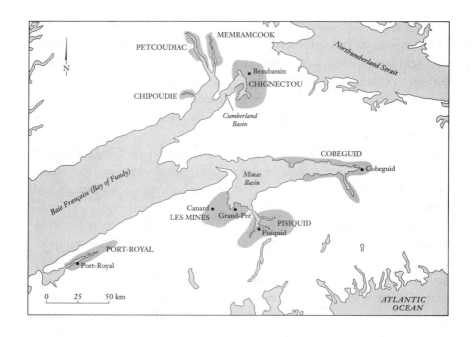

MAP 2. **Acadian Settlements before 1755**
Before the first of the forcible removals began in 1755, there were sizable Acadian villages in various parts of what today are Nova Scotia and New Brunswick. The most populous settlements were in areas with tidal salt marshes, which the Acadians could dyke and desalinate to turn them into highly arable land. The names of Acadian districts are in capital letters; the names of individual villages are in mixed case.

after Halifax was established, the governor offered: "I am firmly of Opinion that the Province cannot be Secure without a good Strength at the Isthmus, both against the French in case of War & The Indians at all times."[19]

For the French the Chignecto area had a double importance. One was as a corridor where land and sea links were made to and from Île Saint-Jean, Île Royale, the Acadian communities of mainland Nova Scotia, and the rest of New France. Baie Verte on the Northumberland Strait was the primary place where French vessels landed for trade and communication; Tatamagouche was the second harbor for that purpose. During the winter months, and sometimes even during the shipping season, officials in Quebec and Louisbourg also sent overland couriers through the Chignecto region. Meanwhile, the second value of the isthmus lay in its Acadian population and the livestock they possessed. The first French settlers had come to Beaubassin in the 1670s, with the community later fanning out to other areas, notably along the Memramcook, Petitcodiac, and Shepody rivers. By 1752 there were nine different villages, and a French census recorded the overall number of "settled" Acadians at more than 1,763, while the total for recently arrived Acadian refugees was 1,113. The administrations at Louisbourg and Quebec had two expectations for those French-speaking, Roman Catholic inhabitants. First, they were to provide livestock and other foodstuffs for the colonists of Île Royale and Île Saint-Jean; and second, they were to support French military expeditions when the need arose.[20]

The British understood the importance of the Chignecto region to the French, which made it all the more important that they find a way to reduce their rival's influence in the zone. An added incentive for the British to drive the French away and take undisputed control was that they foresaw a time when they would want to exploit the timber and agricultural land of the nearby Saint John River area.[21] That could not happen as long as there were hostile forces, French or Native, in the region.

While the boundary commissioners were failing to find a solution to the Chignecto boundary question in Europe, the representatives of Britain and France on the North American side of the Atlantic each resolved to take military steps to strengthen their positions on the strategic isthmus. As in the interior of North America—where in 1749–

50 the French erected Fort Niagara and Fort Rouillé on Lake Ontario and Fort Duquesne where today's Pittsburgh stands—so Atlantic Canada witnessed a number of French strategic initiatives. The reoccupation of Louisbourg in 1749 has been discussed earlier. Around the same time, a military officer from Canada, with orders from Governor La Jonquière, reestablished a post called Fort Ménagouèche at the mouth of the Saint John River. The officer was Charles Deschamps de Boishébert, marquis de Boishébert, a name we will encounter again. French interest in the Saint John River dated back to 1604, to the time of De Mons and Champlain, and they had learned over the course of the next century and a half that the Saint John River was the beginning of an effective inland and overland communications route to the capital of New France, Quebec. When either ice or the British were blocking the sea route to Quebec, the Saint John River and its portages and river connections offered the only link with the most populous part of French North America. In November 1749, a few months after Louisbourg was reoccupied, the French also began to construct two supply depots in the vicinity of Gédaïque (Shediac), on the Northumberland Strait shore that faced Île Saint-Jean. Gédaïque stood along a river route leading into the Chignecto region. The first large French shipment of weaponry and related stores arrived in the spring of 1750. It included four hundred flintlock rifles, three thousand gun flints, ten thousand pounds of lead shot and gunpowder, and two hundred large knives. The matériel made its way up the Shediac River under the supervision of the zealous missionary Abbé Le Loutre, then overland to the Petitcodiac River, and finally downstream to the Beauséjour/Beaubassin district. Also in 1750 the administration at Quebec dispatched a contingent of soldiers, under the command of Louis de La Corne, to establish themselves on Beauséjour ridge, on the Bay of Fundy side of the Chignecto isthmus. They probably erected earthen embankments and a log palisade as interim defenses, with full construction beginning in 1751 on a pentagonal, star-shaped earthwork fortification known as the *fort à Beauséjour*. The fort could house a garrison of a couple hundred men. Soon afterward, on the Northumberland Strait side of the isthmus, the French put up the modest Fort Gaspereau at Baie Verte, the main sea communication link with Île Saint-Jean and Île Royale.[22]

Fixed installations were not the only concern for French officials. There was also the matter of the Acadian population, a people who for decades had sought to walk a neutral line between the claims and pressures from two rival empires and from the occasional pressure exerted by the Mi'kmaq. In 1751 the administration at Quebec issued an ordinance that compelled Acadians living in the Chignecto region to swear oaths of loyalty to Louis XV or else to face the consequences of being forcibly removed from their lands. Louis de La Corne was the officer on the spot to see that the loyalty oaths were taken and that the Acadian men also joined militia companies. La Corne had recently been awarded the Cross of Saint-Louis for his leadership in the 1747 midwinter attack on New England troops at Grand-Pré, where the much smaller French and Native force had completely surprised their adversaries.[23]

While the French were making their moves in the Chignecto region and elsewhere, the British were also making theirs. As soon as they could after establishing Halifax, the British spread out from the initial wooden palisade erected below a dominating hill. They put up posts on the Dartmouth side of the harbor, across the neck of the peninsula that led to Halifax, at Sackville, in Lawrencetown, and beyond. They also constructed forts in or close to two of the Acadian communities of mainland Nova Scotia: Pisiquid, where Fort Edward was erected in 1750, and Grand-Pré, where a makeshift fort was put up in 1749.[24] Meanwhile, the British continued to keep a garrison at the former capital of Annapolis Royal, as they had done since they captured it in 1710. Despite the British place-name and role, the town and surrounding countryside were home to a populous Acadian community. Indeed, most French speakers still called Annapolis Royal by its old name of Port-Royal. Another move that reflected the British determination to establish a loyal presence in the colony was the establishment of Lunenburg in 1753, settled by a large number of "foreign Protestants." For decades some officials had urged the bringing of Protestants, foreign or British, to Nova Scotia, where they would be placed strategically in various Acadian settlements. The idea was that the influx of "loyal" Protestants into or close to the French-speaking, Roman Catholic villages would have a positive influence on the Acadians. The policy was implemented only at Lunenburg, on Nova Scotia's south shore, relatively distant from the largest Acadian villages.[25]

Of the various French and British initiatives, the ones in the contested Chignecto isthmus led to the most drastic consequences. In the spring of 1750, Governor Edward Cornwallis in Halifax dispatched Major Charles Lawrence to proceed with a contingent of troops to the Beauséjour/Beaubassin region to erect a post there. The Acadian villages in the Chignecto region, like Cobequid in central Nova Scotia, had long been well beyond the reach of British administrators at Annapolis Royal. The officials who took over after Halifax was founded in 1749 showed a much greater determination than their predecessors to exercise control in the Chignecto zone. When Lawrence arrived in the area with four hundred soldiers, however, his ships were stranded on a falling tide, unable to come ashore. From a distance they observed that every building on Beaubassin ridge, which numbered more than one hundred and included a church, was on fire or already burned.[26] What was happening was the result of the French anticipating an agreement in Europe on the boundary dispute in the Chignecto region, with the Missaguash River being selected as an agreed-upon boundary between French and British territories. That would have placed the populous settlement of Beaubassin on the "wrong" side, so the French decided to convince or compel the Acadians to move across the Missaguash to the west, or French, side of the river. A French account of the destruction and forcible relocation of the Acadians of Beaubassin stated that on April 25, 1750, "the parish of Beaubassin was entirely burned by the [Natives]." In truth the warriors were carrying out the wishes of Abbé Le Loutre and military officer Louis de La Corne. A Canadian-born officer in the Louisbourg Garrison, René Gaultier de Varennes, was to write six years later that the Acadians "had been forced into the measure of deserting their country, and passing over to the French side, by the violence of Abbot de Loutre, who had not only preached them into this spirit, but ordered the savages, whom he had at his disposal, to set fire to their habitations, barns, etc."[27]

Too late to intervene in what was occurring on Beaubassin ridge—shots were fired on both sides with the result that Lawrence and his troops were driven off—the British returned to Halifax. A much larger force came back to the zone several months later, in September 1750. This time nearly seven hundred British troops skirmished with French, Acadian, and Native men, fended them off, and came ashore. The newcomers made their way to Beaubassin ridge, with its charred ruins, and proceeded to erect a palisade in the form of a square. They called it Fort Lawrence after the leader of the expedition. For the next four years the post was the physical manifestation of British power and aspirations in the Chignecto region.

The French responded in 1751 to the erection of Fort Lawrence. Their answer was a professionally designed, star-shaped fortification on the opposite ridge. That fort atop Beauséjour ridge, known to history as Fort Beauséjour, along with the more basic fort put up at Gaspereau, also in 1751, demonstrated that the French were determined to defend their interests on the isthmus. The sudden sprouting of fortifications along the de facto border between French and British territories intensified an already tense atmosphere in the Atlantic region. In the words of one British lord, Nova Scotia in the early 1750s was in a "motly state neither peace nor war."[28]

Despite the growing tension, there was one subject where the two imperial rivals found common ground. That was on the question of dealing with deserters. Desertion was a huge problem in all European armies, at home and in the colonies. For a brief period in the 1750s there was an agreement in the Atlantic region that allowed the two sides to return each other's deserters. Such an exchange, senior officers hoped, would stop the defections. French officials generally saw themselves as the winners in the desertion game, for they believed more Roman Catholics (usually Irish or Germans) in British service switched to their side than French soldiers fled the other way. An officer at Beauséjour commented that for every soldier the French lost, the British lost ten. That was a gross exaggeration, for in 1752 as many as fifty-two soldiers deserted from the French, but nowhere near five hundred left British ranks at Halifax. In any case, the desertion agreement did not last long. The closer events moved toward open hostilities, the less reason there was for either side to return soldiers to the enemy.[29]

The many military initiatives of the late 1740s and early 1750s on the Chignecto isthmus and around the Atlantic region made many Acadians nervous. In the long-lived phrase of historian Francis Parkman, the would-be neutrals were caught "between two fires." To commit to one imperial side or the other carried grave risks, which few Acadians were willing to take. The end result was that close to half the fourteen thousand or so Acadians in mainland Nova Scotia decided to relocate to what were clearly French-controlled territories. The three primary destinations were the western side of the Missaguash River in the Chignecto region, Île Saint-Jean, and Île Royale.[30]

The French administration on Île Royale followed all developments in the Atlantic region with great interest. In fact, the governor and financial administrator at Louisbourg played a major role in the Acadian migrations that occurred between 1749 and 1754. They and their superiors in France made it a priority to entice the Acadians, along with their cattle, sheep, and pigs, to either Île Royale or Île Saint-Jean. Accordingly, they subsidized the costs of relocation and provided rations to the Acadians for several years. The hope was that the refugees from Nova Scotia would increase the population bases on the two island colonies and use their agricultural skills to render them more self-sufficient. It soon became apparent, however, that the preferred destination for the Acadians was Île Saint-Jean, not Île Royale. Several thousand took refuge on Île Saint-Jean; several hundred came to Île Royale.[31]

Wherever the Acadians settled, their difficulties were not well understood by the administration at Louisbourg. Officials there did not recognize that the vaunted Acadian agricultural productivity back in their Nova Scotia communities had been based on the unrivaled fertility of reclaimed salt marshes—conditions that did not exist on either Île Saint-Jean or Île Royale. When the relocating and relocated Acadians turned out to be a burden, bringing considerable expenses for the Louisbourg administration, the pendulum of opinion swung against the refugees. Financial administrator Prévost and Governor Desherbiers were the first to vent their frustrations with the migrating Acadians. By mid-1751 the minister of the marine himself, Rouillé, described "the subsistence of the Acadian refugees" as a "problem situation." He echoed the officials beneath him and placed the blame on "those who would take indolence too far."[32]

The same years that witnessed increased complexity for the Acadians also saw new challenges for the Mi'kmaq. After the founding of Halifax, the local British administration tried two drastically different approaches, one to win over the Mi'kmaq and the other to eliminate them. The latter approach manifested itself in the use of rangers to fight the indigenous population with the style of warfare that many mid-eighteenth-century Europeans thought was the best way to deal with such warriors: by paying a bounty for Mi'kmaw scalps. The French at Louisbourg used the same policy, only they paid the Mi'kmaq for the scalps of British settlers. The other approach Halifax pursued more or less simultaneously was a treaty-making process. In 1725 representatives of the government of Massachusetts and the chiefs of various tribes from New England, Nova Scotia, and what is now New Brunswick had signed a treaty in Boston. Six months later, in June 1726, a follow-up signing ceremony took place at Annapolis Royal, where representatives of the Mi'kmaq, the Maliseet, the Penobscots, and other nations made their marks on that document, as did the local British administration.[33] The two sides did not view, or later remember, the treaty in exactly the same manner, yet the fact there was a treaty at all was a step in the direction of a more lasting peace. No land was conceded in either the treaty of 1725 or that of 1726, nor in any subsequent treaty in what is now Atlantic Canada. The two sides simply professed peace and friendship. Both sides would commit infractions in the years that followed, yet the incidents did not deter either from continuing to look for solutions to disputes.

In 1752 a portion of the Mi'kmaw population reached a new accord with British officials in Halifax. The Mi'kmaw leaders who signed the treaty viewed it as a renewal of the accords of 1725–26, and Governor Peregrine Hopson and the other members of the Nova Scotia Council shared that perspective. One clause stated: "[A]ll Transactions of the Late War shall on both sides be buried in Oblivion with the Hatchet." Another stated that the Mi'kmaq should "use their utmost Endeavours to bring in the other Indians to renew and Ratify this Peace." That was the most important matter for the British, who knew that some bands were still actively allied to the French at Louisbourg, and their signatures were not on the 1752 treaty. Indeed, the view from Île Royale was that the leading signatory to the treaty, Jean-Baptiste Cope, was a "bad Micmac" who could not be trusted. The French utterly dismissed the treaty signed at Halifax as being "ratified by only ninety to a hundred Indians, men, women and children, all bad subjects."[34] Nonetheless, the Halifax administration hoped that the Mi'kmaq who signed the document would be able to influence the much more numerous pro-French Mi'kmaq to come over to their perspective and stop attacking the British. More than two centuries later, in the late twentieth century, the "harvesting" clauses in the 1752 treaty would have great impact. The Supreme Court of Canada found that the stipulation that the Mi'kmaq were to "have free liberty of Hunting and Fishing as usual" was still in force, giving today's Mi'kmaq special access to certain resources.[35]

A Revolving Door

The swirl of change in Atlantic Canada after 1749 also manifested itself in the administration of Île Royale. In 1751 the minister of the marine, Antoine-Louis Rouillé, comte de Jouy, authorized Governor Desherbiers to return to France. Two years in a colony was more than the long-time ship captain wanted to spend. His successor was Jean-Louis de Raymond, comte de Raymond (ca. 1702–71). Raymond's appointment, which was as commandant, not full governor, marked the first time the top position in the colony was filled by someone with a military background. All previous governors and commandants had been from the "navy" side of the marine department. Prior to embarking for Louisbourg, Raymond was the second in command, or king's lieutenant, at Angoulême, in midwestern France. Before that he had been a lieutenant colonel of the Vexin Regiment.[36]

It turned out that the comte de Raymond, like Desherbiers, would remain on Île Royale only two years. Nonetheless, Raymond made his short stay eventful. For instance, in a bid to increase agricultural production he established several new inland settlements, something rare in a colony where the maritime economy generally dictated coastal communities. Raymond also oversaw an ambitious program of road construction. On the military side of his responsibilities, the comte proposed new redoubts for many undefended harbors on the island. Some of his ideas or actions were scorned by others—such as when he permitted fifteen soldiers to marry on a single day, in the hopes that they would settle permanently in the colony.[37] His secretary, Thomas Pichon, described his employer as "possibly the stupidest of all two-footed animals." Pichon had come across the Atlantic with Raymond and would later begin to work as a spy for the British after falling out with the commandant and being transferred to the French fort at Beauséjour.[38] Yet Pichon was not alone in finding fault with the commandant. Chief engineer Louis Franquet opposed several of Raymond's grandiose projects, especially road construction. Meanwhile, a high ranking officer in the Louisbourg garrison, troop major Michel Le Courtois de Surlaville, drew up a list of no less than sixty-six "foolish mistakes" he felt Raymond had committed during his time at Louisbourg.[39]

One area where the commandant excelled was in the ceremonial aspects of his position. He took his responsibilities as the king's representative seriously and set out to mark "royal" occasions in style. To that end he committed considerable sums of the king's money to pay for lavish displays. The most extravagant example occurred in 1752, when word reached Louisbourg that there had been another royal birth, that of the duc de Bourgogne. The authorities in France asked for a *Te Deum*, the ancient Latin hymn of thanksgiving. Raymond resolved to do much more and ordered the most extensive celebration ever seen on Île Royale. The artillery salutes were long and loud and used up nearly three tons of black powder. That was roughly half the total amount consumed in the entire year. Besides the cannon blasts, a procession through town culminated in musket salvos by lined troops and fireworks and rockets fired into the air. Barrels of wine were also made available to the public, and there was a private ball and banquet for invited guests. To cap off the massive celebration, Raymond asked for a general illumination of Louisbourg. The last effect was achieved by hanging lamps and lanterns from porticoes and pyramids erected in prominent locations.[40]

Despite Raymond's success with the ceremonial side of his position, the many criticisms of the commandant ultimately took their toll. In 1753 the minister of the marine, Rouillé, recalled Raymond to France. Within two years the comte was named the commandant at Le Havre.

The minister of the marine took his time naming a successor to govern Île Royale. Rouillé had been in charge of the navy and the colonies since 1749, and he had seen two commandants spend two years each at Louisbourg. He wanted to find someone who would last longer and at the same time take steps to prepare Louisbourg for the war everyone was expecting. Little did Rouillé know, but he himself was soon to be replaced in the minister's position by former finance minister Jean-Baptiste Machault d'Arnouville.[41] Before that occurred, Rouillé did appoint Île Royale's new governor. In February 1754 he selected Augustin de Boschenry, chevalier de Drucour (1703–62), a fifty-one-year-old career naval officer whose service had begun in 1719. The name by which the officer came to be known came from the village in Normandy, Drucourt, from which the family hailed. Over the course of his career prior to Louisbourg, the naval officer had made sixteen major voyages, including several to the West Indies, two to Louisiana, and one to Atlantic Canada. In 1746 Drucour was captured by the British on the high seas and imprisoned in England for months. At the time of his appointment to the governorship of Île Royale, he was commanding the troops at Brest. Governor Drucour set sail for his posting in the early summer of 1754, accompanied by his wife, Marie-Anne Aubert de Courserac, and eight servants. He would be the last governor of Île Royale.[42]

Around the same time the French were changing governors at Louisbourg, the British leadership at Halifax was also undergoing change. Governor Peregrine Hopson returned to England in November 1753, suffering severe vision problems, though he did not officially step down as the governor of Nova Scotia until 1755. With Hopson's departure, the administration of Nova Scotia passed to military officer Charles Lawrence (ca. 1709–60). Though only an *acting* governor in 1754 and 1755, Lawrence was prepared to make bold decisions. It is worth recalling that at the time Nova Scotia, in contrast to the Anglo-American colonies to the south, lacked any institutions of representative government. On issues lacking clear direction from London, the local governor, with input and advice from an appointed five-man advisory body, the Nova Scotia Council, all of whose members were born in England or New England, determined by themselves the course of action they would take. The only body Lawrence and the council had to answer to, or fear criticisms from, was the Board of Trade in London.[43]

The Wider Context

The warlike buildup in Atlantic Canada in the late 1740s and early 1750s had its echo in the interior of North America, especially in the Ohio Valley. French and British strategic thinkers and military planners scrutinized all reports emanating from the region, trying to figure out what to do next and how to gain the upper hand.[44] The conflict was complicated because there were so many key players: officials in France and Britain, Anglo-American colonists, traders from Canada, and many different indigenous nations. A growing number of Anglo-American colonists wanted to trade and settle in the Ohio country, yet they were prevented from doing so by the real or imagined violence of the French and their Native allies. Even though the Anglo-Americans greatly outnumbered the French of New France, by a ratio of something like twenty to one, they genuinely believed that "if the French had this country [the Ohio Valley], they would in time be masters of all the British colonies."[45] The Anglo-Americans' desire to move into the region clashed head-on with French aspirations to dominate trade with the First Nations and to keep out British settlers. The numerous Aboriginal nations did not care deeply about the European power with which they were to trade. Their priorities were to secure the best goods at the lowest price and to prevent or to minimize European settlements that would alter or ruin their traditional territories.

The hostility in the Ohio country reached a new level in 1754. In April the French captured the British post of Fort George. In May a contingent of Anglo-American militia under the command of George Washington overwhelmed a French party, killing the commander and nine others. The French retaliated in July, capturing Fort Necessity, along with George Washington and the troops under his command. Like Pandora's box, once the conflict had opened, it was not going to close without dire consequences.

Officially France and Great Britain remained at peace until formal declarations of war were exchanged in 1756. In reality an undeniable war began in North America in 1754.[46] The developments in the Atlantic region began to match and then exceed those in the Ohio Valley in 1755. A number of hostile acts led up to that pivotal year. One minor incident involved a military officer from Louisbourg, identified as Loppinot *fils*. He sailed to Massachusetts in the fall of 1753 to learn English, presumably to fill the role of English interpreter in the Louisbourg garrison. The sojourn, however, did not unfold as expected. In February 1755, as planning was under way for an expedition of New Englanders to seize the Chignecto region from the French, Governor William Shirley of Massachusetts ordered the Louisbourg officer placed in prison. Loppinot objected, pointing out that there was no state of declared war. The argument fell on deaf ears, and he was not released until the spring of 1756, when he was exchanged for an English officer captured by the French at Oswego. At that time Loppinot was sent to England, then on to France.[47]

Loppinot *fils* was unfortunate to have been in the wrong place at the wrong time. His detainment, along with all the other events of 1754–55, provided one more indication that after years of posturing and bluff, a moment of truth was arriving for the French and the British in North America. New Englanders were fond of saying that the return of Louisbourg to France by the Treaty of Aix-la-Chapelle was a "loan" they were going to take back at the earliest opportunity.[48] Though they spoke specifically of Louisbourg, the Anglo-Americans really meant it as a shorthand for the French presence in the Atlantic region. As 1755 unfolded, Anglo-Americans and a few British imperial officials were to demonstrate that their boasts were not idle talk.

War in a Time of Peace

The year 1755 started in Louisbourg like the years that immediately preceded it, with an exchange of worried correspondence between officials on both sides of the Atlantic. The dominant subject was British plans and movements. The memoranda contained a mix of fact and rumor, with the focus often on the rumors. Agents reported that there was more activity than usual at the naval dockyards of England, prompting officials in the marine ministry to conclude that "offensive action in America" was in the works. Louisbourg was thought the "premier objet," as Machault d'Arnouville, the new marine minister, expressed it.[49] Its strategic location, its potential as a French naval base, its loss in 1745, and the buildup in Nova Scotia since 1749 all pointed to the capital of Île Royale being a likely target for a British offensive. The dispatches to and from Louisbourg reflected a sense of urgency. Preparations were drawing to what was thought to be a close; full-scale war was coming.

From the perspective of two and a half centuries later, the British were more the initiators and the French the reactors in the decade that began in 1749. Many factors lay behind the difference in the courses adopted by the two powers. The most obvious influences were the massive indebtedness of the French treasury, a burgeoning economy in Britain, increasing British support for colonial ventures, and British superiority on the sea lanes. Despite the advantages the British possessed in the broad imperial context, within the specific setting of Nova Scotia, the administration in Halifax felt vulnerable. Even after founding and fortifying the new capital, officials worried they could still easily lose control of the rest of the territory. The establishments at Halifax and Lunenburg, along with strategically placed forts and blockhouses elsewhere on the Nova Scotia mainland, did not give the administration in Halifax the sense of dominance it felt was needed. British colonists were still greatly outnumbered by Acadians, and the worry over attacks by the Mi'kmaq did not end after a treaty was signed in 1752. There were many more Mi'kmaq who had not signed the accord than had made their mark. That majority was still actively allied with the French.

The one area where the British felt confident was on the high seas. Individual ships of Louis XV were as well built, and sometimes even better built, than those of George II, yet the French king did not have enough of them. In the largest vessel category, ships of the line, France had 45 such ships in 1756, while Britain possessed nearly 130, roughly three times as many.[50] Some French captains may have wanted to be more aggressive at sea, but they were directed not to be. Out of necessity the French naval approach was based on avoidance rather than encounter. Historian George Stanley explains: "French losses bore more heavily upon the French marine than did those of England upon the English. . . . French sailors came to regard it as a victory if they could slip by the British blockade of Brest, Rochefort or Toulon, and make the run successfully to North America. . . . Defensively-minded, the French naval vessels were disposed to look to the fog and wind rather than to their guns to defeat the machinations of their enemy."[51]

British superiority at sea spelled obvious trouble for Louisbourg. Its raison d'être was as a harbor from which in peacetime the French pursued fishery and trade and to which in wartime they might send or shelter ships and troops to protect their interests in the region. Impressive as its bastions and batteries were to North Americans who had not been to Europe, everyone knew that Louisbourg had one major weakness. Aid and reinforcements could come only by ship and from a great distance.

As Charles Knowles observed when he was British governor of Louis-bourg in 1746: "[W]hatever nation sends the Strongest fleet into these seas will always be masters of the Cod fisheries for that year whether there be a Louisbourg or not."[52]

Since the French were not in a position to defeat their rivals in an all-out war at sea, their approach to colonization proceeded differently than did that of the British. They adopted a program of erecting strongholds at a few select strategic locations, of which Louisbourg was one.[53] In the event of hostilities, the leadership of Île Royale expected they would be an early target. Thus when intelligence reports spoke of increased fleet activity in English ports and of fresh provincial troops being raised in Boston, French officials presumed Louisbourg was going to be hit again. France had to act, because to do nothing was to give up on its colonies. Accordingly, in 1755 Louis XV authorized sending seventy-eight com-panies, approximately four thousand troops, to reinforce the *places fortes* of Quebec and Louisbourg. The ships that carried the soldiers had to have most of their cannon removed—which was called to sail *en flûte*—so that there was sufficient room. The naval commander at Brest, Jean-Baptiste MacNemara, with six ships of the line at this command, escorted the vessels bound for New France until they were clear of the French coast, then returned to port. To Quebec were sent four battalions of reg-ular infantry (from the La Reine, Languedoc, Béarn, and Guyenne Reg-iments), who would be commanded by the experienced Jean-Armand, baron de Dieskau. In charge of the squadron to get the soldiers to their destination up the Saint Lawrence River was a man who two years later would be a powerful force at Louisbourg, Emmanuel-Auguste de Cahi-deuc, comte du Bois de La Motte. Meanwhile dispatched to Louisbourg in 1755 were two battalions (from the Artois and Bourgogne Regiments), sent aboard three seventy-four-gun warships and accompanied by a con-voy of other vessels. That squadron was under the command of Antoine-Alexis Périer de Salvert.[54] Taken together, the Artois and Bourgogne bat-talions would add 62 officers and 1,050 enlisted men to the Louisbourg garrison.[55] Roughly speaking, that was going to double the number of defenders in the colony.

Just as the French were gathering intelligence about British military and naval activity in 1755, so the reverse was true. When reports reached

London of French preparations to send a large contingent of Troupes de Terre to Canada and Île Royale, the British authorities issued secret orders to Admiral of the Blue, Edward Boscawen, to cruise off Newfoundland to intercept the French convoy. "If you fall in with any French ships of war or vessels having on board troops or warlike stores you will do your best to take possession of them. In case resistance should be made, you will employ the means at your disposal to capture and destroy them."[56] There was no ambiguity in such orders. Because war between the two nations was still not declared, the orders were secret. When the French ambassador to Britain inquired if it were true that Boscawen had been directed to attack French ships en route to New France, two British "cabinet ministers dined at his house and cheerfully reassured him that such rumours were completely false."[57]

It turned out that Admiral Boscawen's squadron caught up with only three of the French ships, the *Alcide*, the *Lys*, and the *Dauphin Royal*. One French captain hailed his British counterpart and asked in French and in English if their two countries were at peace or war. "At peace, at peace," replied the Royal Navy officer, "followed by shattering broadsides."[58] Two of the French ships were taken, the *Alcide* and the *Lys*, while the third eluded capture and eventually reached Louisbourg. The preemptive British naval action shocked Louis XV and his ministers in France when they learned of it in mid-July. At first, the king ordered strong reprisals against British ships, but by early August he and his officials had decided they did not want to begin a war for which they were not ready, despite the insult and embarrassment suffered. Accordingly, the king modified the instructions already sent out and pulled back from making already poor relations with Great Britain even worse. As a result there were no negative consequences for the British action; they succeeded in capturing ten companies of French regular infantry soldiers (out of the overall total of seventy-eight), two warships, and two hundred thousand livres in specie.[59]

The greatest part of the French convoy eluded Boscawen, so that most reinforcements did reach Louisbourg and Quebec. The Admiral of the Blue was disappointed with his limited success, yet he must have been pleased to learn later in the year that other Royal Navy encounters closer to Europe captured more than three hundred French ships and removed eight thousand French sailors from the high seas.[60] All of this without any official British declaration of war! Following his limited success at sea, Admiral Boscawen proceeded to Halifax. He was soon to play a role in two other major initiatives in 1755. One brought inconvenience and discomfort to Louisbourg, the other outright tragedy to the Acadian population of Nova Scotia.

The squadron commanded by Boscawen stayed around Nova Scotia waters throughout the summer of 1755, calling in occasionally to Halifax. Acting governor Charles Lawrence welcomed the naval presence for the additional protection it offered. Before June 1755 only a single frigate and an armed sloop were in the harbor of the Nova Scotia capital, but after that date there were sometimes as many as seventeen ships of the line and two frigates. The number of sailors totaled over eight thousand. It was a trend that would continue as the showdown with Louisbourg neared. During the summer of 1755, the two British admirals, Boscawen and his second in command, Rear Admiral Savage Mostyn, maintained a rotating squadron off Louisbourg in the hope of taking prizes. They were not disappointed. Between June 8 and September 1, British ships captured no fewer than twenty-four French fishing or merchant ships. The French could not respond with a protective convoy. The best they could do was to keep secret the departure dates of French vessels, so that the British might not learn in advance and lie in waiting out to sea.[61]

Separate from the blockade of Louisbourg, Boscawen ordered a British warship under the command of New Englander John Rous to proceed to the south coast of Newfoundland in August, in the vicinity of Port-aux-Basques. Rous's orders were to destroy the French fishing posts and to remove the French population. Vessels and catches of cod were taken easily, with the prizes brought to Halifax. According to one source, the confiscated cargoes included nearly twenty thousand gallons of rum and brandy. The uprooted French fishers, however, were not kept long in British custody. They were dropped off on the coast of Île Royale, just south of Louisbourg, giving Governor Drucour more mouths to feed.[62]

At Louisbourg the arrival of approximately eleven hundred gray white–coated soldiers of the Artois and Bourgogne Regiments represented the first time regular army regiments had formed part of the garrison on Île Royale. Since its founding in 1713, the colony had known only troops sent by the Ministry of the Marine, predominantly Compagnies franches soldiers, though there were, until 1745, foreign mercenaries as well. The regular army battalions that sailed to Quebec and Louisbourg in 1755 were the first Troupes de Terre to serve anywhere in New France since the 1670s. (There had been an unsuccessful attempt to send out regular troops in 1746, as part of the ill-fated expedition of the duc d'Enville.)[63]

Périer de Salvert, the commander of the squadron that had escorted the Artois and Bourgogne battalions to Louisbourg, stayed in the Île Royale port until August 31, hoping that the squadron Du Bois de La Motte had led to Quebec might join him. That would have greatly increased his chances of getting past the British blockade off the Cape Breton coast when it came time to return to France. While waiting, Périer de Salvert kept his sailors busy strengthening the Louisbourg defenses. Ships carpenters made new gun platforms for the land fortifications, sailors toiled to reestablish existing coastal batteries, and the naval commander saw to it that an entirely new battery, with ten big guns, was established beyond the enceinte on the seaward side, on Rochefort Point.[64]

Meanwhile on the British side, back when the French were first arranging to send reinforcements to Louisbourg and Quebec, the top British officials in Halifax and Boston were planning how to strengthen their own position and weaken that of the enemy. Acting governor Charles Lawrence of Nova Scotia and Governor William Shirley of Massachusetts decided their immediate target in the current context would not be Louisbourg, for that would require massive naval and military support from the mother country. Instead, they turned their attention to other French positions that might be taken with the limited resources available. Their sights turned to the Chignecto region.

Shirley and Lawrence came up with what they thought would be a first step in ridding the Atlantic region of the French menace. Both were experienced hands at wartime maneuvering. In 1744 Shirley had perfect timing when he sent reinforcements from Boston to Annapolis Royal, saving the town from two attacks, one predominantly Mi'kmaw and Maliseet and the other largely French. Then in 1745 the Massachusetts governor had been instrumental in putting together the victorious assault on Louisbourg.[65] Lawrence was a career army officer who had seen battlefield action in Europe before coming to Nova Scotia in 1747 to serve at Louisbourg. Once Halifax was founded, he became a trusted officer of Governors Cornwallis and Hopson. In an August 1754 letter to the president of the Board of Trade, the Earl of Halifax, Lawrence claimed that the French presence in the Chignecto isthmus was "a growing Evil, and the greatest Obstacle that can be imagined to [his] Lordship's design of establishing this Province." The acting governor of Nova Scotia asked for the "least hint" of support from the Earl of Halifax. With that, he would approach Massachusetts Governor Shirley to put together a force to bring about the "Demolition of Beau sejour; And when that is done the French Inhabitants on that side must either be removed to this, or driven totally away by Fire and Sword."[66]

The broad strategy developed by Lawrence and Shirley was to send an expedition to the Chignecto isthmus to capture the two French forts, Beauséjour and Gaspereau. The British commander at Fort Lawrence, Lieutenant Colonel Robert Monckton (1726–82), spent the winter of 1754–55 in Boston to work out the details of the campaign, often quarreling with the man who would be the senior New England officer on the expedition, John Winslow (1703–74).[67]

From the British perspective military strikes against the French forts in the Chignecto region did not require an actual declaration of war because in their eyes the territory was British, not French. In other words it was an operation to reclaim what was rightfully theirs, by virtue of the vague wording in the 1713 Treaty of Utrecht and the failure of the 1748 Treaty of Aix-la-Chapelle to clarify matters. Had it been an expedition against Louisbourg, a recognized French possession, confirmed by the 1748 peace, then the attack would have broken the official peace between the two nations. Sophistry or not, that was the way in which British officials justified a peacetime attack on the French presence at Beauséjour. How different the attitude was in France, where a February 1755 memorandum articulated that their negotiators should prevent war with their imperial rival by offering to establish an uninhabited buffer zone in the Chignecto area that would clearly separate French from British territories.[68]

Thanks to information from Monckton and from detailed reports received from a willing spy, Thomas Pichon—a French clerk at Beauséjour and once the secretary to the comte de Raymond at Louisbourg—

the British knew exactly what the situations were at Louisbourg and in the Chignecto forts. The minister of the marine in France, Machault d'Arnouville, complained to Governor Drucour at Louisbourg that the enemy seemed to have obtained precise information about the French defensive capability in the Atlantic region. He had no idea who was providing it, but he suspected merchants at Louisbourg.[69]

In the specific case of the Chignecto forts, Lawrence and Shirley knew that there were at most 150 trained French soldiers in the garrison at Beauséjour and a much smaller contingent at Gaspereau. Barring massive French reinforcements, Lawrence and Shirley concluded they could put together an expedition to win the day. Accordingly, in early 1755 Governor Shirley raised two battalions, nearly 2,000 men, mostly from Massachusetts. To the provincial recruits were added about 300 British regulars, along with three warships and more than thirty transports. Command of the naval contingent went to John Rous (ca. 1700–1760), a sometime privateer, a member of the Nova Scotia Council, and the officer-in-charge of the devastation along Newfoundland's south coast earlier in 1755.

The British and New England expeditionary force that sailed to the Chignecto isthmus outnumbered the French defenders by approximately fifteen to one, if one counts only the soldiers. With the addition of Acadian militia the ratio might drop to five or six to one, but most Acadians were not enthusiastic about military service and would not contribute much to the defense of Beauséjour. In fact, at various times in the siege to come the French officers worried that the Acadians might desert. Though the vast majority of soldiers in the expeditionary force were Anglo-Americans, overall command of the contingent was given to Robert Monckton, the twenty-eight-year old British commander of Fort Lawrence. Monckton showed a contemptuous attitude toward the provincial soldiers, which grated not only on the enlisted men but on the man who had raised them in Massachusetts, Lieutenant Colonel John Winslow. Winslow, at fifty-two nearly twice the age of Monckton, commanded one battalion in the looming siege of Beauséjour and Lieutenant Colonel George Scott, a career British officer, the other.[70] Three years later Scott and Monckton would both play roles in a much larger British expedition against Louisbourg.

The French commander at Beauséjour must have shuddered when on

June 2, 1755, he learned that an enemy fleet was making its way into the muddy tidal basin below his star-shaped fort. Louis du Pont du Chambon, sieur de Vergor, had arrived at the post in 1754 and knew that an attack was always a possibility, if not a probability. Nonetheless, the appearance of the fleet on that June morning came as a surprise. The commandant had done little to prepare for the moment, other than a minor strengthening of the fort. Hindsight suggests that Vergor would have been wise to have established a detached gun battery close to the shore of the basin, for the cannons of his fort on Beauséjour ridge could not reach any ships that came to anchor there. Moreover, the only possible way the French might turn back an expedition on the scale of that led by Monckton was to prevent a landing. Vergor, however, did not have any detached shore batteries in place when the thirty-four vessels of Monckton's expedition sailed into view on June 2. If he had, cannoneers might have inflicted serious damage on the British ships. The entrance to the anchorage below Fort Lawrence was, and still is, narrow and tricky to navigate. A mere five years earlier, in the spring of 1750, the initial contingent led by Charles Lawrence had floundered when the ships became stranded on the tidal flats in the basin.[71]

The French officers who stood with Vergor on the ramparts of the fort at Beauséjour, studying the ships entering the basin below through a telescope, could tell just by looking at the number of vessels, with hundreds of troops coming ashore in small boats, that it would be difficult for their small garrison to hold out for long. Vergor had participated in the 1744 French capture of Canso and in the 1745 loss of Louisbourg, so he had firsthand experience on both winning and losing sides.[72] Judging by the size of Monckton's expeditionary force, the only hope the French had was for reinforcements to arrive. Vergor quickly sent couriers to Louisbourg, Quebec, Île Saint-Jean, and the Saint John River post with pleas for assistance.

Following the landing of the British and New England soldiers on June 2, besiegers and defenders alike were busy. Each side spent the next ten days strengthening existing positions, reconnoitering and establishing new ones, and making advances and sorties. Raids by Mi'kmaq and Acadians impeded the attackers' progress, yet they could not halt it. First, the besiegers crossed the Missaguash River; then they set up gun batteries on heights of land and fired down on the French fort. The only assistance Vergor received to his call for reinforcements came in the form of forty Maliseet warriors who arrived at Beauséjour on June 13. It was too little, too late. By June 13 the end of the struggle was in sight, though the siege was only beginning in earnest. On that day the besiegers' artillery bombardment commenced. The devastation within the fort was immediate. The following night a courier arrived from Louisbourg with Governor Drucour's answer to Vergor's appeal for troops; the reply was negative. The stronghold of Île Royale was suffering under a blockade by a British naval squadron, and it was impossible for Drucour to send troops to Beauséjour. Vergor wanted to keep the news from the defenders and sheltered civilians, because he knew it would have a devastating effect on morale, but it leaked out. His own staff, notably Thomas Pichon, undoubtedly helped spread the word among the Acadians who had been pressed into service to help defend the fort.

The Acadians were caught in an impossible situation, damned by one side or the other no matter what course of action they followed, regardless of the eventual outcome. While a certain number were willing participants on the French side, the majority wanted no part of the struggle between the two imperial powers. Right from the start of Monckton's attack on the Chignecto region, many Acadians worried that they would compromise their "neutral" status in the eyes of the British if they defended Beauséjour. Accordingly, they asked Vergor to communicate to the besiegers that they had been compelled, on threat of death, to assist the French effort. The effect of the bombardment and the arrival of the news that there would be no more reinforcements convinced most Acadians that their interests were better served if Vergor surrendered. The priority for the Acadians was that Monckton be informed that they had been compelled to take part in the French defense.

It was not a difficult decision for Beauséjour's commandant to capitulate. By June 16 Vergor felt surrender was inevitable and justifiable. His eagerness to end the siege and to include the capitulation of Fort Gaspereau on Baie Verte along with Beauséjour's surprised Monckton. The British commander was happy to oblige, and he granted the honors of war to the French garrison. The siege was over after only four days of actual bombardment. Most Acadians, about three hundred in total, as well as

Mi'kmaw and Maliseet warriors, along with the French missionary Abbé Le Loutre, departed before the British took over the post. When Governor Drucour at Louisbourg wrote the minister of the marine about the loss in the Chignecto region, he offered a pithy assessment: "Le tout est devenu (zero)" (Everything has become nothing).[73]

On June 17, 1755, Monckton renamed the captured French fort Fort Cumberland, after the Duke of Cumberland (third son of George II and commander in chief of the British army). The same day Monckton's soldiers placed the defeated troops on transports for Louisbourg, where they would in turn be put on French ships heading for Quebec. In accordance with the capitulation agreement, the defeated soldiers were not to bear arms against the British for six months. As for Vergor, he too went first to Louisbourg and then on to Canada. His short-lived defense of Beauséjour received much criticism. A French officer at Louisbourg wrote derisively about Vergor and Villeray, the latter being the officer in charge at Gaspereau.

> Seven bombs fell in the fort at Beauséjour, obliging the sieur Vergor to capitulate. He left with honors, on the condition that he not serve for six months. The sieur Villeray imitated the defense of his commander; he gave up the fort at Gaspereau on the same conditions, without waiting for the honor of having them attack him. If the sieur Vergor had thought like a man of war, with a fort that was incapable of holding out until help arrived, he should have burned it and retired, which was easy for him since the enemy did not have him blocked. He held out only three days, during which he lost two officers and four soldiers.[74]

Villeray attempted to shift the blame for the swift double surrender from his commandant, Vergor, to the Acadian population in the Chignecto region. The commandant of Gaspereau maintained that when the over two-thousand-man force of New Englanders and British regulars came ashore below Beauséjour, the local farming population provided them with assistance. Worse still, in Villeray's version of events, the Acadians within the fort at Beauséjour rebelled toward the end of siege, leaving Vergor with no choice but to surrender.[75] It was not a persuasive explanation.

In light of the weak defense at Beauséjour and no defense at all at nearby

Fort Gaspereau, the French authorities put Vergor through a court-martial trial. Yet the commandant had influential friends and supporters, including François Bigot, the intendant of New France, and he was found not guilty. Louis du Pont du Chambon, sieur de Vergor, continued as an officer in the marine troops, and in the early morning hours of September 13, 1759, he found himself in a situation that was decisive for all New France. Four years after his poor showing at Beauséjour, Vergor was the officer in charge of the detachment at the top of a 175–foot cliff overlooking Anse au Foulon, upriver from Quebec. It was the very spot where General James Wolfe and his men made their fateful climb to the Plains of Abraham. Alas poor Vergor: twice the wrong man in the wrong place at the wrong time.

While the victors in the Chignecto campaign were emboldened, the French were reeling. With Beauséjour and Gaspereau lost, the commander of the French post on the Saint John River, Charles Deschamps de Boishébert, burned the fort so that the British could not make use of it.

Since it was only late June 1755, and the military objectives in the Chignecto region had been decisively achieved, the Halifax administration next turned its thoughts to what else might be accomplished with the nearly two thousand New England soldiers signed on for a year. As it turned out, they had a plan waiting for implementation. In 1751 the chief surveyor of Nova Scotia, Boston-born Charles Morris, sent a report to Governor Shirley that urged the Acadians be entirely removed from the colony where he now resided. It was not a novel idea, but no one had previously provided such a detailed plan to achieve that end. Morris had been an officer with the New England contingent overwhelmingly defeated in the Acadian village of Grand-Pré in the surprise midwinter nighttime attack by French and Native combatants in 1747, and that likely colored his opinion of the Acadians. In any case, Morris offered in-depth details on the major Acadian communities and went on to urge that a "stratagem" be found to "destroy all these settlements by burning down all the houses, cutting the dykes, and destroy All the Grain [then] growing." Historian John Mack Faragher describes Morris's logic as "diabolical" and identifies his report to Shirley as the "operational plan for removal" of the Acadians.[76]

For years a succession of British administrators had been annoyed with what they perceived to be a lack of clear loyalty among Acadians, most conspicuously in their refusal to swear an unequivocal oath of allegiance. During the 1740s there were further complaints that some Acadians were complicit in the attacks on Annapolis Royal and the winter attack on the New Englanders at Grand-Pré. When surveyor Charles Morris reported to Halifax in 1751 that "upwards of 1,000 [Acadian] fighting men [in the Chignecto region] . . . [had] all sworn Allegiance to the French," it deepened the mood. (Morris did not mention, likely because he did not know, that the French soldiers had compelled the Chignecto Acadians to swear an oath, under threat of banishment.)[77] When those details were added to the developing atmosphere of a looming imperial war, the mix was ominous. Thus when a dispatch arrived in the Nova Scotia capital in late June 1755 from Colonel Monckton with not only news of his victory at Beauséjour but also mention that three hundred Acadians had participated in the defense of the French fort, the latter detail prompted a harsh reaction from Lawrence and the rest of the Nova Scotia Council. It completely dismissed the clause in Vergor's capitulation that the French commandant had compelled the Acadians to take up arms. On June 25, 1755, the council resolved to remove *all* Acadians from the Chignecto region. The injustice of condemning all for the actions of a minority was not likely argued by anyone at the table. The decision, once taken, was kept secret. It would not be implemented until August.

Having dealt with the Chignecto Acadians—at the policy level, not yet in real terms—Lawrence and the rest of the council decided to tackle the Acadians living in mainland Nova Scotia. As Lawrence's thinking crystallized, the acting governor decided they would be offered one last chance to take the oaths required of British subjects. It is important to add that the British administration rarely if ever referred to the Acadians as "Acadians". They typically called them "French Inhabitants," the "Inhabitants," or "French Neutrals." Colonial French administrations, on the other hand, such as that at Louisbourg, easily and regularly used the terms "Acadiens" and "Accadiens." The difference was more than a nuance. It reveals that the French recognized the Acadians as a people somehow different from themselves, with their own identity or even identities varying from village to village. British administrations made no such distinction. To them the inhabitants who refused to swear the oaths of sovereignty to their monarch were simply French. By "French" they also meant Roman Catholic, which British Protestants in the mid-eighteenth century generally thought a more dangerous quality than foreign ethnicity.

The showdown the Halifax administration was seeking with the Acadians of mainland Nova Scotia during the summer of 1755 occurred in a context that differed drastically from that of only a few years earlier. By late June 1755 the British administration had more forts and block-houses than ever before, it had eliminated the French military presence in the Chignecto region, a Royal Navy squadron was in nearby waters, and there were approximately two thousand New England soldiers at its disposal. The council, led by Lawrence, took advantage of the strong position. It committed to either seeing the Acadians swear the loyalty oaths their status as British subjects required or to ousting them from their long-occupied and highly fertile lands. Decades earlier the administrations at Annapolis Royal were unable or unwilling to be so forceful with the Acadians. Governor Edward Cornwallis commented that the Annapolis Royal administration led by Richard Philipps deserved the "highest punishment" for having accepted in 1729–30 a qualified or conditional oath from the French inhabitants of Nova Scotia. Cornwallis wrote: "[I]t has been called an English Province these thirty four years and I don't believe that the King had one true subject without the Fort of Annapolis. I cannot trace the least glimpse of an English Government."[78]

The expansion of the British presence throughout the region that began in 1749 had advanced far enough by the early 1750s that for the first time it was possible to imagine that land vacated by Acadians would be taken over by British and/or foreign Protestant settlers, whose loyalty would not be in doubt. Wanting a showdown, the Nova Scotia Council sent out a summons in late June 1755 for the Acadian deputies (or representatives) from the districts of Les Mines, Pisiquid, Cobequid, Annapolis, and other areas to come to Halifax. The fate of thousands of men, women, and children were to be determined by the answers the deputies would give to Charles Lawrence's questions.

In developing this approach on the ground in Nova Scotia, Lawrence did not have the specific approval of the authorities in Great Britain. To his way of thinking the current situation was an unprecedented opportunity with no time for delay. To seek input and sanction from London would take months and might not be forthcoming. The summer season still lay ahead, and there were enough troops, warships, and transports in the area—at Chignecto, in Halifax, and patrolling the waters off Louisbourg—to back up whatever action Lawrence and the council chose to take. The acting governor was obviously confident that the decisive measure he was about to implement would not harm or end his career. And indeed, when 1755 did come to an end, Charles Lawrence would receive no reprimands from his superiors in London for what he had done in Nova Scotia. On the contrary, his "acting" appointment ended, and he was confirmed as governor.

On July 3 a group of Acadian deputies from the Acadian villages of Les Mines and Pisiquid arrived in Halifax with petitions that aired *their* grievances before the Nova Scotia Council.[79] No one on the council was the least bit sympathetic to their complaints or their point of view. Lawrence first lectured the deputies on their presumptuousness and lack of loyalty, then asked them to take an unqualified oath of allegiance to George II. He gave them twenty-four hours to mull it over and sent them away into confinement. The Acadian representatives could not have foreseen the full consequences of their refusal. There had been none in the past when similar requests were made by previous British administrations and rejected by themselves or their forefathers. Unfortunately for this group of deputies and the people they represented, both the times and the officials making the decisions had changed. When the Acadian deputies came back in front of the council on July 4, they stated they could not take the oath without consulting their home communities. Lawrence told the deputies that the council "could no longer look on them as Subjects to His Britannick Majesty, but as Subjects of the king of France." When the Acadians then expressed their willingness to take the oath as requested, Lawrence said it was too late. Once an oath of loyalty had been formally refused, they learned, it could not afterward be taken. The Nova Scotia Council imprisoned the deputies on Georges Island in Halifax harbor, a fortified island not far offshore from the settlement of Halifax. The island already had a small prison for Halifax criminals, but the Acadian deputies were, of course, not there for theft or other crimes.[80]

Ten days later, on July 14, Lawrence invited Admiral Boscawen and Rear Admiral Mostyn to attend the next meeting of the Nova Scotia Council, at which the "Security of the Province" was to be discussed. At that meeting, on July 15, the two admirals "gave it as their Opinion, That it was now the properest Time to oblige the said Inhabitants to Take the Oath of Allegiance to His Majesty, or to quit the Country." The expression of such a strong opinion by two senior naval officers confirmed Lawrence and the other council members in their thinking that it was time for ultimatums and deportations.

The second and final encounter between Acadian representatives and the Nova Scotia Council began on July 25. The two admirals, Boscawen and Mostyn, once again joined Lawrence and the other five regular councilors. Because the session began on a Friday, the deputies were given the weekend to mull over the question of taking the oaths. On Monday, July 28, the Acadians returned to tell the council that "they should not be obliged to Take up Arms" under any circumstances. If that was what the king of England and his representatives were trying to force on them, then they were willing "to quit their Lands." All they asked was "that they should be allowed a convenient Time for their Departure." It was bold talk, yet there was no way the Nova Scotia Council and the attending admirals were going to let the Acadians choose either their time of departure or their destination. They feared the six thousand to seven thousand Acadians living in Nova Scotia would move to the nearby French colonies of Île Royale and Île Saint-Jean, as several thousand other Acadians had already done. Such a migration would strengthen the enemy for the coming war. Having brought the issue to a head, the Nova Scotia Council, with Boscawen and Mostyn taking part in the deliberations, decided to deport *all* French inhabitants from the colony. Whether anyone raised the question of applying a policy to everyone, as opposed to individuals, is not known. The council considered sending the Acadian men, women, and children to France but in the end decided the destination would be the Anglo-American colonies. The expectation was that the "French neutrals" would eventually become loyal subjects. No one used the term "assimilation," yet that was the basic idea. Until arrangements could be made, the second group of deputies was sent as prisoners to Georges Island just like the first.

On July 31 Charles Lawrence wrote Monckton, still headquartered at Fort Cumberland, informing him that all Acadians would "be removed out of the Country as soon as possible." The operation was to begin with those in the Chignecto region "who were in arms and therefore entitled to no favour from the government." Lawrence's letter reached Monckton in early August 1755. The colonel made the necessary arrangements. On August 11, 250 Acadian males responded to an order from Monckton and came into Fort Cumberland, the former Beauséjour, to hear an announcement. They were arrested, with most subsequently taken to Fort Lawrence, where they were confined until transported in the fall to the American colonies. At the time the plan was to ship 1,000 to Virginia and 500 each to North Carolina and Maryland. Similar scenes were repeated at Grand-Pré and Pisiquid on September 5 and at Annapolis Royal in December. Most of the soldiers who carried out the roundup came from the New England army raised to capture the Chignecto forts. They and a smaller number of British regulars confiscated all farm animals and crops of the Acadians and then went on to burn the hundreds of buildings (houses, churches, mills, and other structures) that made up the different communities. The idea was to leave no place for individuals or groups to hide or to live. In total the soldiers removed an estimated 6,000 to 7,000 Acadians from along the Bay of Fundy and on the Chignecto isthmus in the late summer and fall of 1755. That was roughly half the total Acadian population in the overall region.[81] The huge scale of the undertaking was fraught with logistical difficulties, which produced some separation of families and generally caused untold human tragedies.

In total the Nova Scotia Council shipped the Acadians to nine Anglo-American colonies from Massachusetts to Georgia. (None were sent to Louisiana, which was a French colony at the time. Large numbers of Acadians would later migrate there voluntarily, many after it had become a Spanish colony.) In the haste of the 1755 operation, Lawrence did not notify officials at the destination ports about the human cargoes heading their way. Rather, a letter explaining the deportation accompanied the Acadian contingents into exile. As a consequence the ports were not at all prepared for the deportees when they arrived. In the case of Virginia officials refused to accept the Acadians at all. After an interval of a few months, Virginia reshipped the entire eleven hundred men, women, and children to England.

Though the Anglo-American and British soldiers were thorough in rounding up Acadians in the summer and fall of 1755, a sizable number escaped. Most fled by water and land to Île Saint-Jean, Canada, and Île Royale, though some hid in what is now New Brunswick, particularly at a refuge up the Miramichi River established by Charles Deschamps de Boishébert. Others stayed on in Nova Scotia, joining with some Mi'kmaq to harass the British in any way they could. As a result "the inhabitants of Halifax were reported to live in constant fear of French and Indian attack during the winter months" of 1755–56. British soldiers and civilians in Annapolis Royal were similarly fearful of straying far from town. In the bloodiest skirmish, which was to occur in December 1757, a guerilla force of Acadians and Mi'kmaq killed twenty-five men of the Forty-third Regiment garrisoned at Annapolis at what came to be known as Bloody Creek.[82]

Around the same time that officials in Halifax were determining the fate of the Acadians, the French in the interior of the continent enjoyed a sudden, dramatic victory over the British. On July 9, 1755, in mountainous terrain near the French post of Fort Duquesne in the disputed Ohio country, a force of 108 French soldiers, 146 militia from Canada, and 600 Aboriginal warriors made a surprise attack on a British contingent of 2,200 men under the command of Major General Edward Braddock. Two-thirds of Braddock's army was killed or wounded, and all supplies were captured. French and Native losses were tiny, 23 killed and 20 wounded. It was a stunning victory that raised the spirits of the French. Two months later, when the deportations of the Acadians were well under way in Nova Scotia, the French and the British met again in the vicinity of Lake Champlain. On that occasion neither side was able to claim victory at the end of "a confused day's fighting."[83]

As 1755 came to a close, both the French and the British could look back on the year as a time of high anxiety. There had been significant losses and victories on each side. Yet while the larger picture was mixed and maybe even a trade-off in the perspective of imperial strategists, with striking French victories at Fort Necessity and Monongahela, there was nothing at all for the French to cheer about in Atlantic Canada. In that corner of North America, the one closest to Europe, the British had made major gains. France's traditional enemy now controlled the strategic Chignecto isthmus, and they had transported six to seven thousand Acadians out of Nova Scotia. The Acadians who had escaped the forcible removal had fled as refugees to nearby French colonies, straining food supplies in those locations.

Surprisingly for twenty-first-century readers, who know of the deportation and devastation visited on the Acadian communities as a major event and tragedy in Canadian history, the "clearance" policy the British authorities adopted in mainland Nova Scotia prompted little reaction in Louisbourg. Governor Drucour's initial interpretation was that it was an act of desperation by the British because they were so weak in the region.[84] Perhaps there was more concern expressed verbally about the Acadians' plight, but it did not leave a paper trail in official correspondence. Did the absence of written comments mean that there was not much concern in Louisbourg about the upheaval in mainland Nova Scotia? Possibly, because French officials had frequently expressed disappointment over the weakness of the Acadians' commitment to the French cause. Moreover, Governor Drucour had two interconnected problems to solve that were caused by the mass removal of the Acadians. One was that the refugees who streamed to Île Saint-Jean and Île Royale had to be fed, and the other was that the French colonies he administered would henceforth not be receiving the supplies of livestock and provisions the Acadians used to sell to them.

Nonetheless, despite the lack of written remarks about the Acadian removal, there is little doubt that French officials on Île Royale felt sympathy for the Acadians as details of their misfortunes came to be known. By the spring of 1756 Drucour and Prévost would be informing their superiors in France of the "unacceptable treatment" the British were showing toward the Acadians, some of whom were hiding in the woods in different parts of the region. Then again, Canadian-born René Gaultier de Varennes, an ensign in the Louisbourg Garrison, did not seem to blame the British for what they had done. He wrote to a friend in Europe in 1756: "[U]pon the whole, I do not see that the English could do otherwise than they did, in expelling [from] their bounds a people, who were constitutionally, and invincibly, a perpetual thorn in their side, whom they could at best look on as secret domestic enemies, who wanted nothing but an occasion to do them all the mischief in their power."[85]

At the end of 1755 Île Royale and Île Saint-Jean were still flying the white flag that indicated they were possessions of Louis XV. On a map the two islands represented a considerable amount of territory. In reality, however, there was only one major fortified place standing in the way of complete British military dominance in the region. That was Louisbourg. (Île Saint-Jean had only a very small garrison at Port-la-Joye.) An army of amateur soldiers from New England had captured Louisbourg in 1745, so the British knew the intended French stronghold could be taken. But since its return to France after the Treaty of Aix-la-Chapelle, Louisbourg was home to more soldiers than ever before, and it was welcoming more French warships more frequently than a decade earlier. Would the increased French defensive capability make a difference, enough to turn aside a second attempt by British men-at-arms to take France's Atlantic bastion? The answer to that question was unknown, indeed, unknowable. It would come down to the size, skill, and determination of two imperial armies and navies, the one to capture the place and the other to defend it. The long conflict over Atlantic Canada was about to enter its endgame.

3

The Match Heightens, 1756–1757

ouisbourg harbor does not freeze over in the twenty-first century, nor did it in the eighteenth. Thus the only times ships could *not* come and go as their captains pleased was when strong winds or no winds at all made it impossible, or when packs of drift ice—from farther north—blocked the entrance or filled the harbor. Blockage by ice packs typically lasted a week or two in spring. Even though the port usually remained open for the winter, Louisbourg was rarely busy between late November and April or May. Compared with the spectacle of the summer, the winter season presented what contemporaries called a "portrait of sadness."[1] Local fishing boats were active in a winter fishery and schooners and other vessels carried on coastal trade (*cabotage*), yet the winter months were not a time when ocean-going warships, transports, and merchant vessels dared to brave the North Atlantic. Strong winds and high seas made winter crossings between France and Île Royale a risky and unusual occurrence. But 1756 was an unusual year. The anticipated war with the British forced the French to take risks they normally avoided.

In late 1755 the French transport *Rhinocéros* sailed from Rochefort to Louisbourg carrying supplies. Île Royale always required a large amount of provisioning from France, and with warfare under way though not yet officially declared, there was a need to increase supplies. At least twenty-four vessels, most of which were sailing from French ports to Louis-bourg, had been seized by a British squadron off Île Royale during the summer of 1755.[2] Officials in France were determined not to allow the place to be lost simply because it ran out of food. The dangerous winter voyage of the *Rhinocéros* was undertaken to build up supplies in the vul-nerable stronghold.

The captain of the transport was Jean Lelarge, a familiar face in Louis-bourg.[3] He had been born in Plaisance in 1712, a year before the coastal French colony in Newfoundland was ceded to the British according to the Treaty of Utrecht. The boy moved to Louisbourg when his family relocated there in 1714. Son of a master carpenter, Jean Lelarge grew up wanting not to build houses like his father but to go to sea as a mari-ner. Louisbourg certainly offered countless opportunities for such a ca-reer. Lelarge took a course in hydrography in the seaport and over time graduated from relatively small coastal trading vessels to large ships that followed the winds and currents from Île Royale to the West Indies. In 1737 Jean Lelarge created a scandal in Louisbourg when he and his girl-friend, Louise Samson, stood up in the parish church during a regular mass and declared themselves to be married. The priest was horrified, interpreting the couple's behavior as a mockery of the sacrament of mat-rimony. Within hours the young people were apprehended; soon after-ward the authorities began court proceedings for sacrilege. The trial went through the necessary stages, and in the end the lovers were chastised for inappropriate conduct but permitted to marry. Their first child was born nine months and nine days after the wedding. It was a boy, Jean Aimable Lelarge, who would eventually eclipse his father's career and become an admiral in the navy of France under Napoleon I. Yet it was the father's seagoing career out of Louisbourg that paved the way for his son.

Jean Lelarge, the father, built a reputation first as a merchant cap-tain, then as a privateer during the war that began in 1744. In the 1750s he made a career leap that few French mariners from nonnoble back-grounds would accomplish during the ancien régime: he became a full-fledged officer in Louis XV's navy. His first trip to Louisbourg in that role, as the commander of a king's ship, was in 1753.

Jean Lelarge knew the risks inherent in his late 1755 voyage from France to Louisbourg and back again and no doubt breathed a sigh of

relief when the *Rhinocéros* reached Rochefort safely on January 8, 1756.
Remarkably, given the season, Lelarge and his crew were then asked to
make a second crossing to Louisbourg. The transport was back on the
high seas again before the end of February. Governor Drucour and financial administrator Jacques Prévost were more than a little surprised when
they saw the sails of the ship appear off Louisbourg harbor on March 26,
1756.[4] The entry of the *Rhinocéros* into port was complicated by packs of
drift ice that blocked the narrow passage. Lelarge attempted to work his
way through the ice and ended up damaging the hull. When a change of
wind cleared the drift ice, sending it out to sea, a local vessel came out
and towed the transport into port, where its cargo was unloaded. Lelarge's stay in Louisbourg was again a short one. Before the end of April
he was back on his way to France, once again risking ice packs and stormy
seas. Now that it was spring, Lelarge also knew that there was an increased
possibility of encounters with British warships.

Trying to Get Ready

The two transatlantic crossings Jean Lelarge made in the depths of winter
speak volumes about the vulnerable situation in which Île Royale found
itself in 1756. Nothing less than the continued existence of the colony
was at stake. The correspondence of royal officials that winter and spring
was dominated by rumors and news of war. Louisbourg was far from the
only worry for marine officials in France, but it ranked near the top because the latest minister and his staff feared a repeat of 1745.

Theoretically, the two winter voyages of the *Rhinocéros* brought sufficient provisions to the large king's warehouse on the waterfront of Louisbourg to last at least a year. Then again, just because supplies made it
to the colony did not mean that all the food was suitable for human consumption. It was not unusual to discover that at least a portion was ined-
ible, either because it had spoiled during the crossing or had been rotten before it left France. Another reality of the transportation business
was that the beginning of hostilities between Britain and France sent insurance rates skyrocketing. That fact, when added to the risk of capture,
produced a drastic decline in overseas merchant shipping. The minister
of the marine, Machault d'Arnouville, complained to the Dunkirk cham-
ber of commerce in September 1756 that its merchants were abandoning

the colonial trade. Yet who could blame them? Many French vessels venturing onto the high seas were being taken as prizes by the British.[5]

Other sources of food and of building materials were similarly drying up for Louisbourg in 1755 and 1756. Livestock was not going to be coming from the Acadian villages of mainland Nova Scotia and the Chignecto region. Those settlements no longer existed, their populations either removed or in flight. New England was another important supply source that was no longer available. Trade with the Anglo-American colonies, especially Massachusetts, had flourished in the 1720s and 1730s and then was reactivated in the early 1750s, to the annoyance of British officials at Halifax. By 1755, however, with war all but declared, New England finally ceased to be an important trading partner for Île Royale. Also gone as a trading partner, for completely different reasons, was the French colony along the Saint Lawrence River. A succession of bad harvests in Canada meant that there was no "surplus" food to send provisions to the sister colony on Cape Breton Island. Canadian harvests would become "progressively worse" in 1756, 1757, and 1758, thereby increasing Louisbourg's predicament and that of the rest of New France.[6]

The reduction, indeed outright elimination, of some of the traditional food suppliers for Île Royale led officials to place unrealistically high hopes on the remaining North American source, Île Saint-Jean. Kitchen plots and large gardens at Louisbourg and elsewhere on Île Royale were important but never sufficient to feed the colonists year round. Governor Drucour and financial administrator Jacques Prévost had envisioned that the transmigrated Acadian population on Île Saint-Jean would be able to send large quantities of livestock, vegetables, and other foodstuffs to feed Île Royale, yet it remained an unrealized goal. With the influx of about two thousand Acadian refugees to Île Saint-Jean in 1755 and 1756, combined with poor local harvests, the island population actually required food assistance from Île Royale. As a result Louisbourg's reliance on its lifeline with France deepened significantly during the mid-1750s. There was no other source but the mother country to send what was needed to keep life going on Île Royale. Flour was at the top of the list because bread remained the staple of the typical European diet.

The spiral of dependence on France grew as time went by, especially when over one thousand soldiers of the Artois and Bourgogne Regiments disembarked at Louisbourg in mid-1755. Lelarge's second trip in the winter of 1756 carried another one hundred new mouths to feed, recruits for the battalions of the regiments.[7]

As troubling as the provision question was at Louisbourg, it was not the only worry. A major problem was the absence of reliable news about developments elsewhere. Events within the region a few months earlier—the loss of Beauséjour and the subsequent wholesale deportation of thousands of Acadians—demonstrated that the British were flexing their military strength in ways not seen before. With Louisbourg the likely next target, Governor Drucour wanted information about troop strength, number of warships, and any other developments at Boston or Halifax. A lack of advance news could prove fatal. Thus the appetite for information was insatiable. The captain of every ship that arrived in port was questioned as to what he had seen during his voyage. It was a rare ship that did not have something to report.[8]

In 1755 the governor of Trois-Rivières, François-Pierre de Rigaud de Vaudreuil, came to Halifax as a prisoner when the British under the overall command of Vice-Admiral Edward Boscawen captured the *Alcide*, the ship on which he was a passenger, off Newfoundland. Because he was a senior officer, Vaudreuil was given considerable liberty as a prisoner in Halifax. He made use of his free time and long rambles to prepare a detailed plan of the port and its fortifications, which he then tried to send to Louisbourg hidden within a "wash ball" inside an officer's trunk bound for Île Royale. Unfortunately for the French, Vaudreuil's plan was discovered before it reached Drucour. It ended up being preserved by the British and eventually made its way to the Library and Archives Canada, where it is one of the best historical plans of the Halifax fortifications in the mid-1750s.[9]

Though Vaudreuil was unable to pass along his information about Halifax, officials at Louisbourg had other sources. One individual mentioned repeatedly when the subject of British troop and naval strength at Halifax came up was an Acadian identified as Gautier, who was praised for the accuracy of his information. This was almost certainly Pierre Gautier, who like his father, the late Joseph-Nicolas Gautier *dit* Bellair, and his brother, Nicolas, was active in support of the French cause throughout

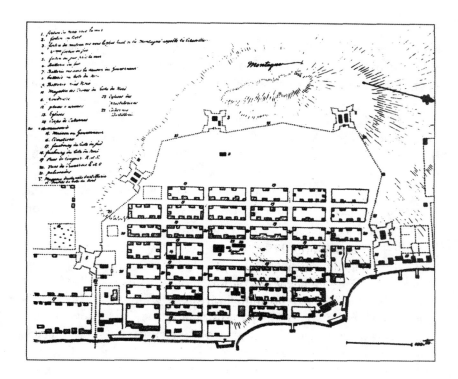

FIGURE 4. **Vaudreuil's Map, 1755**

This is the map that François-Pierre de Rigaud de Vaudreuil drew while a prisoner in Halifax and then tried to send to Louisbourg hidden in a "wash ball." Halifax's enceinte, clearly drawn on the map, was entirely built of wood, five stockaded block-houses linked by a palisade. *Library and Archives Canada, NMC 18532, 77801/142, H2/240/Halifax [1755], 31287.*

his life. Accompanied by unidentified Mi'kmaq, Pierre Gautier made several trips to or close to the Nova Scotia capital during the summer of 1757. He and the Mi'kmaq killed or captured a few British each time, always returning to Louisbourg to report on what they had seen or overheard. (The Gautier family tradition of intelligence work continued into the next generation. A nephew, Louis Mercure, provided a military courier service to the British in what is now the New Brunswick area during the American Revolution.)[10]

Deserters were another valued source of information. When the Mi'kmaq captured a couple of Irish soldiers from the Halifax garrison in the spring of 1756, they first sent them to the commanding officer at Port Toulouse and then on to Louisbourg. When interrogated the deserters provided details on how many ships were in Halifax harbor and what state they were in. The Irish added that there was a deadly sickness sweeping through the port and that a squadron of Admiral Boscawen was expected, whose mission was rumored to be to bombard Louisbourg. The last detail would surely have made the interrogators sit up and take notice. So pleased were the French by the information coming from the Irish deserters that the suggestion arose that the two be sent to France to be incorporated into the Clare Regiment, one of several regiments for foreigners in the service of Louis XV.[11]

The French authorities were not so charitable when it came to their own deserters. When five Compagnies franches de la Marine deserters were apprehended at Louisbourg in July 1756, they were all hanged as an object lesson for the rest of the troops. The sentence was far more severe than peacetime practice, which was to perhaps execute one as an example and accept the rest back in service.[12]

The wartime atmosphere of the mid-1750s inevitably disrupted the normal cycle of life at Louisbourg. The number of couples getting married in the town dropped sharply in both 1755 and 1756 to roughly half the number witnessed in each of the four preceding years. The number of private parties similarly declined. Louisbourg had always had a reputation as a lively place where all social levels consumed much alcohol and enjoyed music, dance, and gambling. The partying usually peaked during the pre-Lenten carnival time, which one resident called the "season of pleasures." Not so in 1756. Carnival in the capital of Île Royale that winter "was the saddest in the world, no dances, no feasts, no marriages. A few meals among the powerful people, lots of gambling among the officers, those [were] the only amusements of [their] meat days."[13]

The war also had an impact on religious life at Louisbourg. In February 1756 the bishop of Quebec, Henri-Marie Dubriel de Pontbriand, issued a pastoral addressed specifically to the clergy and parishioners of Louisbourg. Writing from Quebec, the bishop reminded his distant faithful, who would have heard the message read aloud in the military chapel that served as Louisbourg's parish church, that "earthly powers are nothing before God." He spoke of a lack of righteous behavior on Île Royale, stating: "[I]f the sinners persevere in their disorders, we dare to say it, everything is to be feared for the Colony. And we will perhaps soon see Louisbourg . . . fall a second time into the hands of the Enemy." The military officers from the garrison may well have raised their eyebrows and even grumbled on hearing those words. Their profession led them to believe that fleets and troops would be the determining factors in the conflict with Great Britain, not the moral behavior of civilians. Nonetheless, they likely kept their opinions to themselves until they were outside the chapel. Bishop Pontbriand gave specific directions on how the people of Louisbourg were to raise the spiritual tone in the town. The measures included adding a prayer and antiphon to local church services, having a procession through the streets with a statue of the Virgin Mary on the first Sunday of each month, and exposing the Blessed Sacrament in the various churches of Île Royale on the fourth Sunday of each month.[14]

Around the time Bishop Pontbriand's pastoral reached the colony, a scandalous murder trial was making its way through the courts at Louisbourg. It was a case in which a man and a woman, Pierre LeRoy *dit* Larmement and Anne Lando, were accused of murdering the woman's husband. Their separate trials did not conclude until the summer of 1756 and early 1757, respectively. Nonetheless, the cases must have dominated many a conversation in the colony over the winter. When the conclusions came, both were found guilty. The male was strangled and his body broken on a platform raised on the "public square" of Louisbourg. His cadaver was then taken to the scene of the crime, near the Mira River, where it was placed on a wheel facing skyward. The wife of the murdered man was sentenced to hang on a gallows erected on "the main square of this town, her body burned and Reduced to Ashes to be Thrown to the wind." The punishments were the most grisly in the four-decade history of judicial processes at Louisbourg.[15]

Although the murder case was an incident of marital infidelity carried to a deadly extreme, another case of infidelity in Louisbourg around the same time also ended in a death, though a suicide instead of a murder. That affair involved military officer Pierre Montalembert de Cers and his much younger wife, Marie-Charlotte Chassin de Thierry, daughter of a fellow officer. The bride never made any pretense about loving Montalembert, and his friends tried to dissuade the officer from marrying someone so open about her lack of affection. The wedding went ahead regardless, in September 1755, and soon afterward the bride began an open affair with another officer in the Louisbourg garrison. Montalembert became first distraught, then severely depressed. By the spring of 1757, unloved by his wife and deeply in debt thanks to her expenditures and his own gambling, Montalembert wandered into the woods outside Louisbourg and drowned. His body was not found for months, but everyone in town believed he had taken his own life.[16]

Riveting as the gossip was, the officials charged with administering the colony did not allow their attention to be diverted from the tasks at hand. Île Royale faced enormous challenges as it prepared for a likely attack by the British. In light of what had happened in 1755, the loss of the fort at Beauséjour and the wholesale removal of Acadians, there was precious little time to prepare.

One practical concern was currency. In contrast to the French settlements along the Saint Lawrence River, Île Royale had not yet been forced to issue playing cards as temporary money. Sufficient specie, meaning actual coinage, was always in circulation. In 1756 marine officials in France sent a new supply of coins across the ocean to meet the cash requirements at Louisbourg. Mentioned in the dispatch accompanying the money was the need to pay the soldiers of the Artois and Bourgogne battalions. French officials in Versailles and at Louisbourg understood that the men-at-arms had to be kept reasonably happy. In December 1744 the disgruntled enlisted men at Louisbourg had mutinied and taken control of the entire town. Though they eventually handed power back to the usual authorities, the mutiny was blamed as a contributing factor in the loss of the colony the following spring (1745).[17]

Keeping any garrison at full strength was a never-ending task. There were always illnesses, injuries, discharges, and deaths. In 1756 Louisbourg received six hundred fresh troops from France to replace individuals in those categories. The big question, of course, was how many soldiers were enough. Might Louisbourg need even more troops than the roughly two thousand it had in 1756?[18] The answer depended on the size of the force the British would bring to besiege the place, and there was no way to know what that would be until it happened, at which point it would be too late to increase the number of defenders.

The common thread running through every measure the French authorities took, or worried about, was money. An officer in the marine troops at Louisbourg estimated that the first six months the Artois and Bourgogne battalions were in the colony cost more than three times what the cod fishery had brought in that same year.[19] The minister of the marine provided his own figures on how much the presence of the two regiments of the Troupes de Terre was costing. Machault d'Arnouville stated that the total amount budgeted for Île Royale in the current year was 887,211 livres, of which nearly 40 percent—351,696 livres—was to cover the expenses of the Artois and Bourgogne battalions. The minister warned that such a level of expenditures could not be sustained indefinitely; further increases would not be sanctioned. When François-Marie Peyrenc de Moras took over the marine ministry from Machault d'Arnouville in 1757, he was to issue a similar warning.[20]

The ministers were doing their duty to sound a cautionary note, though it was not the fault of officials on Île Royale that the colony was costing so much. The warfare of the 1750s, actual and anticipated, resulted in a dramatic escalation in the costs of all North American colonies. When one examines the amount of king's money spent on Louisbourg over the years, the totals from the decade that began in 1749 leap out. During the 1720s annual royal expenditures on Île Royale never reached 200,000 livres. In the 1730s the figure climbed to between 300,000 and 350,000 livres. They spiraled upward in 1744 and 1745 to approximately 500,000 livres, but that was wartime. Yet the figures from 1749 onward more than doubled, averaging well over 1 million livres a year, and the

97

first several years were peacetime.[21] That meant that there was roughly the same amount of money spent on Île Royale in its final decade as there had been in its first three decades combined. To put those figures in the wider French colonial context, the annual amount expended at Louisbourg in the 1750s came to rival the total (1.7 million livres) allocated for *all* French colonies in the 1720s and 1730s. Where the overall marine budget in the 1720s had been 9 million livres, in 1758 the minister spent over 42 million livres on his portfolio, and in 1759 the figure climbed to nearly 57 million.[22]

Louis XV and the different ministers of the marine of the 1750s were, of course, troubled by the rising cost of their colonial holdings. How could they not be when the French treasury was suffering severe "financial distress"? The debt was growing by leaps and bounds, and there was no end in sight. Yet what was the alternative? It was either spend money to strengthen key colonial strongholds or else yield them without a struggle to the British rival. Rightly or wrongly, the perception in France was that Louisbourg was a key, sometimes *the* key, to the king's North American possessions. And after all, were the Mi'kmaq, the Maliseets, the Passamaquoddies, and the Abenaki, or the Acadians who had escaped deportation going to have the fighting capacity to hold off the British? None of those groups had sufficient numbers or access to warships, heavy artillery, and organized infantry. And if Louisbourg were lost, then the enemy gained open and unfettered access to the Saint Lawrence River and thus to all French possessions that lay along the great river. Accordingly, the fortified capital of Île Royale loomed large in French thinking of the 1750s as not just important by itself but as a strategic "gateway"—a term used in a 1754 memorandum—to the other colonial holdings.[23]

Since expenditures on Île Royale were already a worry to officials in France, the administration at Louisbourg faced tough choices. The fortifications were not in a good state and in fact had never been as formidable up close as they appeared at a distance. The damp, changeable climate caused continual deterioration. When the British took over the fortress in 1746, the assessment of Governor Knowles and chief engineer John Henry Bastide was harsh: "Upon the whole the General Design of the Fortifications is Exceeding Bad and the Workmanship worse executed." When the French returned to Louisbourg in 1749, they found breaches in the walls and other damaged areas that had not been fully repaired. In a formal statement signed in July 1749 by outgoing Governor Hopson and the engineer Bastide, the enceinte at Louisbourg was said to be "in very bad order." They noted: "[E]very Spring, some part or other . . . falls down, The worst places are at the Faces and Angles of the King's Bastion . . . all the Palissades round the Covered way are Rotten and Useless."[24]

Louis Franquet, the engineer who took over the responsibility for Louisbourg's defensive readiness in 1750, envisioned numerous improvements, which included elaborate outworks. Yet with a British descent seeming imminent from 1755 onward, there was no guarantee that Franquet would have the required block of months or years to complete any major projects. Nor, realistically, were the necessary funds to be authorized in France for such work. As a result there was only a limited use of masonry in the defenses erected after 1749. Earthworks were preferred because they were both faster and less expensive. In the end between 1754 and 1758 the French spent a total of 480,000 livres on the fortifications at Louisbourg. They spent many times that on the wages, equipment, and provisions of the regular infantry battalions and the marine troops that were to defend the place.[25]

Though much less was accomplished at Louisbourg than Franquet hoped, he did oversee a number of defensive works. Or rather, his two assistant engineers, François-Claude-Victor Grillot de Poilly and Nicolas Sarrebource de Pontleroy, both of whom arrived in the colony in 1755, supervised the projects. Pontleroy would leave Louisbourg for Quebec in 1757, where he took over as the chief engineer for Canada. Under Franquet's general supervision, the engineers undertook repairs to the wharves along the quay and construction of a powder magazine in the Brouillan Bastion. That project, begun in 1756, was expected to take three years. Franquet and his staff also advocated improvements in the area of the Princess Demi-Bastion, which fronted the ocean and therefore might be the site of an enemy descent. On the same seaward front, out on Rochefort Point, Périer de Salvert had his naval crew establish an earthwork battery in 1755. The Louisbourg engineers extended that battery two years later, constructing a simple platform that followed the coastline. Another new battery was established on the other side of the harbor, near the lighthouse at the entrance to the port. The King's Bastion, a primary target during the bombardment of 1745, also received some attention, as did the curtain walls on either side that linked to the Queen's Bastion and the Dauphin Demi-Bastion.[26]

The most heavily damaged of all the works in 1745 had been the Dauphin Demi-Bastion, the lowest-lying and therefore most vulnerable spot in the enceinte. Franquet proposed elaborate outerworks to protect it, which the minister rejected. So the Dauphin area stayed more or less the same as the British had left it when they turned over Louisbourg in July 1749. The French chose not to reconstruct the semicircular battery that had been there until reduced to rubble in 1745. Instead, they retained and improved a cavalier battery the British had put up. (The British had wanted to make sure they had a defensive work in the event that the French tried to retake Louisbourg in 1746 or 1747.) The French also constructed an earthwork *tenaille* in the ditch in front of the Dauphin Demi-Bastion between sections of the covered way. The covered way itself was improved when new palisades replaced the old ones.[27]

Out beyond the fortifications on the vulnerable western front, the French engineers took a precautionary measure: they lowered two hillocks overlooking the King's and Dauphin Bastions. Though only slightly higher than the works of the place, the hills had given an important advantage to the New Englanders in the late stages of the 1745 siege when they established batteries on the hills. To lessen their impact in the event of another siege, Franquet wanted the hills cut down. He wanted twelve to fifteen *pieds* removed from the Hill of Justice, but it was not easy going. Workers were unable to lower the hill by more than three *pieds* in 1756. Franquet gave the failure a positive spin when he informed the minister that what was accomplished was less expensive than taking away a greater amount.[28] Cost was always at the forefront of everyone's thoughts when they were writing officials in France. The chief engineer had the laborers back at the task again in 1757.

Franquet and his assistants, Grillot de Poilly and Pontleroy, undertook similar "lowering" measures on the seaward side of the fortress. Close to the coast was a rock outcrop known as Cap Noir, which overlooked the Princess Demi-Bastion. The engineers had holes drilled in the rock, then gunpowder inserted and ignited. Half the feature was blown up and reduced to small fragments, making it impossible for the enemy to use it as an effective gun position. Another precautionary measure taken over the winter of 1755–56 was the preparation of a large supply of fascines. Franquet wrote they would be "indispensable in the event of a Siege."[29]

The various projects carried out by Louis Franquet and the other engineers represented little more than minor tinkering with the fortifications at Louisbourg. Nothing fundamental was altered in the way in which the enceinte at Louisbourg stood in 1758 in comparison with how it had been in 1745. That was not the engineers' fault, for they came up with numerous designs to strengthen the fortifications. Their big ideas, however, could not be carried out because of lack of time and/or money. A French naval officer who arrived in port in June 1757 wrote of the "total abandonment" of the place and of the "consternation and despair" of the inhabitants, who knew how dilapidated the defenses were.[30]

The relatively poor state of the Louisbourg defenses was no secret. British officials in Halifax and beyond learned of the state of the defenses from deserters from the French side and from intercepted correspondence. Even more valuable was the information provided by the well-placed informant Thomas Pichon. Over a period of several years, Pichon passed on to his British contacts everything he knew or heard about Louisbourg, Beauséjour, and other French positions. Nova Scotia governor Charles Lawrence felt well enough informed about Louisbourg to write William Pitt in February 1757 that "the fortifications had undergone little or no alteration since the Restitution of the Place in 1749."[31]

Although French officials did not realize how much the British knew about Louisbourg, they nonetheless recognized that it was only a matter of time before there was another full-scale attack on their stronghold. Their keenest hope was that the British would not be able to make a successful landing, because if they did, the struggle would then come down to whether the French defenders and fortifications could outlast the ensuing siege. No one on the French side was optimistic about the outcome of such a scenario; no one thought Louisbourg was invincible anymore.

War Declared

Long anticipated, the official declarations of war came in the spring of 1756. George II led the way on May 17, 1756; Louis XV followed up on June 9. The delay in making the outright declarations is best explained in terms of the French and the British needing time to assess the balance of power on the European continent. Each side required alliances with other major powers, as no nation could hope to win a war in Europe by itself. It was essential to have allies willing to commit land armies in support of one's own troops. It turned out that the spring of 1756 witnessed a reversal of alliances from the previous war. This time Prussia lined up with Britain, while France, Austria, and the Holy Roman Empire found common cause. Later in the war, in the face of unprecedented British victories, Russia and Spain would also take France's side. In the North American theater, of course, allies such as Prussia and Austria were irrelevant. What mattered on the colonial side of the Atlantic were relationships with the indigenous peoples. Both the French and the British worked hard to maintain or cultivate ties with Aboriginal nations.

The official European phase of the war had no sooner begun than the French had a major success. On May 20, 1756, three days after George II's declaration but three weeks before Louis XV would declare war, a French fleet commanded by La Galissonière gained a victory over British admiral John Byng at Minorca (off the Mediterranean coast of Spain, southwest of Toulon, France). French land forces numbering sixteen thousand under the duc de Richelieu followed up the naval action with an assault that eventually captured Fort Saint Philip on Minorca after a siege of seventy days. Though they surrendered in the end, fifteen hundred British troops put up a valiant defense under the leadership of eighty-four-year old General Blakeney. The victorious Richelieu awarded the defenders the honors of war. The conquest of Minorca so soon after the war had begun brought much rejoicing in France and its colonies. Celebratory *Tè Deums* were held in France and later in the Louisbourg parish church when word of the victory reached Île Royale.[32]

For the losing side the loss of Minorca and the defeat at sea were a terrible blow. Moreover, the contrast between Blakeney's heroic stand on land and Byng's defeat at sea appalled not just the naval authorities but also the British public. Crowds in the streets of London chanted, "Hang Byng or take care of your King." Minorca, it must be noted, had been one of two vital naval stations Britain possessed in the Mediterranean, Gibraltar being the other. Poor Byng soon became the scapegoat for the loss. In March 1757 he was tried on three charges, only one of which stuck: the vague charge that the admiral had not done "his utmost." Found guilty, Byng was shot by a firing squad on the quarterdeck of one of his ships. The incident so impressed Voltaire that he included it in his 1759 novel, *Candide*, where a leading character observes that the British execute an admiral from time to time to encourage the others to do their duty (*pour encourager les autres*). The commander in chief at Portsmouth at the time of Byng's execution, and therefore the officer who signed the order for his death, was Edward Boscawen. This was the same naval officer who in 1755 had been prominent in Atlantic waters and at the Nova Scotia Council when the decision was taken to deport the Acadians. Admiral Boscawen's career was still on the ascendant, and he will once again enter our account of Louisbourg's final decade in the pages that follow.[33]

The setback in the Mediterranean was the first of many disappointments the British endured in 1756. Indeed, there was little that year to lift the hearts of Britons, a time when there were even "widespread fears that the French would invade Britain itself."[34] The invasion never came, but there was a stream of bad news for the British public to absorb. In India Calcutta fell to the Indians, with a well-publicized loss of life in an incident that came to be known as the "black hole." On the North American front, there were defeats on the interior of the continent on two noteworthy occasions. In March, before the official declaration of war, the French took Fort Bull on Lake Champlain. Then in August the forces of Louis XV, commanded by the marquis de Montcalm, captured the complex of British forts at Oswego on the shores of Lake Ontario. Historian Fred Anderson attributes the "collapse" of the British war effort in the Anglo-American colonies to a variety of factors. Chief among them was the confusion that reigned following the change in command of the army from William Shirley to a Scottish peer, John Campbell, Earl of Loudoun. A protégé of the Duke of Cumberland, Loudoun was unfamiliar with the world of colonial politics. The new commander was stymied by the refusal of the Anglo-American legislatures to vote the funds necessary to pursue the war.[35]

While the British and Anglo-American war effort was sputtering, the military leadership of New France seized the initiative in 1756 with French troops, Canadian militia, and Native warriors launching random guerrilla attacks against Anglo-American frontier settlements. Generally speaking, Aboriginal warriors were the most numerous in such campaigns, as well as the most effective in inducing terror among the enemy. Along the Allegheny Mountain range, "from Carolina to New York and down the eastern slopes to within thirty miles of Philadelphia," writes historian W. J. Eccles, "the Anglo-American settlements went up in flames." The psychological impact of the raids on the American colonists and on the British regular soldiers who came to North America was immense. The possibility of being scalped or taken away into captivity to Canada played on people's minds. When it came to an actual combat incident, the whoops and cries of warriors unnerved many European opponents. Some wrote of the "howl of America" and how the screams "struck a panic" in British troops.[36]

Only in what is now Atlantic Canada were the British spared disappointment in 1756. The 1755 capture of the French forts in the Chignecto isthmus, combined with the removal of roughly six thousand Acadians that year, had given the British the definite upper hand. The rounding up and deportation of the neutral French continued throughout 1756, as did the strengthening of the existing British fortifications. Despite such moves the Halifax administration and the British colonists feared attacks from the Mi'kmaq and by groups of Acadians who had escaped deportation. Charles Lawrence, confirmed as governor of Nova Scotia in 1756, placed a new scalp bounty on the Mi'kmaq and sought more troops to "hunt" them. Meanwhile, the threat of Acadian guerilla fighters kept British officials and soldiers at Annapolis Royal close to town. The bloodiest encounter was to occur in December 1757, when Acadian resistance fighters surprised a British wood-cutting detachment and then attacked the soldiers who tried to pursue the Acadians. In the end twenty-six British soldiers of the Forty-third Regiment lay dead, and at least seven others were taken as prisoners.[37]

A seaborne British worry was activity by French warships or privateers. There was no doubt that the Royal Navy was generally the superior force on the high seas, yet British ships and crews were not going to win every encounter. French ships were well built and armed, so the overall advantages of the Royal Navy were small comfort unless a sizable squadron was in nearby waters when it was needed to counteract one or more French vessels. Happily for the establishment at Halifax, there was a British squadron in Nova Scotia waters from May until October 1756.

The mission of the Royal Navy in North Atlantic water in 1756 was virtually the same as Boscawen's in 1755, to seize vessels heading to or from Louisbourg and Quebec. In the words of a Louisbourg officer, writing in August 1756, "[T]he intention of the English . . . is to intercept all assistance and supplies which can come to us from Europe, to reduce our place by famine, and to force us to hand over the keys without firing a shot." Throughout the summer of 1756, British ships of the line and frigates cruised off Île Royale. Their success in capturing French prizes was comparable to what had been achieved the previous year. Between May 22 and October 12, 1756, at least twenty-three French vessels were taken or driven ashore. In addition the British carried out a limited amount of destruction on land, in the form of burning fishing shore establishments as far away as the Gaspé Peninsula. According to a French officer in the Louisbourg garrison, the British landed three times on Île Royale in 1756 in attempts to destroy settlements. On all three occasions they were met by a mix of troops and Mi'kmaq, who killed or captured the landing parties.[38]

When not on rotation near Louisbourg, the British ships were usually at Halifax or on their way to or from the Cumberland Basin, where stood Fort Cumberland (the new name for the French fort at Beauséjour). The most significant single prize taken in 1756 was the *Arc-en-Ciel* (fifty-two guns), captured in June off Scatarie after a long chase and a five-hour gun battle. Reports said the French warship had on board sixty thousand livres in specie and as many as two hundred recruits.[39] The British were delighted with their capture and kept the *Arc-en-Ciel* in Atlantic waters for the next few years, sailing out of Halifax. It would form part of the fleet the British put together to attack Louisbourg in 1758.

Sailing with the *Arc-en-Ciel* when it left France was the frigate *Concorde*. The two ships separated in bad weather near the Grand Banks and went on to different fates. While the *Arc-en-Ciel* was pursued and captured, the *Concorde* initially escaped notice. When later chased, it eluded the Royal Navy not once but twice. On June 10 the *Concorde* slipped into a protected bay on Scatarie Island. When it sailed out, the pursuit began anew. On June 12, the same day the *Arc-en-Ciel* was taken, the *Concorde* headed for Port Dauphin (Englishtown). The British squadron backed off and waited for the French frigate. The captain of the *Concorde* concluded he might never reach his destination, Louisbourg, so he sent a message to the governor and financial administrator to let them know where he was and that he had fifty passengers and about thirty thousand livres in coins. The passengers included military recruits and several stonemasons. Rather than risk capture by heading back out on the open sea, where the British were waiting, the captain off-loaded the passengers and money to a schooner that could sail on the Bras d'Or Lake, going closer to Louisbourg. The men and money could complete their journey by land.[40]

On July 1 a French vessel that had been outfitted at Rochefort, the *Parfaitte Union*, also sailed into the channel at Port Dauphin. It too was being pursued by the British squadron.[41] Both the *Parfaitte Union* and the *Concorde* remained in the vicinity of Port Dauphin for much of the summer. Louisbourg officials hoped that enough French warships might arrive to drive away the Royal Navy ships, but while waiting for that to happen the captain of the *Concorde* erected a temporary shore battery with some of the ship's guns in case the British ventured too close.

As effective as the British squadron was in disrupting, scaring off, and capturing French ships, it was not always victorious. Moreover, there were occasions when no British ships were blockading the harbor entrance at Louisbourg, which created opportunities for the coming or going of French vessels. On August 5 a brigantine from Bordeaux reached Louisbourg with a much-appreciated quantity of wine. French ships even brought in more than a few captures of their own in 1756. Between August 1756 and October 1757, the Admiralty (*Amirauté*) court at Louisbourg processed a total of thirty-nine enemy prizes, worth over 800,000 livres. Those captures lifted French spirits, though they did not alter the overall trend of a tightening noose.[42] As of July 1756, in the words of chief engineer Louis Franquet, the situation in the colony was bleak.

> Nothing new, no news from Canada, the four ships of the line, a frigate and an English snow do not leave our coasts, and Especially they do not lose sight of Port Dauphin where they know are the frigate

Concorde and the *Parfaitte Union*, a merchant ship. From time to time they go promenade the passage of Fronsac [Canso Straight], where they captured not long ago a schooner with 38 beef cattle, and they mistreated another which brought us the same livestock. These little accidents can easily be repaired, but one fears that they will keep the inhabitants of Île Saint-Jean from frequenting us.[43]

A few days after Franquet offered this observation, word reached Louisbourg that a vessel called the *Charmante* had found it impossible to get through the British squadron and was taking refuge at nearby Menadou (Main à Dieu). The governor and the financial administrator quickly sent fifteen shallops—small boats that could stay close to the shoreline—to off-load the cargo of the *Charmante*. They also dispatched by land fifty soldiers to lend armed cover from shore.[44]

The presence of the British squadron off Île Royale was widely known in French marine circles. In mid-July 1756 Governor Drucour received a letter from Quebec from Louis-Joseph de Beaussier de Lisle, commander of a French squadron that sailed up the Saint Lawrence River in May carrying battalions of the La Sarre and Royal Rousillon Regiments. Also on board was Major General Louis-Joseph de Montcalm (1712–59) and several staff officers. On his arrival at Quebec, Montcalm assumed command of the Troupes de Terre on the interior of the continent, taking over from Baron Dieskau, who had been captured by the British in 1755. Beaussier de Lisle and his squadron remained at Quebec for several months. His mid-July letter to Drucour let the governor of Île Royale know that he was soon to set sail, intending to proceed to Louisbourg, unless the ships under his command—two ships of the line and two frigates armed for war—were no match for the British ships patrolling the coast of Île Royale. Should the Royal Navy squadron be significantly larger, Beaussier de Lisle would head directly for France. Beaussier de Lisle sought a letter from the Louisbourg governor in return that would inform him of the situation. Should that not be possible, he asked Drucour to send someone to Cape North, on the northern tip of Île Royale, to light a signal fire if it was impossible for him to enter Louisbourg harbor. Drucour sent back a note encouraging the flotilla to come, and he gave advice on the safest ways to approach Louisbourg.[45]

On July 26 the British ships off Île Royale spotted four distant sails: the squadron commanded by Beaussier de Lisle. Through able maneuvering the French ships succeeded in gaining Louisbourg harbor without incident. They off-loaded three large barrels of money, all their live animals, their shallops, and their sick, who were replaced by two hundred local volunteers. The very next day, at 6:00 AM, the same ships sailed out first to locate and then to escort the *Concorde* into Louisbourg harbor. By that date the *Concorde* had been in the vicinity of Port Dauphin for about six weeks. On the return sail to Louisbourg, the French ships encountered the squadron commanded by Commodore Charles Holmes. An engagement commenced in which most of the French fighting fell to the *Héros*, on which Beaussier de Lisle himself was aboard. The commanders of two other warships, the *Illustre* and the *Licorne*, essentially watched. Though the *Héros* was a seventy-four-gun warship, it had only forty-six cannons mounted at the time. Nonetheless, Beaussier de Lisle engaged in a combat with the *Grafton* (seventy guns) and the *Nottingham* (sixty guns) that was to last six hours. The *Héros* was struck by 182 British cannon balls, 10 of which hit the main mast. Seventy-five of the French crew were killed or injured. In spite of the damage and loss, Beaussier de Lisle did not surrender. On the contrary, the guns of the *Héros* were able to shoot "away much of the rigging in the English ships." In the end neither side was able to claim victory. Beaussier de Lisle and the other French captains returned to Louisbourg and later proceeded to France without further incident. When they reached France, there was an inquiry into why the other French ships had not assisted Beaussier de Lisle aboard the *Héros*. No formal punishment was ever administered, but one of the ship captains hanged himself in the attic of his house, presumably because his reputation had been damaged. The indomitable Beaussier de Lisle would return once more to Louisbourg in 1758.[46]

The coming of colder weather in the fall of 1756 did not bring relief to Louisbourg because there remained so many problems to tackle. At the top level of society a dispute simmered between financial administrator Jacques Prévost and the official who administered the pay and supplies of the Artois and Bourgogne contingents. The conflict was rooted in jurisdictional and personality differences, and it would come into the open early in 1757. Meanwhile, three-way bickering was going on between

Jean Mascle de Saint-Julhien, commander of the Artois and Bourgogne battalions, and local officials at Louisbourg and senior officers in the marine troops. Needless to say, it was not a good time for serious disagreements among those charged with defending the colony.[47]

An emergency situation developed on the night of September 29, 1756, when fire broke out in the garrison bakery, destroying the building. An immediate solution had to be found because bread formed a major part of the diet of the two thousand soldiers in the town, as it did for civilians. Jacques Prévost arranged for the private bakers of Louisbourg to look after the bread needs of the Artois and Bourgogne battalions, while the bakery in the King's Hospital was asked to increase its production for the marine troops. As if provisioning were not already difficult enough, it became further complicated when word arrived that Île Saint-Jean had a poor harvest in 1756 and nothing could be spared for Louisbourg. Rather, Louisbourg would have to send food to help its sister colony. The food requirements for Île Saint-Jean were in fact desperate because the island was home to an additional 1,400 Acadian refugees from Nova Scotia. If rations were not sent, the Louisbourg administration learned, livestock on Île Saint-Jean would have to be slaughtered. That would have a disastrous impact on Île Royale the following year, for Louisbourg relied on Île Saint-Jean as its only remaining source of fresh meat.[48]

Jacques Prévost summarized the bleakness of the food situation at Louisbourg in a late November 1756 dispatch to the minister of the marine. It was Prévost's responsibility to solve provisioning problems, but the British blockade and other complicating factors meant there was little the administrator could do. Instead, he asked the minister, Machault d'Arnouville, to send more assistance. Prévost's position required that he use a tone that was calm and measured. Nonetheless, the dire nature of the situation came through.

> We can no longer rely absolutely on the commerce of France or that of Canada for the subsistence of the colony. It's from the storehouses of the King that people today generally draw flour and all that they need to live. . . . It will be advantageous for the Security of the country and for the operations that we try against the enemy to have sent here the required foodstuffs. If there is not always enough for two years

in advance in the storehouses of the King during the war, we will be obliged to withdraw the population and famine will Follow.[49]

Machault d'Arnouville likely shuddered at Prévost's assessment. Île Royale was asking for more provisions, more protective convoys, and more risks. It added up to one thing: more expenditures.

Machault d'Arnouville must have winced again when he read a petition drawn up in early December by eight of the marine officers on Île Royale. The officers were feeling the effects of the shortages in the colony, where runaway inflation was driving up the cost of everything. According to the petition: "We have dived into the greatest misery and the absolute necessity to contract debts that we predict we can never repay." They asked the minister to help them with their plight. Without saying it directly, the marine officers were undoubtedly hoping their pay scale might be increased to something comparable to that of the officers of the Artois and Bourgogne battalions in the Louisbourg garrison. What a time to be minister of the marine! On top of all the other worries Machault d'Arnouville had to face—food shortages, British blockades, and inadequate fortifications—here was a group of company captains complaining about their personal indebtedness. The very men upon whom the defense of Île Royale might soon hinge! The minister wrote Governor Drucour in early 1758 that the king would not agree to raise the allowances of the marine officers, but he did suggest that a fund could be created for the most needy.[50]

The community at Louisbourg likely began the winter of 1756–57 in a fairly gloomy mood, though a few remained optimistic or tried to put on a brave face. Chief engineer Louis Franquet, for instance, was clearly looking to the future when he assigned an assistant engineer, Grillot de Poilly, to take a late-winter tour around Île Royale. Grillot de Poilly did as he was ordered and prepared a report that commented on the outlying settlements. He also updated map information, recommended improvements, and identified needed repairs to fortifications.[51]

Hundreds of leagues away, in the French colony along the Saint Lawrence River, Canadians were particularly upbeat as the 1756 season of warfare drew to a close. The war with Britain had started well in their theater. One Quebec merchant trumpeted: "The English on this continent are in dire distress, the poor devils don't know which saint to turn to, for as you know they are not acquainted with many. It is estimated that since last year we have killed 4,000 of their men without counting those they lose every day by destitution and desertions."[52] If there were those who actually believed that the setbacks in 1756 were weakening the British will to carry on the war in North America, they were to be disappointed by the events of 1757.

Fresh Resolve

It is axiomatic that war and politics are interconnected, sometimes interchangeable. Therefore, it was inevitable that the disappointments endured by the British in 1756 would have an impact on the politics back home. With expectations for victories running high, those responsible for disappointments paid dearly, as we saw with Admiral Byng, who paid with his life for a naval defeat off Minorca. So it was that the government led by the Duke of Newcastle suffered for having been in charge of the war during a period of bad news. Pressure from the public, as well as insider intrigues, brought about changes in government. The individual touted to correct the situation was William Pitt (1708–78). Pitt was a skilled orator and someone who at times had a tremendous following. "He could rally London and the great merchant towns to his banner," writes historian J. H. Plumb. "His attitude was their attitude; his voice, their voice."[53] Partly because of the support Pitt generated among the public and partly because of the nature of his views, he was neither liked nor trusted by Newcastle or George II. They found his criticisms of spending money to send troops across the English Channel to Hanover particularly annoying. Still, there were few who would deny that the "Great Commoner," as Pitt was known, possessed the abilities required in the crisis that developed in the latter half of 1756. One of his traits was a supreme confidence in his own ability. Witness his declaration: "I am sure I can save this country, and nobody else can."[54]

William Pitt joined the cabinet in December 1756, at which time he was given responsibility for the Southern Department. The position gave him a role to play, but not the domineering one he wanted. Disagreements with other cabinet members over the war policies led to Pitt's dismissal in April 1757. If the British war effort had been going better at the time, it might have been the end of Pitt's ascendancy. Yet the expected victories had still not materialized, so there was an ongoing public outcry in support of Pitt. By late June the war had still not improved in Britain's favor, and William Pitt was asked to rejoin the government, this time on his own terms. He became secretary of state, with ultimate control over both foreign affairs and how the war was waged. He was forty-nine years old and finally exactly where he wanted to be. As one biographer has written, without much exaggeration: "During the next four years Pitt's biography is to be found in the history of the world."[55]

Though Pitt was the top figure and public face of the war effort, he was certainly not a one-man administration. His capable and experienced staff came to include the equivalent of a joint chiefs of staff in the persons of First Lord of the Admiralty George Anson and the commander in chief of the British Army, John Ligonier. Both men were veteran campaigners. Sixty-year old Lord Anson was renowned for his round-the-world cruise of the early 1740s; seventy-seven-year old Ligonier was a Huguenot from the south of France who had emigrated to England as a young man, joined Marlborough's army, and gone on to take part in twenty-three general actions and nineteen sieges without a wound.[56]

The tide for the British war effort actually began to turn for the better a few days before Pitt came back into government on June 29, 1757. On June 23 Robert Clive won a convincing victory, though vastly outnumbered, at Plassey, India. It was a victory that "opened the way for British dominance over Bengal."[57] Important as the gain in India would ultimately prove to be for British imperial interests throughout the nineteenth and early twentieth centuries, the campaign in North America was the focus for William Pitt in the mid-eighteenth century. The new secretary of state believed the key to winning the overall war lay not in Europe but on the other side of the Atlantic Ocean. To be sure, there were those who disagreed, including the captain general of the British Army, the Duke of Cumberland, who was in charge of the war effort in Europe. Cumberland maintained that Britain's troops were best deployed on the nearby continent, protecting Hanoverian interests, rather than on the faraway North American continent fighting the French and their Native allies.[58]

After Pitt assumed full control of the British war effort in June 1757, his vision prevailed. He contended Britain's armies could never win land victories in Europe that would be decisive enough to allow him to dictate favorable terms in any treaty. France and its European allies were land-based powers with large armies and strong fortresses. That did not mean that Pitt ignored the European theater, because he did not. Yet it was on the high seas and in North America where he thought Britain was, and needed to be, dominant. It was a bold insight: to win a European conflict through gains in North America. Gone was the piecemeal approach to colonial wars in which the balance of power shifted ever so slightly. Pitt's vision was as simple as it was far reaching. The goal was to put an end once and for all to France's holdings in North America.[59]

The important first step in accomplishing Pitt's goal was for the Royal Navy to enforce more or less continuous blockades of the major French naval ports of Brest, Rochefort, and Toulon. That would prevent Louis XV's navy from being a factor in the war. The fewer French warships at sea, the more France's ocean-going commerce and colonies would be vulnerable to British preying. Once the role of the French navy was reduced, Pitt envisioned Louisbourg and Quebec falling, thereby forcing a surrender of all New France. Next Britain would go after the sugar islands of Martinique and Guadeloupe, then the slave-trading center of Gorée (off today's Dakar, Senegal). To Pitt's way of thinking, victory over France was a matter of providing sufficient resources in the hands of the right admirals and generals.

Fleets of Empire

While William Pitt's willingness to make decisions about how, when, and where to allocate military and naval resources gave him a clear vision, no vision by itself ever won a war. The secretary of state and his senior staff positions were not personally going to sail the ships, open the siege trenches, or direct musket fire against the enemy. Victory required many thousands of combatants, who would have to come from the British army, Royal Navy, and engineering corps, as well Anglo-American troops and sailors, and even some Native fighters. In light of the setbacks already endured, it would be no easy matter to defeat the French and the Aboriginal nations allied to their side. In the interior of North America, Britain's enemies had demonstrated resilience, tenacity, and military ingenuity. The defeats of 1756 stung the British. It was going to take more effort and more resources than had thus far been brought to bear.

The cost of sending the British forces to North America was enormous, yet the island nation was able to make the financial commitment. As historian Jacques Mathieu observes: "In this maritime and colonial struggle, England can bring to bear four times as many ships of the line and five times as many men as France. Beyond that, William Pitt obtains from the British Parliament financial credit which is 25 times that agreed to in France, to undertake an offensive war." By way of contrast, in George Stanley's phrase, the best the French could muster was "rationed help." Money may not be everything, but it helps if one is seeking to wage a successful war on several continents.[60]

In the course of 1757, Britain sent approximately eleven thousand regular infantry soldiers to North America. The commitment was not only much larger than France's, but it also revealed a new emphasis on using regulars, or "redcoats," in American campaigns. Up until that point the usual way to wage war against French positions was for individual colonies or a combination of colonies to raise provincial soldiers, militiamen, from their own populations for short campaigns, with professional soldiers from Britain in the minority. The new policy was a "dramatic reversal" of past approaches and an indication of London's new determination to use all available resources to dominate North America.[61]

Meanwhile, in France two dominant figures directed the war effort in 1757: the minister of war, Pierre-Marc de Voyer de Paulmy, the comte d'Argenson, and the minister of the marine, whom we have already mentioned many times, Jean-Baptiste de Machault d'Arnouville. The former had little to do with colonial matters, though it was his ministry that provided the battalions of the Troupes de Terre that were sent to Quebec and Louisbourg in 1755. Machault d'Arnouville, like his predecessors, was responsible for practically everything that related to the navy and the colonies. Since assuming control of the marine ministry in 1754, Machault d'Arnouville wondered each year thereafter when a British attack on Louisbourg was going to occur. Like Pitt he recognized that whoever had the upper hand in terms of sea power would probably prevail in the Atlantic region. The losses and damage British squadrons had inflicted on French shipping in 1755 and 1756 had been costly, and the minister anticipated that 1757 might be worse. While not knowing exactly what the enemy was planning, Machault d'Arnouville wanted to be ready. His intelligence reports suggested there was to be a major expedition against Île Royale, so he gave orders for a major naval contingent to sail to Louisbourg. Three squadrons were to make their way to the colony over several months. The embarkation ports were Brest and Toulon, though the home base for some of the ships was Rochefort. The squadrons were to set out early in the year, in the hope that they would reach Louisbourg before a British blockade was in place. If they all made it to the destination, Île Royale would have eighteen ships of the line and five frigates. It would be by far the largest French naval force ever seen in the colony.[62]

Machault d'Arnouville did not remain in his portfolio to see matters through to a conclusion. Two days after the first squadron left France on January 30, 1757, Louis XV signed *lettres de cachet* to send both the minister of the marine and the minister of war, the comte d'Argenson, to their country estates. The king's mistress, Madame de Pompadour, irritated not with the ministers' conduct of the war but with their attitudes toward her, was behind the dismissals. The king did allow Machault d'Arnouville to retain his position as keeper of the royal seals. The new minister of the marine was François-Marie Peyrenc de Moras, whom historian Jonathan Dull describes as lacking Machault d'Arnouville 's genius, "but he was honest and conscientious." Peyrenc de Moras was France's controller general of finances, a post he retained for six months. Theoretically, the double responsibility meant Peyrenc de Moras would have to convince only himself to find money for the navy and the colonies. With the war being waged across much of the globe, the cost of the conflict escalated to unseen levels. The annual total for the marine ministry would reach over 42 million livres in 1758 and almost 57 million livres in 1759.[63]

Peyrenc de Moras did not countermand Machault d'Arnouville 's decision to send three naval squadrons to Louisbourg, for he shared the sentiment that Île Royale was a probable British target. On the contrary Peyrenc de Moras asserted to Drucour: "[I]f the reunion of naval forces destined for Louisbourg can reach there in time, the Enemies will not dare undertake anything against that place."[64] Putting his own personal stamp on the defense of Louisbourg, Peyrenc de Moras sent a dispatch to chief engineer Louis Franquet, letting him know that if Governor Drucour died, he was to take over as commandant until a new governor was named. The engineer was a surprising choice because the sixty-year old was in poor health and sixty-four-year-old Jean Mascle de Saint-Julhien, commander of the Artois and Bourgogne battalions at Louisbourg, was the more experienced campaigner. Peyrenc de Moras likely selected Franquet because Mascle de Saint-Julhien had a reputation of being difficult to get along with, but the engineer's ailing health made him a poor choice.

The three French squadrons that set out for Île Royale in 1757 carried massive firepower. All together the eighteen ships of the line and the five frigates carried over fourteen hundred cannons. In other words the floating fortresses possessed nearly ten times the killing power of the land-based fortifications at Louisbourg. There were fewer than 150 artillery pieces mounted permanently in the town.[65] Nothing like the 1757 fleet had ever been seen before in Louisbourg harbor, nor would it be again.

The first squadron to set sail included five ships of the line (one eighty-gun, two seventy-four-gun, and two sixty-four-gun) and a thirty-two-gun frigate, and was under the command of Joseph de Bauffremont, prince de Listenois. The flotilla left Brest on January 30 and sailed first to Sainte-Domingue (Haiti), then north to Île Royale. It reached Louisbourg on May 23. The second squadron sailed from the Mediterranean port of Toulon on March 18, commanded by Jean-François de Noble du Revest. It was comprised of four ships of the line (one seventy-four-gun and three sixty-four-gun) and arrived at Louisbourg on June 15. The final squadron was the largest of the three, with nine ships of the line (two eighty-gun, four seventy-four-gun, and three sixty-four-gun) and two thirty-two-gun frigates. The commander was Emmanuel-August de Cahideuc, comte du Bois de La Motte, who was seventy-four years old and a veteran of many campaigns. One of his adventures had been in 1755, when he was in charge of the squadron that carried a large contingent of Troupes de Terre to Quebec. The British sought to intercept Du Bois de La Motte's squadron on its way back to France in 1755, but the wily commander eluded them by sailing up the Strait of Belle Isle and along Newfoundland's northern coast, something no large French squadron had tried before. One naval historian writes that Du Bois de

La Motte had performed "superbly" in 1755, guiding his fleet back to France without any losses, while another castigates him for being "apathetic and timid" in his refusal to sail from Quebec to Louisbourg to assist Périer de Salvert's squadron.[66]

When Du Bois de La Motte reached Louisbourg in 1757, he assumed overall command of all naval ships assembled there. His squadron left Brest on May 3 and reached Île Royale on June 19. Two weeks later, on July 2, he allowed two warships, along with a transport and three merchant ships, to set off for Quebec. They carried with them two battalions of the Berry Regiment destined for service in Canada. At least one of the lower-ranking French naval officers thought the decision was a mistake. In his opinion the Berry troops could have been put to better use defending Louisbourg.[67]

Frequently when ships reached Île Royale after long voyages—four to six weeks was the average length of a crossing from France—a number of the sailors had to be hospitalized. The situation at Louisbourg in 1757 was worse than anything seen before. Back in February, before the squadrons left Brest or Toulon, sailors aboard two of the ships developed typhus. This occurred, according to a naval officer, because one of the warships went to the aid of a merchant vessel that had the sickness on board. If that indeed was the cause, the humanitarian act would end up having deadly consequences on a vast scale. The fever spread quickly aboard the warships, with four hundred men put ashore before the squadron sailed from France. Unfortunately, that did not eradicate the typhus. Other sailors fell ill during the crossing to Louisbourg, with some dying. Around the same time troop ships sailing to Canada were also carrying the epidemic. Between May and October 1757, 250 soldiers in the regiments of the Troupes de Terre died at Quebec. The impact at Louisbourg was even greater. There were so many sick sailors in the capital of Île Royale that they could not all be accommodated in the King's Hospital in the center of town. In July 1757, reported Jacques Prévost, the sick from the ship were placed in twenty-four houses located outside the walls of the town and around the harbor to reduce the chances of the disease spreading. Yet the situation became progressively worse in the summer and fall.[68]

Though the sickness carried by their sailors was a worry to the French naval officers, those officers had been pleasantly surprised that there was no British blockade when their squadrons neared Louisbourg. An officer aboard the *Inflexible* described the reaction of Lieutenant General Du Bois de La Motte: "This general also expected to find before the place some forces to oppose his entrance and he was much surprised at the conduct of the enemy. The English nation, which had flattered itself to make a second exchange of Louisbourg for Port Mahon [Minorca], had not acted in such a manner as to succeed this year, while on our side we may be gratified at the happy junction of our squadrons."[69]

All the rumors had pointed to a major British expedition against Louisbourg, so what had happened? Where was the Royal Navy? The short answer is that despite William Pitt's enthusiasm for a combined operation against the French positions in North America, the senior military and naval officers had not been able to put a force to sea as early as the leadership wanted. While the French had sent one squadron across the ocean at the end of January, another in mid-March, and a third in early May, the British ships and troops were held up by logistical problems. The plan was for them to sail in February or March under the command of Admiral Francis Holburne, yet the departure from Cork, Ireland, was repeatedly delayed. Holburne finally set off to cross the Atlantic on May 7; it would be July 10 before the warships and transports finally reached Halifax. By that time all three French squadrons were safe, though sick, at Louisbourg.

Late though the British fleet was in arriving in Atlantic waters, Holburne was in command of a formidable armada: fifteen warships, several sloops, and forty-five transports. The soldiers on board came from seven regiments (1,000 men of the Royal Second Battalion and 700 men each from the Seventeenth, Twenty-seventh, Twenty-eighth, Forty-third, Forty-sixth, and Fifty-fifth Regiments of foot). All together they totaled 5,200 men at arms. The plan was for the ships to sail to Halifax, where they would join up with the more than 6,000 troops that were to sail north from New York, led by Lord Loudoun, commander in chief of the British Army in North America. Once they made their rendezvous, Loudoun and Holburne were to determine whether they should proceed against Louisbourg or Quebec. The eight-year-old settlement at Halifax did not yet possess all the facilities of a major servicing port for the

British fleet, but its location made it an excellent staging harbor for an expedition against either French stronghold.[70]

At roughly the same time Admiral Holburne was preparing to set sail from England, Lord Loudoun was in New York with about 6,300 soldiers (officers and enlisted men of the Twenty-second, Twenty-eighth, Forty-second, Forty-fourth, and Sixtieth Regiments) and accompanying siege material. Clearly Loudoun's plan to capture Louisbourg before the end of June 1757 and then go on to capture Quebec before winter set in was not on schedule. By mid-June, still in the New York area, Loudoun would be doing well to launch an attack on one or the other French stronghold, not both. To help Loudoun make up his mind as to which one to go after first, William Pitt sent his commander in North America a letter stating that his preference was Louisbourg, though he left the final decision to the commander.[71]

Loudoun agreed Louisbourg should be the first target, and he committed to proceeding to Halifax to rendezvous with Holburne's fleet. However, there were not enough warships at New York to escort the hundred or so vessels Loudoun had gathered to make the voyage to Nova Scotia. The only protection available was Rear Admiral Sir Charles Hardy's fifty-gun warship and several small cruisers. A sail to Halifax was risky. If the expedition encountered French warships heading to or operating out of Louisbourg, Loudoun's force could be disrupted. A few, some, or many of the vessels might be captured or sunk. That was an enormous gamble, for it placed a sizable British force at the mercy of a French squadron known to be in the general area. Loudoun measured the risks and then courageously, or foolishly, set sail for Halifax on June 20.[72]

Fortunately for Loudoun and the British, the French were not in the right place at the right time. Bauffremont's squadron was looking to intercept British ships but found none in the waters it covered. The reason why more of Du Bois de La Motte's overall fleet was not out patrolling the seas can be found in the orders given to the commander before he left France. The minister of the marine emphasized that the three squadrons were being sent to defend Louisbourg, not to wage an offensive campaign. Moreover, recall that many of the French ships had just arrived at Louisbourg, and a large number of the crew were seriously ill. Of course, had the senior French officers only known—which they could not—that there was a virtually unprotected British flotilla sailing from New York, they would surely have sent more warships looking for it. Instead, Loudoun, Hardy, and their force reached Halifax safely on June 30.[73] Having attained the rendezvous point before Admiral Holburne, Loudoun ordered his troops to carry out military exercises so they would be battle ready when the time came.

According to Captain John Knox, who was sailing in the fleet commanded by Admiral Holburne, the transatlantic crossing took "seven weeks and five days." He notes: "[T]hough we had a good deal of rough, blowing weather, with thick fogs to sour our passage, yet upon the whole we esteemed ourselves peculiarly fortunate." The ships finally arrived in Halifax harbor on July 9, ten days after Loudoun's force. Nearly one thousand of the soldiers from England had to be placed in houses that served as interim hospitals. Though ill, they were not afflicted with typhus, as were many of Du Bois de La Motte's sailors at Louisbourg.[74]

Holburne, Loudoun, Hardy, and other senior officers now had to decide their next step: Louisbourg or Quebec? The source of their uncertainty was the lack of precise information on the size and strength of the French fleet within Louisbourg harbor. They dispatched the versatile Captain John Rous—who in 1755 had destroyed the French settlements on the Newfoundland shore, commanded the naval portion of the attack on Beauséjour, and voted as a member of the Nova Scotia Council to deport the Acadians—to proceed with four frigates on a reconnaissance trip to Louisbourg. Poor weather and fog delayed Rous on his mission, and it was three weeks before he was able to return to Halifax.

While the senior British officers were waiting to decide their next course of action, they put some of their enlisted men to work planting a large garden "to supply the sick and wounded of the army with vegetables" for the anticipated siege of Louisbourg. The activity later became a "source of ridicule" back in Great Britain, where the expectation was that the army would be engaging the French on battlefields, not growing cabbages. Vegetable gardens aside, many units did make use of the available waiting time for warlike practice. Officers put their men through drills of coming ashore in small boats, simulating an amphibious landing. The rehearsals irritated some who were anxious to get on with the real thing. One officer complained bitterly to Loudoun: "We only carried on this Sham attack to Loiter away time . . . our behaviour this Campaign would furnish laughter to all Europe, and the French in particular, who would have a Farce at Louisbourg representing our Transactions at Halifax."[75]

Far from Nova Scotia events of importance were occurring in the wider war on the North American continent. The French in Canada followed with interest Loudoun's withdrawal of most of the British infantry regiments from New York and the Mohawk River frontier, for it presented them with a golden opportunity. In late July 1757 the governor general of New France, the marquis de Vaudreuil, sent Major General Louis-Joseph de Montcalm to attack Fort William Henry on Lake George with a force of about eight thousand French regulars, marines, militia, and Native warriors. The British defenders numbered about twenty-four hundred. Six days of French artillery bombardment forced a surrender on August 9. When the British marched out of Fort William Henry, an incident occurred that was immediately regretted by Montcalm and soon regarded in British circles as an act of infamy. Warriors attached to the French side attacked the unarmed columns of British prisoners, killing perhaps fifty and carrying off about six hundred. Montcalm restored order, and Vaudreuil eventually recovered approximately four hundred of the soldiers who had been carried off.[76] Nonetheless, the British interpretation of the events at Fort William Henry as a massacre would have a long life. One of the first places it made its impact felt would be at Louisbourg the following year.

Defending the Colony

The months before the arrival of the French squadrons at Louisbourg in May and June 1757 had not been easy. The winter was long and unpleasant. In the words of chief engineer Louis Franquet, "Winter here was very hard in every way, as much for its length, by the rigor of the weather, as by the absence of the sweet things of life." The month of May brought more to complain about when more than eighteen inches of snow fell during the first twelve days of the month.[77]

Like the bad weather the worries of the top officials on Île Royale continued without relief. One concern was the knowledge that spies based at Louisbourg were apparently passing information on to the British.[78]

Little did anyone suspect that Thomas Pichon, former secretary to the comte de Raymond, had been a primary source until 1755, when he went to England. Rather, Louisbourg officials pointed to deserters and exchanged prisoners as the likely guilty parties. And no doubt the British were obtaining information from those individuals. Certainly the French were obtaining reports about what was going on in Halifax from the same sources. Drucour and Prévost resolved to be as careful as they could about the impressions they were passing on to enemy prisoners in their care, for they would eventually be exchanged. It was important that they not take back to the British tales of hardships and shortages at Louisbourg. That was a difficult subject to conceal, however, for the top problem for the French administration in the spring of 1757 was indeed the food situation.

In May 1757 Governor Drucour and financial administrator Jacques Prévost held back nothing when they wrote to the minister of the marine: "Of all the food shortages the Colony has suffered through up to the present time, there has not been one as severe as it is currently. And if the Enemies undertake some enterprise against this Place, it is certain that famine will be inevitable. We are in the fifth month of the year, Monseigneur, without provisions and without sea forces. All winter long there was not a family with an ounce of flour."[79]

Drucour and Prévost added that since commerce had virtually ended, the colony was subsisting on rations and provisions distributed from the king's storehouse. Without explaining how they were doing it, the two officials stated they were taking "precautions to hide the sad state of the Country from the public, in order that word did not leak to [their] neighbours." One doubts they were able to hide much, given the winter that the local families had endured. The only bit of good news the governor and the financial administrator could pass along to the minister was that local privateers had taken a few prizes from the enemy. In one instance a sizable quantity of flour and grain had been captured. The flour was distributed to Louisbourg residents, while a portion of the grain was used to feed poultry, with a surplus sent to Île Saint-Jean, where the plight of the settlers and Acadian refugees was even more dire than on Île Royale. It was a weary and worried Drucour who commented in mid-June about Île Saint-Jean: "Happy are those who have perished (of which the number is rather large); they are delivered from many evils."[80]

The arrival of the three squadrons from France might have wiped out whatever food supplies were in Louisbourg, yet it did not. The warships carried sufficient provisions to tide the crews over for a while, but what after those provisions ran out? The minister of the marine soon sent out eight ships from Rochefort with another three months provisions for the crews of the ships.[81]

While Drucour and Prévost were worrying about food, Louis Franquet was fretting about the fortifications. Rather than commit to a particular project for the 1757 building season, Franquet wanted to wait and see what the British were going to do. If they launched an attack, he reasoned, there was insufficient time to begin any major changes. If there was no attack, then he hoped to raise the revetment of the King's Bastion by at least eight feet and to get on with other minor work. As it was, routine maintenance was a major challenge by itself. The chief engineer wrote: "This place is falling into so much decay that each day presents new reparations . . . and as the attack can take place only on one of the two fronts facing the ocean, we give all our attention to those areas." To show that he was staying within the money allocated for fortifications work at Louisbourg, Franquet closed one letter to the minister with a reference to his "industriousness in economizing the King's funds."[82]

By mid-June, with two naval squadrons already in the harbor and Du Bois de La Motte's expected any day, Franquet and the other officials could relax somewhat about an enemy attack. The larger the fleet, the less likely it was that the British would try to make a landing. On June 18 the engineer wrote the new minister of the marine, Peyrenc de Moras, concerning the projects that were completed or in progress. The palisades and traverses of the covered way outside the Queen's Gate were finished. The glacis was being worked on. The parapet on the right face of the Princess Demi-Bastion was now five feet higher. They would soon get back to blowing up more of the outcrop known as Cap Noir (Black Rock). The stones, bricks, and sand required for a proposed powder magazine were delivered. The work on the coal wharf was completed. The parapet of the left face of the spur battery was raised three feet and thickened by twelve feet; then three embrasures were cut. Traverses were finished on the covered way of the Dauphin Demi-Bastion. Two épaulements were constructed to make the postern tunnel on the right flank of the King's Bastion less visible. The nearby hills were lowered a few more feet. Three thousand fascines were prepared, some of which were already used while the rest were set aside in the event of a siege. It was quite a list, and it was only June 1757. There were still many weeks of work ahead for Franquet to supervise.[83]

Following the arrival in port of Du Bois de La Motte, the third squadron from France, the nature of the military work undertaken at Louisbourg changed drastically. One reason for the change was information obtained from a British deserter the Mi'kmaq brought to Louisbourg on July 7. According to the deserter, a massive army and navy were assembling at Halifax. Their intention was to come up the coast and besiege the French stronghold.[84] The news prompted a switch from the main enceinte at Louisbourg, which had always been Franquet's primary concern, to considering ways to defend locations up and down the coast in close proximity to the harbor. Du Bois de La Motte, the lieutenant general of the fleet, was not showing his seventy-four years and henceforth assumed the dominant role in determining the priorities for the defense of Louisbourg. In contrast to Franquet the priority for the naval commander was to prevent the British from making a landing in the first place. If the enemy could not get his soldiers ashore, reasoned the veteran officer, there could be no siege. Moreover, with the huge fleet Du Bois de La Motte had at his disposal, French warships should be able to thwart any blockade. An anonymous officer aboard the sixty-four-gun warship the *Inflexible* described how the admiral took charge of preparing the defense of Louisbourg.

> Immediately after his arrival the general began his inspection of the fortifications of the place, with which he was not satisfied; his inspection went all along the coast, on the south side as far as Gabarus, which is the locality where the enemy effected his landing in 1745, and on the north side as far as Laurenbec. Having found in these parts several points suitable for a landing, he immediately ordered detachments from all the ships, with officers, to work the entrenchments, and establish batteries at each point, and no work was stopped until everything was complete. He caused the fortifications to be repaired and increased as well in the interior as on the exterior of the

place, where we increased the batteries and levelled a height which commands the grand cavalier of the Dauphin gate. . . . Ile Royale, a place of much renown, required such an inspection in order to be put somewhat in a state of defence.[85]

The author of this account clearly thought Du Bois de La Motte was the only one making the decisions about where and how the landing areas near Louisbourg were going to be defended. That is surely a simplistic interpretation brought on by the officer's pride in his commander and his arm of the service. Governor Drucour and the director of fortifications, Louis Franquet, undoubtedly offered advice, or at least consent, before any entrenchments and batteries were erected. Apparently they welcomed Du Bois de La Motte's ideas and leadership, for there is no documented evidence that either Drucour or Franquet resisted or resented his initiatives. On the other hand, Jacques Prévost, the financial administrator, did rile the naval commander. Prévost initially refused to provide certain supplies for the French troops detached to the positions along the coast, beyond the walls of Louisbourg. Du Bois de La Motte straightened the matter out by marching to Prévost's house, which he "threatened to set . . . on fire, and to send him back to France, if everything which the store contained was not ready by the next day."[86] The seventy-four-year old naval commander was obviously not someone to suffer interference or opposition. Even after he left the colony in the fall of 1757, officials on Île Royale would continue to make respectful, almost deferential references to his ideas and projects in their letters to France.

Before Du Bois de La Motte's arrival, Franquet and Drucour had gone outside the walls of Louisbourg and inspected landing areas along the coast that they thought might be suitable for an enemy descent. Though nothing they proposed was as far-reaching as the projects initiated by the visiting naval commander, Drucour and Franquet were aware that steps had to be taken to prevent, or at least slow down, a British landing. One precautionary move by Governor Drucour was to send a company of marine troops to Port Dauphin in the interior of the colony to wait there and serve as a small reserve force. In the event of a successful British landing at or near Louisbourg, the soldiers were to join forces with Native allies and refugee Acadians camped at Gabarus Bay to wage a guerilla campaign "on the rear of the enemy." Another project was the establishment of a defended post at the specific part of the shoreline where New England soldiers had come ashore in 1745. Drucour and Franquet envisioned placing detachments of soldiers and abatis (felled trees with the branches or roots facing the enemy) in various locations.[87]

When Du Bois de La Motte arrived in port, he saw the defense of the landing areas on either side of Louisbourg harbor as the highest priority. The lieutenant general had at his disposal a large labor pool—the healthy sailors from his disease-afflicted squadrons—that could carry out the necessary work. A naval officer recorded that six hundred of the "best soldiers" off the vessels were selected, placed in companies of fifty men each, and assigned to shore duties.[88] Even if Drucour and Franquet had wanted to implement the projects undertaken by Du Bois de La Motte, they did not have the manpower to do so.

The work along the coast took place both northeast and southwest of the Louisbourg harbor. Laborers created a few small artillery positions, but mostly they constructed parapets of earth or fascines, laid abatis on beaches, and established lines of communication between different posts. In the summer of 1757 the coastal posts above and below Louisbourg became the temporary homes to hundreds of regular French infantry, Compagnies franches de la Marine troops, Native warriors, local militia, and Acadian refugees turned volunteer fighters. The warriors included not just Mi'kmaq from Île Royale and Nova Scotia, but also Mi'kmaq from across the Atlantic region and Native warriors from other nations. A French officer in the Compagnies franches, who was detached to the coast from June 6 to September 15, stated that when one contingent of warriors left their positions on July 15 to go look for appropriate birch bark for their canoes, they were replaced by a force of 100 Mi'kmaw and 110 Kennebec ("Canibas"), Maliseet, and Abenaki warriors. In total, according to the officer, about 3,000 men-at-arms were posted at the different landing spots during the peak moments of the summer of 1757. The French officer, used to giving and taking orders in a clear-cut European-style chain of command, was frustrated by the Abenaki custom of holding daily councils to decide on a course of action. The officer's estimate of 3,000 men posted to the defensive posts along the coast appears to have been on the high side. A list drawn up by military officials stated there was a total of 2,468 men, sixty-eight cannons, and two mortars at coastal positions created outside the walled town of Louisbourg in 1757.[89]

It would be repetitive to describe all the defended positions in detail, for one example illustrates the kind of preparations that were undertaken. At Grand Lorembec (Big Lorraine), to the northeast of Louisbourg, a contingent of the garrison troops, the Compagnies franches de la Marine, camped at the ready. They had three pieces of artillery: one cannon of eighteen livres and two of twelve livres. The only part of the beach where a landing was thought possible was covered with an abatis. A raised embankment overlooked the spot, from which the soldiers would direct musket fire if the British attempted a descent. Other defended positions to the north of Louisbourg harbor were Petit Lorembec, Anse à Gautier, and the cove behind Lighthouse Point. Right at Lighthouse Point itself, which was a rocky outcrop at the entrance to the port, on the right-hand side of ships entering the port, Du Bois de La Motte had a battery erected in 1757. This was the spot where in the late stages of the 1745 siege New Englanders had erected a siege battery that soon silenced the French guns on the nearby Island Battery. Du Bois de La Motte ordered three guns mounted at Lighthouse Point *en barbette*, that is, eighteen- and twelve-livres cannons firing over an earthwork embankment. Guns mounted there would mean that any enemy vessel that tried to force its way into the harbor would be caught in a crossfire between Lighthouse Point and the Island Battery on the other side of the narrow channel.[90]

The French regarded the beaches to the southwest of Louisbourg as the most likely to attract a British landing attempt, so they were more heavily defended than the positions to the northeast, mentioned earlier. In 1745 the French had been completely unprepared for an enemy landing at any coastal location. They had thought the marshy terrain between the coast and the fortified town represented a sufficient barrier. The Anglo-American provincial soldiers demonstrated how wrong that assumption was. The New Englanders made a beachhead a few kilometers to the south of the fortress, beat off a last-minute attempt by the French to drive them off, then proceeded overland to launch their assault against the fortified town. They constructed sleds to haul their weapons and supplies through the marshy areas the French had thought were impassable.

The two best locations for a landing south of Louisbourg were Pointe Platte (Flat Point) and Anse de la Cormorandière (Kennington Cove). The former was closer to Louisbourg and was where the New England-ers had descended in 1745. Since both offered excellent potential as land-ing beaches, neither could be overlooked. After Du Bois de La Motte carried out his initial inspection and provided sailors to do much of the work, both areas were turned into well-defended positions. Detachments of five hundred troops from the Artois and Bourgogne Regiments were sent to each cove, as well as Compagnies franches de la Marine soldiers, militia, and Native warriors. Some warriors came from as far away as the Miramichi region (in modern-day New Brunswick).[91]

At Pointe Platte the French established several well-entrenched posi-tions, again with abatis on the beaches. Directly behind the landing ar-eas, the defenders erected an earthwork parapet about four hundred me-ters long. On the left they raised an earthwork redan and a small battery (two six-livres cannons) to provide enfilading fire along the beaches. De-tachments of the Artois and Bourgogne battalions and a contingent of Compagnies franches troops camped nearby. One communication path connected the area to Louisbourg, and a second extended up the pen-insula. On the extreme right side of the Pointe Platte peninsula was an-other fortified area, with more abatis and another parapet. Native war-riors camped in that area, though which nation they were from was not recorded.[92]

The most extensive defenses constructed by the French in 1757 were at Anse de la Cormorandière. The gently curving shape of the cove ex-tended roughly eight hundred meters, with two stretches of sandy beach separated by rock outcrops. It was easily the best landing area within marching distance of Louisbourg, so the French toiled long and hard to make it unwelcoming to the enemy. They covered each beach in abatis and constructed parapets of earth and fascines behind the entire shore. They mounted two six-livres cannons on the left flank of one beach and placed a single six-livres cannon overlooking the second. To provide more

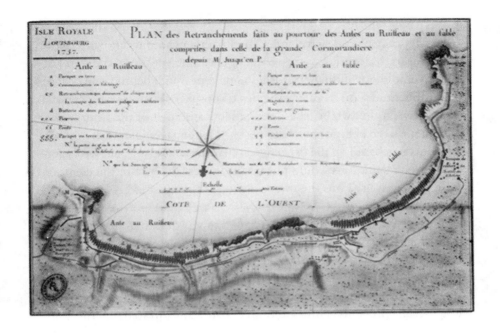

FIGURE 5. **Preparations Ashore, 1757**

Thinking a British invasion was imminent, which it was, visiting naval commander Du Bois de La Motte led the drive to create a range of defended positions at the most likely landing spots north and south of Louisbourg. This particular plan illustrates what was done at Anse de la Cormorandière (today's Kennington Cove). To be noted on the plan are the abatis (felled trees) on the beaches, the communication path, and the places where the troops were camped. *Courtesy of Archives nationales de France, Marine, B4, vol. 285.*

firepower they placed swivel guns, small-caliber cannons known as *pierriers*, in various locations. Native warriors camped at the farthest end of the cove; soldiers of the Artois Regiment kept watch behind one beach; a contingent of Compagnies franches troops were posted at the central area between the two beaches; and officers and men of the Bourgogne Regiment were behind the other beach.[93] The placement of the different units was based on the expectation that the soldiers of the Artois and Bourgogne battalions would put up the stiffest defense in the event of a British landing. Thus they were posted at the most likely landing areas, the beaches.

Though the leadership considered the soldiers of the Troupes de Terre as the mainstay of a defense of Louisbourg, they also had high hopes for the Aboriginal warriors. Although the number of warriors was relatively small, about three hundred, the French believed that their style of irregular warfare would have an unsettling and demoralizing impact on the enemy. The previous century and a half had demonstrated that the British and the Anglo-Americans had a deep dread of such warfare. Yet in truth the British response to Native warriors and the way in which they fought revealed a striking ambivalence. On the one hand, the British consistently proclaimed a sense of moral superiority over the French and especially their Native allies. The enigmatic James Wolfe, who looms large in the following pages, expressed the prevailing view among his countrymen when he boasted, "Britons breathe higher sentiments of humanity, and listen to the merciful dictates of the Christian religion," in contrast to their enemies. In truth the British eagerly employed as many of their own warriors as they could, as well as creating their own irregular troops, and both adopted essentially the same measures they liked to denounce the French and their allies for using.[94]

The surest indication of the high value the French placed on the warriors' contributions to the defense of Louisbourg in 1757 is found in the money spent on supplying the Mi'kmaq, the Maliseets, and other allies. The cost of keeping the warriors around for an extended period in the summer of 1757 reached an all-time high for that particular category of expense. Louisbourg officials spent over sixty thousand livres on weapons, tobacco, and assorted merchandise to support their Native allies. Another dimension to the relationship between the two peoples was the religious connection. With so many warriors camping at coastal positions, French missionary Abbé Pierre Maillard saw to their spiritual needs as Roman Catholics. In July he officiated at an outdoor Mass, said in the Mi'kmaw language at Gabarus Bay. Another insight into the relationship between the French and their allies comes from the journal of naval officer Louis-Auguste Rossel. He described a scene in which a chief made a speech to Du Bois de La Motte that included the comment "that they were brothers and ready to spill all their blood in the service of the King their father." The chief then placed a number of scalps at the feet of the lieutenant general and sought his encouragement to bring back more of the same. Du Bois de La Motte replied to the chief and the assembled warriors that "they should not delay in making their good intentions a reality."[95]

August and September 1757
Captain John Rous sailed back into Halifax harbor in August, completing his mission to obtain information on the French fleet at Louisbourg. Rous had learned from a captured French vessel that Louisbourg was sheltering ten French warships and three thousand soldiers. That would turn out to be a gross underestimate of the French naval presence, but the British at the time knew no better. Lord Loudoun and Admiral Holburne soon held a joint council of war to discuss their next step and decided to drop the attack on Quebec and concentrate on taking Louisbourg. They felt the relative weakness of the French, based on Rous's information, gave them a reasonable chance of success. After all, they had about eleven thousand regular troops and a fleet that was larger than what they thought the French possessed. The new plan called for Holburne to use a portion of his fleet to lure the French ships out of Louisbourg harbor to engage them in naval combat. If the French fell for the trap, then a landing by soldiers would follow.

Before the plan was implemented, however, the British commanders learned the situation at Louisbourg was not what Rous had told them. Found aboard a French ship captured on August 4 was a complete list of the warships at Louisbourg. Put simply, Du Bois de La Motte's ships outnumbered and outgunned Holburne's, which changed everything. Loudoun sent a note to Holburne asking the admiral if his fleet was "sufficient to attempt the reduction of Louisbourg with any probability of success at this advanced season." Holburne replied that "there [was] no probability of succeeding" given the size of the enemy's fleet and the time of the year. After all the buildup, that exchange put an end to the attempt to capture Louisbourg in 1757. Lord Loudoun sailed back to New York, escorted by a protective shield of warships under the command of Admiral Holburne.[96]

The admiral, however, still yearned to inflict at least a little damage on the French ships at Louisbourg. He likely also thought of how Admiral Byng had recently been hanged for not doing his "utmost," a vague failing he hoped not to duplicate. After seeing Loudoun safely back to New York, Holburne returned to the waters off Île Royale with twenty-two frigates and ships of the line. They appeared off Louisbourg on August 19. After having anticipated an invasion fleet for months, the French naturally wondered if this was finally it. It did not seem so because there was no sign of transports carrying large numbers of troops. Just in case the transports were to follow, the Louisbourg leadership gave the orders for "all the troops" to go to Gabarus Bay, where the New Englanders had brought their soldiers ashore in 1745.[97]

Within Louisbourg harbor and immediately offshore, the two massive flotillas squared off like armies in a classic land battle. A French plan details the standoff as it appeared on August 19.[98] Arranged offshore were the warships under Admiral Holburne's command, not in a continuous line but clustered in threes and fours between Cap Noir to the south and Lighthouse Point to the north. Within the harbor were an equal number of French warships, which Du Bois de La Motte had anchored so as to maximize their broadsides out to sea. There was only one way into the port, and the French commander had sixteen of his ships in the shape of a triangle, with the base blocking the entrance to the port. The front line contained seven ships of the line (three eighty-gun, three seventy-four-gun, and one sixty-four-gun); the second line had five ships (two seventy-four-gun, one seventy-gun, and two sixty-four-gun); while the third (one seventy-gun and two sixty-four-gun) and fourth lines (a single sixty-four-gun) completed the triangle. The sixteen ships were anchored so that the rows presented a solid mass, with—on paper at least—the ships in the first two rows able to fire their heavy artillery without

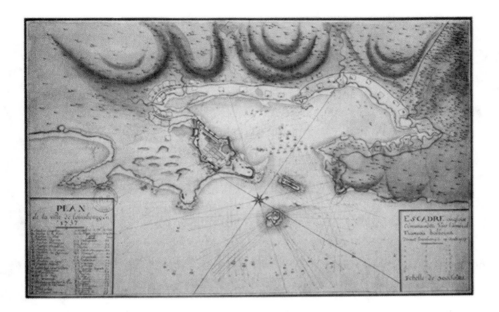

FIGURE 6. **Naval Standoff, 1757**

This French plan depicts the impasse of two massive naval squadrons in the fall of 1757. Admiral Francis Holburne's Royal Navy squadron is shown in a line off the coast from Louisbourg, while its French counterpart, the squadron of Emmanuel-August de Cahideuc, comte du Bois de La Motte, is illustrated moored in a triangle blocking the entrance to the port. *Courtesy of Bibliothèque nationale de France, Cartes et Plans, Atlas Ge D 1348.*

hitting one another. Behind the triangle, moored not far from the Royal Battery, were four smaller warships (one thirty-six-gun and three thirty-two-gun) as a reserve.

The spectacle of the two massive fleets squaring off with thousands of crew and more than a thousand pieces of artillery on each side would never again be duplicated in the waters of Atlantic Canada. A forest of British masts and sails towered outside the harbor, matched by an even denser forest of French masts compressed into a tight wedge inside the harbor. It was a sight to inspire a mixture of awe and dread in the inhabitants of Louisbourg. How the encounter would end was not at all clear when people went to bed on the night of August 19.

On the morning of August 20, according to a French naval officer who was an eyewitness, Holburne and his squadron came as close to shore as they dared "to make a good reconnaissance, and after his examination went seaward, then made for Halifax, where he [Holburne] remained eight days shut up in his room without speaking to anyone." It was an imaginative interpretation by the French officer, who was undoubtedly recording the gossip circulating in the stronghold of Île Royale. The truth of the matter was that Holburne had decided to devastate as many of the French ships within Louisbourg harbor as possible. To accomplish that he needed to prepare two fire ships, which would be sent into the crowded port to do their damage. Initially the admiral thought the fire ships could be prepared at Tor Bay, along the eastern shore of Nova Scotia, but he decided at length to head back to Halifax and carry out the work there.[99]

The departure of Holburne's flotilla brought relief to the capital of Île Royale once it was confirmed that the British ships had indeed sailed away. The French leadership reduced the number of defenders at the entrenched positions along the coast. Du Bois de La Motte decided that whatever the future held, it was a suitable occasion to celebrate the Roman Catholic faith and Louis XV. The timing for such a celebration was perfect. August 24 was the eve of the feast day of Saint Louis, the medieval king of France who was later beatified, and the following day was the date on the church calendar when the French world usually held its most lavish celebrations. To mark the occasion in 1757, the lieutenant general of the fleet "ordered all the ships to dress and discharge all their artillery in succession, to be followed by a continued musketry fire. . . . On the 26th, the ships were similarly dressed, and fired each 15 guns, the general firing first." The salutes of the French armada in port reverberated a long time and generated an enormous cloud of smoke.[100] The rejoicing, it turned out, was premature.

On September 16 the French spied a British man-of-war and a frigate off Louisbourg. The two vessels briefly came within artillery range and were immediately driven away. The British were back, undertaking a reconnaissance. For the next several days the French saw the sails of a sizable Royal Navy squadron, though at a great distance.[101] Admiral Holburne's ships were keeping well out of the range of Louisbourg's cannons, but close enough to capture vessels should any attempt to sail in or out of Louisbourg. Sooner or later, the British admiral reasoned, Du Bois de La Motte's fleet would have to head for France. Supplies were insufficient for them to spend the winter on this side of the Atlantic.

A waiting game began, with sailors from both sides keeping a watchful eye on the weather. Fall was, and is today, a time when tropical storms and hurricanes sweeping up from the Caribbean sometimes hit Atlantic Canada. Friday, September 23, the wind was "pretty fresh with heavy sea." The next day there was a "strong wind and very heavy sea . . . in the evening the wind increased in violence." Both the French and the British naval commanders knew a storm was coming and took precautions. Yet whatever they did, it was not enough. Nothing could have prepared them for the storm that hit. In the early hours of September 25, a Sunday, at one hour past midnight, the wind picked up speed. "By 3 o'clock it was furious with an awful sea."[102] The blast was to last about twelve hours. It was, in the words of the chevalier James Johnstone, a Scottish Jacobite serving as an officer in the Louisbourg garrison, "the most furious tempest ever known in the memory of man."[103] The windstorm and surging seas of the hurricane wreaked havoc. Water flooded the Louisbourg quay wall, driving soldiers from their posts. Du Bois de La Motte's ships suffered damage to their masts, rudders, and hulls. One eyewitness offered the following description:

> If at noon the wind had continued for another hour and had not changed to the S. and S.W., nine or ten of our vessels, including

that of our general, would have been in imminent danger of being driven ashore. It is impossible to imagine such a dreadful spectacle as that which met our eyes. The frigate *La Bénaquise*, the cable of which parted, was instantly thrown up on the beach, along with 25 merchantmen, several of them high and dry. More than 80 boats and skiffs of the squadron were tossed by the waves and smashed most of them on shore, a number of the men aboard them perishing. More than 50 schooners and boats met the same fate.[104]

The destruction inflicted on the French ships and boats within the anchorage was more than matched outside the harbor. Nine ships in Admiral Holburne's squadron suffered broken masts and bowsprits, with the *Tilbury* (sixty guns) wrecked on the rocks of the coastline. The *Sunderland* found "the Sea Breaking constantly" over it and was forced to throw four of its upper-deck guns into the sea. It found itself less than a mile from shore when the wind at last began to let up. Holburne later wrote William Pitt that "had the Wind continued to blow onshore but one hour longer every Ship of the Squadron must unavoidably been lost."[105] In the case of the *Tilbury*, it went ashore near Saint-Esprit, with the captain and 120 of its 400–man crew drowned. French troops and a contingent of 150 Mi'kmaq rounded up 280 survivors and brought them into Louisbourg. The French worried the Mi'kmaq might slaughter their bitter enemies, yet it was a groundless fear. The warriors treated the shipwrecked British sailors like victims of a tragedy, not as invaders. One of the captured British ensigns was John Thane, whom the French learned had been an assistant to Admiral Peter Warren when Louisbourg had been captured in 1745. Since Thane was an officer and therefore deserved better treatment than the enlisted men, Governor Drucour put him up in a government building. But because of Thane's past involvements against Louisbourg, the governor directed that he be one of the last of the prisoners exchanged and sent to Halifax.[106]

Holburne's scattered and dismasted vessels were theoretically vulnerable to a concerted French attack, if Du Bois de La Motte had sent some of his undamaged vessels out of Louisbourg harbor looking for them. Here was the second chance the very same summer for the French to strike a blow at British sea power. As with the missed opportunity with Loudoun's voyage from New York to Halifax a few months earlier, the occasion passed without any action taken. Why Du Bois de La Motte did not authorize even a few ships to take advantage of the situation is a matter for speculation. He did have a large number of vessels needing repair from the hurricane, and there was the matter of the deadly typhus sweeping through the crew. The seriousness of the disease was made clear by a French officer who stated that while the squadron was at Louisbourg 850 sailors perished and nearly 300,000 livres were spent on healthcare.[107] In addition to those practical reasons, there was the matter of the orders the senior naval officer had been given before he left France. The priorities articulated by the minister of the marine were to defend Louisbourg and to keep the fleet safe. As a result Du Bois de La Motte concluded that it was better to repair and to keep in sight all the warships under his command than to send some out to attack the storm-tossed British squadron limping back to Halifax.

Around the same time that the storm was buffeting Holburne's and Du Bois de La Motte's ships at Louisbourg, indecision was taking its toll on a British initiative off the coast of France. Throughout September 1757 a sizable expedition—about 8,500 soldiers aboard transports, commanded by Lieutenant General Sir John Mordaunt; sixteen ships of the line under the leadership of Vice-Admiral Edward Hawke; and an assortment of frigates, fire ships, and bomb ketches—stood poised to strike at Rochefort, the naval arsenal that lay inland up the Charente River along France's Atlantic coast. The initial British idea for offensive action in that region had come from the ruler of Prussia. Frederick I wanted his British ally to do something in the war that would compel French troops to pull back from the front in the German states. William Pitt took the idea and made it his own. He selected Rochefort as a vital spot that was vulnerable to a coastal landing followed by a flanking action to attack the arsenal from the rear. It was a bold idea, yet indecisiveness and a lack of cooperation between the commanders of the navy and the army doomed the expedition. The British fleet moored in the Basque roads off the Charente estuary for more than a week, gaining nothing other than the temporary capture of the Île d'Aix. The overall venture was said to have cost one million pounds, and when the fleet sailed back to England in early October with nothing to show for the time and money, there was enormous disappointment in Britain. The outcry rivaled that over the loss of Minorca in 1756, though this time no scapegoat was hanged.

Pitt felt the sting of criticism because he was closely associated with the Rochefort project. One officer who had taken part in the expedition, and who was more than a little annoyed by the opportunity that had been not just missed but not even attempted, was James Wolfe (1727–59). Only thirty years old, Wolfe was quartermaster general and chief of staff of the land forces. On many occasions he had urged action; he may even have gone ashore to reconnoiter the position near Rochefort. The enthusiasm of the young officer impressed his superiors in what was otherwise a dismal failure.[108]

Though hardly a veteran of many campaigns, James Wolfe identified the mistakes in the Rochefort fiasco. In a private letter to an old friend, the young officer itemized a long list of the lessons he had learned. One of the most important, he felt, was the need for close cooperation between army and navy in joint amphibious operations. Some of the others pertained specifically to the navy ("an admiral should endeavour to run into an enemy's port immediately after he appears before it"), while others concerned the army ("the generals should settle their plan of operations, so that no time may be lost in idle debate and consultations when the sword should be drawn"). Common to all the lessons he had learned was the need for bold action, indeed, what many others would call rash measures. Wolfe felt that war is by "its nature hazardous," and success is often determined by "chance and fortune." Where such reflections might have made many military men shake their heads, James Wolfe expressed the opinion that the "the loss of 1,000 men" is sometimes "an advantage to a nation," as "gallant attempts raise its reputation and make it respectable."[109] Heady talk, though in Wolfe's case he would get opportunities to put his words into practice. The first such opportunity was to come sooner than he might have guessed, not on the coast of France, but across the ocean at Louisbourg. There he would have a fresh opportunity to demonstrate how bold acts might make a difference.

Aftermath

In early October 1757, the aide-major of the marine troops at Louisbourg, Jean-Chysostome Loppinot, composed a letter in which he identified the three factors that had saved Île Royale in the year that was winding down. First, there were the delays the British had encountered in dispatching their warships across the ocean. Second, there was the unprecedented windstorm of September 25. Third, there were "the three squadrons that protected [them] throughout the campaign." He added, "It is to be hoped that next year we will be able to congratulate ourselves on similar circumstances." Loppinot was correct in his assessment, and he knew he would only have to wait until the spring of 1758 to see if there would be "similar circumstances."[110] The winter ahead was a waiting period.

The three French squadrons that protected Louisbourg in 1757 readied to sail back to France throughout the first half of October. When they finally embarked, Du Bois de La Motte sailed without about four hundred ill sailors. He would have liked to have left behind about one thousand more, but he did not want to burden a colony that was already facing a difficult provisioning situation. Drucour and Prévost did not want to keep any more ailing sailors than was absolutely necessary. In fact, once the sick sailors were put on board the departing French ships, Louisbourg officials ordered their bedclothes burned.[111]

Whether Du Bois de La Motte expected the sickly sailors to make it back to France, few did. As historian James Pritchard puts it: "Ships became floating hells." By the time the fleet reached Brest on November 22–23, reported a naval officer, there were 2,000 fewer sailors than there had been when the squadrons left France months earlier. And the death toll was not final, for the ships were carrying more than 2,400 stricken crew back to Brest.[112]

Having learned of the plight of the French crews aboard the ships coming from Louisbourg, seamen from along the Brittany shoreline came out to meet the ships and went on board to help bring the vessels into port. Once ashore at Brest, there was nowhere to put the sick. Two warships had already arrived from Quebec, with one thousand sick of their own, so the local hospitals were filled. Consequently, the typhus-stricken crews from Louisbourg were placed in makeshift settings. Fifteen temporary hospitals were set up, with physicians and surgeons who had come from elsewhere in France. The improvised hospitals turned out to be unsanitary and overcrowded, and it was not long before the typhus spread throughout Brest and into nearby areas of Brittany. For a while there were between fifty and eighty deaths a day. A French surgeon offered a grim description: "The stench was intolerable. No person could enter the hospitals without being immediately seized with headaches; and every kind of indisposition quickly turned to fatal fever, as in the old days of the plague." Over the course of the next several months, "upwards of ten thousand people" perished, including the commander of one of the squadrons, Noble du Revest. Almost half the deaths were civilians from Brest and neighboring areas. It was a tragedy of enormous proportions in one of France's most important naval bases. The scale of the suffering in late 1757 and early 1758 would make it even more difficult than usual for the French navy to put experienced crews on their warships for the coming campaign in the summer of 1758. As Jonathan Dull comments, the effect of the typhus outbreak was a "blow to the French navy as serious as the loss of a great battle."[113]

Although typhus and scurvy struck the French squadrons after they left Louisbourg, the British fleet under Holburne made out much better. After the great windstorm of late September, the fleet split into two parts. Some vessels headed directly for the mother country; others remained in colonial waters, with the necessary repairs being made at Halifax. William Pitt sent word that eight ships of the line were to spend the winter in the Nova Scotia seaport. Commodore Alexander Colvill assumed command of the ships, and twenty-eight artificers were hired in Boston and Halifax to carry out the needed work. The plan was that the ships would be ready to intercept French shipping coming to Île Royale at the earliest opportunity in the spring of 1758. This marked an important departure. A few ships had overwintered at Halifax previously, but never before had eight ships of the line remained in port to be ready for early the following spring. Neither Admiral Holburne nor Rear Admiral Hardy stayed in Halifax—they both returned to Britain—and neither liked the approach. They did not think Halifax had a properly equipped naval yard of sufficient accommodations, which it did not, yet it was Pitt who was making the decisions. The ships of the line that remained in Nova Scotia in the care of Commodore Colvill were the *Northumberland*, the *Terrible*, the *Kingston*, the *Orford*, the *Arc-en-Ciel*, the *Sutherland*, the *Defiance*, and the *Somerset*, as well as the frigate *Portmahon* and the sloop *Hawke*.[114]

As the autumn of 1757 moved into winter, there was much to fret over at Louisbourg. Those who were able to put aside worries about the blockade and attack that were looming again for 1758 faced other pressing issues that had to be addressed. Royal officials pondered what they were going to do about an anticipated shortage of coins in the local economy. There was the request by the Sisters of the Congregation of Notre-Dame to go "home" to Canada because of their financial distress at Louisbourg. The religious community had been in Louisbourg since 1727, providing education and moral guidance to girls and young women, so its withdrawal would be a loss. And there was a perceived need to split the functions of the Bailliage (lower court for civil and criminal cases) and Admiralty courts, which had been combined under one judge for most of the past decade.[115] As important as these and other issues seemed to some in Louisbourg, they paled in comparison to the general anxiety over the war.

Louisbourg had two obvious requirements if it was going to continue as a French stronghold beyond 1758. The first was to have a naval presence in the harbor that matched or outmatched whatever the British were going to send overseas. A reprise of the three squadrons sent to the colony in 1757 would be ideal, though this time without the sickness. The second priority was for more men-at-arms. At the end of 1757 the Louisbourg garrison counted 2,015 soldiers.[116] That was nearly three times as many defenders as Louisbourg had in 1745, yet those numbers provided little comfort. The British land troops rumored to be available for expeditions against Louisbourg and Quebec were said to total about 15,000 men, nearly four times the size of the Anglo-American army that had conquered Louisbourg in 1745.

During the anxiety-ridden summer of 1757 the French had been able to position as many as three thousand men-at-arms at the landing coves to the north and south of Louisbourg, and they still had some soldiers on the ramparts inside the fortress. That was possible because Du Bois de La Motte had assigned many sailors to land roles and at least three hundred Native warriors had come to the French fortress.[117] Would 1758 witness a reprise of such outside assistance? It was an unanswered question over the winter of 1757–58. If the naval presence in 1758 were to be smaller, or if the sailors who came were kept aboard their ships, would that not mean that the coastal positions would be less well manned than they had been in 1757? And what if fewer, or none at all, of the Mi'kmaq, the Maliseet, and the Abenaki came in 1758? The French would certainly ask for similar support from their Native allies, but it was impossible to know if they would arrive again in such numbers. Such uncertainties made the arithmetic of defending the coastline a worry.

Lieutenant General Du Bois de La Motte had deep worries about the vulnerability of Louisbourg before he set sail for France in October 1757. He let it be known among the local administration that he "had not found enough troops for the defense of the country." He informed Drucour and Prévost that when he returned to France, he was going to ask Peyrenc de Moras, the new minister of the marine, to send two more battalions of infantry regiments to the colony. That Du Bois de La Motte specifically requested regular infantry troops, and not more Compagnies franches de la Marine soldiers, was not surprising. Virtually all the military and naval officers who came from France had low opinions of the marine ministry's own troops. Michel Le Courtois de Surlaville, troop major at Louisbourg in the early 1750s, articulated that perspective when he stated: "[T]he soldier of Canada is worth nothing."[118]

As they did each autumn, before the last ships sailed for France and the colony was cut off from communication with the mother country until the next spring, the governor and the financial administrator of Île Royale sat down to compose letters to the minister that looked both backward and ahead. In their letters of September and October 1757, Drucour and Prévost covered the routine details of administering the colony, as their positions required, yet it was obvious that war preparedness was the abiding concern. They asked that another large flotilla be sent out as early as possible in 1758, and they requested extra artillery specialists and more companies of marine troops. There was no mention of additional Troupes de Terre, which they knew Du Bois de La Motte was urging, for their assessment of the troops needed on Île Royale differed from that of the naval commander. Drucour and Prévost were not specifically looking for more regular infantry because of the two years of bitter rivalry they had witnessed since the first infantry battalions arrived at Louisbourg in 1755. Getting along with Mascle de Saint-Julhien and the other officers of the Artois and Bourgogne battalions had not been easy for the governor and the financial administrator. They much preferred to deal with marine officers. To give their preference an impartial basis, the two Louisbourg officials cited the substantially lower cost of the marine companies in comparison to the regiments of the Troupes de Terre. For the same amount of money, they pointed out, one could have more than twice as many Compagnies franches soldiers as regular infantry troops.[119]

In Prévost's separate letter to Peyrenc de Moras, the financial administrator made clear the depth of his resentment toward both the Troupes de Terre and the squadrons that had been at Louisbourg in 1757. He stated he had endured abusive behavior from the commander of the infantry regiments, Mascle de Saint-Julhien, and also from the naval officers and seamen. Regarding Mascle de Saint-Julhien, the financial administrator complained about his overbearing ways and his refusal to communicate. As for the naval presence in port, Prévost wrote that the seamen had broken every window of his residence, and there were other humiliations. He did not blame Du Bois de La Motte for what had occurred, but he did express his wish that there be no repeat of such incidents when fresh warships arrived in 1758.[120]

The minister of the marine was also to hear about the friction at Louisbourg from the naval officers when they returned to France. They too complained about the squabbles with Prévost and went on to undermine his career by letting Peyrenc de Moras know about the high-stakes gambling taking place in his residence. Some individuals, including a few of the officers themselves, were said to have lost as much as 15,000 to 20,000 livres at Prévost's house. The minister subsequently let Prévost know that such gambling was illegal and had to stop. On the more significant issue of relations between the military and the civil powers during a time of war, however, Peyrenc de Moras took the side of Drucour and Prévost. In April 1758 the minister would write to all concerned that they had to demonstrate harmony and unity. Friction and disunity would be fatal to the colony. In recognition of the difficulties Drucour and Prévost had already had with Mascle de Saint-Julhien, Peyrenc de Moras named Mathieu-Henri Marchant de La Houlière as the new overall commander of the Troupes de Terre at Louisbourg. Marchant de La Houlière was then in France but was to sail to Île Royale in the spring.[121]

The cantankerous Jean Mascle de Saint-Julhien, commander of the Artois and Bourgogne battalions, who had regularly clashed with Drucour and Prévost, sent a much different assessment to the minister. In late 1757 Mascle de Saint-Julhien listed all the things he thought were wrong with the defensive situation at Louisbourg. The batteries were rotten; there was a shortage of artillery swabs and pricks and not enough cannonballs; one face of the King's Bastion was so dilapidated sheep could pass through to drink in the ditch; some revetments were ready to disintegrate in a heavy rainfall, making them an "agreeable staircase for the enemy." What Peyrenc de Moras thought when he read Mascle de Saint-Julhien's litany of complaints is not recorded.[122]

While Drucour, Prévost, and others were beseeching the minister of the marine to send another large fleet to Île Royale in the spring of 1758, chief engineer Louis Franquet wrote Peyrenc de Moras about the risk of such an action. He was not arguing against it, but he wanted to point out that if the British were able to set up a blockade and make a successful landing, then the ships sent to defend Louisbourg would be trapped inside the harbor and ultimately lost. In that scenario the more ships sent to the colony, the more ships might be taken by the enemy. Defeatist or realist, Franquet's perspective gave the minister something to think about regarding the risks involved in continuing to defend Louisbourg in 1758. As for letting Peyrenc de Moras know about his own workload and accomplishments, Franquet explained how he was getting the stronghold ready for a possible spring assault.[123]

As winter closed in on Île Royale, it was inevitable that the ordinary colonists wondered how severe the tribulations of the coming months were going to be. Spring threats by the British may have seemed a long way off, since first they had to survive the period when the harbor was usually closed to the outside world. Hunger was perhaps their greatest worry, for nothing was ever certain in a colony so dependent on food imports. Between storms at sea and blockading British fleets, there was no guarantee that shipments of provisions from France would get through. All marine officials in France could do was their best.

On October 1, 1757, four ships carrying provisions sailed from Brest bound for Louisbourg. Later in the month another ship left Brest, and two more set off from Bordeaux. Each carried quantities from the four major categories of provisions in the eighteenth century: flour, salted meats, vegetables, and butter. In November Peyrenc de Moras made arrangements for additional ships to proceed to Île Royale, with more of the same kinds of supplies. They were to sail in convoy escorted by armed frigates. Not every vessel reached its destination. One that was lost was the *Chariot Royal*, whose captain was Louisbourg-born Jean Lelarge. One morning Lelarge spied sails on the horizon and, correctly assuming they were British, took evasive action. He successfully led his lightly armed ship away from that threat only to run directly into the HMS *Tor Bay*, a seventy-four-gun warship commanded by Augustus Keppel, a future First Lord of the Admiralty. Keppel began a pursuit that lasted most of the day, and in the end Jean Lelarge's luck ran out. He was taken prisoner, then sent back to France in a prisoner exchange. Dispatched to Louisiana in 1758, where he became seriously ill, Lelarge was to die in Rochefort in 1761, after having been an invalid for two years.[124]

One supply ship that was successful in reaching Louisbourg in late 1757 flew a Portuguese flag. Its captain stated that the flag was the only thing that enabled him to get past the British warships, since those two countries were still at peace. Accordingly, Peyrenc de Moras requested more ships from neutral countries be utilized in sending supplies to the French colonies overseas.[125]

Meanwhile on Île Royale, financial administrator Jacques Prévost reacted to the local shortage of flour by increasing the amount of rice that residents received in their rations. Louisbourg civilians accepted the change without protest, which gave them a ration that was one-third flour and two-thirds rice. The soldiers and the bakers who produced the soldiers' loaves apparently required more convincing. The bakers initially resisted using rice as a substitute for one-third of the flour. With time, stated Prévost, the soldiers "were shown the advantage of this treatment for Health, and that nothing was lost by replacing flour" with rice. The men were now adding the new-style bread to their evening and morning soups.[126]

All rumors at Louisbourg during the fall and winter of 1757 pointed to a major British assault, once spring conditions made naval and military operations possible. The British ships and troops wintering in Halifax were no secret to the French on Île Royale. At Versailles the precarious situation in which the colony of Île Royale found itself was discussed at the highest levels. A letter written on December 21, 1757, with the marginal notation that it was "taken to the king," revealed the enormous costs involved in keeping Louisbourg going. The price of a full year's subsistence for ordinary colonists, Native allies, and Acadian refugees was projected, then doubled in the event an additional year's provisions would be required.[127] The bottom line was that Île Royale was to be retained, whatever the cost.

Three days later Peyrenc de Moras composed a letter to Drucour and Prévost that outlined his major concerns. First, the fortifications had to be ready for the bombardment to come. Second, the minister was going to send fifty *canoniers-bombardiers*, artillery specialists, to help out with the defense. He stated that he saw no advantage to increasing the number of marine troops, which is what Drucour and Prévost had requested, but then in another memo written later the same day he suggested that 300 to 320 recruits might be sent to Louisbourg. Third, Peyrenc de Moras would arrange for a shipment of six iron mortars, six small pieces for the artillery school, and a quantity of mortar bombs, cannonballs, and gunpowder. Fourth, the minister was going to send two years' worth of provisions to guarantee that the colonists on Île Royale and Île Saint-Jean would not suffer severe shortages.[128] Conspicuously absent from the measures listed by Peyrenc de Moras was any mention of the most crucial element in any defense of Louisbourg: the number of warships that would be sent overseas. Had Peyrenc de Moras not yet made up his mind on that question? Was he waiting for the epidemic at Brest to die down so he could better assess what naval resources, both ships and personnel, were available?

On the British side of the imperial struggle, the expectation was that 1758 would at last see a breakthrough in their war effort. The first two years had witnessed a string of setbacks, of which the loss of Fort William Henry in North America, retreats and defeats by British and Prussian forces in Europe, and the unsuccessful expeditions against Louisbourg and Rochefort stood out. The fallout from the failures was rough for some commanders. Sir John Mordaunt, in charge of the land force in the Rochefort expedition, was not executed like Byng had been, but he was court-martialed. Lord Loudoun, commander in chief in North America, was abruptly recalled to England and replaced by Major General James Abercromby. Within the Royal Navy there were similar shifts in assignments. The individual directing the various personnel changes was the political leader, William Pitt. To be sure, Pitt was receiving advice on who should be removed and who the new appointees should be. His capable and experienced advisors were the First Lord of the Admiralty, George Anson, and the commander in chief of the British Army, John Ligonier.[129]

As 1757 drew to a close, William Pitt articulated his resolve for success in 1758. He put aside the "Losses & Disappointments of the last inactive and unhappy Campaign." Writing to the governors of the Anglo-American colonies, Pitt asked them to do their part by raising twenty thousand soldiers to fight the French in the interior of the continent. The mother country would shoulder the costs of the "Arms, Ammunition, and Tents, as well as to order Provisions." Pitt committed to sending as early as possible in 1758 additional British regular troops and supporting naval vessels. In his year-end letter to Major General Abercromby, the newly named commander of the British war effort in North America, Pitt offered a detail not contained in the dispatches to the governors, one that concerned Louisbourg. "I am to begin with acquainting you, in the greatest Confidence, that the King has come to a Resolution to allot an adequate proportion of His Forces in North America, amounting . . . to upwards of Fourteen Thousand Men for the Siege of Louisburg." Pitt stated that the operation should begin by April 20, 1758, "if the season [should] happen to permit." The commander of the expedition had not yet been selected, but that would be looked after shortly.[130]

For Pitt, Anson, Ligonier, and the other senior military and naval leaders on the British side, the commitment to win the war with the French in North America was not waning. Only time and the course of events would reveal whether the renewed resolve would be rewarded.

4

Beginning of the End, Early 1758

The people of Louisbourg made a valiant effort to enjoy themselves during the winter of 1757–58. Throughout the cold, dark season they did their best to put aside worries about blockades, food shortages, and a looming British assault. January 1758 offered a chilling mix of rain and snow, yet spirits remained high. The new year began, according to a diarist, with a customary "Day of Ceremony." The entry is cryptic, but one imagines an official occasion, perhaps a levee that involved the governor and/or the financial administrator doing something in public. The diarist, the engineer Grillot de Poilly, added only that it was an event "carried out dutifully: many Compliments and little sincerity." Whatever the event was, it may have been similar to what went on in Canada around the same time. The diarist Madame Bégon wrote about the "day of *folies*" and "true extravagance" that took place in Montreal on January 1.[1]

On January 12, 1758, the annual pre-Lenten period of festivities known as carnival began at Louisbourg. It was a celebration in many Roman Catholic countries, with its occurrence shifting each year depending on the date for Easter. The church frowned on pre-Lenten partying, but that disapproval had little effect on the custom. At Louisbourg in 1758 as in previous years, carnival meant several weeks of parties and wedding celebrations. Music, dancing, drinking, and gambling were the principal amusements, with impressive buffets of cold dishes (*ambigus*) served at some events. Between January 12 and February 19, 1758, which extended into Lent by a few days, Grillot de Poilly attended ten parties. Presumably there were other gatherings over the same period to which the engineer was not invited, especially those offered by the civilian half of Louisbourg society. Grillot de Poilly recorded going to two revels hosted by Governor Drucour and one each put on by the Artois and Bourgogne battalions. Financial administrator Prévost and the wealthiest merchants in town must have similarly opened their houses to friends and associates during the carnival of 1758, but if so, Grillot de Poilly was not one of their guests.

Beside references to pre-Lenten parties, Grillot de Poilly's diary offers another indication that Louisbourg was in a mood to be amused during the winter of 1758. The engineer recorded a humorous exchange in a local catechism class. The story was circulating in town that a child had made a funny reply to a priest when asked what was meant by *Espérance*. The expected reply was that it was the expectation for eternal life, but the Récollet heard the girl say: "Oh yes, my Father, in the name of the Father, the Son, and the Holy Ghost, l'Espérance is a big sergeant in the Artois Regiment who sleeps with my mother every night."[2]

Marriages and baptisms provided other occasions for joy and celebration in the winter of 1758. Weddings during the coldest season of year were common at Louisbourg as they were elsewhere in New France, because the church forbade marriages during Advent (most of December) and Lent (usually in February and March), and summer marriages were rare in the busy seaport. The result at Louisbourg was that more marriages took place in November and January than any other time of year. The year 1758 was no exception, with six weddings in January and four more in early February. One of those February events required a dispensation because it occurred in early Lent. There were no marriages in the rest of February nor in March because of the interdiction of weddings during that period of self-denial. On the birth front the Louisbourg parish welcomed eleven babies in January, six in February, and twelve in March.[3]

The inhabitants of Louisbourg also found entertainment in early 1758 in the night sky. In the world before the invention of electrical lighting, people were very aware of celestial occurrences. In the winter months on Île Royale, at about 46 degrees latitude north, the night sky begins early, around 5:00 PM. On January 23, 1758, Grillot de Poilly recorded that the moon was "a great red color and [there was] a darkening as if it was an eclipse." The phenomenon caught his attention on the way to a ball, which lasted until 4:00 AM and featured high-stakes gambling. In March, well after Lenten austerity had replaced the party atmosphere of carnival, the night sky had an even more spectacular event. On March 4 people thought they were seeing "a Comet: it was a Star that appeared in the west that was bigger and clearer than the others." Three nights later Grillot de Poilly wrote: "[T]he Planet that we had taken for a Comet, it's Venus." He followed its course across the heavens using a telescope belonging to Jacques Prévost. The feature was visible once more on March 13, with the engineer describing it once again as Venus. Grillot de Poilly acknowledged that the popular opinion in the town was that it was a comet, yet he dismissed the interpretation.[4] In truth, the hoi polloi, and not the engineer, were right. For it was in March 1758 that the comet predicted by English astronomer Edmond Halley (1656–1742) made its return through the night skies of the Northern Hemisphere after an absence of seventy-six years.

One surmises that diversions in the form of house parties, childish jokes, and celestial happenings were welcome to Grillot de Poilly and others at Louisbourg because the day-to-day reality of the winter of 1758 was grim on most fronts. Two separate fires in town in February damaged or destroyed buildings, and it was also in February that offshore drift ice began to play havoc with arrivals to and departures from the port.[5] The drift ice was an annual occurrence and usually just a temporary inconvenience. Yet in 1758 the quantity of ice and the number of weeks it lingered along the coast was exceptional; it was also long enough to try people's patience because it threatened their provisioning lifeline with France. Then again, if ice packs were disrupting French shipping, they were having the same impact on British warships expected to be coming across the Atlantic and up the coast from Halifax. In that case perhaps the ice was not something one wished away too quickly.

French Preparations

Events and decisions in France during the first five months of 1758 were crucial to the defense of Louisbourg. During this time Louis XV and his latest minister of the marine, François-Marie Peyrenc de Moras, figured out what, who, and how much would be sent to the overseas colonies. The three most important aspects were warships, troops, and food.

In early 1758 an optimist in France might have said the war in North America was going fairly well. All the major strongholds were still in French hands, and their side had actually captured a few British forts in the interior of the continent. A pessimist, however, would have pointed out the cumulative disastrous effect that British dominance on the high seas was having on both France's trade and its navy. To cite a few examples, imports from the French West Indies dropped by more than 50 percent in 1757, and insurance rates rose by more than 50 percent. As for the French navy, only one ship of the line had been lost in 1757, yet it still trailed Great Britain in both the number of warships capable of setting to sea and the number of sailors to man them. In mid-1757 the Royal Navy had ninety-six ships of the line in service; France had forty-two. On the personnel front the six thousand sailors killed by typhus in the aftermath of their voyage back from Louisbourg were going to be sorely missed. As things stood in early 1758, France could muster about thirty-five thousand sailors; Great Britain more than sixty thousand. The duc de Choiseul (Étienne-François duc de Choiseul, 1719–85), who in late 1758 would take over France's foreign affairs portfolio, felt that France had made a serious error in not keeping pace with its British imperial rival in terms of naval capability. He would write Louis XV that attention on the land campaign in Europe "brought with it neglect of the war at sea and in America, which was the real war."[6]

Two of the key figures at Louisbourg, Drucour and Prévost, spent part of the winter of 1757–58 writing to Versailles reiterating requests already made and explaining that outdoor work could not be undertaken during the cold months. The only large project that could be pursued was the preparation of barracks facilities for the additional troops expected from France. The financial administrator did find something new to mention to Peyrenc de Moras when he complained how the captains of king's ships in recent years had left behind anchors on the harbor bottom when they sailed from Louisbourg. Prévost called it a waste to the service and informed the minister he was recovering the anchors.[7] One wonders if Peyrenc de Moras shared the view that the retrieval of the anchors warranted the effort, given what else was unfolding.

Other than processing paperwork and making sure the troops were drilling in readiness for an expected attack, the civil and military authorities at Louisbourg were left to wonder whose sails would first appear on the horizon when spring came and in what numbers. The reports circulating at Louisbourg alleged that seven warships were wintering in Halifax and that British land troops consisted of three regular infantry battalions and two thousand Scottish Highlanders.[8]

At Versailles some decisions about Louisbourg took no time at all. It was easy, for instance, to promote Jacques Prévost from a *commissaire* to a *commissaire-général* of the marine. That meant a step up in the financial administrator's status and brought with it an increase in his salary. Another easy decision related to the hundreds of sick sailors left behind when Du Bois de La Motte had sailed from Île Royale the previous fall. The ones who had recovered their health were to resume their duties on the ships that would be sent to the colony in 1758. On another medical matter Peyrenc de Moras informed Drucour and Prévost that six new Brothers of Charity of Saint John of God, the order that had long operated Louisbourg's hospital, were to sail to the colony, along with six assistants, to replace the brothers who had passed away in 1757.[9] More complicated for Versailles was the continuing challenge of sending provisions to the beleaguered island colony. The colony's once flourishing fishery, the peacetime base on which the economy rested, had virtually shut down after the hostilities commenced.[10] Accordingly, four ships with flour and rice set sail from France for Louisbourg in late December 1757. An additional four ships from Saint-Malo and five more from Rochefort were supposed to leave before the end of January 1758, with other vessels slated to depart a month later. The minister directed that if all ships arrived, Drucour and Prévost were to send some of the flour on to Quebec. Alas, such optimism was not borne out. British ships captured three of the first convoy and the fourth went missing. Despite considerable expense and effort, nothing had been accomplished. There was simply no certainty about feeding Louisbourg.

Indeed, nothing that involved traveling on the high seas was guaranteed. French ships were regularly lost sailing to and from their colonies in the West Indies. One large convoy that left Saint-Domingue in November 1757, bound for France, ran into a winter storm and was so damaged and dispersed that only fifteen of the original forty-one ships had attained France or Spain by the end of February.[11]

Though Île Royale was one of Peyrenc de Moras' prime concerns, along with the West Indies, the minister also had advice for Île Saint-Jean. He directed the local commandant, Gabriel Rousseau de Villejouin, to have the settlers live close together rather than spread out. In that way, Peyrenc de Moras explained, the inhabitants could more easily join together to resist an attack.[12] Villejouin must have shaken his head. If the British were to descend on Île Saint-Jean with any kind of force at all, it was not going to matter how close the settlers lived. The colony needed a large number of trained soldiers and a squadron of warships to defend itself. Villejouin had neither and no hopes that he ever would.

On the broad scale of worries, France's highest priority in the Atlantic region in 1758 could not have been simpler: hold on to Louisbourg. Early in the year Louis XV made the decision regarding additional troops for Île Royale. The king concluded that two more battalions of regular infantry were needed, as had been requested by Du Bois de La Motte. The units selected were the Cambis Regiment and the Volontaires Étrangers. Each was to send its second battalion, each of which contained 680 men at full strength. The king also authorized a contingent of 300 more Compagnies franches de la Marine soldiers to fill out the ranks of the garrison troops, and as well 10 artillerymen from Rochefort. Once the cannoneers reached Île Royale they were to select and train 40 sailors from the fleet to form a second artillery company. The arrival of all the additional soldiers would bring the number of trained troops at Louisbourg to a round figure of 3,500. By comparison Quebec in 1759 was to have about 14,000 defenders, or four times as many. On the other hand, Louisbourg had nearly twelve times the 300 men-at-arms posted to Fort de Chartres, the largest French garrison in the Illinois country along the Mississippi River.[13]

The troops selected to go to Louisbourg in 1758 were not all French. As the name suggests, the Volontaires Étrangers was composed of foreign volunteers who provided their services to Louis XV in return for a wage, a uniform, rations, and a place to sleep. The regiment was raised in 1756, the latest in a long line of non-French soldiers fighting in the service of French kings. (The practice continued after France became a republic, in the form of the Foreign Legion.) The tradition dated back to 1480, when the Cent-Suisses became the personal guard of Louis XI. Historically, the Swiss provided the largest number of France's foreign troops, followed closely by German-speaking soldiers and lesser numbers of Irish, Scots, Italians, and other nationalities. During the Seven Years' War about 48,000 foreigners fought in the different regiments of France. Île Royale had already known foreign troops, for between 1722 and 1745 Louisbourg had a detachment of the Karrer Regiment in its garrison. The Karrer soldiers were primarily German-speaking and Protestant. The contingent took a lead role in the mutiny of December 1744 and was not sent back to Louisbourg in 1749.[14]

The Volontaires Étrangers were therefore the second "foreign" troops to serve on Île Royale. As of 1758 the Volontaires were one of sixteen German-speaking regiments in French service, which added up to about nineteen thousand soldiers. The regiment of Volontaires Étrangers was organized in three battalions, with the second dispatched to Louisbourg. The color of their coats was the usual gray white worn by most French troops, including the Artois and Bourgogne regiments already at Louisbourg. But where Artois and Bourgogne uniforms had red as the accent color in their waistcoats (and with the Bourgogne in their breeches and stockings as well), the uniforms of the Volontaires Étrangers had green cuffs, collar, and waistcoat.[15]

While the Volontaires Étrangers went to Brest to prepare to sail to Louisbourg, the battalion of the Cambis Regiment proceeded to Rochefort, from which it would sail. The Cambis Regiment had a history stretching back to 1676, when it was raised for service in Italy. Over the course of the next eighty-two years, the regiment earned a distinguished reputation. Most recently, in 1757, both of its battalions camped along the coast in Brittany in anticipation of a British descent that never materialized. A colonel and 39 officers led each battalion, with approximately 685 NCOs, soldiers, and drummers. The enlisted men were organized in sixteen companies of ordinary musket men and one company of grenadiers. The basic uniform was the usual gray white coat of French regiments, distinguished by a red collar and cuffs. The breeches were gray white, and the tricorn black with silver and gold lace trim.[16]

The second Cambis battalion arrived in Rochefort in February 1758, where it was outfitted with the equipment and supplies it would need. Lists kept by the commissariat provide a detailed picture of all the matériel issued to the Cambis troops. Each soldier received the standard clothing articles (knitted cap, woolen stockings, shoes, and four shirts), while the contingent as a whole took with it 1,500 spare caps, 2,315 pairs of shoes, 2,260 shirts, 1,200 haversacks, 700 sleeveless vests, 1,200 pipes, 100 pairs of scissors, 24 razor stones, and much more.

The minister of the marine's hope was that both the Cambis and the Volontaires Étrangers battalions would arrive at Louisbourg before the Royal Navy established their usual blockade. The transatlantic crossing typically took four to six weeks depending on the winds and weather. Since the British had overwintered a sizable force at Halifax, the French expected an attack on Louisbourg might begin as early as April or May. (The speculation was correct, for it was Pitt's hope that an assault on Île Royale would commence around April 20.) Though the French minister wanted to get the Troupes de Terre overseas before the British began their blockade, it did not happen. Peyrenc de Moras would not learn about it until much later, but Louisbourg sighted the first British sails on March 31.[17]

As of March 11, 1758, neither the Volontaires Étrangers battalion in Brest nor the Cambis battalion in Rochefort had left French waters, though the Volontaires were at least in the final stages of preparation. The disruptions caused by the typhus epidemic carried to the naval port in Brittany in late 1757 likely lay behind the delay. The command of the squadron that was to carry the troops from Brest to Louisbourg was entrusted to Beaussier de Lisle, who was already familiar with North American waters. He had acquitted himself well in a combat off Louisbourg in July 1756, and in 1758 his squadron was to contain four ships of the line—the *Entreprenant* (seventy-four guns), the *Bienfaisant* (sixty-four), the *Capricieux* (sixty-four), and the *Célèbre* (sixty-four)—as well as two frigates, the *Comète* and the *Aréthuse*. Two other vessels, the *Juste* and the *Echo*, were to carry provisions, especially flour.[18] By itself Beaussier de

Lisle's squadron did not measure up to the ships sent to Louisbourg in 1757. There were no eighty-gun ships and just one of seventy-four guns. But then the squadron from Brest represented only one of three named to go to Louisbourg in 1758. The other two were simultaneously being readied at Rochefort and Toulon.

Beaussier de Lisle's squadron from Brest reached Île Royale on April 28, a day when there happened to be no British ships blocking the entrance to Louisbourg harbor. The very next day nine ships of the Royal Navy appeared, but by then all French ships were safely in port. Already anchored at Louisbourg, having preceded Beaussier de Lisle by a few days, were the *Apollon* (fifty guns), the *Chèvre*, and the *Prudent* (seventy-four guns). The last-named ship was commanded by Jean-Antoine Charry, marquis des Gouttes. Des Gouttes would end up as the most senior French naval officer at Louisbourg in 1758, so he would play a dominant role in the decision making in the weeks to come.[19]

The Cambis battalion's route to Louisbourg proved much more complicated than that of the Volontaires Étrangers. By mid-March 1758 a British squadron under the command of Admiral Edward Hawke was patrolling the Atlantic coast of France, lying in wait for any French vessels that tried to sail in or out of the Charente River, where Rochefort was located. As the vessels carrying the Cambis troops were getting ready to leave Rochefort, Admiral Hawke struck. On April 4 a portion of Hawke's squadron surprised French vessels near the Île d'Aix. A line of British ships, under full sail, swept in and attacked five ships of the line, two frigates, and about forty merchant vessels. The French ships cut their cables and fled in haste. The shallow-draft merchant vessels were able to move onto the mud banks, temporarily out of harm's way, but the warships were not so fortunate. The large French vessels wanted to make their way up the winding Charente River toward Rochefort, but an ebb tide stranded them at the mouth of the river. Their crews spent the night waiting for the next flood tide. When it came, Admiral Hawke sent in two small, shallow-draft ships to inflict more damage. The French responded by throwing overboard guns, stores, and ballast to lighten their loads, as well as buoys to mark the locations for later retrieval. The French ships successfully made their getaway, hauled up the Charente by men onshore hoisting the cables. The British, meanwhile, cut adrift the eighty or more buoys the French had placed to mark the jettisoned items. Hawke's squadron had not captured or destroyed any French vessels, yet it had delayed by about a month the departure of the French squadron bound for Louisbourg. The ships carrying the Cambis battalion were still at Rochefort, while the Volontaires Étrangers were already at Louisbourg. Following the incident at the mouth of the Charente River, French marine officials revised their plan to send one thousand muskets and a large quantity of black powder to Louisbourg. They shifted the munitions from Rochefort to Brest because they expected other ships to be sailing from the Breton port before any was able to leave Rochefort.[20]

It turned out that the vessels transporting the Cambis soldiers were not able to set out on the high seas until May 2, 1758. The squadron's commander was the Louis-Charles, comte du Chaffault de Besné, who was responsible for the *Dragon* (sixty-four guns), the *Belliqueux* (sixty-four), the *Sphinx* (sixty-four), the *Hardi* (sixty-four), the frigate *Zéphyr*, and the merchant ship *Brillant*. The *Belliqueux*, the *Sphinx*, and the *Hardi* all sailed *en flûte*. The late date of their departure meant they were unlikely to reach Louisbourg until early or mid-June. As with Beaussier de Lisle's squadron that had left earlier from Brest, Du Chaffault de Besné's ships were smaller and carried less firepower than Du Bois de La Motte had brought to Louisbourg in 1757.[21]

The third squadron Peyrenc de Moras directed to sail for Île Royale in 1758 was by far the largest of the three. It was comprised of fifteen vessels, including eight ships of the line. Its port of origin was Toulon, on the Mediterranean, where a former governor general of New France, the marquis de Duquesne, was acting commandant of the fleet. The squadron that was ordered to go to Île Royale was commanded by Jean-François Bertet de La Clue-Sabran, who had been at Louisbourg for a couple of months in 1751.[22]

Had La Clue-Sabran's armada been able to sail out of the Mediterranean, it would have made a huge contribution to the defense of Île Royale. Unfortunately for the French, a British squadron commanded by Vice-Admiral Henry Osborne prevented that from happening. Though Britain had lost its base at Minorca in 1756, it retained Gibraltar, on the

Spanish peninsula. Operating from that base, Osborne's squadron effectively blockaded the Strait of Gibraltar and the Spanish port of Cartagena, where many of La Clue-Sabran's ships were moored. Osborne's preventative action began in February 1758 and lasted for months. By July he decided it was too late for the French ships to make the transatlantic crossing and influence the outcome at Louisbourg, and his squadron returned to England. La Clue-Sabran came to the same conclusion and returned to Toulon. Thus the largest contingent of ships identified to go to Île Royale in 1758 would make no appearance there.[23]

In addition to the three major squadrons slated to go to Île Royale in early 1758, Peyrenc de Moras sent a number of individual ships or small groups overseas en route for Louisbourg. One noteworthy vessel was the *Formidable* (eighty guns), which put to sea from Brest on May 11 with Charles de Blénac-Courbon on board. The minister of the marine had given Blénac-Courbon, up until then the commandant at Brest, orders to assume the overall command of the French defense at Louisbourg. The appointment was perhaps slightly influenced by the month or so Blénac-Courbon had spent in the stronghold of Île Royale in the summer of 1750, when he was a captain of a ship cruising the Grand Banks protecting French vessels, though his more recent record of command at Brest was obviously much more important. The *Formidable* was approaching its destination on June 9, not quite four weeks after setting out, when the crew spied a large squadron of British ships off Louisbourg. Blénac-Courbon may have given some thought to fighting his way past the blockade; or to coming back a few days later to see if the situation was improved; or to finding another way to reach Louisbourg—for instance, overland after dropping anchor in an unguarded harbor elsewhere on Île Royale—but if he did, he rejected those possibilities. Instead, the man the minister had selected to lead the defense of Louisbourg decided that his best option was to return to France. He was back in Brest on June 26, where he once again took command of the port. As a consequence Governor Drucour was to retain overall command at Louisbourg throughout the summer of 1758, with the marquis des Gouttes in charge of the French warships. Would Charles de Blénac-Courbon have made different decisions than Drucour was going to make? Undoubtedly, for we all react differently in times of crisis. Would those decisions have affected the outcome? We will never know.[24]

Native Allies

There is no documentation to inform us about any discussions that took place during the winter and spring of 1758 among the leaders of the different Aboriginal nations implicated in the struggle over Louisbourg. Yet discussions there must have been. Ever since Louisbourg was founded in 1713, the various nations in the northeastern corner of the continent had shown varying levels of interest in the French colony. The Mi'kmaq, especially the bands residing on Île Royale and in eastern Nova Scotia, were the ones who maintained the most frequent and deepest ties with the administration at Louisbourg. On the other hand, a few Mi'kmaw bands had signed a peace and friendship treaty with the British administration at Halifax in 1752.

From the French point of view, an alliance with the Mi'kmaq, the Maliseet/Passamaquoddy, the Penobscots, and the Kennebecs was vitally important. It was through relationships with the indigenous peoples that the French had long counterbalanced the more populous British and Anglo-American presence on the easternmost portion of the continent. In the words of the marquis de Duquesne, governor general of New France from 1752 to 1755, "these Indians [were] the mainstay of the colony" who "should never be permitted to conclude peace with the English." Duquesne directed Abbé Jean-Louis Le Loutre to convince the nations within his sphere of influence to strike against the British of mainland Nova Scotia "without delay, provided it [did] not appear that it was [he] who gave the order." The support and encouragement the French gave their allies in the Atlantic region was not unusual. It was an approach followed across North America wherever the French had imperial interests. Fred Anderson succinctly describes the sweep of Louis XIV's and Louis XV's colonies in North America as "less a French dominion than a multicultural confederation knit together by diplomacy, trade, and the necessity of defending against English aggression."[25]

Officials at Louisbourg strove to maintain the relationship with their allies, especially the Mi'kmaq, who were the closest nation. There were annual allocations in the French colonial budgets for firearms, provisions, and missionaries. The costs were comparable to those in Canada. Historian Catherine Desbarats calculates that the portion for gifts "typically amounted to less than 5 percent of colonial expenditures and never more than 10 percent." From the French perspective, it was an efficient use of funds, for it "would have cost considerably more to maintain an equivalent number of additional soldiers." According to a memoir written at Louisbourg around 1739, presents made to the Mi'kmaq each June or July included the following items: fifteen thousand gun flints, thirty-five quintals (hundredweight) of gunpowder, sixty quintals of lead pellets, three quintals of lead balls, forty-five muskets without bayonets, and eighty picks or spades. With the outbreak of full-scale warfare in the 1750s, there was an increase in the quantity of war-related "gifts" sought by the Mi'kmaq and provided by the French. In late 1757 an estimate was made in France that as many as seven hundred Aboriginal allies might have to be subsidized on Île Royale for a five-month period in 1758, more than double the number of warriors at Louisbourg in 1757. Colonial officials were more than willing to make the expenditure if it helped keep Île Royale in French hands.[26]

While subsidies directed toward Native allies came from the king's treasury, the individuals closest to the First Peoples themselves were the missionaries. No particular order had a monopoly on this kind of work. What mattered was a willingness and an ability to live and work with the people they served. As it turned out, the two most influential missionaries in Atlantic Canada during the 1750s were Abbé Jean-Louis Le Loutre and Abbé Pierre Maillard. Both were Spiritains (Ordre du Saint-Esprit) by training, yet each was sent to the colonies under the auspices of the Seminary of Foreign Missions (Séminaire des Missions Étrangères). The two men, and others like them who are less well known today, worked long and hard to sustain the connection between the two interests they served, those of France and those of their parishioners. On Île Royale Abbé Maillard balanced the sometimes competing interests from 1735, when he arrived in the colony, until the end of 1758. After the fall of Louisbourg, Maillard and a few other missionaries would continue to serve their Native parishioners, but in the context of a British regime. Not surprisingly, Maillard's accommodation drew accusations of treason from French quarters. That turn of events was, of course, unseen in early 1758, when the missionary was still working tirelessly to further the interests of Louis XV. Until the late summer of 1758, Maillard operated out of Île de la Sainte-Famille (Chapel Island) on the Bras d'Or lake, not far from the French community at Port Toulouse (St. Peter's).[27]

The best any missionary could aspire to in serving a Native group was influence, not control. Chiefs and elders of the band or nation ultimately decided whether warriors would take part in a campaign and if so, to what extent. In late 1757 or in early 1758, meetings were undoubtedly held, separately, among the Mi'kmaq, the Maliseet/Passamaquoddy, the Penobscots, and the Kennebecs to determine their involvement in the defense of Louisbourg for the coming spring and summer. No sources shed light on their deliberations. Whatever factors were debated, the end result was that significantly fewer warriors traveled to Louisbourg in 1758 than had been there in 1757. Although the French hoped there might be seven hundred warriors, only about seventy, or 10 percent, actually came to participate in the defense. The many weeks warriors had spent at Louisbourg coastal positions in 1757, without any action, may have been a disincentive to return there. A similar decline had been seen before, in the summer of 1744, when Annapolis Royal was attacked on two separate occasions. About three hundred Mi'kmaq and Maliseet took part in the first assault; less than a tenth that number participated in the second attack a few months later.[28]

Despite the absence of documents informing us about their thinking in 1758, other sources reveal the general attitude of the Mi'kmaq toward warfare in general. Similar sentiments and ideas may have been shared by other Native allies in the Atlantic region. The starting point for the Mi'kmaq was that the land on which they lived and harvested resources was theirs alone, regardless of the claims and treaties of European powers. The idea that they had inhabited the region since the first ages of the world was forcefully and poetically expressed in a 1749 letter sent by chiefs to the new British administration at Halifax: "[T]his land belongs to me. I have come from it as certainly as the grass, it is the very place of my birth and of my dwelling, this land belongs to me."[29] As a consequence the Mi'kmaq maintained they had a right and a duty to defend their homeland against any who tried to deprive them of it.

Notwithstanding a long adherence to Roman Catholicism, dating back to 1610, when Chief Membertou was the first to adopt the Christian faith at Port-Royal, older and more traditional belief systems were still alive among the Mi'kmaq. Abbé Pierre Maillard did not call it "syncretism," yet he did relate how one orator appealed to the moon to guide them on what were called "nocturnal journeys" in a time of war: "By the favor of thy light it is, that we have often struck great strokes in war; and more than once have our enemies had cause to repent their being off their guard in thy clear winter-nights. Thy pale rays have often sufficiently lighted us, for our marching in a body without mistaking our way; and have enabled us not only to discover the ambushes of the enemy, but often to surprize him asleep."[30]

The sun was even more important than the moon, as revealed in this extract from a Mi'kmaw speech Maillard heard around 1753. The soliloquy formed part of a declaration of war against the British. "Sun! Be thou favorable to us in this point, as thou are in that of our hunting, when we beseech thee to guide us in quest of our daily support. Be propitious to us, that we may not fail of discovering the ambushes that may be laid for us; that we may not be surprized unawares in our cabbins, or elsewhere; and, finally, that we may not fall into the hands of our enemies. Grant them no chance with us, for they deserve none."[31]

The missionary elaborated on why the Mi'kmaq asked specifically not to be surprised or otherwise captured by their enemies. "There is nothing they do not think themselves permitted against their enemy, from whom they, on the other hand, expect no better quarter than they themselves give." Another French commentator from the 1750s, an officer in the Louisbourg garrison, offered this opinion on the warfare of the Mi'kmaq.

> War is considered by these people as something very sacred, and not lightly to be undertaken; but when once so, to be pushed with the utmost rigor by way of terror, joining its aid towards the putting the speediest end to it. . . . It is not then, till after the maturest deliberation, and the deepest debates, that they commonly come to a resolution of taking up the hatchet, as they call declaring of war; after which, there are no excesses to which their rage and ferocity do not incite them.[32]

Officials on the French side, at Louisbourg and elsewhere, valued their Native allies precisely because the British and the Anglo-Americans feared their sudden raids and sometimes terrifying treatment of prisoners. Writing specifically of the Mi'kmaq, Maillard characterized the feasts they held when wars were declared or commenced as being marked by "a mixture of devotion and ferocity."[33]

The customs of the Mi'kmaq surrounding warfare were not an exclusive male domain. Women sometimes played key roles in motivating the warriors to fight fiercely. Jesuit missionaries had commented on the way in which women encouraged warriors in the Canadian interior in the 1630s.[34] Abbé Maillard noticed the same phenomenon a century later in Atlantic Canada. The French priest recalled the words one elderly woman spoke at a feast where the men were implored to defend "our nation" from "the insults of our enemies."

> You men! Who look on me as of an infirm and weak sex, and consequently of all necessity subordinate to you, know that in what I am, the Creator has given to my share talents and properties at least of as much worth as yours. I have had the faculty of bringing into the world warriors, great hunters, and admirable managers of canoes. This hand, withered as you see it now, whose veins represent the root of a tree, has more than once struck a knife into the hearts of prisoners, who were given up to me for sport.[35]

Inspired by the women of their community, Mi'kmaw men formed a fighting force that could be highly effective in guerilla warfare. The question before the French at Louisbourg in 1758 was how much of a factor would guerilla warfare involving the Mi'kmaq, the Maliseet/Passamaquoddy, the Penobscots, and the Kennebecs be in the coming struggle at Louisbourg.

British Measures

In the early months of 1758, William Pitt and the senior military and naval staff in Great Britain made their decisions about which French colonial holdings they were going to strike in the coming campaign season. Their side had not yet enjoyed much success in the North American theatre, yet Pitt was not losing faith, at least not that he was admitting. Still, he wanted a breakthrough and committed even more troops and ships overseas than he had in 1757. By mid-1758 "there were more British soldiers in North America than in all the British garrisons and field armies in continental Europe."[36]

Like the French, the British were sending more and more regular troops into the fray in North America. That was a significant change from the seventeenth and early eighteenth centuries, when the main combatants in the colonies were colonists or colonists and Native warriors. The attacks on Louisbourg in 1745 and Beauséjour in 1755 and even the initial deportation of Acadians in 1755 were all carried out primarily by Anglo-American troops. From 1756 onward, however, provincial soldiers from New England, Canadian militia, colonial-based French marine companies, and Native warriors began to slip into the background, supplanted by thousands of regular infantry troops sent from the mother countries. Of the two nations the British demonstrated the greater willingness, or ability, to send line regiments across the ocean. While Peyrenc de Moras arranged for a total of about 6,800 infantry troops to strengthen New France during the Seven Years' War, Pitt sent roughly 32,000 redcoats.[37] That imbalance in land forces more or less mirrored the imbalance in warships, both in favor of the British.

As discussed earlier, the first step in Pitt's North American strategy for 1758 took place in the waters close to France, where the Royal Navy tried to cut off the provisioning and sending of warships and reinforcements to all French colonies, not just New France but also the West Indies, India, and elsewhere.[38] Admiral Osborne enjoyed total success in the Mediterranean theater, while Admiral Hawke caused delays to ships leaving from Rochefort. The end result was that the French naval force that made its way to Louisbourg in 1758 was much less formidable than its predecessor in 1757.

The British recognized that to succeed in North America they would have to achieve dominance over both sea and land approaches to their targets. To capture Louisbourg and Quebec they would have to control the waters and make amphibious landings; to take Duquesne, Carillon, Montreal, and others, they would have to mount overland campaigns out of the Anglo-American colonies. The various campaigns required an enormous commitment from the Royal Navy and unprecedented numbers of British regular troops. Pitt obtained approval to send twenty-four thousand soldiers into the American theater in 1758, fourteen thousand of which were to join the campaign against Louisbourg. The expectation was that the Cape Breton stronghold would fall quickly and the military and naval force would move on to tackle Quebec. The remaining ten thousand fresh soldiers were for the thrust into the interior of the continent, where Fort Duquesne was the first target. To support the redcoats in that campaign, twenty thousand colonial Americans were raised in provincial regiments.[39] On paper the two-pronged approach sounded simple.

The logistical challenges of transporting, feeding, and controlling armies and navies the size the British were mustering in 1758 were enormous. The total of all the combined land forces—British regulars, Anglo-American provincials, and rangers—expected to take part in the various 1758 campaigns and for the defense of the springboard at Halifax came to over forty-seven thousand soldiers. In addition roughly fourteen thousand sailors would be required for the ships heading for Île Royale.[40]

The top positions in the British army and the Royal Navy each possessed a breadth of experience and carried out responsibilities with aplomb. George Anson had returned as First Lord of the Admiralty in June 1757, after being out of the position for a year. Lord John Ligonier took over as commander in chief of the army in October 1757, though he had direct responsibility over only the troops in Great Britain. Because of the importance of the war in the far-flung imperial theaters, Parliament gave approval for thirty thousand of the overall ninety thousand regulars in the British army to serve overseas.[41]

Pitt, Ligonier, and Anson selected the commanders who were to lead the offensives planned for 1758. Named in late 1757 to replace Lord Loudoun as the overall commander in chief in North America was Major General James Abercromby. He was to handle the advance northward through the British American colonies into the interior of New France.[42] The expedition against Louisbourg, however, was more complicated than the strictly land campaign because of the vital role that would be played by the navy. Close coordination between the two services was essential, as the failures of 1757 at Rochefort and Louisbourg had demonstrated. Those who had failed the year before did not receive a second chance. In their place Pitt, Ligonier, and Anson chose two new faces to head the expedition to Île Royale. They handed the control of the army for that campaign to a relatively unknown officer, one who had never been to North America before, the forty-one-year old lieutenant colonel of the Fifteenth Regiment of Foot, Jeffery Amherst (1717–97).

Selected to lead the naval operation was forty-seven-year old Edward Boscawen (1711–61), already familiar with the waters and strongholds in Atlantic Canada.

Lord Ligonier was the one who proposed Amherst be given command of the land forces. He was familiar with the younger officer's organizational abilities because Amherst had served as his aide-de-camp a decade earlier. Amherst's methodical planning and coordinating abilities left a lasting impression. However, Ligonier did not find it easy to convince first Pitt and then George II that Amherst possessed the skill and experience to command the army for the expedition to Louisbourg. After all, the officer had not yet commanded a regiment in the field, and his only campaign experience was as an aide-de-camp. It was an incredible jump to be suddenly given the responsibility for fourteen thousand soldiers on a crucial campaign. Nonetheless, the others eventually accepted Ligonier's choice. The appointment was finalized on December 30, 1757, at which time Amherst was serving on the European continent. In early January 1758 an order was issued for the young officer to return immediately to England, so he could lead the campaign against Louisbourg with the temporary rank of "Major General in America." The order, however, did not reach Amherst for several weeks, and then he had to journey back to England. In the meantime, preparations were well under way for the naval squadrons under Hawke and Osborne to hem in French ships along their own coasts and for a flotilla that would make the strike against Louisbourg.[43]

As for Edward Boscawen's appointment, Admiral Anson had every reason to feel confident that he was the best man to lead the naval operation against Île Royale. Anson's appreciation for Boscawen's abilities dated back at least a decade, to when the younger officer served as a ship captain under Anson's command during the 1747 victory over La Jonquière off Cap Finistère, Brittany.[44] Boscawen was to sail to Louisbourg aboard the same ship, the *Namur*, that he had captained in that 1747 sea battle. Neither Pitt nor the king needed to be convinced, as they did about Jeffery Amherst, that Boscawen was the right choice. Boscawen was well known and had a reputation as a problem solver. He was expected to demonstrate that quality in working out campaign details with the less-experienced army commander, Jeffery Amherst.

Boscawen's appointment came later than did Amherst's. He was named

Admiral of the Blue and commander in chief of the Louisbourg-destined squadron on February 8, 1758. Little more than two weeks later, on February 24, Boscawen set off at the head of a squadron of twenty-three ships of the line and dozens of transports carrying soldiers, equipment, and provisions. Amherst, on the other hand, was at Portsmouth until March 16, when he left aboard the seventy-four-gun *Dublin*. Neither commander made a quick crossing. Boscawen's convoy was slowed by the transport vessels, so that it was May 12 before the huge flotilla arrived at the rendezvous of Halifax.[45] Amherst's crossing was lengthened unnecessarily when the captain of the *Dublin* spied a French East Indies ship near Brest and gave chase. He eventually made the capture and found that its cargo included valuable rosewood and 700,000 pounds of coffee. There ensued another search for a vessel that could escort the rich prize back to England. The two diversions, chase and search, added about two weeks to Amherst's travel time across the ocean. It was May 28, two weeks later than Boscawen, before Amherst saw the Nova Scotia shoreline.

While Boscawen and Amherst were making their way overseas, other preparations for the campaign against Louisbourg were under way in New York and Halifax. Transports carrying battalions of various regiments—the Royal, the Royal Americans, the Fifteenth, the Twenty-second, the Twenty-eighth, the Thirty-fifth, the Fortieth, the Forty-fifth, the Forty-seventh, and the Sixty-third—set sail from New York, bound for Halifax, in late April. They were organized in four brigades. Meanwhile in Halifax the experiment of overwintering several warships in port had proven a success. Having a sizable flotilla and a number of regiments on the North American side of the Atlantic was supposed to give the British an extra advantage in the coming campaign. Blockading activity off Île Royale could begin earlier than usual, and at least some soldiers and sailors would avoid the illnesses and diseases induced by ocean crossings.[46]

The individual in command of the British ships at Halifax before Boscawen arrived was Sir Charles Hardy. He moved to second in command when the superior officer arrived. Hardy reached Halifax from New York on March 19. About three weeks later he began cruising off the northeast coast of Cape Breton with eight ships of the line and two frigates. It was one or more of those vessels that the engineer Grillot de Poilly observed on April 12 and duly recorded in his diary. Grillot de Poilly stated that a British ship of the line came within a league of the shore between Pointe Blanche (White Point) and Pointe Platte (Flat Point), hoisted a red flag, fired two blasts from its cannon, then turned, and sailed back out to sea. It was, one supposes, a symbolic beginning to the 1758 assault on Louisbourg. There would be many more sightings of British sails through the rest of April and into May.[47]

In the first five months of 1758, Hardy's squadron captured no fewer than ten French prizes in the waters off Île Royale, all of which were escorted to the Admiralty court in Halifax.[48] Some were more valuable than others. Captain John Knox, in the garrison at Halifax, made special note in his diary of a French ship that carried fifteen hundred thirteen-inch mortar shells, four hundred barrels of powder, seven hundred barrels of flour, four hundred barrels of pork, four chests of money, and twelve hundred "stands of arms."[49] Officials in Louisbourg must have winced when they learned of the loss.

While Sir Charles Hardy's ships were cruising off Louisbourg, the land forces already in Halifax were busy preparing fascines and gabions for siege batteries that would eventually be needed. Ninety carpenters from New England constructed six prefabricated blockhouses that could be put together in a matter of hours after a landing, as well as a huge sling cart with wheels eight feet high so that one could "transport Cannon over Marshy Ground." The carpenters also learned how to "draw" masts for vessels, should the need for replacements arise. At the same time a selection process was under way in the infantry units. The British command wanted to have a highly mobile force of specialized light infantry that was capable of moving quickly and easily during an amphibious landing and could subsequently deal with Native warriors and French irregulars who might attack the siege camps. Major George Scott of the Seventieth Regiment was put in command of over one thousand men. Five hundred were rangers from New England (whose captains were Benoni Danks, Joseph Gorham, James Rogers, and John Stark). The remaining soldiers were drawn from regular British regiments, with twenty or thirty marksmen selected from each regiment except the Seventy-eighth, which provided one hundred. This large light infantry corps was dressed in green and blue and outfitted "for easier brushing through the Woods; with Ruffs of black Bear's Skin round their Necks." An eyewitness described them as follows: "Their clothes are cut short, & they have exchanged their heavy Arms, for the light fusils."[50]

The commander of this light infantry strike force, Major George Scott, is an intriguing figure. In the early 1750s he was Thomas Pichon's main contact on the British side when the French clerk was handing over maps, letters, and general information about the strengths and weaknesses of Louisbourg and Beauséjour. In 1755 Scott commanded one of the two battalions during the siege of the French fort at Beauséjour. Years later, in 1767, he would perish following a duel on the Caribbean island of Dominica.[51] In 1758, as we will see, George Scott and his light infantry were to play a crucial role at the pivotal moment in the attack on Louisbourg.

Still in Halifax in the spring of 1758, Scott and his men, along with others from the line regiments, rehearsed landing on the beaches near Louisbourg. An eyewitness offered this account:

> During the recess there [*sic*] stay at Halifax afforded them, the Generals did not fail to accustom the Troops to what they were soon to encounter. Some Military operations were dayly carried on. They frequently landed in the boats of the Transports and practised in the Woods, the different Manuvres they were likely to act on the Island of Cape Breton. In all these operations you may imagine that Gen. Wolfe was remarkably active. The Scene afforded Scope for his Military Genius. We found it possible to land 3500 Men in the Boats belonging to Transports, and when the boats from the men of War assisted, 5000 Men could be landed.[52]

Though the preparations struck some observers as thorough and well conceived, James Wolfe found fault. Wolfe, named as one of three brigadier generals to serve under Amherst, arrived in Halifax on May 8 and immediately channeled his energy into the tasks at hand. In acerbic letters to friends and family in England, the thirty-one-year old officer had no end of complaints: his side required more troops; the Anglo-American rangers were contemptible; and there were too many poorly prepared soldiers in the regular regiments. The only two units to make a positive impression on the hypercritical Wolfe were the Highland regiments raised in 1757, Montgomerie's (Seventy-seventh) and Fraser's (Seventy-eighth). There was an irony in this. Many if not most of the Scottish officers and men had been enemies of James Wolfe back in 1745, when the then eighteen year old had been aide-de-camp to General Hawley in putting down the Jacobite sympathizers. Wolfe apparently forgave and forgot and wrote from Halifax on May 12, 1758: "[The] Highlanders are very serviceable soldiers, and commanded by the most manly corps of officers I ever saw."[53]

As the days and weeks of preparation ticked by in Halifax, impatience grew among the British officers and enlisted men. By mid to late May, everything and everyone were nearly ready. The only important elements still missing were a small contingent of soldiers and one important individual. Jeffery Amherst, the officer named to command the land troops, was still somewhere out to sea aboard the *Dublin*. Rather than wait for him, Admiral Edward Boscawen began to issue orders for both services. He called for all the soldiers and sailors to take regular exercise and to keep their living quarters clean so that they remained "in health and vigour." On May 21 Boscawen put out a lengthy order on the assault landing that was planned for Louisbourg. It detailed that the boats belonging to the hospital ships would be exclusively for the wounded; other boats would be for the rescue of those who fell into the sea by accident. As for the soldiers in the landing boats, they were to carry only what they absolutely needed, which was defined as their immediate arms and ammunition and enough bread and cheese in their pockets to tide them over for two days. Furthermore, no one in the landing parties was to fire his weapon or fix his bayonet until he was on dry land. Tents, blankets, and six days of provisions would be sent ashore after a foothold was achieved.[54]

The delays involved in setting out from Halifax frustrated James Wolfe, as he made clear in a personal letter: "The latter end of May and the fleet not sailed! What are they about? Why are they not landed at Louisburg?" In the same letter Wolfe sketched the invasion plans as they then stood. Since the British knew the French were entrenched along the beaches of Gabarus Bay, to the south of Louisbourg, the current thinking was that Wolfe would land with about three thousand soldiers along the Mira

River and then advance overland to attack the stronghold from the landward side. While that roundabout operation was under way, Wolfe explained in his letter, other British forces were to land at Lorembec and Baleine, to the north of Louisbourg. Wolfe acknowledged that the plan might change once Amherst arrived or upon a closer examination of the situation when the fleet reached the shores of Cape Breton.[55]

On the evening of May 24, the same date Wolfe wrote the letter venting his frustrations about the delays in setting off for Louisbourg, the brigadier general blew off steam at a huge party at the most celebrated of Halifax's many drinking establishments. Wolfe hosted and paid nearly one hundred pounds for the pleasure of forty-seven diners and drinkers at the Great Pontack House. The three-story inn stood along the Halifax waterfront and was the venue for auctions, theatrical plays, meetings, and general merriment. Wolfe's guests were presumably fellow officers—whether from the army, the navy, the artillery, or the engineering corps—and they made a concerted effort to give themselves a memorable evening before they set off to discover their destinies at Louisbourg. Ten musicians entertained the party, and there were fifteen servers, one for every three diners. By the end of the night, meaning the early hours of the next morning, the revelers had consumed, or at least paid for, forty-seven full meals, seventy bottles of Madeira, fifty bottles of claret, and twenty-five bottles of brandy.[56] They must not have been expecting to do very much the next day.

With Major General Amherst's whereabouts still unknown, Admiral Boscawen and the senior army officers decided they should not wait any longer in Halifax. The stakes were too high, including for their own careers if they indulged in what officials in London and public opinion decided was an unnecessary delay. Admiral Byng's fate was a fresh memory, especially for Boscawen. On May 27 the admiral composed a short note to William Pitt, informing the secretary of state: "We have on board the Transports Thirteen Regiments of Foot, and all the Train of Artillery, and Ordnance Stores. . . . I will lose no opportunity of proceeding to sea as soon as the wind and Weather will permit." The following day the armada made its way out of Halifax harbor and turned north, toward Cape Breton Island. Such a spectacle of masts and billowing canvas people in the port had not seen before and never would again on such a scale.

There were over 150 vessels in the convoy, including 23 ships of the line, 18 frigates, and perhaps as many as 127 transports.[57]

The personnel on board the vessels totaled over twenty-five thousand soldiers, sailors, and support persons. The vast majority were men, but there were women as well, for army regulations permitted up to six women per company per regiment. A detailed list of the transports reveals several hundred women in total. They were there to perform a range of cleaning and cooking tasks, and they received victuals in return. They were not, however, to be involved in any combat. Admiral Boscawen's orders made specific mention that: "No women to be permitted to land, until the men are all on shore, and until their tents, blankets, provisions, and necessaries are likewise landed."[58]

Soon after the armada left Halifax's harbor, a sail was spied, coming down the coast from Cape Breton. When it came alongside the lead ships, off Cape Sambro, people recognized it as the *Dublin*. After more than ten weeks at sea, Major General Jeffery Amherst had finally arrived. With the expedition under way for Louisbourg, more than a month behind the target date set by Pitt, Amherst caused no further delay. The commander in chief of the army gathered up his possessions aboard the *Dublin* and made a shift to the largest of the ships in the flotilla. Henceforth, until the campaign would be decided one way or the other, Jeffery Amherst was to live aboard Edward Boscawen's flagship, the *Namur*. At 175 feet long, weighing 1,814 tons, with a crew of 780, the *Namur* was a powerful headquarters from which the two overall commanders were to issue their orders.[59]

The British force was in a buoyant mood as it drew near Louisbourg. Aside from James Wolfe, most felt they had sufficient resources to get the job done. The will to succeed was characterized by a jaunty self-confidence, a vital part of the job of being an eighteenth-century military leader. Senior officers were, and were expected to be, glib on the eve of battle and in the face of an enemy. They hoped their witty remarks might be repeated among the men who served beneath them. Edward Boscawen, schooled in the spirit of the era, had a quick retort when an aide informed him upon his arrival in Halifax a few weeks earlier that some French warships and transports had already made it into Louisbourg harbor. The admiral replied: "I am glad of it; if all the fleet of France goes in, I will follow them; there is room enough for us all;—the more we find there, the more captures I will make." It was precisely the sort of remark officers were supposed to make. As Boscawen must have hoped, his rejoinder circulated among all ranks assembling in Halifax. Around the same time, James Wolfe penned a similar remark in a letter to his uncle in England. On the subject of the number of enemy ships in Louisbourg harbor, Wolfe added: "If they had thrown in twice as much we should not hesitate to attack them; and for my part, I have no doubt of our success."[60]

The British expedition against Louisbourg grew larger again when it neared its destination and merged with Sir Charles Hardy's squadron, which had been patrolling the harbor mouth and nearby coast for weeks. It became, and would remain, the largest single armed force ever mounted by Great Britain in North America with over 27,000 combatants. The expedition mounted in 1759 to blockade and besiege Quebec would have a larger naval contingent (about 18,000) but a smaller number of soldiers (8,640), making for a combined force that was slightly smaller than that sent to attack Louisbourg in 1758.[61]

At the Last Minute

Even before the warships under Sir Charles Hardy first appeared off Louisbourg in mid-April 1758, the leadership on Île Royale started to implement a plan of defense. Governor Drucour did not know for sure that a seaborne assault or landing attempt was about to take place, but he and his senior officers wanted to be ready if it did. On April 1, 1758, Drucour ordered one of the senior officers in the Artois battalion, La Tour du Chemin, to take command of the Island Battery when the time came for it to be manned. As of May 3 the governor had not yet given the signal to send La Tour du Chemin and his contingent to the Island Battery. It was a cold and windy spot at the best of times, and given the dreary weather that continued throughout April and into May 1758, the governor hesitated putting soldiers there before it was necessary. Meanwhile on April 21, when Hardy's squadron was known to be cruising offshore, the French leadership dispatched a detachment of artillery specialists to man the battery on Lighthouse Point, on the opposite side of the entrance to the port.[62]

Drucour's greatest hope—and deepest worry—concerned the size of the fleet that France would be sending to defend the colony. Only when the vessels had safely reached port would he have a clear idea of whether Louisbourg and Île Royale could be defended. The first ship to arrive was the *Gloucester*, presumably a merchant vessel, on April 11. The *Apollon* followed four days later. It was a fifty-gun ship out of Rochefort that carried a crew of 400 and brought with it "foodstuffs for the Colony and other supplies." On April 24 the *Prudent* (seventy-four guns, crew of 680) sailed into port, followed by a flute, the *Chèvre*. The commander of the *Prudent* was the marquis Jean-Antoine Charry des Gouttes, who assumed control of the naval defense of Louisbourg once he reached port. The weeks ahead were to witness many occasions when he would have profound disagreements with Governor Drucour over how best to employ the French ships in the harbor.[63]

If Louisbourg's spirits soared when the *Prudent* sailed past Lighthouse Point into the harbor, they soon sagged. Word spread round the port that some of the other warships sent from France were delayed, diverted, or lost to the British. Moreover, "two-thirds of its Crew [the *Prudent*] were sick; and it carrie[d] 50 recruits which [were] the dregs of humanity." Jacques Prévost reported ten days later that 250 sailors off the *Prudent* were in one hospital and the rest of the crew in another. On April 27, a day that witnessed a mix of snow and fog, observers from Louisbourg spotted five vessels off the ice-covered coast. Initially thought to be British, the ships were soon determined to be French. Grillot de Poilly recorded that it was likely part of the squadron commanded by La Clue, expected to be coming from Toulon. Of course, the engineer could not know those ships had not made it out of the Mediterranean. The following day, April 28, the five vessels sailed into port: it was the squadron from Brest commanded by Beaussier de Lisle. The ships were the *Entreprenant* (seventy-four guns, crew of 680), the *Célèbre* (sixty-four guns, crew of 550), the *Capricieux* (sixty-four guns, crew of 550), the *Bienfaisant* (sixty-four guns, crew of 550), and the *Comète* (seventy-four guns, grew of 680). Aboard as passengers were the second battalion of the Volontaires Étrangers. On the last day of April another French ship, the *Fidelle*, reached Île Royale, though not Louisbourg. The *Fidelle* anchored at Port Dauphin, where it stayed for a while, unable or unwilling to attempt to run the blockade at Louisbourg.[64]

On May 1, a day after six British vessels were spotted off the coast, Drucour and chief engineer Louis Franquet left the walled town of Louisbourg to examine the most likely landing beaches. Soon afterward Drucour sent soldiers to those locations, first to repair the damage the winter weather had exacted on the parapets and the abatis and then to guard them round the clock. Drucour explained in a note to the minister of the marine that by sending six hundred soldiers to the entrenched positions he was also making room in the barracks for the newly arrived Volontaires Étrangers.[65]

During the first week of May, Governor Drucour, financial administrator Prévost, and chief engineer Franquet took stock of the situation and composed letters to the minister of the marine, Peyrenc de Moras. Their matter-of-fact summaries were not exactly defeatist, yet there was none of the bravado British senior officers were expressing at the same time. Given that the authors of the letters knew Peyrenc de Moras would not receive the letters for another month or so, at which point the fate of Louisbourg might perhaps have been decided, the memoranda were not written because the authors were expecting assistance. The true purpose was to demonstrate to the minister that the officials were doing everything they could to serve the king's interest, despite the odds mounting against them. In that sense the letters were not so much assessments of Louisbourg's readiness for an assault as epistles to protect or enhance the writers' reputations and careers.

As it turned out, Peyrenc de Moras would not be the one to read the letters from Louisbourg. At the end of May 1758, Louis XV granted the minister of the marine his wish, that he be allowed to retire with a pension. Historian Jonathan Dull describes Peyrenc de Moras as "exhausted and overwhelmed by his terrible responsibilities." Overseeing the navy and colonies was no longer a plum portfolio. The first person the king offered it to after Peyrenc de Moras turned it down, but the commandant of Toulon and lieutenant general of the fleet accepted. Claude-Louis d'Espinal, marquis de Massiac, became the latest minister responsible for Louisbourg, Quebec, New Orleans, and the rest of the overseas French world. Promoted to become a deputy minister to give advice to Massiac on the colonial side of his portfolio was a former financial administrator of Île Royale, Sébastien-François-Ange Lenormant de Mézy.[66]

When Massiac finally read the letters composed in Louisbourg in early May, he did not find much good news. One positive item was that Beaussier de Lisle's squadron of five ships, carrying the Volontaires Étrangers, had arrived. Another was that there was no shortage of provisions in the port. Some foodstuffs had even been sent on to Canada. The bad news took longer to relate. The *Dianne* (thirty-six guns, crew of five hundred) was known to have been chased by the British, and it may have been captured. It carried supplies and uniforms needed by the Artois and Bourgogne battalions. Also in the probably lost column were four merchant ships from Saint-Malo and one from Bordeaux that had accompanied Beaussier de Lisle's squadron. Massiac was, of course, not surprised to learn that the entire squadron from Rochefort, under the command Du Chaffault de Besné, had not reached Louisbourg by early May. The minister knew well that Admiral Hawke had delayed those ships and that it would be early June before they reached Île Royale. Drucour and Prévost warned that when the ships did arrive, they had best be carrying a supply of bedding material (sheets, covers, and straw mattresses) for the Cambis and Volontaires Étrangers soldiers because there was not enough bedding in the colony for any more troops. Yet another worry for the Louisbourg administration was a shortage of hard currency. The local royal officials had not paid the Artois and Bourgogne soldiers for months, not since January 1, 1758. It did not need to be said that such a situation could lead to unrest and possibly a mutiny.[67]

As for the state of the fortifications, Massiac learned from Franquet that the long winter had caused extensive deterioration. Rain and snow had washed away one-third of the repairs at the King's Bastion. On the left flank, because of a breakdown in the masonry, seven feet of turf had been added. The engineer explained that the turf would not support the weight of a man, which made it clear to the minister how well it was going to stand up to British bombardment. Given the lack of time to do anything major, Franquet resigned himself to carrying out small tasks. He added some mines to the gallery in front of the King's Bastion and additional palisades to the covered way.[68]

When Drucour and Prévost wrote the minister about the looming

British assault, they painted a discouraging picture. As of May 3 nine enemy ships had been sailing back and forth across the entrance to the harbor. The Louisbourg officials correctly assumed they were the ships that had overwintered at Halifax. To obtain a better idea of how many more British vessels might be on their way, the governor sent word to traditional Native allies that he wanted enemy prisoners, not scalps, because he required information. Drucour informed the minister that with the certainty of an attack he had summoned to Louisbourg the detachments from the outports of Port Toulouse and Port Dauphin, as well as any able-bodied civilians capable of bearing arms and serving in the militia. The extra bodies were needed to augment the garrison within the fortified town and to defend positions at possible landing sites along the coast. Also on the manpower front, Governor Drucour sent a message to the Compagnies franches officer Charles Deschamps de Boishébert in Quebec to come to Louisbourg's assistance. Boishébert had a reputation for assembling large numbers of irregular forces—Native warriors, French soldiers, and Acadian militia—to help defend the Atlantic realm of New France. Drucour asked Boishébert to come as quickly as possible. Another appeal the governor mentioned to his superior in France was a call he had made to "Isle St. Jean for the Acadian youth with all the Mickmacks of Miramichy and of that Island." Pointedly, Drucour added for the minister's benefit: "I find they delay a lot."[69]

The unstated purpose of the dispatches Governor Drucour sent to France in early May was to let the minister know that the odds were stacked against a successful defense of Louisbourg. He had asked for more ships, more troops, and more warriors, and if others could not deliver, well, one did not win wars with good intentions. An example of Drucour's frustration with how events were unfolding was his comment to the minister that the four twelve-*pouce* mortars that had just arrived aboard the *Apollon* could not be used. The bombs in the fortress were slightly larger and thus would not fit in the mortars.[70]

After sending off a couple of letters to France in early May, Governor Drucour would not compose any further correspondence to the minister for more than a month, not until June 10. By then there would be a lot to relate. For the rest of May and into early June, the governor was preoccupied with preparing Louisbourg's defensive posture. On May 14, for instance, Drucour issued orders to the senior officers he selected to be in command at the three most likely landing beaches. He named the commander of the Artois battalion, the irascible Mascle de Saint-Julhien, to take charge at Anse de la Cormorandière (Kennington Cove). For Pointe Platte, Drucour chose the commander of the Bourgogne battalion, Marin Michel du Bourzt. Finally, for Pointe Blanche, Drucour selected the lieutenant colonel of the Volontaires Étrangers, Henry Valentin Jacques d'Anthonay. A signal was agreed upon—two cannon blasts from the cavalier battery at Louisbourg's Dauphin Gate and the beating of the drum call, the *générale*. When the three officers heard the signal, they were to hurry to their assigned posts and take command.[71]

A good source for the events at Louisbourg during the spring of 1758 is the diary of military engineer Grillot de Poilly. In addition to daily weather and wind conditions, Grillot de Poilly recorded everything he observed or heard concerning the preparations to defend the colony, such as the sending of five hundred soldiers to the entrenched positions along Gabarus Bay on April 29. Tents and cooking pots were sent the next day. Then on April 30 the grenadier company of the Volontaires Étrangers, who had arrived in port two days earlier, finally came ashore. The next day, May 1, the rest of the contingent disembarked. On May 3 the entire battalion underwent a review, presumably by Governor Drucour.[72]

Beginning in late April British reconnoitering missions along the coast of Île Royale were a common event. On April 30 a British skiff came so close to Cap Noir, just beyond Louisbourg's Princess Demi-Bastion, that a detachment of French soldiers went to make sure the small boat did not come ashore. Other exploratory looks by the British, usually in a frigate, took place on May 8, 11, 12, 14, and 15. The French drew the obvious conclusion: the British were studying the shoreline and the extent of defenses between Pointe Platte and Anse de la Cormorandière. When a British frigate came too close to Louisbourg itself, apparently to see how many ships were in port, the French seaward batteries opened fire, but the frigate was not hit. Down the coast, at the presumed landing beaches, the French could not drive the British off in early May because their artillery pieces were still being set up. And even when the French batteries were established, the ordnance was neither as powerful nor as concentrated as the guns in the fortified town. The beaches were to have only a handful of moderate caliber cannons and a few swivel guns.[73]

From the British perspective the coastal reconnaissance of April and May generated reasonably good information about the French positions, which was communicated to Amherst and Boscawen when they arrived off Louisbourg. Another valuable piece of the puzzle was a detailed plan of attack drawn up by Brigadier Samuel Waldo, one of the senior officers of the New England siege of Louisbourg in 1745. Waldo had forwarded the document to William Pitt in November 1757.[74]

On May 1 Drucour and Franquet investigated the coastal positions as far as Pointe Blanche. From that day on, laborers toiled at strengthening the retrenchments. As for the initial contingent of soldiers living in tents along the coast during a cold and wet spring, they were relieved by replacements on May 7. Around the same time, the first of the Native warriors and Acadian refugees arrived. Their numbers were small, but every additional body was welcomed. On May 7, 11 Mi'kmaq and 11 Acadians arrived. Two days later the French commandant from Île Saint-Jean, Gabriel Rousseau de Villejouin, brought in a detachment of 90 Acadians. On May 12 word reached Louisbourg that 17 Acadians from Île Saint-Jean were at Port Toulouse and on their way. Then on May 18 the missionary Abbé Pierre Maillard came into town with 28 Mi'kmaq from Île Saint-Jean. All told, the arrivals added about 150 men-at-arms.[75]

The Acadians and the Native warriors were envisioned to serve primarily as irregulars, or skirmishers. The expectation was that they would help regular French soldiers defend the beaches against an enemy descent; then if the British made it ashore, they would harass their camps. In anticipation of the latter necessity, Drucour ordered supply depots established inland, where soldiers and warriors would obtain needed matériel and food. The first depot was established on a property along the Mira River on May 10. Five days later, following a war council at the governor's residence, a second cache of food provisions and military stores was created "for the use of the troops who [would] be thrown into the woods in the event of a siege." The council of war also decided to prepare fire ships (*brulôts*) in the event that the British tried to force their way into the harbor.[76]

As May unfolded, with continual preparations for war, the worries intensified within the Louisbourg community and its military leadership. Grillot de Poilly recorded on May 14 that the enemy had captured two

French coastal traders (*caboteurs*); two days later he noted that three larger merchant ships had been intercepted. On May 19 the story reached town that a vessel carrying "every kind of foodstuff" had made it to Port Dauphin but then had to flee. One of the few ships to make it past Hardy's blockade squadron was from Saint-Malo; it sailed safely into Louisbourg harbor on May 20. Around the same time Drucour dispatched two officers with fifty men each to Anse à Gauthier, north of Louisbourg. The relatively small size of the detachments revealed that the governor did not expect a major assault in that location. Many more defenders and much higher ranking officers were camping along the beaches to the southwest of Louisbourg: Pointe Platte, Pointe Blanche, and Anse de la Cormorandière. The cold, wet weather was taking a toll on the soldiers in those spots, even though they were relieved weekly. Grillot de Poilly commented on May 22 that the number of sick soldiers had outstripped the capacity of the one-hundred-bed King's Hospital in the heart of Louisbourg. Overflow patients were placed in the chapel, the sacristy, and officers' rooms of the hospital.[77]

Many days in May 1758 were foggy, which meant there was much guesswork among the inhabitants of Louisbourg concerning British activity out to sea. On May 21 Grillot de Poilly interpreted the sounds of offshore cannon fire as "signals for the English to keep themselves together." A week later, around 7:00 PM on the evening of May 29, the people within the fortified town heard a series of loud cannon blasts, followed by musket fire. The sounds came from the coast to the north of Louisbourg. The interpretation was that the British were attempting a landing along the least protected shoreline between Anse à Gauthier and Lorembec. The drummers of Louisbourg began at once to beat the générale to signal an emergency. Troops hurried to the assembly points around town, as did the civilian inhabitants. Grillot de Poilly records that the civilians were ready to fight, "carrying themselves with will and confidence." Before long everyone discovered that it was a false alarm; there was no enemy landing in progress. What had been heard through the fog was a running sea fight off shore, the end of which saw three French frigates, first the *Echo* (thirty-two guns) and then the *Bizarre* (sixty-four guns) and the *Aréthuse* (thirty-six guns), get past the British squadron into Louisbourg harbor. No one knew it at the time, but these French vessels would be the last to make it safely into port before the arrival of the huge British fleet making its way to Louisbourg from Halifax.[78]

As May came to a close, the inhabitants of Louisbourg and the soldiers and sailors defending them had lived through long weeks of unseasonably cold weather and fretful anticipation. When and where the enemy attack might come, and with what force, remained unknown. Worry was a routine part of daily life, as it had been since the mid-1750s. Was it too much to hope for a repeat of 1757, when an invasion loomed yet did not materialize? Might there be another windstorm to put an end to the current threat?

Around 7:00 AM on the morning of June 1, 1758, the people of Louisbourg discovered that the British presence off the coast had grown overnight. No longer was there only Sir Charles Hardy's squadron in their waters, which had been nuisance enough. When Governor Drucour was summoned to see the new situation, which he did around 8:00 AM, he counted seventy sails. He knew instantly that the arrival of the enemy armada marked a turning point, for he began that day a diary, the first line of which described the sighting of the British sails offshore. As the winds were contrary, he added in his journal, the ships were not yet able to come closer than four or five leagues. They were staying down the coast in the vicinity of Anse de la Cormorandière.[79]

The appearance of the large enemy fleet led Drucour to order the drummers to beat the générale. The senior officers he had already picked to go to the three expected landing beaches were to set off to assume command of those areas. Drucour also sent a lieutenant and twenty-five men overland to the Mira River to study the situation there.[80] (As discussed earlier, the earliest British invasion plan envisioned James Wolfe landing along the Mira and advancing from that direction.)

While the French military was scurrying about their business, several thousand civilian parishioners at Louisbourg prepared to fulfill a religious obligation. Thursday, June 1, 1758, was the octave of the Corpus Christi, normally a feast day of great festivity and ceremony. The traditional highlight of the occasion was a procession of the Blessed Sacrament through the streets past kneeling worshippers. Despite the military activities under way, the procession went ahead as planned. Moreover, the procession at Louisbourg that day was accompanied by artillery salutes from the cannons of the fortress and from those of the ships anchored in the harbor. The civil, religious, and military officials in the colony did not allow the arrival of a massive enemy fleet and a concern about saving gunpowder to cancel their celebration of one of the most important days of the Roman Catholic church calendar. After the Corpus Christi procession was over, male civilians capable of bearing arms joined the military preparations. One hundred civilian volunteers were dispatched to Anse de la Cormorandière, where Mascle de Saint-Julhien and his officers found them tasks or positions. The rest of the "bourgeois," as Grillot de Poilly described them, were ordered to proceed, when the signal was given, to the crenelated wall of the Princess Demi-Bastion, which faced the ocean. The untrained civilians could be sent there because it was thought an unlikely place for the British to attempt a landing.[81]

The best news to reach Louisbourg on June 1, 1758, came in the evening. Around 8:00 PM two officers of the Cambis Regiment reached Governor Drucour with the message that the troops of their battalion were finally on the soil of Île Royale, and they were making their way overland toward the stronghold. The ships carrying the Cambis battalion had crossed the ocean in twenty-seven days and moored in Saint Anne's Bay on May 29. Realizing the seaward approach to Louisbourg was blockaded, the commander of the squadron, Du Chaffault de Besné, proceeded to the relatively safe anchorage of Port Dauphin. For two days the troops remained on board five ships while their officers assessed the situation. Finally on May 31 two Cambis officers were ordered overland to Louisbourg to let Drucour know that the battalion was on its way. The officers also carried the latest dispatches from Versailles.[82]

The news of the imminent arrival of the 680–man Cambis troops must have spread swiftly throughout Louisbourg and down to the coastal positions. The battalion was already a month late, and many must have feared the ships carrying the soldiers were either captured or returned to France. Yet here they were, two of their officers at least, on the very day the British fleet appeared off the coast. The timing was perfect.

With the Cambis battalion a few days' march from Louisbourg, Drucour could mentally add them to the complement of military personnel defending the place. Once they reached the town he would have roughly 3,500 professional soldiers under his overall command. If one added the several hundred local militia to the total, along with the 150 or so Acadian and Native fighters, there would be over 4,000 land-based defenders. Drucour did not know it, but the besieging army was more than three times that figure. In fact, the British force had twice as many drummers (258) as the French had artillery specialists (120).[83] Of course, Drucour was not intending to meet the enemy in a pitched battle, in which case he would not have had a chance. As long as his defenders were not outnumbered by more than three or four to one, then he might have a chance. At least that was the standard ratio expected between besiegers and besieged. Then again, Louisbourg was not a typical fortified place. What Drucour was defending was many weeks sail from any significant reinforcements, and its site was low lying, easily commanded by artillery established on nearby hills. The best, and maybe the only, hope that Drucour had was to prevent the British from getting ashore in the first place. As long as the enemy stayed on board their ships, they could not capture Louisbourg, no matter how big their fleet was. Reduced to that simple fact, Drucour needed only enough defenders and sufficient artillery at each potential landing beach to repel the enemy.

The other "weapon" in Drucour's arsenal was the ships in the harbor, under the command of the marquis Charry des Gouttes. There were thirteen good-sized ships in port, with crews totaling 3,870 sailors. He could not add the four warships and the merchant vessel that transported the Cambis troops to Port Dauphin to the list, for there was little likelihood they would ever make it past the blockade and into port. In fact, he did not expect them even to try. It was not much compared to what he could see of the British fleet massing down the coast.[84]

As night fell on June 1, Governor Drucour and his senior officers went to their beds realizing they had, or were soon to have, all the resources they were going to get to defend Louisbourg. Over six hundred Cambis troops would be marching into town in the next couple of days, and there was still reason to believe that Boishébert would show up with a sizable contingent of irregulars. But that would be it. The conflict that had been building for a decade was coming to its moments of truth. All too soon the participants on both sides would find out if those moments would be of glory or of despair.

5

This Time for Real, June 1–7, 1758

The showdown building on and offshore at Louisbourg in the early days of June 1758 involved an enormous cast of characters. Including civilians, there were perhaps as many as thirty thousand individuals on the attacking side and ten thousand on the defending side. The names of only a few of those people appear in this narrative—invariably those at the top of the chains of command or individuals who left a written account or did something noteworthy. Despite the inevitable focus on leaders and decision makers, it is important to emphasize that the attack and the defense of Louisbourg in the summer of 1758 touched the lives of thousands of men, women, and children. Hundreds of people whose names we do not know were to die; hundreds more were injured; and thousands were eventually uprooted and sent across an ocean.

Dramatis Personae

Most of the central figures in the dramatic confrontation developing at Louisbourg in June 1758 have already made an appearance in the preceding pages. A few have not, and this section will mark their entry into the story. Regardless of whether the key players have been introduced to this point, it is worth pausing to offer a more complete portrait of the various individuals charged with leading either the defense or the attack.

The governor of Île Royale, Augustin de Boschenry, chevalier de Drucour, was the man who had the final say on how best to defend the stronghold of Île Royale in 1758. He held that distinction by default, not choice. Had the British fleet been less imposing in the spring of 1758, Drucour would have been relieved of his overall responsibility for the defense of the colony. Before he retired as minister of the marine at the end of May 1758 and was replaced by the marquis de Massiac, Peyrenc de Moras had selected Charles de Blénac-Courbon, the commandant at Brest, to take over the defense of the stronghold of Île Royale. Blénac-Courbon spied an imposing flotilla of enemy ships as his ship neared its destination, and he sailed back to Brest, leaving the governor in charge of the defense of Louisbourg in 1758.

Drucour turned fifty-five years old in March 1758, when he was in his fourth year as governor of Île Royale. Prior to that, most of Drucour's career had been on the naval side of the ministry of the marine. He entered the service at Toulon in 1719, and in the years that followed he gradually rose through the ranks and took part in sixteen major voyages to destinations as far-ranging as Stockholm, Constantinople, Martinique, and Saint-Domingue (Haiti). In 1730–31 he took part in the campaign against the Natchez in Louisiana. Drucour was en route to what is now Atlantic Canada in 1746, in the attempt to recapture the long-disputed territory of Acadie/Nova Scotia, when the British captured him on the high seas. Released in 1747, Drucour went on to receive his first appointment as a ship captain in 1751. At no point in his career did he seek a land-based appointment in a colony. Nonetheless, such an opportunity came his way in 1754, when the then minister of the marine, Machault d'Arnouville, offered him the governorship of Île Royale. Drucour declined the posting, claiming that a lack of family wealth made him ill suited for the job. He was not playing hard to get, because he knew governors were supposed to carry out their duties in a way that entailed many personal expenditures. In his case, though his family was noble (with its roots in Drucourt in Normandy), he was without significant income. Machault d'Arnouville persisted, however, and the career naval officer bowed to the pressure. He set sail to become the governor of Île Royale, based at Louisbourg, in the early summer of 1754. Accompanying him overseas was his wife, Marie-Anne Aubert de Courserac, and eight servants.

Madame Drucour (Courserac) was one of the few wives of high-ranking French officials to join their husbands on Île Royale, as most preferred to stay in France. It is not known how active a role Madame Drucour played in Louisbourg society before 1758, but she was to become prominent that summer.[1]

It is impossible to know for certain how the general populace in Louisbourg felt about Governor and Madame Drucour, though there is a hint that the governor was respected and perhaps even admired. In the words of one Louisbourg military officer, an individual generally highly critical of the leadership in the colony: "Our Governor is certainly a perfect man of honor." The qualities the officer was singling out for praise are unknown, but it seems that the governor could not be faulted for his willingness to live up to the hospitality and entertaining responsibilities of the position. Lacking deep family pockets, Drucour borrowed heavily while at Louisbourg, putting himself in a debt from which he would never escape.[2]

Though the chevalier de Drucour bore ultimate responsibility for the defense of Louisbourg in 1758, he turned for advice to the senior military and naval officers in the garrison and in port. Forty-one-year-old Mathieu-Henri Marchant de La Houlière was the person the king designated to command the land forces. At the time of his selection for the assignment, Marchant de La Houlière was king's lieutenant at Salces, near Perpignan in the south of France, where he had been since 1735. A veteran of nine sieges in Europe, Marchant de La Houlière could bring battle-hardened experience to the decisions he would make at Louisbourg. On the other hand, one who knew Marchant de La Houlière stated: "[He possessed] talent and goodwill, he has seen lengthy service, but nevertheless he is not one of those men made to command." As it was, Marchant de La Houlière's appointment came so late that there was no guarantee that he would even reach the colony. He sailed from Brest aboard the *Bizarre* on April 21, and as luck would have it, this ship was one of the last to slip past the British blockade and into Louisbourg harbor, on May 31. Better late than not at all, yet Marchant de La Houlière had reached his destination too late to make any meaningful changes in the defensive positions already established. The day after his arrival, June 1, was when Drucour set the defensive posture in place, in response to the large number of British sails that were spotted off Gabarus Bay.[3]

Marchant de La Houlière's naval counterpart at Louisbourg was Jean-Antoine Charry, marquis des Gouttes. Des Gouttes made it into port on April 24, in command of the seventy-four-gun warship *Prudent*. Rank and seniority determined the command structure, so des Gouttes, as the highest ranking naval officer at Louisbourg, automatically took charge of all the warships in the harbor. He would have to defer to Governor Drucour in the event of a disagreement on a major issue, something that was to occur repeatedly, with major consequences, in June and July 1758. When it came to routine matters, such as the deployment of the ships, men, and matériel to carry out an agreed-upon strategic decision, des Gouttes made the decisions alone.

The marquis des Gouttes was originally from Moulins in the Massif Central, close to the center of France. Despite the distance from the ocean, the family developed an attachment to the sea. His father was the commandant of the Gardes-Marines at Rochefort, a grand uncle had been lieutenant general of the navy, and Jean-Antoine Charry's own career began in 1725 as a naval cadet. He was promoted to lieutenant in 1741 and captained his first ship of the line in 1746. His one and only stay in Louisbourg would be brief, a matter of months, yet filled with long hours of deep anguish.[4]

Another key person on the French side was chief engineer Louis Franquet, who had joined the army at the age of twelve. He had served in infantry regiments for more than a decade and then in 1720 was admitted to the engineering corps. A veteran of many campaigns and sieges in Europe, Franquet first came to Louisbourg in 1750 to suggest ways its defenses could be strengthened. There were trips to France and Canada in the years that followed, and from 1754 onward he held the title of director of fortifications for all New France. Regardless, Louis Franquet spent more time at Louisbourg than anywhere else in the colonies, producing many elaborate designs for improved defenses. By the late 1750s Franquet was beset by debilitating health problems. In 1758, aged sixty-one, he was suffering from scurvy, dropsy, and probably other ailments. Ill and not very mobile, he was sometimes forced to give directions to subordinate engineers without actually seeing a given situation for himself. One assistant, the diarist Grillot de Poilly, described his superior as "a man of war, loving good . . . a gentleman and a good citizen; but unfortunately an illness which undermined his health had so weakened the body that the spirit of the man was lost, he only had moments."[5] Governor Drucour undoubtedly wished his chief engineer were in better shape to deal with the crisis facing them in June 1758.

One important figure at Louisbourg was neither soldier nor sailor nor engineer. Jacques Prévost de la Croix was the financial administrator (*commissaire-ordonnateur*) of Île Royale and primarily preoccupied with budgets and ledgers. He and his staff controlled the provisions, clothing, and some of the services, such as the hospitals, on which the soldiers and sailors depended. Moreover, it was Prévost who bore the responsibility of speaking on behalf of the civilian population. Senior military officers generally did not care to hear what Jacques Prévost had to say, but the man had a guaranteed seat at the war council table. Prévost was from Brest, of a family that had joined the nobility of the robe in his grandfather's time. Like his father and three of his brothers, Jacques entered the commissariat department at the marine arsenal in Brest. He first came to Louisbourg in 1734, aged nineteen, as principal writer and moved into higher and more demanding positions after he became the protégé of Île Royale financial administrator François Bigot. Injured during the siege of 1745, Prévost returned to France with the rest of the inhabitants. In 1746 he was shipwrecked as part of the failed expedition to recapture Louisbourg and Acadia. The following year he was named controller at Quebec but while on route to Canada was taken prisoner by the British off Cap Finistère. Prévost later returned to France and in 1749 was appointed financial administrator for Île Royale.

His promotion brought many turbulent moments, for Prévost had numerous personality and jurisdictional clashes with different governors and senior military officers during the decade he held the post.[6] Rightly or wrongly, the military officers resented Prévost's emphasis on following procedures and reducing expenditures. One officer, a Scottish Jacobite in French service, described the *commissaire* as a "finished rascal, vain and proud as a peacock, of the most obscure birth." Those above Prévost in the marine ministry, however, appreciated his administrative talents. When his career in Louisbourg came to an end, he went on to serve in a variety of capacities in France.[7]

The final person to be mentioned on the French side was someone who was not at Louisbourg in early June 1758 but whose arrival was eagerly awaited. That was thirty-one-year old Compagnies franches officer Charles Deschamps de Boishébert, a native of Quebec, who had a reputation for leading successful campaigns of irregular forces in Canada. Officials on Île Royale and the general populace hoped Boishébert would help them out during the coming siege of Louisbourg. Summoned from Quebec by Drucour in the spring of 1758, Boishébert brought with him five Compagnies franches officers from Canada, five cadets, and seventy volunteer soldiers, some of whom were Compagnies franches regulars. The expectation was that hundreds of Native warriors and Acadian resistance fighters would join Boishébert as he advanced toward Louisbourg. If that happened, a large force capable of forest warfare might make a significant difference to the defensive effort.[8]

Boishébert and his initial contingent left Quebec on May 8 aboard three vessels. Because of bad weather they did not reach Miramichi (in modern-day New Brunswick) until June 9. There Boishébert added seventy Acadians and sixty Native warriors to his force. Rumors of its imminent arrival at Louisbourg, with wildly inflated estimates of its size, waxed and waned in the days and weeks that followed. Such talk gave hope to the defenders and spread a measure of anxiety among the British.[9]

Turning to the British side, two figures towered over a cast of many thousand. One was Jeffery Amherst, in charge of the land forces; the other was Edward Boscawen, commander of the fleet. Both were considerably younger than those leading the French forces. At the start of June 1758, Major General Amherst was forty-one, and Admiral Boscawen was forty-six, though he would celebrate his forty-seventh birthday in August. Despite their relative youth, William Pitt and his closest advisers thought each possessed the leadership skills required to bring the British side a victory at Louisbourg.

Jeffery Amherst was from Kent, England, where his father and grandfather had been lawyers. His own military career began, so to speak, when he became a page for the Duke of Dorset, who subsequently helped him obtain an ensign's rank in the army at age fourteen. Recommended to General John Ligonier "as a young man of uncommon ability," Amherst became Ligonier's aide-de-camp in Germany. He served in that capacity at the battles of Roucoux, Dettingen, and Fontenoy. The protégé next joined the Duke of Cumberland's staff, where he continued to impress. His rise in the ranks took a major step in 1756, when he became lieutenant colonel of the Fifteenth Foot. Two years later came an even greater leap. In early 1758 William Pitt, on the recommendation of chief of staff General Ligonier, selected Amherst to command the expedition fitting out at Portsmouth to wrest Louisbourg from the French. One of Amherst's preeminent qualities was said to be his "absolute self-control," a trait that set him apart from other young officers, like James Wolfe, who were prone to rash decisions. Another description of the rising officer was that he was "grave, formal and cold," which is perhaps how self-control appears to those who do not value it highly.[10]

In analyzing Amherst's account of the campaign in North America, historian G. M. Wrong notes that the major general was "kindly, thoughtful for others, so hard working that he is up sometimes at two in the morning." Other observations were that Amherst was "free from vanity" and "watchful to effect economy in the service, [and was] careful for the comfort of his men." Wrong could find fault with the commander of the land forces at Louisbourg only for his "excessive caution." James Wolfe would certainly have agreed with the last assessment. In many private letters written at Louisbourg, Wolfe hinted that the siege would have ended sooner if Amherst had made bolder moves.[11]

Amherst's naval counterpart at Louisbourg, Admiral Edward Boscawen, was a good fit with the commander of the land forces. Both leaders were meticulous planners, and neither let service rivalries or personality conflicts get in the way of collaboration. The harmony they found in their overall joint command was a quality often missing on the French side. Of course, the cliché from the world of sports is that winning teams are happier than losing ones.

Boscawen had links on his mother's side with some renowned names in British military history, notably the Churchill family. His own career at sea began in 1726 at the age of fifteen. By the time he was twenty-one, he had passed his naval exams and become a lieutenant. His postings then took him many places Great Britain had a colonial or strategic interests: the Mediterranean, the West Indies, the East Indies, and North America. Before the 1758 expedition, Boscawen had taken part in several combats, including the convincing 1747 victory over the French off Cap

Finistère (Brittany). In both 1744 and 1755, when hostilities erupted between Britain and France in separate wars, Boscawen was the first British officer to capture enemy ships. In one encounter he was wounded in the shoulder by a musket ball. The injury caused him thereafter to tilt his head slightly forward, prompting the nickname "wry-necked Dick." He earned a different nickname, "Old Dreadnought," from the crew of a ship he commanded as a young captain. Though Boscawen was a strict disciplinarian, ordinary seamen apparently liked and respected him because of his persistent efforts to improve their health and comfort. As previously noted, Boscawen was in Atlantic Canada in 1755, to command a squadron intercepting French ships heading for Louisbourg and Quebec and to play a role in the forcible removal of the Acadians. That same year Boscawen became a vice-admiral. Three years later, in February 1758, he was named Admiral of the Blue and commander in chief of the naval forces bound for Louisbourg. While naval assignments took up most of his time, Edward Boscawen did have a seat in Parliament, representing a district in Cornwall, though he rarely attended sessions. In the 1758 campaign at Louisbourg, Admiral Boscawen was ably served by his experienced second-in-command, Sir Charles Hardy.[12]

The army officers immediately below Amherst in the command structure deserve an introduction as well. There were three brigade commanders: Edward Whitmore, Charles Lawrence, and James Wolfe. Each received the same rank, a temporary assignment as a "brigadier in America," yet their responsibilities differed widely as did the mark they left on the course of events at Louisbourg.

Edward Whitmore was by far the oldest of the senior British officers at Louisbourg; he turned sixty-four in 1758. His long career included an unsuccessful expedition against Quebec in 1711 and a role in putting down a Jacobite uprising in Scotland in 1715. Whitmore subsequently spent over twenty years in Ireland, then moved on to the West Indies in 1740, Flanders in 1745, and back to Scotland for the battles of Falkland and Culloden in 1746. In 1757 Whitmore was named colonel of the Twenty-second Foot and sent to Halifax. As the expedition against Louisbourg took shape in the early months of 1758, Edward Whitmore found himself named to command one of the brigades under Amherst's overall command. Fellow brigade commander James Wolfe described

Whitmore him as "a poor, old, sleepy man," but then Wolfe was critical of everyone around him. Others on the British side were more charitable toward Whitmore. Montague Wilmot called him a "truly amiable Person," and Jeffery Amherst said he was "a worthy Good Man." It sounds like the faint praise it probably was.[13]

As for Charles Lawrence, by 1758 he had already left an indelible mark on Atlantic Canada. Lawrence joined the British army in 1727 and subsequently served in the West Indies, the War Office, and on the European continent. In 1747 he was at Louisbourg, then under British occupation, as a newly promoted major of the Forty-fifth Regiment. Lawrence proceeded to Halifax when it was founded in 1749 and in 1750 established a fort that was named after him atop Beaubassin Ridge in the Chignecto region. In 1753 he oversaw the establishment of a "foreign Protestant" settlement at Lunenburg. Two years later, as acting governor of Nova Scotia, Charles Lawrence played the leading role in the decision to forcibly remove every Acadian from Nova Scotia. Those who admired him, which did not include any Acadians, described Lawrence as an "enormous, bluff, and competent man."[14]

The third of Amherst's brigade commanders was James Wolfe, who at thirty-one was the youngest of the senior officers. Wolfe came from a military family, and grew up in Westerham, Kent, four miles from Amherst's home. Wolfe's father and uncle were both high-ranking officers in the British army, and his younger brother was to serve as well. James Wolfe began his career with an appointment at age fourteen to the regiment in which his father was colonel. He soon switched into the Twelfth Foot and later into the Fourth Foot. He saw action on the European continent at the battle of Dettingen and then in Scotland during the Jacobite uprising of 1745–46. In 1748 he was made a major of the Twentieth Foot, then acting colonel in 1749. During the winter of 1752–53 Wolfe went on leave and spent six months in Paris. In 1757 he was the quartermaster general of the failed expedition against Rochefort. Soon afterward the battalion he commanded was split off from the Twentieth Foot and converted to a new regiment, the Sixty-seventh, of which he became the colonel. It was the highest substantive rank he would ever reach.[15]

Wolfe had a reputation for bold actions, a quality William Pitt and General John Ligonier were looking for in their quest to reenergize the stalled campaign in North America. As one historian puts it, Wolfe's superiors knew he was "half-mad with enthusiasm, and might in a fit of enthusiasm run his army into a very perilous position."[16] To balance the risk Pitt and Ligonier placed the unpredictable Wolfe under the command of the always-prudent Jeffery Amherst. James Wolfe arrived in Halifax on May 9 and chafed at the weeks of waiting that followed. At last, in the early days of June 1758, Wolfe found himself off the coast of Louisbourg and eager to make a descent. Tall and gangly with bright red hair, often brandishing a cane, Wolfe soon became the most recognizable figure on the British side in the 1758 expedition.

The individuals sketched here, French and British, were the principal decision makers at Louisbourg in 1758. We cannot name the thousands of combatants beneath them in their respective command structures, but we can make a few general points. The most obvious is that the combatants were virtually all male. We insert the word "virtually" because there is the occasional mention of women doing more than cooking, cleaning, and other camp activities during the Louisbourg campaign. The most celebrated is Marie-Anne Aubert de Courserac, Madame Drucour, wife of the French governor. In an attempt to boost the morale of the defenders, Madame Drucour walked the Louisbourg ramparts daily throughout the siege to fire three symbolic cannon blasts to keep up the spirits of the French soldiers.[17] Meanwhile, on the British side in at least one instance women became actively involved in the campaign. James Wolfe noted in a letter written just after the end of the siege that the soldiers "worked with the utmost cheerfulness, and upon one occasion several women turned out volunteers to drag artillery to the batteries."[18] Such an involvement appears to have been exceptional. More commonly, women on the British side were associated with camp life, such as the selling of rum. Admiral Boscawen asked Amherst at one point during the siege to banish "that pernicious liquor . . . from [his] camp." He averred, "I know the women of the Highlanders, & the Royals to be notorious sutlers."[19]

The wars of the twentieth and twenty-first centuries leave the impression that most enlisted men are young and get whipped into shape by an older complement of officers, NCOs, and longtime permanent soldiers. The data on eighteenth-century armies sometimes presents a slightly different picture. It was era when more emphasis was placed on the "steadiness and experience of veterans rather than the headlong courage of youth." Thus, the average age in the Prussian army of 1783 was 31.6, while that of the British army in America at the time of Revolutionary War was about 30. Recent research on the Fifty-eighth Foot (Anstruther's), one of the regiments raised in 1757 and sent to Louisbourg, reveals that its soldiers were closer to the modern model, for 79 percent were under thirty and 89 percent had been in service for one year or less. Meanwhile, records on the wounded from all regiments in three separate British campaigns (Braddock's in 1755, Louisbourg in 1758, and Guadeloupe in 1759) similarly point to an age profile that has soldiers enlisting in their early twenties. On the French side the average age of the Compagnies franches soldiers in the Louisbourg garrison during the period 1751–53 was twenty-seven. With little turnover in the years that followed, the average age of the one thousand or so Compagnies franches troops in the fortress in 1758 would have been about thirty-two. Comparable figures are not available for the four battalions of the Troupes de Terre that came to bolster Louisbourg's garrison between 1755 and 1758.[20]

Of course, average ages reveal nothing about those who were much younger and much older. The eldest of the combatants on the British side at Louisbourg was likely Sergeant Donald Macleod in the Seventy-eighth/Sixty-third Regiment (Fraser Highlanders). Macleod was seventy years old at Louisbourg and still in active duty as a sergeant. In 1759 he would go on to Quebec, where he was injured on the Plains of Abraham. Years later, at the age of eighty-seven, MacLeod enlisted in Clinton's army in New York during the early stages of the American Revolution.[21] It is impossible to say how many soldiers were in their fifties and sixties, but there were likely more than a few. Recall that in chapter 4 we discussed the impact that the seventy-four-year old French naval officer, the dynamic comte du Bois de la Motte, had on Louisbourg's outlying fortifications in 1757.

Besides age it is important to at least mention questions of ethnicity and race. In a conflict that was ultimately a struggle between France and Great Britain, about which power would be preeminent in northeastern North America, it is easy to assume that the combatants facing off at Louisbourg in 1758 were French and British. We need to recall that the battalion of the Volontaires Étrangers that reached Île Royale in the spring of 1758 was composed of not French but foreign nationals fighting in the service of Louis XV. The other French regimental battalions and the Compagnies franches de la Marine troops would have had at least a few non-French soldiers in their units as well. On the British side the understandable desire was to recruit only soldiers who were likely to be loyal to the ruling monarch. That meant there were fears and instructions to reject or avoid Roman Catholics, whether they be French, Scottish, or Irish. Swiss and Germans were no problem as long as they were Protestants, like the royal family, who were from Hanover yet invited to sit on the British throne in the early eighteenth century. Despite the injunctions against Catholic enlisted men, the need for men in ranks meant that more than a few Roman Catholics were wearing the redcoat. When recruiting for British regiments took place in the Anglo-American colonies, the direction was not to enlist any runaway servant, "Negro, Mulato, or Indian." That instruction related to men who might bear arms in regular service, for there was a already a tradition of black men and boys serving as drummers and musicians, just as there was a desire to have Native warriors to participate as "irregulars" in ranger companies.[22]

Offshore, Onshore

The first British ships of the massive armada that set off from Halifax on May 28 arrived off the coast of Louisbourg on June 1. Governor Drucour observed "70 sails" that day, which means that the rest of the vessels were either not tall enough to be seen from the Louisbourg ramparts or had not yet reached Gabarus Bay. It was not until around 4:00 PM on June 2, for instance, that the *Namur*, carrying Amherst and Boscawen, sailed into the bay. As of June 7 nearly two hundred vessels were either anchored within Gabarus Bay or cruising near Louisbourg harbor. That total consisted of 24 ships of the line, 19 frigates, sloops, fire ships, and other armed vessels, and 150 transports.[23]

Soon after the *Namur* arrived on June 2, Amherst, Wolfe, and Lawrence reconnoitered the shoreline along Gabarus Bay. Edward Whitmore was not with them because the ship carrying him had not yet reached the rendezvous spot. Following their visual inspection of the shoreline, Amherst, Wolfe, and Lawrence decided to abandon the preliminary plan of attack drawn up in Halifax, which called for Wolfe to land three thousand men along the Mira River and then march overland while the brigades under Whitmore and Lawrence tried to effect landings at Lorraine and Baleine north of Louisbourg harbor. From what they could see through their telescopes of the coastline near Louisbourg, the three senior officers decided it would be better to make the main descent at a beach closer to the French stronghold. That would eliminate having a long advance overland, using up valuable time. Such a direct approach would inevitably mean more British casualties, for the landings were going to be attempted exactly where the French were most prepared. But so be it, concluded Amherst, Wolfe, and Lawrence. The quality of the landing beaches at Pointe Blanche, Pointe Platte, and Anse de la Cormorandière was too good to ignore. So what if those beaches received entrenchments and soldiers in 1757 and were manned again in early June 1758? The British leadership convinced themselves that the forces under their command would be able to overcome whatever resistance the French defenders might put up.[24]

After studying the "Chain of Posts" the French had on the beaches, Amherst, Lawrence, and Wolfe "made a Disposition for landing in three places the next morning, in case the Troops arrived." At the time only about one-third of the troops were available. Most of the remaining transports came in the next day. When June 3 dawned, however, Amherst decided a descent could not be attempted because "the surf on shore was so great, it was impossible to land." The commander rescheduled the descent for the following day.[25]

Sometime on June 3 Jeffery Amherst sat down aboard the *Namur* to compose an address to all the officers and enlisted men under his command. His expectation was that a landing was imminent, and he wanted to offer words of inspiration as well as practical instructions. Amherst could not speak personally to the thousands of men aboard the two hundred or so vessels bobbing off Gabarus Bay so copies of his address were distributed and read aloud on each ship. As a written text, the six-page eve-of-battle speech offers a revealing insight into what was on Major General Amherst's mind as military action loomed.[26]

Amherst began his remarks by encouraging everyone under his command to show "Zeal & Valour" because "His Majesty & the Nation . . .

[had] their Eyes fix'd on the Operation of this great Fleet & Army." The troops were to pay "exact Obedience to all orders" and "to live in Friendship & Harmony amongst each other." The commander reassured his listeners that their well-being was a concern of the senior officers. There was a "sufficient Quantity of Provisions and Stores"; "there will be an Hospital, and in time, it is hop'd there will be fresh meats for the Sick and Wounded." Following the words of comfort, the major general issued a few warnings to potential malcontents. The "least Murmur or Complaint . . . [would] be checked with the greatest severity, and Backwardness in sights of the Enemy [would] be Punished with imediate Death." Likewise, anyone who deserted to the enemy would be "hang'd with Infamy as a Traitor."

Amherst then spelled out what he was looking for from the officers, NCOs, and ordinary enlisted men. Regular infantry soldiers were to advance on the French positions, "discharge their Pieces loaded with two Balls and then rush upon them with their Bayonets." With the Highlanders the direction was a little different. Their specific commander was encouraged, "when He [saw] occasion, [to] order His Corps to run upon them with their drawn Swords." Finally, the major general spoke of the light infantry, especially formed for the Louisbourg campaign. Their primary role, in Amherst's words, was "to oppose the Indians, Canadians and other Painted Savages of the Island, who [would] entertain them in their own way." Though Amherst had never before set foot on North American soil, he had deep-seated opinions about the Native warriors his troops might encounter. He elaborated at length on what he took to be the "barbaric" tendencies of the Native allies of the French, describing them as "the only Brutes and Cowards in the creation who were known to exercise their Crueltys on the Sex [women], and to Scalp and mangle the poor sick Soldiers and Defenceless Women." Amherst asserted that the light infantry troops would make "[t]hese Howling Barbarians . . . fly before them." It is unlikely that the major general was consciously or cynically trying to "demonize" the enemy as a motivational device for the ordinary enlisted men. Far more likely the commander of the land forces at Louisbourg had read and heard, and accepted at face value, many accounts about forest warfare in North America. This section of his address was aimed to reassure the troops, and perhaps himself, that there was nothing to fear from the Native warriors he thought were waiting on the shores near Louisbourg.

Amherst's speech then switched to how the landing and subsequent operations were going to unfold. He could not, and did not, show the slightest doubt that everything was going to proceed smoothly, with the possibility of simultaneous landings in different parts of the island. Once ashore, Amherst affirmed, "the Business [was] half done." Siege camps would then be established "slightly Entrenched or Pallisaded, that the men [might] ly quiet in their Tents." Sentries would keep a lookout for "miserable lurking Mickmacs whose Trade [was] not War but Murder." Amherst's return to the subject of the Native allies of the French under-scores just how deep was his fear and hatred of such warriors. It was a sentiment that would lead him, only a few years later, to sanction the idea of spreading smallpox-infested blankets among Britain's Aboriginal en-emies in the Ohio country.[27]

The rest of Amherst's address focused on practical matters. Drunk-enness was forbidden as a general rule: "[B]ut a Man who is Drunk on any kind of Duty will be Punish'd without mercy." There were injunc-tions to the soldiers to show respect and obedience where appropriate and to keep firearms and equipment in good repair and a state of readi-ness. The commander admitted this might not be easy because "the Air of Cape Breton is moist & foggy," and there was a risk of "the Dews Drop-ping of the Trees, when they [were] in search of ye Enemy." Amherst's most explicit directions were given to the light infantry unit, which he expected to lead the way during the landing. The commanding officer put forward a few combat platitudes. "Pushing at the Enemy when they see them in Confusion & that the Ground favours their Efforts, never to pursue with too much eagerness, nor to give way but in a very great inequality of Numbers, they must avoid huddling togather & running into a Lump."

On June 4, the day after the commander's address to the troops, Am-herst recorded that "the Wind and Surf were so very high that Admiral Boscawen told [him] it was impracticable to land." It was a similar story on June 5, when there was "a great swell and Fog in the morning." The days were ticking by, and in the back of the minds of both Amherst and Boscawen must have been the failed attempts at Rochefort and Louisbourg the year before, when the British came away empty handed. The careers of the commanders of those two campaigns suffered as a consequence, and neither Boscawen nor Amherst nor any other senior officer wanted a repeat.

When Amherst woke on June 6, he noted there was "an Appearance of Change of Weather . . . [he] was resolved to seize the first opportunity." He gave the signal between 5:00 and 6:00 AM for the soldiers to prepare for a landing. By 8:00 AM "all the Men were in the boats," and the assault on Louisbourg was imminent. Then the fog moved in, the swell of the waves increased, "and the Admiral again declared it impracticable to land." The next day, June 7, the weather was once more poor in the morning. It improved in the afternoon, with the swells subsiding, and Amherst and Boscawen expressed "great hopes of landing at day break the next morning." That would be June 8.[28]

Historian J. S. McLennan maintains that Admiral Edward Boscawen took a great risk by anchoring the huge British fleet in crowded quarters in Gabarus Bay in the early days of June 1758. McLennan points out that the prevailing easterly winds and the poor visibility caused by fog that first week of June gave the French at Louisbourg a definite advantage, if only they had exploited the situation. The historian cites assistant engineer Grillot de Poilly, who claimed that the commander of the fleet at Louisbourg, the marquis des Gouttes, "might have immortalised himself" by launching a strike against the British fleet when they did not expect it. Grillot de Poilly envisioned the French naval commander sailing out of Louisbourg harbor with six warships to make a sudden descent on the British fleet, whose ships would have difficulty maneuvering and defending themselves. With his ships emerging out of the fog with a good wind at their back, des Gouttes "might have driven in to the fleet and with his six vessels destroyed it entirely." Such was Grillot de Poilly's assessment. Of course, the engineer provided this assessment after the fact, with the clarity that hindsight always provides when we know what happened instead. The engineer added that the captain of the sixty-four-gun warship *Bizarre*, which had made its way past Sir Charles Hardy's squadron into Louisbourg harbor on May 29, proposed precisely the same course of action. The more senior officers, presumably des Gouttes and Drucour, dismissed the idea, giving "to his project the name of the vessel he commanded," bizarre.[29]

The boldness of an unexpected French attack on the much larger British fleet at Gabarus Bay in early June 1758 still has an appeal for armchair admirals. From where Governor Drucour and the marquis des Gouttes stood, however, the proposed maneuver carried more risks than rewards. Suppose the French warships did not devastate the enemy fleet, which after all was much larger than that of the French. Could the individuals responsible for the defense of Louisbourg justify to themselves, and later to their superiors in France, that it was a heroic failure? If the bold stroke failed to destroy or weaken Boscawen's fleet, and there were still enough British ships of the line around to force an entry into Louisbourg harbor, would not the British have been able to make even quicker work of Île Royale than otherwise? And thus move on to attack Quebec the same season? Back in February 1758 no less a figure than William Pitt had instructed Boscawen that if at all possible he would "not omit attempting to Force the harbor of Louisbourg . . . as the Success of that Operation [would] greatly tend to shorten and facilitate the reduction of that Place."[30]

Still, what if? Could a half-dozen French warships realistically have made it past Hardy's patrol of the harbor entrance, then outdueled two dozen British ships of the line and nearly as many frigates and sloops in the crowded anchorage of Gabarus Bay? Success would have required incredible good luck as well as skill and daring. Of course, the element of surprise can be a powerful equalizer. Yet it seems unlikely that the surprise would have been maintained if there had been any cannon fire from either side as the French ships tried to slip out of the harbor past Hardy's squadron. The cannons of the British ships would certainly have signaled Boscawen's fleet if they suspected the French were leaving Louisbourg. On the other hand, if the fog was so thick that it cloaked a French exit and advance, those very conditions would have posed grave risks to the French ships as they attempted to make their way along the rocky coast toward Gabarus Bay. Grillot de Poilly commented that the worst thing that could have happened with the surprise attack was that the six French warships would have been lost. The land-based military engineer obviously did not grasp the value of those ships to the king's navy and treasury and as a deterrent keeping the British from entering the harbor and shortening the coming siege. Warships were not something one casually sacrificed, like an advance earthwork battery. The cost and consequences were in completely different leagues. Moreover, Grillot de Poilly likely did not know that Governor Drucour had specific orders from the minister of the marine to do everything he could to prolong a siege at Louisbourg. Sending outnumbered warships to attack the British fleet was a high-stakes gamble Drucour chose not to take.

To return from the topic of what might have happened at Louisbourg to what actually did occur in early June 1758, the French made themselves busy at the potential landing beaches while Amherst and Boscawen were waiting offshore for the right surf conditions to launch their amphibious assaults. On June 2 Governor Drucour ordered reinforcements sent to all landing spots. After sunset the French thought they detected a British feint toward Anse à Gauthier, to the north of Louisbourg. Additional troops marched to that location, while a call went out to all available troops and militia to proceed to the seaward front of the town. There, between Rochefort Point and the Princess Demi-Bastion, soldiers and armed civilians waited all night. It proved to be a false alarm. Meanwhile, on June 3 the British began to bombard French positions at Anse de la Cormorandière, south of Louisbourg. The firing continued all day long, primarily from the twenty guns on board the frigate *Kennington*. The bombardment injured several and killed a French cannoneer and a civilian (the usher of the Superior Council). The French returned fire throughout the day, killing three and wounding six on board the British frigate. Around 6:00 PM the British gunners got lucky when one of their shots struck a supply of French gunpowder. The resulting explosion destroyed the surrounding retrenchment.[31]

The rough seas of June 4 convinced the French, as they did Boscawen and Amherst, that there would be no attempted landing that day. French attention turned instead to the *Kennington*, which was seriously damaging the entrenched defenses at Anse de la Cormorandière. With heavier ordnance, the French believed, they could force the British frigate to move back, thereby reducing its effectiveness. The officer in charge at Anse de la Cormorandière, Mascle de Saint-Julhien, asked Drucour for more artillery pieces. The governor turned to the naval commander, des Gouttes, and requested 250 sailors, some to help bring the additional cannons to Anse de la Cormorandière and the rest to go to Pointe Platte.

As it turned out, the *Kennington* pulled back on June 4 and stopped firing. Observers on shore thought the British frigate had suffered damage to its rudder. When the rough and foggy conditions continued on June 5 and 6, the defenders had more time to strengthen their positions. They moved two mortars and three twenty-four-livres guns to Pointe Platte and to Anse de la Cormorandière. On the afternoon of June 5, Drucour traveled to the latter area, undoubtedly on horseback, to see the situation firsthand. The fog was so thick he could not even make out the British ships offshore.[32]

When the governor returned to Louisbourg on June 5, he learned that about half the Cambis troops were now at the Mira River, still a day or two from town. The other half had not yet left Port Dauphin. They were waiting for small boats to take them to Baie des Espagnols (Sydney harbor), from which they would proceed overland to Louisbourg. Drucour cannot have been pleased. As soon as weather conditions improved, the British would presumably be making a descent. The governor needed every able-bodied man-at-arms he could muster to drive the enemy back. That meant a lot of bodies because the potential landing areas were numerous and spread out to the north and the south of Louisbourg. Indeed, the fortified town itself had relatively few trained defenders in early June, mostly at coastal positions. Drucour wanted the 680 soldiers of the Cambis Regiment installed somewhere along the coast to help repel the enemy. That many veteran soldiers might be enough to keep the British from making it ashore.[33]

Between noon and 1:00 PM on June 6 the first contingent of the Cambis troops marched into Louisbourg. That same day a group of thirty Native warriors arrived in Louisbourg from the Halifax area. The Cambis troops were split up, with some sent to Pointe Platte and others to Pointe Blanche. First, however, they were given "some soup and some warmth." The physical needs of the soldiers camped at the remote, cold, and damp coastal entrenchments were also attended to. They were sent shoes and socks as well as portions of wine and spirits for the morning and evening. Grillot de Poilly commented: "[W]e are beginning to untie the purse strings; it is certain that the good will of our troops requires such considerations."[34]

Grillot de Poilly and Drucour differ on exactly how many men-at-arms were at the various entrenched positions along the coast on June

1. Demi-Bastion Dauphin
2. Bastion du Roi
3. Bastion de la Reine
4. Demi-Bastion Princesse
5. Bastion Brouillan
6. Bastion de Maurepas

Lighthouse

Royal Battery

Lighthouse
Point

Pointe à
Rochefort

Island
Battery

Cap Noir
(Black Rock Point)

ATLANTIC
OCEAN

Pointe Blanche
(White Point)

0   0.5   1.0   1.5 km

Anse de la
Cormorandière
(Kennington Cove)

Gabarus Bay

Pointe Platte
(Simon Point)

MAP 3. **Louisbourg, 1758**
This modern map provides an orientation for the key events during the early stages
of the 1758 siege. The amphibious landing led by Brigadier James Wolfe occurred at
Anse de la Cormorandière, while other flotillas made feints to land at Pointe Platte
and Pointe Blanche, headlands closer to Louisbourg. Once ashore the British established base camps on both sides of Freshwater Brook, roughly half way between
Anse de la Cormorandière and the fortified town of Louisbourg.

6, though their numbers were not far apart. Anse de la Cormorandière was judged the top priority because it had between 970 and 985 defenders. Pointe Platte had between 620 and 710, while Pointe Blanche was guarded by between 200 and 250. Only Grillot de Poilly offered figures for the Island Battery (100 men) and the distant settlements of Port Dauphin and Port Toulouse (30 soldiers between the two of them). Both diarists mention a reserve force posted at the Montagne du Diable in the Gabarus area. The governor said the reserve was made up of 150 men, while the engineer gave the number as 192.[35] The idea of a reserve was excellent, though in the era before motorized transport it was important that the distance not be more than a few hours walk away. It was no easy matter to march troops from one location to another. There were roads and paths through the woods, but the distances were considerable. Drucour ordered the defenders to move wherever the need was greatest when the attack came, which sounded fine on paper but might mean little in the heat of an attack. With so many possible landing spots along the coast on both sides of Louisbourg harbor, it would be fortuitous if the French reserve force happened to be close to where the British landed.

At the end of the first week of June 1758, Governor Drucour had roughly two thousand men-at-arms—a mix of regimental soldiers, Marine troops, and Acadian and Native irregulars—at various scattered positions along the coast and another two thousand soldiers and militia standing guard within the walls at Louisbourg. Everywhere the manpower was spread thinly. The coastal positions were remote from one another, and even within the fortress the enceinte, or perimeter, extended 2.72 kilometers. Since individual defenders needed time away from their posts on a regular basis, there were more likely about seven hundred defenders in position on the walls of Louisbourg at any given time. Unlike the interior of New France, where the Canadian militia was a well-trained and highly regarded military force, Louisbourg had no such tradition. Still, better late than never, so in early June, the military organized the male civilians of Louisbourg into a structured militia. Each night a sizable force of men-at-arms, probably soldiers and militia, camped between Rochefort Point and Cap Noir, just in case the British tried a landing in that area.[36]

When the sea swells finally subsided on June 7, the hopes of Amherst

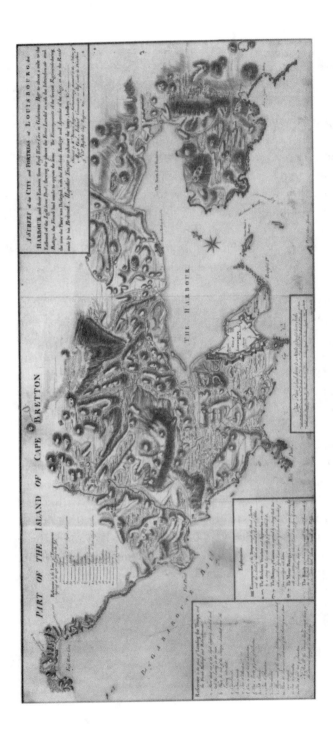

FIGURE 7: **Lay of the Land**

This British map drawn in 1758 shows essentially the same area as map 3, only this time with the various heights of land emphasized. *Courtesy of William L. Clements Library, University of Michigan.*

and Boscawen rose. The descent, already put off for five straight days, might finally occur. Accordingly, the two British commanders decided they would confuse and misinform the French defenders about what was soon to be attempted and where it was going to unfold. On June 7 Amherst and Boscawen sent a small convoy of sloops close to the mouth of Louisbourg harbor. The vessels carried a supply of artillery pieces and the Twenty-eighth Regiment (Bragg's), recently arrived from Halifax. The sloops sailed past the harbor entrance in the direction of Lorembec and Anse à Gauthier. The action was a diversion, made in the expectation of thinning out the French defenders. The men of the Twenty-eighth Regiment were to remain bobbing offshore to the north of Louisbourg harbor until they heard or saw a signal that the time for the real descent had arrived.[37]

The British maneuver drew the response Boscawen and Amherst wanted. Drucour interpreted the sloops sailing past the port entrance as a sign that a landing was going to be attempted where his forces were the weakest. The governor ordered one detachment of soldiers to Lorembec and another to Anse à Gauthier. In other moves on June 7, Drucour sent an eighteen-livres cannon by boat down the coast to Pointe Platte, presumably quite close to shore. The journey overland would have been safer, but it would have taken longer. The commander of the French forces clearly did not feel that time was on his side.[38]

At noon on June 7, Major General Amherst issued operational orders for an amphibious landing, either later that day or early the next morning. The orders superseded those of June 3 and 4.[39] Once weather and wave action permitted, three divisions of rowboats filled with soldiers were to set out from the fleet moored in Gabarus Bay and head for three separate beaches. Amherst stressed the need for an element of surprise. He was not going to reveal until the last moment which beach was the primary landing area.

6

Attack and Defend, June 8–July 27, 1758

As midnight struck on June 7 and the calendar rolled over to June 8, sailors extinguished nearly all the visible lights on the British transports anchored in Gabarus Bay. The only exceptions were at the waterline, where lanterns hung over the sides of three vessels as signals. Near the waterline of the *Violet* were three lanterns, which according to Major General Jeffery Amherst's specifications, indicated where the boats making up the right wing of the assault were to form. That was the "white" division, commanded by Brigadier Edward Whitmore. Over the side of the *Saint George* were two lanterns, the signal for the "blue" division under Brigadier Charles Lawrence. The *Neptune*, to the left of both the *Violet* and the *Saint George*, had a single lantern suspended above the water. Near there, Brigadier James Wolfe's "red" division was to gather. Wolfe's flotilla was the smallest of the three contingents, but the one chosen to be the primary assault force. Over the next two hours, under complete cloak of darkness, all the troops chosen for the landings, or more accurately the two feints and the one true landing, lowered themselves from their transports into the boats waiting below. Amherst's orders of June 7 stated there was to be a "profound silence throughout the whole army, and, above all things, the firing of even a single musket must be avoided." The major general wanted to keep the

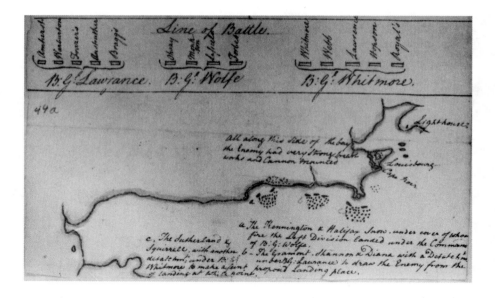

FIGURE 8. **The Assault Landing**

This British sketch shows the three divisions clustered behind warships prior to their setting off for the French-held coastline. The explanation above the drawing, titled "Line of Battle," places Wolfe's division in the center, between Lawrence's and Whitmore's. In truth, Wolfe's flotilla was the one to the far left, which set off for Anse de la Cormorandière (Kennington Cove). *Courtesy of William L. Clements Library, University of Michigan.*

French waiting or sleeping onshore to be guessing as long as possible about when and where the amphibious landing would take place.[1]

French accounts uniformly describe the British landing craft they saw on June 8 as barges. In fact, there appear to have been three types of small boats in the "motley flotilla" used by the British: whaleboats, flat-bottomed *bateaux* from New England, and the small boats off warships. Coincidentally, the British were developing a new design for standardized shallow-draft, flat-bottomed boats that could effectively transport large numbers of troops ashore, but those boats would not enter the service until after the 1758 attack on Louisbourg.[2]

June 8

Every soldier taking part in the British assault was in his designated longboat by 2:00 AM. Whitmore's white division was to row for Pointe Blanche, the headland closest to Louisbourg. The *Sutherland* (fifty-gun ship of the line) and the *Squirrel* (twenty-gun frigate) were to cover their advance with heavy firing. The men in that division were not to make a landing, just to make it look as if that were their intention. The feint would force the French to keep their troops on Pointe Blanche. The regiments making up Whitmore's division were the First (Royals), the Seventeenth (Forbes's), the Forty-seventh (Lascelles'), the Forty-eighth (Webb's), the Fifty-eighth (Anstruther's), and the Second British Americans (Sixtieth, Second Battalion). The Twenty-eighth (Bragg's) Regiment was also listed as part of the white wing, but it had sailed the day before to wait off the coast to the northeast of Louisbourg, near Lorembec and Anse à Gauthier.

The blue contingent under Charles Lawrence had instructions to make for Pointe Platte, with artillery cover to come from two frigates, the *Diana* (thirty-two guns) and the *Shannon* (twenty-eight guns), and a sloop, the *Gramont* (eighteen guns). As with Whitmore's division, the objective of the flotilla under Lawrence was to tie down French defenders in their entrenchments, thereby reducing the possibility that reinforcements might arrive at the one beach where the British were actually going to attempt a landing strike, Anse de la Cormorandière. Lawrence's orders did, however, give him the possibility of making a descent at or near Pointe Platte, or alternatively, if it looked as if the descent directed at Cormorandière was succeeding, to land there. The soldiers in the blue division came from the following regiments: the Fifteenth (Amherst's), the Twenty-second (Whitmore's), the Thirty-fifth (Otway's), the Fortieth (Hopson's), the Forty-fifth (Warburton's), and the Third British Americans (Sixtieth, Third Battalion). The Seventy-eighth (Fraser's) Regiment, also known as the Sixty-third, was listed as part of Lawrence's wing, yet it actually formed part of the division commanded by James Wolfe.

Amherst's orders to Wolfe were that he was to lead the red division ashore on June 8, at what the French called Anse de la Cormorandière. The landing boats that made up the red flotilla formed near the *Neptune*, to the left of Lawrence's wing, with the *Kennington* (twenty-gun frigate) and the *Halifax* (twelve-gun snow) to provide artillery cover when the moment came. The youngest and most active of the three brigadiers and the most eager to go into battle regardless of the risks, Wolfe was the logical choice to lead the assault on French shore positions. In addition to his other qualities, Wolfe was generally well liked by his soldiers because he respected them, as was demonstrated by his habit of addressing them as "Brother Soldier."[3] Assisting Wolfe in leading the contingent ashore were Major Alexander Murray, who had overseen the deportation of the Acadians from Fort Edward/Pisiquid (Windsor, Nova Scotia) in 1755, and a Colonel Fletcher. An even more important figure in the landing contingent was Major George Scott, a career military officer who had induced Thomas Pichon to spy for the British back in the early 1750s and who had played a prominent role in the siege of Beauséjour in 1755.[4] In the spring of 1758 at Halifax, Scott had put together a light infantry unit especially for the task at hand. He selected 550 marksmen from different British regiments and 500 irregular soldiers from the Anglo-American colonies with an eye to forming a mobile contingent that could handle itself in the North American style of woodland warfare. Its primary mission on the morning of June 8 was to find a way ashore at Anse de la Cormorandière, not an easy task given the felled trees (abatis) blocking the two main beaches and the artillery and musket fire the French were going to direct at the landing areas. The British did not know exactly how many French soldiers and Native warriors there might be in the entrenched positions, but they hoped the feints by the white and blue flotillas would at least keep reinforcements away from the red as they made their landing.

In addition to Scott's complement of light infantry, Wolfe's division contained handpicked soldiers of the First (Royals), the Fifteenth (Amherst's), the Seventeenth (Forbes's), the Twenty-second (Whitmore's), the Thirty-fifth (Otway's), the Fortieth (Hopson's), the Forty-fifth (Warburton's), the Forty-seventh (Lascelles'), the Forty-eighth (Webb's), the Fifty-eighth (Anstruther's), the Sixtieth, Third Battalion (Moncton's), the Sixtieth, Second Battalion (Lawrence's), and the Seventy-eighth/Sixty-third (Fraser's). Each soldier going ashore at Anse de la Cormorandière, both light and regular infantry, carried his food with him, enough bread and cheese in his pockets to keep him going for two days.[5] The rest of what would be needed to sustain the assault—tents, blankets, provisions, field artillery pieces, and other essentials—would be sent ashore after the troops secured a foothold.

The matériel involved in the 1758 siege deserves more than a passing mention. The scale of the undertaking was such that an enormous quantity of stuff was needed to support the soldiers and sappers once they were on land. In terms of artillery the British had 51 brass guns and 37 iron pieces ready to go ashore, with 24–pounders being the most numerous in both cases. As for shot, the British had over 43,000 iron cannonballs (of different calibers) and much smaller quantities of tin case shot, bag shot, and grapeshot. There were also 52 mortars to be taken ashore, all but one of which were brass. Most were small, highly portable mortars; thirty with a 4 2/5 inch diameter and ten with 5 1/2 inch. There were over 45,000 fixed fuses and nearly 42,000 shells, mostly for the smaller mortars. Other items to support the siege included 115,000 sandbags, 105 scaling ladders, 150 mantelets (screens or curtains, usually of rope, put up to protect artillerymen from enemy fire), nearly 726,000 musket cartridges with ball, 2,027 pick axes, 814 wheelbarrows, 2,336 spades, and 902 hand hatchets.[6]

Before the order was given to the red, white, and blue divisions to set off for shore, Admiral Boscawen ordered Commodore Philip Durell to row close enough to land to determine if the rolling surf was going to pose a problem. It would be a disaster if the boats flipped over or were driven against rocks. Durell's advice had led to the delays on June 5 and

7. This time Durell "found there was a Surf on the Shore, but not such as to prevent Boats landing." It was what Amherst and Boscawen were waiting to hear. Thousands of troops in hundreds of longboats were soon to be on their way. The only remaining matter, a vitally important one, was fifteen minutes of preliminary bombardment of the French shore positions. At 4:00 AM on June 8, at which time Boscawen wrote that the sun was beginning to rise, the *Kennington* and the *Halifax* began to fire at the entrenchments of Anse de la Cormorandière. The *Diana*, the *Shannon*, and the *Gramont* did the same for Pointe Platte and the *Sutherland* and the *Squirrel* at Pointe Blanche. Physical evidence of that bombardment came to light 229 years later. During the hot, dry summer of 1987, the ponds on Pointe Blanche dried up, and archaeologists counted twenty-two cannonballs and a large mortar fragment. At last, about 4:15 AM, the landing boats received their signals. The sky was lightening; the descent was under way.[7]

From their positions onshore, the French made out what looked like two flotillas of small boats. The larger one was heading to the left, toward Pointe Blanche, the smaller one toward Anse de la Cormorandière. The French could not know which was a feint, nor that the smaller contingent contained handpicked light infantry, irregulars, and Scottish Highlanders. Rather, it looked to the French for many minutes as if Pointe Blanche were the primary British target. The French commander at Pointe Blanche, d'Anthonay of the Volontaires Étrangers, ordered his two eighteen-livres cannons to open fire at the boats heading toward his headland. Grillot de Poilly recorded that "in spite of that the shallops kept advancing." Similarly at Pointe Platte the French artillery on shore pressed an active fire at the oncoming enemy flotilla. Meanwhile, within the town of Louisbourg, which was a few kilometers away, the sudden sound of prolonged cannon fire down the coast prompted a swift reaction. Drummers played the *générale*, the beat that signaled an immediate call to arms. Drucour, or senior officers, ordered a contingent of troops to proceed immediately to Pointe Blanche, the closest headland and another to nearby high ground until it was determined where the need was greatest.[8]

At Anse de la Cormorandière and there only, the French officers ordered the defenders to hold their fire until the advancing British boats came within close range. The commander of the Artois battalion, Mascle de Saint-Julhien, was in charge of the defense of the cove, so it would be his decision when the muskets and artillery would have their deadliest impact. Amherst would later write: "Enemy acted very wisely, did not throw away a Shot till the Boats were near in shore, and then directed the whole of their Cannon and Musketry upon them."[9]

Mascle de Saint-Julhien finally ordered the men lining the shore of Anse de la Cormorandière to fire around 5:00 AM. Sergeant James Thompson of the Seventy-eighth Regiment (Fraser Highlanders) was in one of the British landing boats and later offered an eyewitness description of what it was like advancing toward the shore. He recalled that only the officers and NCOs were seated, at the rear of the boat; the ordinary soldiers were packed so closely they had to stand. There was not even room for rowers in Thompson's boat, which was towed by a boat that had rowers. The Scottish sergeant related that when the French opened fire with their cannons, swivel guns, and muskets, the shots "came whistling about [their] ears." According to Thompson, "Nothing could be like it, and as our ships of war kept up a fire upon the batteries to cover our landing, there was a terrific hulabaloo." Any shot that happened to hit a tightly packed longboat had a deadly effect. Thompson recalled that one twenty-four-pounder French cannonball did strike the boat he was in and "did a great deal of mischief."

> It passed under my hams and killed Sergeant McKenzie, who was sitting as close to my left as he could squeeze, and it carried away the basket of his broadsword which, along with the shot, passed through Lieutenant Cuthbert, who was on McKenzie's left, tore his body into shivers, and cut off both legs of one of the two fellows that held the tiller of the boat, who lost an astonishing quantity of blood, and died with the tiller grasped tight in his hand! After doing all this mischief, the shot stuck in the stern post. Although this shot did not touch me, the thighs and calves of my legs were affected and became as black as my hat, and for some weeks I suffered a great deal of pain.

Sgt. Thompson's boat took many more hits over the next few minutes, so many that it would have sunk except that there were Highlanders on board. The Scottish soldiers used their plaids, which contained twelve yards of double-width tartan, to stuff the holes and keep the boat afloat. Weeks later, the boat would be "taken home to England as a great curiosity, for she was completely riddled with shot-holes, and nearly a bucket-full of musket balls and other small shot was taken out of her."[10]

Many boats endured similar hot fire. Major Alexander Murray recorded that there were "about 60 shot holes in [his] boat, yet nobody in her wounded." The onslaught from the French shore positions was terrifying to most, exhilarating to a few. One British sergeant stood up in one of the boats and shouted: "Who would not go to Hell, to hear such music for half an hour?" His exultation was short lived; a musket ball killed him moments later. In another incident a lieutenant opened his mouth wide to give a command, when "a musket ball went through it, and passed out at his cheek."[11]

The deadly fire from French cannons and muskets was not the only worry for the British soldiers coming ashore. There was also high surf, for the sea had grown rougher after Commodore Durell gave his assessment that the landing could proceed. A few heavily laden landing boats overturned on their way to shore, and some soldiers, weighed down by heavy uniforms, went to their deaths in the cold Atlantic water. An eyewitness wrote: "One Boat in which were Twenty Grenadiers and an officer was stove, and Every one Drowned."[12]

The British soldiers in Wolfe's red division were under strict orders not to return the French fire. Their muskets had to be loaded when they set foot on the landing beach, so they could storm the entrenched positions and not stop to reload. Under the stress of battle, at least one unnamed soldier, a member of the Fraser Highlanders, disobeyed the order. When the soldier seated beside him was shot and killed by fire from shore, the man instinctively raised his musket and returned fire. He picked a Native sniper positioned atop a rock outcrop along the Anse de la Cormorandière as the one who had fired the deadly shot. Though his boat was bobbing in the heavy surf, the Highlander hit his target. The warrior tumbled "down like a sack into the water . . . there was not a word said about it, but had it been otherwise he would have had his back scratch'd if not something worse. This shot was the best I have ever seen," offered another member of the regiment.[13]

Watching from the safety of the *Namur*, Admiral Boscawen was keeping track of the length of time each stage of the assault was taking. From his point of view, the intense fire from the French entrenchments at Anse de la Cormorandière lasted about fifteen minutes. Fifteen minutes may not sound long when one reads it in a book, but to those caught in the fierce French fire in the early morning hours of June 8, it must have seemed like an eternity. With casualties mounting and some boats overturned with men flailing and drowning in the water, James Wolfe signaled a retreat. The red division began the slow process of turning and rowing back to the transports through clouds of smoke and rolling surf. A landing would have to wait for another day, perhaps in another location. The brigadier's thoughts likely turned fleetingly to the original plan, before Amherst arrived, that had called for Wolfe to land along the undefended Mira River and then proceed overland toward Louisbourg. That longer yet safer approach was looking as if it might be the way the British would have to go to make a landing.

In the haze and hurry of the British retreat from Anse de la Cormorandière, with dozens of boats swinging round to head back to the transports, three boats went their own way. The men commanding and steering the three "barges" veered to the east, which may have looked to French observers onshore, if they could see the boats at all through the smoke blanketing the cove, as if they too were turning to head out to sea. They were not. Quite by accident the soldiers in the three British boats found themselves in an area that was out of sight of the entrenched French positions. When the officers in the boats—Lieutenants Hopkins and Brown and Ensign Grant—realized what they had achieved, they quickly decided to attempt a landing. The surf was riding high and rolling hard ashore, yet the officers ordered the men to row toward a narrow beachfront between two rock outcrops.

Meanwhile, out on the choppy waters of the Anse de la Cormorandière, James Wolfe, red division commander, and George Scott, in charge of the irregulars, noticed that three boats of redcoats were making their way ashore in an area "free from the Enemy's fire." Separately Wolfe and Scott ordered their boats and those nearby to proceed to the same spot. Wolfe, recounts an admiring biographer, stood up in the bow of his boat, with its flagstaff shot off, and used his cane to wave the troops on. Then, close to shore, the brigadier leaped into the water and led a charge up the cliff. Though undoubtedly embellished, the story does illustrate that Wolfe did immediately recognize the opportunity presented by the three boats that had made it ashore and did not hesitate to personally lead more soldiers to the same location. Had Wolfe and Scott not followed up so quickly, the advantage gained by the initial British contingent might have been lost.[14]

In the first three boats were about fifty infantry. They jumped out as soon as their boats scraped the gravel bottom of the shoreline. Unknown to the French, the enemy was on firm land. Two days later the commander of the French land forces, Marchant de La Houlière, would write that the enemy descended in an area thought to be "inaccessible" because of the rocks. How fatally wrong that assessment was![15]

The first British troops ashore quickly attached their bayonets to their muskets, which had been forbidden as long as they were in the tightly packed boats. Officers Hopkins, Brown, and Grant looked at the steeply rising ground in front of them—a virtual cliff—and ordered their men to climb. There was still no French fire, so it was clear to the British that no one knew where they were. The element of surprise would be on their side when they reached the top. Whether that would be enough, they were soon to discover.[16]

In climbing the cliff face there was no attempt to keep units together. In the words of one who was there on the beach, the men of the light infantry, Highlander, and regular grenadier units "intermixed, [then] rushed forward with impetuous Emulation, without Regard to any previous Orders." Another eyewitness wrote that it was the irregulars recruited and trained by Major Scott who made the difference when the British went over the top of the cliff and surprised the French positions: "Ye Rangers Started them first, they Ran and Hollow'd and fired on behind them and they [the French] left their Brest work."[17]

One British account of the events of June 8 used the words "eager Impatience" to describe the attitude of the troops going ashore. Such impatience is understandable, for the soldiers had spent months anticipating the moment, with many practicing landings while they were in Halifax. Yet the entire first week after they arrived off Louisbourg was marked by one delay after another, with the soldiers eager to get out of the crowded transport ships. The final wait—undoubtedly the worst of all except for those who enjoyed putting their lives on the line—was the quarter hour the red division endured as sitting ducks for French musket and artillery fire, all too aware they had orders not to return fire. The unexpected discovery of a landing place out of French sight lines suddenly turned a morning doomed to defeat into a moment of possible success.[18]

When Mascle de Saint-Julhien, overall commander at Anse de la Cormorandière, learned that the enemy had come ashore beyond the left flank of the entrenched positions and was attacking French troops in that area, he ordered the nearby Artois and Bourgogne soldiers to reinforce the threatened post. Long before they would arrive, however, the startled defenders on the left flank gave way. The British were coming at them from higher ground, a completely unexpected angle, and the defenders felt outnumbered, even though they were not, at least not initially. All too soon Mascle de Saint-Julhien saw his left flank yield and then outright flee. Suddenly his worry was that the British might come ashore in sufficient numbers to cut off all the remaining troops at Anse de la Cormorandière. If that happened, if the one thousand or so French and Native defenders at the cove were denied access to the road that led to Louisbourg, then Louisbourg's defense would be further weakened. In the heat of the moment, Mascle de Saint-Julhien decided that it was better to order the retreat of all remaining troops back to the fortified town than to risk their capture. Had the commander chosen instead to hurry all his soldiers to stem the tide of British coming up the cliff from the beach, the outcome on June 8 might have been different. If he had only known how few British there were ashore—150 men in the first wave—he undoubtedly would have marshaled his forces to drive them back into the sea. But Mascle de Saint-Julhien did not know that. An anonymous French diarist wrote that the hasty withdrawal from Anse de la Cormorandière to Louisbourg was "more a flight than a retreat." As a result boatload after boatload of British soldiers came ashore almost unopposed. And once they noticed the French were fleeing their positions all along the cove, the British began to land at the far end of Anse de la Cormorandière as well as at the initial spot. Any French defender straggling risked becoming trapped between the two contingents.[19]

French accounts of the events of the morning of June 8 say little about

how and why the British suddenly appeared at the top of the cliff overlooking Anse de la Cormorandière. All they knew was that their cover-
age of the cove was not as complete as they had believed. There was little
or no desire to dwell on the lack of foresight or preparedness. Yet it was
more than mere water under the bridge, for so much effort had gone into
establishing and manning the coastal entrenchments in 1757 and 1758.

The failure to prevent the British from coming ashore at the cove on
their very first attempt to land stunned the leadership in Louisbourg.
Assistant engineer Grillot de Poilly began his journal entry for June 8
with the words: "Fatal day for France." French accounts do not make it
clear as to any decision-making role that Mathieu-Henri Marchant de
La Houlière, overall commander of the land forces, played on June 8.
One French participant in the siege mentions in passing that Marchant
de La Houlière was injured at the time of the British landing, and that
"he was hampered by a bad leg, which prevented him from acting as he
would have wished." Where and when that injury occurred and how it
influenced the course of events on June 8 is unknown.[20]

The psychological impact on the Louisbourg leadership of the successful British landing was pronounced. A certain pessimism had always been
lurking in the background, and it came to the fore after the withdrawal
from Anse de la Cormorandière. Marchant de La Houlière composed
a letter to the minister of the marine on June 10 in which he stated that
"in spite of the works undertaken and the Excessive expenditures," the
fortifications at Louisbourg were in terrible shape. That being said, he
assured the minister: "[W]e will hold out, Sir, as long as it will be possible for the honour of the Arms of the King, and our own."[21] An official
aboard the *Prudent*, the seventy-four-gun warship anchored in the harbor, wrote: "[W]e are waiting for providence to decide our Fate." The
siege had not even begun in earnest, yet the leadership at Louisbourg
was close to acknowledging that they were doomed.[22]

Looking back on what unfolded at Anse de la Cormorandière on the
morning of June 8, 1758, we recognize three factors that snatched imminent victory away from the French and handed it to the British. First,
the French unleashed their fire on the British landing attempt before the
enemy actually set foot ashore. Amherst, a considerable distance away
aboard the *Namur*, thought the French did well to hold their fire as long

as they did, until the landing boats came close to shore. Yet the anonymous author of "An Authentic Account" was much closer to the action. His conclusion was that if the French had waited just a little longer, until the British boats were actually on the beach and the soldiers entangled in the abatis (upended trees), "the consequence [would have] been much more fatal to [the British], few if any of whom would have escaped." Another British diarist, an officer named Gordon, agreed: "Had the Enemy permitted the Troops . . . to have landed in the Cove, They must certainly have put it out of our power to have troubled them afterwards . . . we afterwards must have been at their mercy." Such a terrible death toll of British soldiers pinned down and immobile on the landing beach would likely not have led to the accidental discovery of a short stretch of shoreline beyond the left flank. A major loss of life would almost certainly have forced Amherst to reconsider making a direct assault on the landing areas closest to Louisbourg. The earlier British plan, to land on the Mira River and proceed overland, would have involved a long, slow advance through brush and bog.[23]

The second factor that altered the outcome of the morning's assault was the absence of someone assigned to an elevated lookout area with a view of all possible landing areas at Anse de la Cormorandière. A year earlier, when the British were off the coast in 1757 and Du Bois de La Motte was overseeing the establishment of entrenchments at the cove, a lookout had been posted on the ridge—the "magpie's nest"—that looked down on the small stretch of shore where the three British boats ended up landing. Was it cockiness or incompetence on the part of Mascle de Saint-Julhien that the post was not manned in 1758? It was probably a bit of both. On the topic of the "magpie's nest," the author of an anonymous French journal commented: "[U]nhappily we had not posted someone there, I do not know the reason." A British diarist offered, charitably, that "the Difficulty of Landing at this place was such that they [the French] thought the Devil himself would not have attempted it." If Mascle de Saint-Julhien had made sure someone was in that location on June 8, he and the other defenders would have known about the attempted British landing as it was occurring, instead of after the fact. Presumably, the closest French defenders would have had little trouble repulsing such a small contingent.[24]

The third factor that turned the tide for the British on June 8 was that in the short, pitched battle that took place when the British came over the cliff and raced down to fight the surprised and panicked French, there was no nearby reserve force to come to the defenders' support. In fact, Mascle de Saint-Julhien had no effective reserve anywhere at Anse de la Cormorandière. The defenders were strung out, too busy firing at retreating British boats to realize that an impromptu landing had taken place. Without support the French quickly ceded the ground and handed the British the descent, which only moments earlier they had vigorously denied.

The swift turn of events on the morning of June 8 could not have been predicted, for it involved sheer good luck for the British and disastrously bad fortune for the French. James Wolfe, the officer in command of the red division, made no attempt to claim what happened as being part of any plan. He wrote in a private letter: "Our landing was next to miraculous. . . . I wouldn't recommend the Bay of Gabarouse for a descent, especially as we managed it."[25]

Coming Ashore

Once they gained a foothold at Anse de la Cormorandière, the British moved swiftly to secure the position. They worried that a French and Native force might counterattack, yet there was no such attack. Mascle de Saint-Julhien and those under his command believed that the enemy was ashore in sufficient numbers to rout them, so their thoughts were for their own safety, and to not be captured and therefore lost for the next stage in the defense of Louisbourg. A sergeant in the Seventy-eighth Regiment recorded that his compatriots "seeing the French run away, could not resist the temptation of giving them a chase." The British officers did not send their men after the French, nor did they lead them; it was simply an instinctive reaction on the part of the Fraser Highlanders. "In an hour and a half or so they all came back again to a man . . . and almost every man of them brought in his prisoner and some had two." One of the French prisoners was an officer who was incensed that his sword had been taken from him. The officer insisted that it was enough to have lost his liberty, that as an officer he was entitled to keep his sword. The Scottish soldier who had captured the French officer was Duncan McFee, described by one who knew him as "a wick'd rascal as ever lived, and as bold as lion." McFee wanted the weapon as a war prize and would not return it to the Frenchman under any circumstances. The adjutant of McFee's company sought the advice of the colonel of the regiment, Colonel Fraser, to see if there was a way to appease the officer and still keep McFee happy. They decided that McFee should sell the sword to a British adjutant, who would then give it back to the French officer. The following day Duncan McFee noticed the French officer again wearing the sword and became infuriated. The British officers had to restrain McFee from hurting the captive and taking the trophy one more time.[26]

Though the British enlisted men, especially the Highlanders, had not been ordered to chase the French from Anse de la Cormorandière, and from Pointe Platte and Pointe Blanche as well, the eagerness the soldiers had shown for pursuit made a strong, positive impression on their officers. It was the sort of energy and combativeness they longed to see among their troops and was all the more remarkable with the Highlanders since some had been enemies of the English a mere dozen years earlier during the Jacobite uprising in Scotland. The redcoats gave up their pursuit of the French only when the heavy guns mounted on the walls surrounding Louisbourg fired at them. The warning shots stopped the British in their tracks, and it did them a favor. The cannon blasts revealed the range of the fixed artillery at Louisbourg. Consequently, the attackers learned where they could safely establish their opening siege positions.

The French flight from Anse de la Cormorandière was costly in more than the strategic ground given up and the number of soldiers lost as prisoners. There was also the abandoned matériel, in the form of artillery and other supplies. It was the same story at Pointe Platte, where the French commander ordered the troops to withdraw quickly to the protection of the fortress when he learned what was happening at Anse de la Cormorandière. Thus the French at Pointe Platte left behind swivel guns, cannons, and stores. Only at Pointe Blanche did the officer in charge order the matériel destroyed, though the cannons were neither blown up nor spiked. The British haul of weapons from the three main French coastal positions totaled seventeen cannons, two mortars, and fourteen swivel guns, as well as associated stores and supplies.[27]

The fighting that occurred on June 8 had not lasted long. The British bombardment of the French shore positions began around 4:00 AM, followed by the advance of the boats filled with British soldiers. Around 5:00 AM the French began their "very smart Fire at the Boats . . . which continued about 15 minutes, when it ceas'd, part of the Troops having Landed and driven the Enemy out of their Entrenchments." The subsequent pursuit of the fleeing soldiers and warriors heading toward Louisbourg continued for the next couple of hours. By 8:00 AM the fighting was essentially over for the day. Major General Amherst stated that the British losses were 4 officers killed and 5 officers wounded; 5 NCOs killed and three wounded; and 41 enlisted men killed and 55 wounded or missing. Another British source provides different numbers and distinguishes between both ranks and land and sea service. Whatever the totals, drowning brought about the greatest number of deaths, more than French artillery and musket fire, and rolling seas continued to be troublesome for days to come. Admiral Boscawen would later inform Amherst that "there were above a hundred boats lost in landing the troops and provisions." On the French side Governor Drucour placed the French losses at 114 men, a figure that included dead, injured, deserted, and captured. The last-mentioned category was by far the largest. Taken as prisoners on June 8 were 4 French officers and about 70 enlisted men, who were transferred to vessels moored along the coast.[28]

Of the many dead bodies littering the shore at Anse de la Cormorandière, the British were especially fascinated by the Native sniper the Highland sharpshooter had picked off as his boat was coming toward the beach. Amherst described him as "an Indian Chief," a man of "extraordinary size." Word of the height and girth of the man spread throughout the British troops, provoking so much curiosity that the cadaver was dug up not once but twice. The second occasion was at the request of Amherst himself, who wanted to see with his own eyes just how big the man was. Had it been a French soldier of a similar large size, one presumes, there would not have been the same interest. Indeed, the author of the account in which the disinterment of the cadaver is mentioned went on to state that the reason the body was "shown to the troops was to give them a dislike to the savages who were very numerous about the country. . . . this savage had been dug up for the purpose of giving [their]

Highlanders an opportunity of indulging in their favourite mode of inflicting casualties upon dead bodies, as they were consider'd to be mere Cannibals."[29]

By 1758 a mix of horror and fascination had long characterized the British view of the indigenous tribes of North America. A morbid interest in the large corpse at Anse de la Cormorandière was one manifestation of the phenomenon; so too were excesses committed by the British soldiers as they came ashore. An officer in one landing party wrote his wife that the British gave chase to the defenders, killing "a great many of the French and some Indians. . . . The men scalped the Indians & some peasants, but the soldiers were treated with the greatest humanity; we took a good many Prisoners." One imagines that the men the officer described as "peasants" were not wearing uniforms and therefore were French or Acadian militia. Olaudah Equiano, a highly literate slave aboard one of the British ships, wrote that he held in his hand on June 8 "the scalp of an Indian king, who was killed in the engagement; the scalp had been taken off by an Highlander." The antipathy between the British and their Native enemies ran deep.[30]

The success the British enjoyed in getting their troops ashore on June 8 did not extend to the supplies the soldiers needed. The height of the surf increased throughout the day, preventing the besiegers from sending field artillery, tents, and other stores. Had the French within the walls of Louisbourg realized the shortages the British were enduring, they might have organized a counterstrike on the somewhat vulnerable enemy contingent.

It would be June 9 before the first of the British tents made it to land. On June 10, recounted Amherst, "the surf still continued and it was with great difficulty that, we got anything on shore." To keep the men on land busy, and to prepare for possible counterattacks by French or Native skirmishers, the officers had their men erect defensive works of earth and stone at the rear of the siege camps that were being established. On June 11 the weather finally improved enough for the first British artillery pieces to be landed, six-pounders. It would be another full week, June 18, before the first of the larger artillery, twenty-four-pounders, made it to land. So rough were the sea conditions, according to Boscawen, that "there were above a hundred boats lost in landing the Troops and provisions." The figure is so high that it must include the losses of June 8 as well as on the days that followed. The transfer of stores from ship to shore was still continuing on July 3.[31]

Despite the delays in landing matériel, the quartermaster general of the besiegers was ashore by June 9 and began selecting locations for the main camps. Attacks by French and Aboriginal forces were a constant worry for the British—whether from Louisbourg or from the detachment Boishébert was rumored to be leading toward Île Royale. In truth, Boishébert's force was still at Miramichi on June 9, and it would be June 26 before his contingent would reach the Strait of Fronsac (Canso). The British had no way of knowing that and were obligated to expect the worst, so they started constructing defensive positions soon after the landing. They also established "Roads through the Camp and to the Cove where the Artillery &c was landing." More roads and many other defensive features would be added later.[32]

The progress made during the first few days after the landing at Anse de la Cormorandière was slow but steady. Although heavy surf conditions slowed them down on June 9, 10, and 11, the British hoped that the work undertaken laid the foundation for the siege to come.

Preparing to Defend

By noon on June 8 all the defenders who had been at Anse de la Cormorandière, Pointe Platte, and Pointe Blanche were safely inside the walls of Louisbourg, except for those who had died, been captured, or deserted. Since the enemy was now ashore, Governor Drucour decided that two of the four outlying batteries had to be abandoned. The governor reasoned that the Royal Battery, along the north shore of the port, and the battery on Lighthouse Point, on the opposite shore of the harbor entrance, were too vulnerable to garrison. It would be only a matter of days before the British could attack them from the rear. Accordingly, Drucour ordered that the guns of the Royal Battery be brought within the fortress and those at the battery on Lighthouse Point be spiked. Even with those two harbor defenses abandoned, the French would still be able to keep British warships from entering the harbor and putting a quick end to Louisbourg. The remaining outer works were the well-armed Island

Battery and a battery on Rochefort Point, not to mention the warships within the anchorage.

If certain outlying fortifications were no longer tenable, then what about the houses and other buildings that stood beyond the walls of Louisbourg? That was an easy decision. Drucour and his senior staff ordered that all structures in the Fauxbourg and Barachois areas outside the Dauphin Gate as well as part way along the north shore of Louisbourg harbor were to be burned. They wanted to eliminate anything that might provide cover for a British advance. On the afternoon of June 8, fifty soldiers of the Volontaires Étrangers left the protection of Louisbourg, intending to spike the twenty-four-pounder left behind at Pointe Blanche. They turned back when they saw that the enemy already occupied the location. Word reached Louisbourg about 3:00 PM that the other half of the long-awaited Cambis battalion was at the careening facility on the far side of Louisbourg harbor, having marched in from the Mira River, where they had spent the previous night. Around 8:00 PM a few hundred additional defenders arrived when the contingent previously assigned to be a reserve force at the Montagne du Diable—Acadian refugees, Louisbourg militia, and others—came into town. As night fell on June 8, Governor Drucour ordered all combatants to sleep on the covered way. It was rumored that the British were advancing in three columns against the place, and the governor wanted each man-at-arms to be ready.[33]

The rumor was groundless; there was no enemy assault that night. When June 9 dawned with thick fog and heavy rain, the order went out to decrease the guard on the covered way. The British were not going to launch an assault in such weather if they couldn't be sure of keeping their powder dry. The most important event of the day for the defenders was the war council Drucour held, attended by all senior military officers. Such discussions were not meant to be public knowledge, yet word of a profound difference of opinion between the military and the naval forces at Louisbourg was soon circulating beyond the meeting room. Grillot de Poilly, who was not present for the debate, summarized the gist of disagreement in his diary, at least as he heard it secondhand. The heart of the matter was that the naval officers, led by the marquis des Gouttes, had submitted a letter to Governor Drucour asking permission to sail out of the harbor after dark descended, if the wind permitted. Since the British had succeeded in coming ashore, reasoned the ship captains, the colony was doomed. They argued that it was only a matter of time before the town capitulated, which in turn meant that every French warship would either be destroyed or taken over by the enemy and, of course, their crews taken prisoner. A much better option, for des Gouttes and the captains, was to sail away, allowing the king's ships and their several thousand sailors to fight again another day, somewhere else. The naval commander asked that Drucour give his answer in writing, so that it was on the record that the destruction of the ships was the governor's decision.[34]

The members of the council, all military men, did not welcome the idea that it would be best to cut one's losses and abandon the soldiers and civilians of Louisbourg to their fate. Did Drucour and the military men give it at least a few moments reflection, or did they just reject it outright? We really don't know. Certainly, the naval captains' basic point was valid; if the ships stayed in Louisbourg harbor, they were more than likely going to be either destroyed or flying British flags before long. Yet the truth is not always easy to hear, and besides, Drucour and his officers may not have cared if the marquis des Gouttes' assessment was accurate or not. They had what is often a safer refuge: they were following orders. And on that ground the council rejected the suggestion to let the warships leave the harbor, the governor writing back to des Gouttes and his officers that the orders from the minister were to hold out at Louisbourg as long as possible against the British, so as to prevent the enemy from making an attempt on Quebec the same summer. Keeping the ships in the harbor, quite simply, would prolong the siege. The most Drucour would grant the commander on June 9 was that three ships could sail away. One was the frigate *Comète*, which left that night for France with news that the British had made a successful descent. The other two vessels allowed to leave were the sixty-four-gun *Bizarre* and the thirty-two-gun frigate *Echo*, both of which were to sail for Quebec. Drucour felt it important for the record to note that this was the third time he had to tell des Gouttes to leave the ships of the line in the harbor so they could contribute to the defense of Louisbourg.[35]

The three French vessels permitted to leave did indeed make their way safely out of the blockaded harbor, which prompted Major General

Amherst to observe: "[H]ow very difficult it is to block up the Entrance to the harbour, it appears to me to be impossible." The British would eventually capture one of the ships, the *Echo*, on June 16. It was brought back to Louisbourg on June 19 as a British prize.[36]

One naturally wonders if Governor Drucour anguished over the decision to retain the ships of the line within Louisbourg harbor, rather than bow to the ship captains' desire to sail away before their vessels were damaged or captured. Drucour surely saw the logic in des Gouttes' argument, yet as the governor of Île Royale he knew the decision expected by his superiors in France. It would be months before Drucour would learn the reaction of the king and the minister of the marine, but eventually he did find out. Soon after the governor's June 10 memorandum reached Versailles, the minister composed a note affirming that "His Majesty approved that [Drucour] insisted to retain the Ships of the line in the roadstead of Louisbourg, . . . it [could] only produce the best effect to inspire the garrison and all those" who were defending the place.[37]

Soon after the Louisbourg war council rejected his request, the marquis des Gouttes wrote France to put his point of view on the official record. The commander of the naval force stated that he would rather have engaged the British in a combat at sea than anything. Nonetheless, he accepted the war council's decision to keep the ships in port and therefore prolong the coming siege. Like Marchant de La Houlière in a separate letter, des Gouttes placed the blame for what he felt was the impending loss of Île Royale on the nonarrival of additional warships at Louisbourg. If there were more ships, observed both des Gouttes and Marchant de La Houlière, the French could have launched a preemptive attack on the enemy fleet that was anchored in Gabarus Bay before the landing and saved the colony. Reading these letters two and half centuries later, one is struck by how the siege had not even begun and the senior French officers were all but conceding defeat and trying to figure out what had gone wrong. One specific action that reflected the defeatist attitude was the notification of the ships still anchored at Port Dauphin, the *Brillant* and two merchant ships, that they should sail away and save themselves.[38]

In developments on land at Louisbourg, the grenadiers of the Volontaires Étrangers went outside the walls of the town on June 9 to provide protection to fifty workers. The laborers filled sacks with dirt to be used on the ramparts and elsewhere to strengthen the fortifications, and they toiled to lower a nearby hill (one with a lime kiln) that was judged to be a location the enemy might use as an artillery position. When night fell on June 9, one-third of the garrison stood at the ready on the glacis, another third were in their rooms fully clothed, and the final third were allowed to sleep.[39]

On June 10 the first reliable reports of what the British were up to reached officials at Louisbourg. One or more individuals had left the fortress to see what they could of the enemy's activities down the coast, and the word that came back was that the British were establishing camps on either side of the brook that spilled into the ocean near Pointe Platte. This was no surprise because the brook offered a source of fresh water, and in 1745 the New Englanders had camped in the same general area. Judging by the number of tents observed, it appeared there were going to be between 10,000 and 12,000 soldiers camped in that area. After recording that estimate in his journal, Governor Drucour added: "[W]e are preparing to put up all possible resistance." Drucour wanted five special companies formed by volunteers from the soldiers of the Troupes de Terre battalions and the Compagnies franches de la Marine. The newly organized companies were to make sorties and bring back information about enemy movements. In another move a force of one hundred Acadian refugees under the command of a few Compagnies franches officers was sent into the woods with a mandate to take prisoners, for the information they might provide. In other activity that day more bags of dirt were brought inside the town to make the casemates in the King's Bastion more bombproof. The expectation was that those casemates were going to shelter women and children during the coming days of bombardment. Though that stage of the siege lay in the future, Governor Drucour and his senior officers knew the enemy would eventually be erecting gun batteries on the nearby hills, just as the New England besiegers had done in 1745. As a consequence the governor and his advisers concluded: "[I]t would be good to anchor a frigate so that it could fire upon the hills behind us, we hope that will happen." The frigate selected to harass the enemy advance on that landward front was the *Aréthuse*, commanded by Jean Vauquelin. A seasoned seaman and fearless in battle, the thirty-one-year old non-noble Vauquelin did not have a commission in the French navy. He was attached to the service only because of the pressing need for officers. Yet in the days ahead it would be Vauquelin and his crew who stood out for what they would accomplish.[40]

Calm before the Storm

Though the French were worrying about a British attack on the town soon after the June 8 landing, such a sudden assault was not on Jeffery Amherst's mind. The commander of the British land forces wanted to lay the groundwork for a lengthy, successful siege rather than begin one prematurely. Amherst's methodical approach irked James Wolfe, who complained in his private correspondence that more could have been accomplished much sooner with a more energetic campaign. At least a few of the French defenders within the walls of Louisbourg were similarly puzzled. Grillot de Poilly, the engineer, confided in his diary on June 22: "I understand nothing about the slowness of their movements."[41]

From Amherst's perspective there were two main priorities in the period immediately after June 8. One was for his forces to seize control of the terrain that wrapped nearly around the French stronghold, as far as there was land, because the ocean, controlled by the Royal Navy, was on one side. The ground Amherst wanted to control formed an arc that extended from Pointe Blanche on the Atlantic coast across the inland heights close to the fortified town, then continued along the north shore of the harbor, and concluded at Lighthouse Point and the seacoast that contained Anse à Gauthier and Lorembec. The other priority was to complete the logistical infrastructure to conduct a siege. Most of that work was carried out a safe distance from the fortress, with the biggest undertaking being the construction of a temporary city—or base camp—for the approximately fourteen thousand soldiers involved in the land campaign. Amherst and Boscawen assigned thousands of sappers, soldiers, and sailors to the work, which was carried out on a massive scale and in quick order. The total area covered by the 1758 siege camps was 2,500 square meters. Prefabricated blockhouses brought from Halifax were assembled, and extensive camps, roads, batteries, redoubts, and other features built from scratch in the woods and on the hills in the vicinity of the fortress. Amherst provided the overall direction, but the details were worked out by nearly a dozen engineers led by Colonel John Henry Bastide and by the artillery unit commanded by Lieutenant Colonel George Williamson. On at least one occasion, on June 17, Amherst, Bastide, and Williamson traveled together on horseback to reconnoiter "the whole ground as far as [they] could."[42]

In short order the British transformed a large portion of the landscape near Louisbourg—so much so that the vestiges of the work remain visible 250 years later, if one knows where to look in the forest that has since grown up. The quartermaster general placed the regimental camps on a series of low hills close to the brook that ran into the ocean near Pointe Platte, a stream that provided the soldiers with fresh water. The most visually dominant aspect of the camps was the hundreds of tents, but the British also erected structures that were either built entirely of stone or had stone foundations and earthen walls. An archaeological survey in 1987 revealed the presence of three powder magazines, a redan, a redoubt, and five sentry posts at approximately five hundred different camp sites. Military engineers generally directed the work, which was executed by soldiers and sailors. Writing to Amherst from Lighthouse Point on June 19, James Wolfe commented: "My whole affair now is the spade and pickaxe." So it had to be, for until the batteries were constructed, the bombardment could not begin. An anonymous British officer observed that the engineers had at their disposal "thousands of workmen," which meant a lot could be achieved in a short period of time. At the Grenadiers Redoubt, for instance, 2,200 men put up a huge earthwork in two days. Once completed, it was "capable of holding 4 or 500 men, and the Parapet Cannon Shot proof."[43]

At the same time as thousands of British combatants were carrying out construction projects well beyond French artillery range, decisions had to be made regarding how to take control of the terrain closer to the walls of Louisbourg. Colonel Bastide, in charge of the engineers, was a strong advocate of establishing an initial battery on Green Hill, where New Englanders had erected an effective battery in 1745.[44] From there the British would gradually fan out and advance closer to the fortress, one hill at a time. Yet an even higher priority for Major General Amherst and others was to seize Lighthouse Point, directly across from the fortified town. In 1745 the New Englanders had not realized the strategic

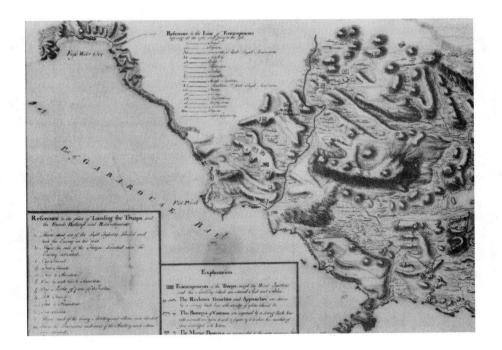

FIGURE 9. **Coastline and Camps**

This is an enlarged detail from figure 7, with emphasis on the three beaches the British advanced toward in the early morning hours of June 8. At the top of the map, identified as Fresh Water Cove, was what the French called Anse de la Cormorandière. In the middle of the map is Flat Point, or Pointe Platte, while on the lower right is White Point, or Pointe Blanche. Close to the middle of the map, extending inland from Flat Point and on both sides of the brook, the British established their siege camps, indicated by numerous rectangles. *Courtesy of William L. Clements Library, University of Michigan.*

value of the Lighthouse Point location until late in the siege. Once they erected a battery there, however, they were able to silence the French guns on the Island Battery in short order, and not long afterward Louisbourg surrendered. Having learned from the experience of 1745, Amherst wanted to begin the assault in 1758 by taking control of Lighthouse Point as soon as he could. From there British gunners could target both the Island Battery and the French warships moored in the harbor.

To lead the contingent to capture Lighthouse Point, Amherst chose Brigadier James Wolfe, who had shown his courage and creativity during the landing a few days earlier. For this next assignment Amherst gave Wolfe command over 1,350 officers and enlisted men selected from twelve different regiments. The force made its way to its target by marching around the harbor along the north shore, while the artillery it would eventually need was sent by sea. In a related move Major George Scott led 400 light infantry and rangers to the northeast end of Louisbourg harbor. Scott was ordered to "there lay in Ambush" and to provide cover to both the detachments sent by sea to Lorembec and to Wolfe's force on its way to Lighthouse Point. The contingents under Wolfe and Scott left base camp separately while it was still dark on the morning of June 12, around 4:00 AM. Each man carried six days worth of provisions, and collectively they had as many hatchets as could be spared, forty rounds of ammunition, and "Tents and Camp necessaries for every Eight men."[45]

A thick fog in the early morning hours of June 12 kept the sailors aboard the heavily armed French warships anchored in Louisbourg harbor from noticing that a British advance was taking place, though for their part the British were able to hear activity and voices aboard the French ships. When the fog lifted later in the day, the French realized the British were already on Lighthouse Point. They had reached there about 2:00 PM. It was no mystery to the French what the enemy had in mind. They knew Lighthouse Point offered commanding positions from which to bombard their ships and the Island Battery. On the afternoon of June 12, the French fired a few shots at the British contingent digging in at Lighthouse Point, and the next day, June 13, there was an all-out effort to disrupt the British work party. The guns of the Island Battery, the battery on Rochefort Point at the end of the Louisbourg peninsula, and the French ships in the harbor pounded the area as best they could.

Ironically, many of the cannons the French fired from their land batteries were likely of English manufacture. A supply of forty-five English twenty-four-pounders had been sent from Brest to Louisbourg in 1750 and kept in service thereafter.[46]

Though the priority for the French warships was to bombard and thereby disrupt and delay the establishment of British batteries on Lighthouse Point, the marquis des Gouttes did find time on June 13 to meet with all the ship captains under his command aboard his own ship, the *Prudent.* The discussion revolved around the need to save at least some of the ships by getting them out of the harbor before the British began to sink them one by one. The captains unanimously agreed that sailing away from Louisbourg was the wisest course, though no one was willing, not yet anyway, to disobey Governor Drucour and leave without his approval. No one informed the governor that the naval officers were making tentative plans to act in what they thought was the best interest of the king, regardless of what he thought.[47]

On Lighthouse Point the construction continued after dark and on foggy days, when French gunners could not be sure where they were firing. During the night of June 14 the British safely landed fresh supplies for Wolfe's force as well as the first of their cannons and mortars. The work on the redoubts, batteries, and communications lines continued for several more days and nights, with additional artillery landed and mounted. Finally, on June 19, eleven days after the landing at Anse de la Cormorandière and a week after Wolfe and Scott marched their contingents around Louisbourg harbor, a mortar battery and a battery of howitzers and cannons were ready to fire from Lighthouse Point. Wolfe was clearly pleased with what he and his men had accomplished in a short period, under severe French bombardment. He wrote Amherst: "About ten this night you will see my signals. Are you not surprised to find that I have a battery here?" The reason Wolfe selected this time must have been because he wanted to wait until dark was descending, which on June 19, close to the summer solstice, is late in the day. As Wolfe had informed Amherst, the night sky of June 19 was lit first by signals and then by mortar bombs. Governor Drucour described how it appeared to him: "As night descended the enemy lit fires on the coast and on the hills close by and to the northwest of the harbor and town. They lit signal flares and not long after they began to bombard the ships of the line.

FIGURE 10. **British at Lighthouse Point, June 1758**

Once the British landed their stores and artillery, Major General Amherst decided the first military targets would be the Island Battery and the French ships in the harbor. To achieve that end, Amherst ordered James Wolfe to lead a contingent to Lighthouse Point, from which both targets could be hit. This engraving by P. Canot, based on a sketch drawn on the spot by Captain Charles Ince, depicts the arrival of the British contingent to set up their artillery. Louisbourg's Island Battery is partly hidden by the lighthouse, though a puff of smoke indicates French cannon fire from there. *Courtesy of Parks Canada, Fortress of Louisbourg, National Historic Site of Canada, Photo Number: M 96 01.*

They fired about 120 bombs, of which one fell on board the *Prudent*, injuring several sailors and others." Wolfe's gunners fired at their targets all night long.[48]

The bombardment from Lighthouse Point on the night of June 19/20 ended the waiting and wondering among the French leadership. They had wrongly expected assaults on the town's defenses soon after the landing. The days that followed saw only minor skirmishes as both sides sought either to gather information or to establish positions beyond the walls of the fortified town. The deadliest encounter occurred June 13, when the British drove back a French sortie from the fortress. Grillot de Poilly recorded that five French officers were injured and twenty enlisted men killed or injured. The encounter may be what gave rise to the rumor that spread through Louisbourg the following night that three columns of the enemy were advancing on the town. The drummers beat the *générale*, and all regular troops and militia hurried to the ramparts and the covered way. By 11:00 PM, with no sign of the British, the defenders were told to return to their beds. Suddenly the drummers were again playing the *générale*, and everyone hustled back to his position. Once more it was a false alarm. One can only speculate whether the British were deliberately doing something to stir things up inside the French stronghold or whether the defenders were merely skittish.[49]

The absence of reliable information about British movements certainly gave birth to anxiety among the French. Governor Drucour wrote on June 13: "Our knowledge of the enemy's forces . . . is imperfect." Grillot de Poilly showed the same uncertainty: "[I]t is said that the Enemy is in force at the Lighthouse and at Anse à Gauthier." While the French leadership was waiting to see what the enemy would attempt, it used the time available to carry out projects within the town. One was to strengthen the most vulnerable portions of the enceinte. Another was to move gunpowder from the casemates in the right flank of the King's Bastion to the icehouse (a well with a roofed structure over the top) and to lime kilns near the Maurepas Gate. Those structures were made bombproof, as well as such structures could be, in case the features were hit. As for the vacated casemates of the King's Bastion, they were selected as the location to which women, children, and other vulnerable civilians were to go once the British bombardment of the town began.[50]

The best French hope for reliable information about British intentions lay in capturing someone from the other side. Similarly, the British placed a high priority on finding out what they could from their prisoners. Specific orders on June 9 directed that "[a]ll French prisoners . . . be brought to Major-General Amherst." There were a good many such prisoners to choose from after the June 8 landing, whereas the French did not have any British prisoners until June 17, when they took a sailor into custody. Two days later Drucour and the other senior officers welcomed an Irish deserter from a British regiment. There would be other deserters from the besieging side later in the siege, which is odd given that both sides were sensing a British victory. A deserter to the French side was not likely to find long-term relief. The French questioned the men from the British side thoroughly, seeking details about the size and nature of the enemy forces. They recorded the numbers they were given on troops, ships, ill, and injured; they noted that the besiegers believed it was "certain that they [would] take Louisbourg." There were many on the French side who would have agreed, though certainly not in public. On the other hand, some things the Irish deserter revealed were encouraging. He claimed there were only 10,000 British soldiers, many of whom were sick. It was his opinion that most had been pressed into service and did not want to be there. He added that 1,200 men had been lost in the landing on June 8. Could Drucour and Marchant de La Houlière believe the deserter, or was he embellishing his story to please his listeners? The desire to see a ray of hope in their predicament ran strong inside the walls of Louisbourg. Moreover, a 1,000 to 1,200 casualty figure for the British during their June 8 landing was what they had already sent to the minister of the marine in France in a dispatch aboard the *Comète*, so the deserter's numbers were a corroboration. In truth, the British casualties in the descent had been 61 killed or missing and 115 wounded.[51]

While the French were trying to sort fact from fiction about the besiegers, there was one rumor they hoped was true. That concerned the projected arrival of Charles Deschamps de Boishébert and a large force of irregulars that was supposed to be nearing Louisbourg. The word was that anywhere from 700 or 800 to 1,200 men were in the contingent. Of course, until Boishébert actually arrived, it was all speculation. Unknown to anyone inside the walls of Louisbourg, Boishébert's force was nowhere near its rumored size, and it would be June 28 before it would make it to Port Toulouse (St. Peter's), in the southeastern corner of Île Royale. It would then have to find a way to make it to Louisbourg, avoid capture by the British, and have an impact on the siege. It was a tall order, but then there was not much else on which to base French hopes.[52]

During the eleven-day interval between the British landing and their first artillery cannonades, Governor Drucour sent a French drummer to the British camp with a letter for Major General Amherst. The declared purpose was to inquire about the health of the French officers who had not made it back into town on June 8. Drucour stated in the letter to Amherst that he wanted to know if the missing officers were alive and being cared for. A secondary purpose was almost certainly that Drucour hoped the messenger might come back with information about the enemy's camp and its lines of attack. Certainly Amherst viewed the French drummers as being on an "intelligence" mission. The British commander issued orders that any French drummers were to "be stopped by the first Sentry" and kept back "so that he [could not] see any of [their] works or the Camp." Amherst sent a letter to Drucour via the drummer that the French officers were being cared for with the same attention as his own British troops. He concluded with the comment that "if there was something in the camp which could be useful to either the person or the table of [His] Excellency, [Amherst] would be charmed" to send it to him. Three days later Amherst showed that he meant what he said; he sent two pineapples—which by the mid-eighteenth century were symbolic of high status and hospitality—to Governor Drucour's wife. Madame Drucour was not to be outdone by Amherst's courtesy. The following day, June 18, she sent him a basket containing fifty bottles of Burgundy wine.[53]

The gift exchange gives the impression that the siege was a courteous affair, which it was in comparison with what was to become the "total" warfare of the nineteenth and twentieth centuries. Yet we must not make too much of the pineapples and the wine, which were after all enjoyed by a handful of leaders on the two sides. For the thousands on the front lines, whether inside or outside the walls of Louisbourg, or aboard ships within or without the harbor, their lives were filled with hardship and toil and sometimes suffering. For the vast majority of defenders and besiegers in 1758, there were no gifts at all.

The Bombardment Gets Results

The British bombardment unleashed on the night of June 19 from mortar and gun batteries on Lighthouse Point was unsettling to the senior French naval officers in the harbor. Their ships received only a few hits in the first day or two, but they knew that once the British gunners found the range, their vessels were going to be easy targets. Clearly the captains had to shift their ships away from where they were anchored in midharbor. On June 21 the captains of the French king's ships moved them as far as they could away from Lighthouse Point, to the end of the harbor that was closest to the fortified town. The new position brought relief, though everyone knew it would be temporary. Once the British opened batteries on the hills overlooking Louisbourg, which was only a matter of time, the ships would be well within the range of those guns.

Of course, it pained the French ship captains to imagine their ships sunk while at anchor, so they decided to make a new case to the governor. Des Gouttes went in person to Drucour's quarters, apparently at 9:00 AM on June 22, to make a different argument than the one he had communicated by letter two weeks earlier.[54] With British artillery now in play, the loss of the ships was no longer hypothetical. The naval commander proposed allowing some of the ships to sail away from Louisbourg and others to be sunk in the narrow entrance channel to the harbor. Drucour took the proposal to the war council, and they agreed. On June 22, after only three days of heavy firing from the batteries on Lighthouse Point, the council authorized two warships to sail for France. Des Gouttes selected the seventy-four-gun *Entreprenant* and the sixty-four-gun *Célèbre*, with the remaining ships of the line, frigates, and other vessels to stay in the harbor to await the outcome of the siege. There were not likely to be any more opportunities to sail away from Louisbourg because of another council decision. That was to block the entrance to the harbor. Marchant de La Houlière mentioned six ships would be sacrificed: three warships and three large merchant ships.[55] Their masts and spars, it was hoped, would prevent British warships from coming into the port to blast the town from that angle. The sinking of block ships, of course, also meant that no more large French vessels would be getting out. The *Entreprenant* and the *Célèbre* would have to sail before the barriers were sunk in the channel. That some of these vessels were to be

FIGURE 11. **Town under Siege**

The unknown painter of this scene may not have had much training as an artist, but his bird's eye view of Louisbourg during the siege of 1758 is a fascinating eyewitness interpretation. This detail from what is a very large painting gives an excellent indication of the French defenses—palisades and masonry escarp walls—as well as the close-packed civilian community within the walls. *Courtesy of Library of Congress, Washington DC.*

sunk must have surprised a few people. A mere two days earlier, on June 20, three of them—the king's ships *Apollon* and *Chèvre* and the merchant ship *Ville de Saint-Malo*—had been identified as vessels to become hospital ships for the sick and injured.[56]

Notwithstanding the decision, as evening fell on June 22 no French ships had attempted to leave Louisbourg and none had been sunk in the channel. Governor Drucour recorded only that it was foggy and there was insufficient wind, "which prevented the ships of the line from leaving." Grillot de Poilly had a different interpretation of what happened. He had heard that the orders for the *Entreprenant* and the *Célèbre* to sail for France were issued, then rescinded. The engineer wrote that those making the decisions, code words for Drucour and the marquis des Gouttes, were showing "vacillation and irresolution." Meanwhile, other opinions were circulating in the besieged town. The author of an anonymous journal wrote that the warships were going to set sail "without the consent of the governor," which he felt demonstrated the lack of coordination between the naval and the land forces in their collective defense of Louisbourg.[57] To be sure, the close cooperation on the British side between Amherst and Boscawen was not found within the walls of Louisbourg. Yet it is hardly a fair comparison. The French were in a virtually impossible situation once the British forces came ashore. Had Drucour and des Gouttes possessed the advantages the British did, their relations may indeed have been more harmonious. In any case, despite the war council decision to send away a few warships and to scuttle others to block the harbor channel, nothing was done to achieve either project. They were subjects the French would have to revisit soon enough.

On June 24, after five days of bombarding French ships and the Island Battery, Major General Amherst felt it was time for another gentlemanly gesture. Accordingly, on June 24 he sent a drummer to Drucour with a letter and two more pineapples for Madame Drucour. If Amherst hoped to receive more wine, he was disappointed. Perhaps the period of bombardment had soured the governor and his lady on sending any kind of return gift. Instead, Madame Drucour gave the messenger two *louis* for his trouble, had her husband express appreciation for the fruit, and sent along clothing and other effects for the use of the French officers and enlisted men who had been captured on June 8 and afterward. Governor

Drucour was miffed by the latest gift from Amherst, commenting that the general wanted to exchange his "wine cellar for pineapples."[58]

There was not the slightest hint in Amherst's letter that Drucour should consider surrendering. Both leaders knew the code of siege warfare, which called for the attacker's progress to be much further advanced than it was by late June before the subject of capitulation could be raised.

On the same date that Amherst's second gift of pineapples arrived, June 24, Drucour sent a courier into the forest with a letter for Charles Deschamps de Boishébert, who was said to be at or approaching Port Toulouse. For weeks everyone at Louisbourg had been expecting the renowned officer to bring them relief and reinforcements. The governor's letter offered detailed instructions on how Boishébert should make his way to Louisbourg, given the scale of the enemy siege force. Included in the lengthy note was news that there was no longer a cache of gunpowder, musket balls, and food near the Mira River. Those provisions, placed in that location with the Boishébert expedition in mind, had been scavenged by some of the Mi'kmaq following the British landing on June 8. Drucour blamed the missionary Abbé Pierre Maillard, who was with the warriors when the cache was carried off. The governor felt the missionary "should not only have made every effort to prevent the stores from being taken away, but, moreover, ought he not to have remained in the town? His staying would have meant the Indians remained as well, and they numbered about sixty."[59]

The governor's note was not good news for Boishébert, as he was short of provisions and fatigued from an expedition that had begun seven weeks earlier in Québec. Soldiers travel on their stomachs, even irregular forces. Nonetheless, there was an object enclosed with Drucour's letter that undoubtedly brought a smile to Boishébert's face. That was the cross and ribbon of the Order of Saint-Louis, which the king had awarded the Compagnies franches officer. Drucour stated that he was sending it along because by putting on the medal during the current campaign, Boishébert would be an inspiration to those he led: "[I]t can only have a good effect, those who follow you must be pleased by the favor the King gives you and it will inspire emulation." The medal likely did have a positive effect on everyone traveling with Boishébert, for membership in the Order of Saint-Louis was highly regarded. Regardless of inspiration, the expedition still needed provisions, powder, and shot if it were going to be effective against the British lines and camps in the woods around Louisbourg.[60]

The last week of June dramatically advanced British interests and set back those of the French. By the evening of June 25, the British battery on Lighthouse Point had all but silenced the guns of the Island Battery. French artillerymen were still able to fire the occasional mortar from the island, but without much effect. British gunners, using heavier artillery pieces supplied by Admiral Boscawen, continued to strike at the battery to prevent the French from carrying out extensive repairs. Wolfe removed the lighter artillery from Lighthouse Point for use in new batteries that were going to be established on the north shore of the harbor. The advance on that front and on the hilltops closer to the fortified town of Louisbourg was the next step in the British siege plan.[61]

With the Island Battery knocked out, it was finally time to establish a strong position on Green Hill, which overlooked the French stronghold at a distance of about nine hundred meters from the Dauphin Demi-Bastion and the Dauphin Gate. Once a battery was set up on Green Hill, the long-range bombardment of Louisbourg and its enceinte would begin. This would not only damage the town and undermine the French will to fight; it would also provide cover for subsequent batteries that were to be erected ever closer to the fortress walls. For the third time during the campaign—the first two being the initial landing at Anse de la Cormorandière and then the securing of Lighthouse Point—Amherst turned to James Wolfe with a key assignment. On June 26 the brigadier led two hundred fusiliers and four companies of grenadiers up to Green Hill. They encountered resistance from French soldiers on a sortie from Louisbourg, but the British outnumbered them and forced a withdrawal. By nightfall Green Hill was under Wolfe's control.

With sustained artillery fire from the guns in the Dauphin Demi-Bastion and on board the warships anchored in the harbor, the French did everything they could to make it difficult for British engineers and sappers to make progress in establishing batteries. The besiegers responded by raising protective embankments of fascines and gabions. In a different attempt to slow British progress at Green Hill, Native warriors were occasionally active on the edges of the British zone. At the end of June there was a small skirmish and pursuit at Anse de la Cormorandière, in which the British killed and scalped two warriors.[62]

While the British advance on the landward approaches to Louisbourg was still in its early days, their already-established batteries continued to aim at French ships riding at anchor. A direct hit was rare, but when one occurred—the *Capricieux* was struck at 7:00 PM on June 29—it sent a signal that sooner or later every ship in the harbor was going to be destroyed or captured. When Drucour heard from a new British deserter that the enemy was planning to send its warships into Louisbourg harbor within two days, the governor revived the idea of sinking ships to block the narrow harbor channel. He discussed the scheme with his senior officers for three days, a delay that prompted Grillot de Poilly to offer more criticisms in his diary. The assistant engineer, as was his wont, blamed the indecisiveness entirely on the naval officers. From what he had learned, the ship captains delayed matters first by asking for a war council and then, when the time came to sink the chosen ships, by providing only two-thirds of the men required, all of whom were drunk. That any block ships were sunk at all—as some were around 3:00 AM on June 29—Grillot de Poilly attributed to "the diligence and activity of Monsieur Drucour." The governor ordered soldiers from the garrison and civilian sailors from the town to carry out the project. The crews off the frigates that were sunk were redeployed to join the defenders in town. A British observer commented that the French scuttled the vessels in the harbor entrance "in such hurry that they left their Mizen Sails out & masts standing so that [the British] could see their main Tops out of the water, & sails spread." The next night, according to another British source, two more French vessels were "sunk at the Harbours Mouth, and the masts of the others cut away." The ships selected to block the channel were the *Apollon*, the *Fidèle*, the *Chèvre*, the *Biche*, the *Ville de Saint Malo*, and possibly one other merchant vessel.[63]

Intoxication of combatants—the French sailors who were incapable of sinking the block ships—was also a problem on the British side. Wolfe informed Amherst on June 20 that the detachment sent to Lorembec were "all drunk and asleep,—sentries, guards and all. The rum was sold to them by the masters of the ships" on which they sailed. The brigadier wanted Major General Amherst to punish those responsible. Specific orders had previously been issued that no "Liquors of any kind [should] be permitted to be sold at any place but at the fixed market" in the regimental camps, but obviously that directive was not being fully observed.[64]

When June came to a close, the British had been ashore for a little more than three weeks. In that span, in the words of British officer Alexander Murray, major of the Forty-fifth Regiment, they had "knocked down their Island Battery and raised four redoubts to begin [their] first Parallel." All that was accomplished with relatively few casualties; only around a dozen British lives had been lost since the June 8 landing. Murray wrote his wife that some "were lost by their own rashness & folly in running out before [their] own Guns & braving the Enemy by opprobrious names." To be sure, there had not been many engagements with the French over the three-week period. The British had concentrated on constructing camps, roads, embankments, and batteries in their slow but steady advance toward the ultimate prize. Yet what action had occurred had definitely favored the besiegers. The key French harbor defense, the Island Battery, was silenced, and their warships driven from their initial mooring in the center of the harbor to six hundred yards closer to the town quay, as far as the shallow water permitted.[65]

The sinking of French block ships during the night of June 28–29 left the embittered marquis des Gouttes in command of five ships of the line (two seventy-four-gun, the *Prudent* and the *Entreprenant*, and three sixty-four-gun, the *Bienfaisant*, the *Capricieux*, and the *Célèbre*). Those ships and the thirty-six-gun frigate *Aréthuse* launched cannon shot and mortar bombs to slow down the construction of enemy batteries, but they could not halt the work altogether. The most effective vessel to hinder British progress on the western approaches to Louisbourg was the *Aréthuse*, commanded by Jean Vauquelin and anchored in shallow water adjacent to the *barachois* outside the Dauphin Gate. It kept up a steady fire, with brave sailors taking their turns atop a mast to advise the cannoneers where to aim their guns. In that way the *Aréthuse* effectively hindered British construction of siege batteries. It was one of few bright spots on the French side. One report recounted that on the night of June 30, the *Aréthuse* fired one hundred rounds at the workers in the vicinity of Green Hill. Amherst even mentioned the impact the French frigate was having in a letter to William Pitt. Another British officer commented that "the Work of the Epaulement much interrupted by the Enemy's Fire particularly from Le Arethusa Frigate Stationed as High up the Harbour as the depth of Water would permit." On June 30 Wolfe issued orders for new batteries closer to the walled town "to take possession of two Eminences not far from the West Gate," which among other things would "force the frigate out of its present situation." For the next few days the British focus was on eliminating or driving away the *Aréthuse*.[66]

Though the efforts of Vauquelin's crew aboard the *Aréthuse* were the most significant element in the defense of Louisbourg in late June 1758, it was not the only initiative. Within the walls of the town the French moved additional pieces of heavy artillery to the ramparts of the King's, Queen's, and Dauphin Bastions, which faced the hills where the British were constructing their batteries. Simultaneously, the defenders added thousands of bags of earth to take the impact of British cannonballs, which were soon going to be launched against the fortifications. On June 29 the French sent out a small detachment beyond the protective enceinte "to set fire to the Block House" the British had erected. The soldiers surprised and overpowered the British guard and put a barrel of pitch inside the structure but were driven away by British reinforcements before they could set it alight.[67]

Meanwhile, across the Atlantic Ocean word of the enemy's landing near Louisbourg reached the court at Versailles. The *Comète*, carrying the dispatches of June 10, reached Port-Louis on the coast of Brittany on June 28. The packet traveled overland for two days, then was opened by the marquis de Massiac, the newly installed minister of the marine. Massiac composed return letters to the governor and other principals in the colony—Drucour, Prévost, des Gouttes, Marchant de La Houlière, and so on—though realistically he must have wondered if his correspondence would reach them. Regardless, the minister expressed the king's disappointment over the news of the successful British landing and added that the expectation was that the colonists would put up "the most vigorous defense."[68]

Closing In

With the coming of July the combined attack on and defense of Louisbourg moved into a new phase. The end result was not in doubt, but the British wanted it to come sooner, while the French did everything they could to delay it as much as possible. Nearly a month after the British had come ashore down the coast from the French stronghold, Jeffery Amherst felt the pressure building to bring the assault to a close. The commander of the land forces sounded almost apologetic in a July 6 letter to William Pitt when he explained the length of time it was taking to reduce the French stronghold. "The many difficulties of landing every thing in allmost a continual Surf, the making of Roads, draining and passing of Bogs, and putting ourselves under Cover, renders our Approach to the Place much longer than I could wish, but I beg leave to assure you, Sir, that no time shall be lost in advancing and I doubt not, but, the necessary Precautions being taken, our Success will be very certain."[69] Major Alexander Murray, in a private letter composed the same day, told his wife that victory was certain but progress was slow. "Gen. Amherst goes on carefully & will not lose any lives he can save by carrying on approaches; well he is an amiable man."[70]

Meanwhile, the pressure mounting on the French was of an entirely different sort. Governor Drucour and the other senior officers were obligated to find ways to prolong the siege, at least if they wanted to emerge at the end of the struggle with their reputations and careers in tact. Indeed, if the defense took an especially long time, some honor could possibly be gained. The civilians within the walls of the town, however, were worried not about honor but survival. By early July only a few cannonballs or mortar bombs had struck the town, those that had overshot the primary target: the French ships anchored close to the town. That was unlikely to remain the case much longer, however, since enemy batteries were under construction ever closer to the urban settlement. The civilians knew that extensive property damage and possibly a large loss of life were looming.

The British batteries erected in late June and early July were atop hillocks that looked down slightly on the walls of Louisbourg. Marchant de La Houlière attributed the shift in emphasis on the part of the British to the fact that sunken ships were now blocking the harbor entrance. He believed that once the besiegers realized they could not send in warships to bombard the town from the harbor side, they would be obligated to attack the place from the landward side, in traditional siege style. The French senior officer was correct. At dusk on July 1, Wolfe "and his Grenadier Companies marched and took Post on the Eminences . . . within 7

FIGURE 12. **The Besiegers' Perspective**

Painted by British artillery officer Thomas Davies from the "centre redoubt" of the siege positions, this work appears to have been executed on July 21, the day British gunners struck and sunk three of the French ships in port, the *Entreprenant*, the *Célèbre*, and the *Capricieux*. Davies shows a great many smoke plumes in his painting, some of which are coming from advance British batteries in the middle ground and some from burning French buildings in town or their ships in the harbor. Running across the horizon in the background is a portion of the Royal Navy's blockading fleet. *Courtesy of Royal Artillery Institution, England, N9265.*

or 800 yards of the West Gate [Dauphin Gate]." With the British firing from that range, it would not be long before the houses and storehouses of Louisbourg were hit. From that point on, civilian casualties were a certainty. Though Major General Amherst directed the artillery commander, Lieutenant Colonel George Williamson, "to direct his fire as much as possible at the defences, 'that we might not destroy the Houses,'" such precision was not possible. In fact, the French later came to believe that the British were deliberately targeting civilian areas.[71]

The first of the French defenders to crack under the pressure of British artillery fire were the captains of the five ships of the line. Their vessels and the frigate *Aréthuse* were the principal targets for the British cannoneers after the Island Battery was knocked out. Jean Vauquelin, captain of the *Aréthuse*, did not request an escape from what he was enduring, but his counterparts aboard the much larger ships did. In the first few days of July they moved their seventy-four-gun and sixty-four-gun vessels even closer to the Louisbourg quay wall. Alas, it was too close; three of the vessels grounded when the tide retreated. The captains complained that their crews were serving no purpose in the defense of the town and asked first des Gouttes and then Drucour if they might go ashore to help out in the landward defense. The captains said all that was required on each ship was a skeleton crew, because the large vessels were now sitting ducks for British gunners. Since each ship carried a crew of between 550 and 680 men, that meant there could be more than 2,000 additional bodies to carry out construction tasks and to man the ramparts.

The mass exodus from the warships did not take place immediately. Jacques Prévost, the financial administrator, caught wind of the idea and intervened. Prévost wanted the crews to stay where they were and the ships to continue to play an active role in the defense of the town. On the evening of July 3, however, the ship captains obtained what they wanted, permission to come ashore. When British artillery landed four "hot shot" aboard the *Prudent* around 7:00 PM, the shots started a small fire. The fire was contained, but the incident prompted an officer from the ship to appeal to des Gouttes and Drucour to allow all but fifty sailors to come ashore. The governor wrote des Gouttes that he "would adhere to whatever he judged appropriate to do." The next day, July 4, the captains and many sailors began to take up positions in the different bastions of the fortress. Jacques Prévost ridiculed the officers for their hasty departure from the warships in a letter to the minister: "[T]hey have however only lost three men and a cabin boy to the fire by the English." Yet by July 6 des Gouttes had "disembarked with the greater part of his crew" from the *Prudent*. What sailors were left on board continued to fire the ships' guns at British artillery positions as long as they could.[72]

While the ship captains were trying to abandon their floating targets, French land forces were launching a few sorties. Detachments left the fortified town on several occasions in early July to obtain firewood and to hinder British construction efforts. They fired their muskets at the besiegers and engaged in some hand-to-hand fighting. Both sides suffered casualties, with each in their accounts minimizing their own losses and inflating those of the other side. The largest French sortie contained eight hundred men and left the fortified town between 1:00 and 2:00 AM on July 5. The commander of the Volontaires Étrangers, Henry Valentin Jacques d'Anthonay, led the force. It was expected to surprise and overpower the British at their advance batteries, with a particular goal of destroying the eighteen six-inch mortars that the French believed were damaging the ships of the line and the *Aréthuse*. Sending out such a sizable sortie was a bold move, yet it was not successful. Drucour wrote in his diary that when their "troops neared the causeway and the adjoining heights they saw the enemy, which appeared to be lined up ready for battle and in numbers much superior to [their] own." Overmatched, d'Anthonay called for a quick retreat. It turns out that the British had anticipated the French might try something of that nature and so maintained "a Party of Light Infantry Posted at the Foot of a Bridge over the Barrasoy [*barachois*] every night to prevent the French from crossing."[73]

The French had a second disappointment on July 5. Around 8:00 PM British gunners finally forced Vauquelin to move the *Aréthuse* away from the spot it had occupied for a few weeks. The ship and its crew had taken enough hits, suffered enough casualties. As one British observer put it: "[T]he frigate whose Fire had done so much mischief in retarding the Works on the right and killing many men at the Epaulment . . . left her station about 8 o'clock this night, and hauled under the Town." The *Aréthuse* joined the ships of the line that had already anchored in front of the Louisbourg quay days earlier.[74]

To counteract the noose tightening on the town, the French leadership ordered a continuous fire on the British advance batteries. Throughout the first week of July the guns on the ramparts of the bastions and on the French warships blasted away. Amherst wrote Pitt that the "great cannonading from the Town and the Shipping" was directed at Wolfe's work on the advance batteries. While the continual French firing was hampering the British, at least one person within the walls, the engineer Grillot de Poilly, thought it a "useless" waste of munitions. Worse still, in his opinion, was that the constant firing from the ramparts was noticeably damaging the French fortifications. The assistant engineer lamented that no one would listen to him: "I have the voice of a man who cries in the desert." Amherst appears to have agreed with him regarding the aimlessness of some of the French fire. A few weeks later, writing in retrospect, the major general wrote Pitt: "[T]he Enemy have fired very wildly and have thrown away a great quantity of Ammunition." Wanton and self-destructive the French fire might have been, yet it did slow the British construction of new batteries. Moreover, and this was perhaps the most important aspect for the subsequent careers of the French commanding officers, the active defense gave them something to recount to the minister in France. Louisbourg was almost certainly going to be lost, and they did not want their careers to suffer the same fate.[75]

In early July Drucour gave the British the benefit of the doubt when their cannon shot and mortar bombs occasionally carried beyond military targets into civilian parts of the town. On July 6 the French governor attributed the British bombardment of that night to poor visibility. "It was a foggy night, the enemy threw several bombs in town, one of which fell on the King's Hospital, where two of the religious were injured and the surgeon major of the Volontaires Etrangers was killed." Judging by the journals of the British leadership, there was no remorse at all about inflicting damage on civilian areas. The day the hospital was struck, one officer commented: "The Bomb Batteries chiefly confined their Fire to the Town, and many shells burst in it." The next day, July 7, the same observer offered that the "Batteries very well Served against the Shipping, and some shells thrown into the Town." A note that James Wolfe sent to Amherst was probably indicative of the skeptical way in which the besiegers viewed French complaints about the damage done to civilian areas. "When the French are in a scrape, they are ready to cry out in behalf of the human species; when fortune favours them, none more bloody, more inhuman. Montcalm has changed the very nature of war, and has forced us, in some measure, to a deterring and dreadful vengeance."[76]

Wolfe's mention of Montcalm was a reference to the incident a year earlier, in August 1757, when after the British surrendered at Fort William Henry, some of France's Native allies attacked a large number of unarmed British prisoners as they were marching away from the fort. Approximately two hundred prisoners died. Montcalm put a stop to the slaughter and decried what had happened, but the British regarded the incident as an example of French treachery and kept its memory alive for years. In the quotation, Wolfe appears to use what happened at Fort William Henry as a justification for bombing civilian areas within Louisbourg. The orders issued at Louisbourg on July 14 elaborated on the theme. They stated that because the French had violated the "Law of Nations" at Fort William Henry, the capitulation of the British officers and enlisted men a year earlier was "null and void." This was relevant because some of the besiegers at Louisbourg had given their word at Fort William Henry that they would refrain from bearing arms against the French for one year. The British orders stated that if the French should capture any of those individuals and "any violence follow thereupon," the British would "retaliate on the Persons of the French Prisoners now in [their] hands." Clearly, what had happened a year earlier in the distant interior of North America was very much on British minds as they closed in on Louisbourg. Looking ahead, one might anticipate that if Amherst and Boscawen were able to force Drucour to capitulate, they were not going to be generous in their terms of surrender. Indeed, in 1759 when James Wolfe was in charge of the assault on Quebec, he wrote that he intended "to set the Town on fire with Shells, to destroy the Harvest, Houses & Cattle . . . to send off as many Canadiens as possible to Europe, & to leave famine and desolation behind [him]."[77]

Governor Drucour made an attempt to lessen the impact of the British bombardment on the people of Louisbourg. On July 7, 1758, he sent a note to Amherst and Boscawen asking them to agree to a "safe" area where an interim hospital could be established for the French sick and wounded, out of harm's way. The British co-commanders took time to prepare their replies, which provided a lull in the firings from both sides. That allowed Drucour, Franquet, and Marchant de La Houlière to go beyond the walls and investigate the situation at Cap Noir. It was probably during the same truce that a British officer and a lady friend strolled close to an enemy position, where they engaged in a lengthy conversation with the French officer in charge. The British lady and the French officer discovered they were possible cousins. She asked if she might "pick a salad, this was accorded her." At the end of the truce, Drucour received two letters, one each from Amherst and Boscawen, both in French, the language of diplomacy. The messages were not what the governor wanted. The British commanders proposed that Drucour place his sick and wounded either on Battery Island or aboard a British ship. Those were the only two locations Amherst and Boscawen would consider as zones where their bombs and shot were not going to land. Drucour declined the offer, and the artillery assault on the town and its defenses began anew. That same day, July 7, Drucour dispatched an emissary by sloop, under a flag of truce, with a supply of necessary items for the French prisoners aboard British vessels. He sent along a bag of money for one of the French officers and a salad for Sir Charles Hardy, second in command of the British naval contingent. Hardy sent back word to Drucour that everything was distributed as requested. He added that he regretted he could not reciprocate with anything for Madame Drucour.[78]

Though the toll of dead and injured was growing on the French side, by the end of the first week in July it was nowhere near enough for the leadership to consider surrendering. Marchant de La Houlière, commander of the land forces, stated on July 7 that nineteen officers were injured and one hundred enlisted men were out of service. Still trying to think aggressively, the French were completing a nine-gun battery atop the Queen's Bastion and planning on adding nine more artillery pieces to a work near Cap Noir. On the night of July 8/9, the defenders made a bold sortie to attack British positions close to Louisbourg. The area they chose was on the Cap Noir–Queen's Bastion front, which had been relatively quiet. Recent activity by the British made it look as if the enemy were preparing to launch an assault from that zone. The sortie was a preemptive strike.[79]

The decision to send out a large force was taken at 9:00 PM on July 8. Lieutenant Colonel Marin of the Bourgogne battalion led six hundred to seven hundred men, drawn from all units serving at Louisbourg, out through the Queen's Gate between midnight and 1:00 AM. The force made its way in two columns to the foremost enemy siege works. British accounts written after the fact claimed that the French were "much in Liquor." Whether the French had fortified their courage with alcohol before setting out, Marin's force completely surprised the British workers. They inflicted many casualties with bayonets, because they did not want to fire muskets and warn other British units. French laborers who had come along with the sortie set about destroying what the British had constructed, while the French soldiers moved on to the next British position, which they took as well. The element of surprise eventually vanished. When it did, the British rallied to stand their ground. Marin's contingent held the captured positions for about an hour, then pulled back to Louisbourg, taking with them thirty prisoners, including an officer and an engineer. French losses for the evening totaled one officer and seventeen enlisted men killed. The British claimed they had five fatalities (including a sleeping captain, the Earl of Dundonald), seventeen wounded, and eleven missing. At dawn on July 9 the French asked for a truce to bury their dead, which the British granted.[80]

The week that followed saw few dramatic developments in the attack and defense of Louisbourg. Heavy rain hindered activity on both sides for several days. Nonetheless, the British continued to bombard the town and its fortifications day and night. The cumulative effect of the artillery fire prompted the engineer Grillot de Poilly, on July 8–9, to begin making separate entries in his diary for daytime and nighttime events. For instance, Poilly recorded that during the night of July 12–13, the enemy constructed a "type of 1st Parallel at the foot of the height he occupie[d] in the center." Over the next day and a half the engineer observed and heard more work on different sections of the parallel. The night of July 14 was exceptionally quiet, with no bombardment after midnight, so Grillot de Poilly walked out to the farthest French sentry position, where he could hear the sounds of British sappers working. The next day everyone realized the different sections of the first parallel were now connected. Grillot de Poilly expected the British to open new batteries from a new, closer location, and he was not disappointed. Amherst wrote Pitt that on the night of July 14 tracings were made for four new batteries of twenty-four-pounders that would "destroy the defences" of Louisbourg as well as "a Battery of seven Mortars, with some twelve Pounders to ricochet the Works and the Town."[81]

In addition to constructing advanced batteries, the British busied themselves with the supporting infrastructure of roads and *épaulements*. To protect soldiers and laborers from French artillery fire, there was an ongoing need to erect new or renewed gabions and fascines. The work called for huge labor forces, so 500 men were assigned each day for construction or repair chores. On the other side of the siege, the French were regularly employing 150 laborers around the enceinte, some of whom were sailors off the warships. To disrupt the slow but steady enemy advance, the French directed artillery fire from the guns on the ramparts and from the warships at different British advanced positions. Drucour and his senior advisers thought the area around Cap Noir was going to bear the brunt of an attack, so they strengthened it with additional artillery. Amherst observed the French activity in that area and assumed it was "to hinder [the British] taking Possession near that Point." He added, contrary to Drucour's thinking, that the area of Cap Noir was "of no Consequence."[82]

On July 15, around 10:00 PM, the night sky over Louisbourg lit up. The sudden, bright glow came from British rockets fired from Lighthouse Point. The reason for the illumination was soon apparent: a French ship was attempting under cloak of darkness to maneuver past the sunken French block ships to leave the harbor. The commander of the British squadron, Sir Charles Hardy, responded with his own signals and set out to intercept the French vessel. By the light of flares the British could see that the departing ship was the *Aréthuse*, the very frigate that had hindered the enemy advance on the landward side. Governor Drucour had given Vauquelin permission to sail for France on July 7, after the frigate had been forced to relocate closer to the town's waterfront. No longer could its crew and guns play a role in the defense of Louisbourg. To leave the port, however, its commander, Vauquelin, needed a night with poor visibility. Otherwise, he had little chance of eluding the British squadron sailing back and forth past the harbor entrance. On July 15, eight days after receiving permission to leave, Vauquelin felt he had the required conditions.

The *Aréthuse* was not just trying to escape from Louisbourg; it was also carrying dispatches from Drucour, Prévost, and Marchant de La Houlière to the minister of the marine. These were updates on the progress of the siege, with each author taking time to praise the heroism of two individuals: Vauquelin in command of the *Aréthuse* and the chevalier de Queue in charge of the French battery on Rochefort Point. (The chevalier de Queue was the second officer from the *Apollon*, sunk as a block ship on June 28–29.) The *Aréthuse* did make its way past the masts and rigging of the French block ships and began to sail away. James Wolfe was at one of the batteries that fired at the frigate, and he observed two or three howitzer shells land "into his stern, and to shatter him a little with . . . 24 pound shot." Wolfe commented, "I much question whether he will hold out the voyage," but he was wrong. The French frigate was neither caught nor sunk by Hardy's squadron, and it completed its voyage to France. Jean Vauquelin and his crew reached Bayonne safely, from which the dispatches brought from Louisbourg were sent on to Versailles.[83]

There was one person aboard the *Aréthuse* who was not part of the crew, a passenger whom neither Drucour nor Prévost had authorized to leave port. This was the chevalier des Rochers, a naval officer from one of the ships of the line. The marquis des Gouttes had charged him to go to France to explain in person to the authorities why the ship captains at Louisbourg had taken their actions during the siege. Des Gouttes knew that Drucour and Prévost were annoyed with the ship captains, especially their repeated requests to sail away from the colony, and the naval commander wanted to make sure that his side of the story was heard. For their part, after they learned about what des Gouttes had done, Drucour and Prévost wrote the minister to let him know that it was the marquis who had authorized the chevalier des Rochers's clandestine departure. The ongoing friction between the land and the naval officers on the French side stood in sharp contrast to the cooperative relationship Amherst and Boscawen had forged between their respective forces at Louisbourg.[84]

The night after the *Aréthuse* sailed away from Louisbourg, Governor Drucour heard musket fire at the far end of the harbor. Optimistically or perhaps desperately, Drucour interpreted the sounds as the long-awaited arrival of Boishébert and his contingent. There was no way for the governor to confirm that was the case, yet he thought it plausible. Whatever the size of the contingent, the irregulars might make some difference. Unknown to Drucour and everyone else confined within the walls of Louisbourg, Boishébert had actually arrived on the Mira River in the interior of Île Royale on July 1, and over the days that followed he sent detachments of 100 to 150 of his 500–man force either to reconnoiter or to attack the British camps. They inflicted some casualties and captured a few prisoners, but the skirmishes were little more than a nuisance to the besiegers. Fatigue and illness took its toll on Boishébert's force, which in turn led to desertions by some of his men. The militia who had joined at Port Toulouse and some of the Native warriors were the first to leave, believing what they were attempting was futile. Some deserters passed information on to the British about Boishébert's intentions and location. It was not long before the renowned Boishébert had only 140 men at his disposal, which meant he could do even less to hinder the enemy. At that point the French officer essentially gave up the mission he had come so far to carry out. He sent a note to Drucour, which the governor received on July 16, to let him know "the critical situation" he was in, so that Drucour could not accuse him of "slowness" in doing his duty "to follow his instructions in harassing the enemy."[85]

Also during the night of July 16, using darkness as cover, James Wolfe ordered four companies of grenadiers and some other troops to advance to the low hills overlooking the west gate of Louisbourg, the Dauphin Gate. The detachments toiled all night "throwing up intrenchments" a mere 250 yards from the walls of the fortress. When the French heard the work under way, they unleashed a "Fire [that] was extremely hot all night from the Town with Grape, round and Shells." French artillery action continued the following day. Major General Amherst put it succinctly in his summary for July 17: "[A] great fire continued from the Town and Shipping." The British responded in kind, hoping to give some cover to the work being undertaken close to the French enceinte. Drucour recorded that in the afternoon he saw a British engineer and several officers reconnoitering the landscape, who then left two stakes to align future work. That night, July 17–18, in an attempt to interrupt the British advance, French soldiers on the covered way unleashed heavy musket fire; from the cannons on the ramparts came a bombardment of grapeshot. At first light the following morning, Drucour could see that the enemy had taken possession of the Hill of Justice—named after the occasional hanging that had taken place in the past. The governor wrote that he expected the next night the British would "join all these little heights by a communication trench." Accordingly, he ordered a continuation of the musket fire and grapeshot directed at the advanced enemy positions.[86]

At this stage of the siege, with the British front line within French musket range and the British bombardment of the town continuing on a daily and nightly basis, the death toll began to climb sharply on both sides. One British account states that over the forty-eight hours of July 17–18, eighteen of their officers and men were killed. And the French fire continued, preventing the British from adding a second parallel between the Hill of Justice and Lime Kiln Hill. Meanwhile, a French deserter on July 19 informed the besiegers that within the walls of Louisbourg twenty French "were killed, two Guns dismounted and a Mortar rendered useless that same day." The next day, July 20, the British severely damaged or silenced two French positions: the spur battery that extended into the harbor near the Dauphin Gate and the cavalier battery that stood nearby. They also struck one of the ships of the line, knocking down its masts. No official was tracking civilian casualties as they were the military deaths, but the engineer Grillot de Poilly did note on July 21 that they had "a great many people injured and killed either by the cannon or the bomb."[87]

On the afternoon of July 21, a fiery spectacle captured everyone's attention. Between 2:00 and 3:00 PM a British mortar bomb struck the *Célèbre* (sixty-four guns), anchored with four other French warships close to Louisbourg's quay. At once there was a loud explosion, for the bomb chanced to land on powder cartridges stored on the poop deck. The fire that broke out quickly spread out of control. Within moments the wind carried sparks from the *Célèbre* to the sails of two ships moored nearby, the *Entreprenant* (seventy-four guns) and the *Capricieux* (sixty-four guns). They too began to burn, which led to more explosions "for as they became Hot they went off." The only remaining French ships of the line, the *Prudent* and the *Bienfaisant*, were not touched. The former was upwind, and the crew on the latter were able to maneuver the vessel out of danger.[88]

The blazes in the harbor brought to the British lines a sense of jubilant fascination. At first some thought the French were deliberately scuttling their own ships rather than see them turned over to the enemy. Mesmerizing though the scene was, British officers did not allow the artillery batteries to let up on the French. The quay area where the French were frantically trying to limit the damage to men and ships became a primary target. Major General Amherst reported later to Pitt that the three ships "burned very fast and [the British] kept firing on them the whole time to try to hinder the Boats and People from the Town to get their Assistance." More than a few of the British likely shared the mixed emotions of one officer, who commented that "in short to humanity tho' an Enemy, the Scene was very Shocking." The conflagrations aboard the *Célèbre*, the *Entreprenant*, and the *Capricieux* lasted for hours, with the vessels and their billows of smoke gradually drifting with the tide away from Louisbourg town and toward the part of the harbor near the *barachois* pond. Governor Drucour wrote in his journal that by 7:00 PM the ships "were nearly consumed, they [the British] continued to batter the King's and Dauphin bastions." The French cavalier battery in the Dauphin Bastion was no longer able to respond.[89]

The sudden and dramatic destruction of the three warships forced Drucour and the war council to cancel an ambitious plan they had developed. The idea had been to strike against the enemy advance positions in the early morning hours of July 21 with a sortie of twelve hundred soldiers, divided in half to attack two different points. Artillery fire from two of the ships of the line was supposed to precede the sortie and support it. Yet when the marquis des Gouttes and the other ship captains did not maneuver the warships into position for the bombardment to begin, the sortie had to be delayed. Now, with the burning of three vessels later that very day, there would be no further opportunities to have naval artillery fire for any sortie. Grillot de Poilly offered this observation in his private journal about the inability of the French naval and land forces to work together: "Things which should combine for good take place with slowness, and our ills multiply each day." Further, he noted that the Louisbourg garrison was down to two thousand men, including the contingents off the naval ships. Deaths, injuries, illnesses, and desertions had obviously taken their toll. Six weeks earlier, before the British landing on June 8, Louisbourg had roughly four thousand defenders.[90]

British hopes were rising as fast as those of the French were sinking. With the town and its fortifications taking a constant pounding, its warships no longer a factor, and British sappers beginning a new parallel less than 250 yards from the body of the place, the sand in Louisbourg's hourglass was running out.

Given the discouraging state of affairs, the inhabitants of Louisbourg must have been astounded on the evening of July 21 to learn that a British officer, a lieutenant of the Royal American Regiment, had deserted to their side. Soon enough everyone learned the rumor was false. The officer had not deserted but, according to a British source, had lost "his way in going his rounds [and] was made Prisoner . . . near Cape Noir."[91]

The situation within the beleaguered fortress soon grew worse. Near daybreak on July 22—about 4:00 AM, say the French sources—British batteries on both the right and the left front unleashed a massive bombardment. Colonel George Williamson, in command of the artillery, trained thirty-seven cannons, eleven mortars, and a large number of other pieces on the town and its defenses. The main targets were the King's, Queen's, and Dauphin Bastions. Grillot de Poilly recorded that many cannonballs and mortar bombs flew past the fortifications and landed in the heart of the community. He figured that between eighty and one hundred people were killed or injured. One bomb crashed through the roof of the King's Bastion barracks, a Louisbourg landmark since the 1720s. Initially there was thought to be little damage other than to the roof, but a half hour later a fire broke out that could not be extinguished. A British eyewitness wrote: "About 8 this Morning the Citadel Barracks took fire by a Carcass and burnt with great violence; all the above mentioned Batteries playing extremely smart the whole time." The blaze in the barracks lasted until 5:00 PM, completely gutting the building. With Louisbourg's citadel area in flames, Amherst "ordered Col. Williamson to confine his fire as much as he could to the Defences of the Place that [they] might not destroy the Houses." It was a humane intention, though the ordnance of the period was not capable of pinpoint accuracy. The inhabitants of Louisbourg did not notice any letup in the bombing of civilian sectors. Grillot de Poilly wrote on July 23 that "the Enemy during all this time crushed the town with its cannon and with its Bombs." It was the same on July 24: "The cannon of the besiegers criss-cross throughout the town and destroy many people. The Bombs assail us everywhere." An anonymous French diarist wrote: "[T]he fire of their Cannons and the Bombs destroys many people in town." The night of July 23 brought another flaming disaster. This time it was in the Queen's Bastion, where a large wooden barracks that had been erected by New Englanders during their 1746–48 occupation of Louisbourg and used by French troops since 1749 was struck repeatedly. A major blaze erupted that could not be controlled. An appeal for help went throughout the town, yet Grillot de Poilly stated assistance was slow in coming and offered grudgingly. The massive building and two nearby houses were consumed in flames. In fact, if the wind had not changed direction, the fire might have destroyed much of the town.[92]

While the British were stepping up their attack, the French defense was flagging. Illness, injury, fatigue, and reduced numbers were taking an obvious toll. Deserters from Louisbourg became more and more common. They provided the British with details on how desperate conditions were within the walls, for instance, that the French "could not stand to their own guns, on account of [British] Bombs, and that [the British] had killed a good many within these two or three days." Another sign of desperation and an indication of a shortage of munitions was that the French began to use as projectiles "all sorts of old Iron and any stuff they could pick up." The use of scrap metal continued as long as the French were able to fire. The decline in the firepower of the defenders spurred on the besiegers, for the British had monitored where the French artillery fire was coming from and with what frequency and accuracy since the beginning of the siege. With each passing day more and more French guns and mortars were falling silent. The British noted on July 22, for instance, that the new battery of four twenty-four-pounders they were setting up fifty yards beyond the existing parallel "did not meet with the obstruction [they] might have expected, the Enemy only firing a Shot now and then." On the following days, July 23 and 24, it was more of the same: "the Enemy's Fire much decreased, a Shot now and then from the remaining ships." Finally, Amherst and the senior officers could see breaches beginning to open in the walls of the Queen's, King's, and Dauphin Bastions. Some of the damage, according to a French diarist, was from the firing of the fortress artillery: "[O]ur own Cannons destroyed our weak Ramparts as much as the Enemies." Whatever the cause, the standard protocol for sieges in the mid-eighteenth century was that "practicable" breaches had to exist for both sides to agree that the conflict had run its course. It was a protocol of fundamental importance for the careers of military officers. Drucour had to be able to tell his superiors that he had put up a satisfactory defense, or suffer the consequences.[93]

Checkmate

Nearly seven weeks had elapsed since the morning of June 8, when the British were fortunate to find their way ashore at Anse de la Cormo-randière. As July 25 dawned, besiegers and defenders alike knew that Louisbourg could not hold out much longer. At daybreak Wolfe sent a note to Amherst informing him that an advanced five-gun battery was completed and ready to have its cannon mounted. If everything went well, the brigadier wrote, "we may batter in breach this afternoon." He added that the engineer Samuel Holland had "carried on" the trenching beyond the position of the new battery, to within fifty or sixty yards of the French glacis. Wolfe would later recall, looking back on July 25, that the British enlisted men "were animated with perfect rage against [the French], and asked impatiently when [they] were to storm the town."[94]

Admiral Boscawen was as impatient as the rest of the British leadership to bring the siege to an end. He resolved on July 25 to send two contingents, a total of six hundred sailors and marines, into Louisbourg harbor in small boats once darkness fell. The commander of one contingent was Captain John Laforey; the other was Captain George Balfour. Their mission: capture or destroy the two remaining French warships, the seventy-four-gun *Prudent* and the sixty-four-gun *Bienfaisant*. The latter vessel had been active on July 24, firing at British trench positions. Boscawen wanted its guns silenced. The admiral decided that Balfour and Laforey would carry out their mission at midnight, as the clock turned to July 26. When Amherst received word of Boscawen's plan, he committed to providing a diversion that would support his colleague's initiative. The commander of the land forces "ordered all the Batteries at night to fire into the works as much as possible to keep the Enemy's attention to the Land."[95]

Around midnight one contingent of British small boats began to row quietly for the *Prudent* and the other for the *Bienfaisant*. The sailors and marines were armed with cutlasses, pistols, and hatchets. Boscawen wrote later that the stealthy approach was "favoured with a dark Night." French accounts spoke of a thick fog blanketing the harbor. The noise and confusion created by British artillery fire at the landward fortifications did indeed keep the French focused in that direction. Amherst added even more of a diversion when he ordered a feigned assault on the covered way of Louisbourg. Everything worked as planned; the French kept their eyes and manpower on the landward front, though it needs to be said that French exhaustion and the reduced number of sailors on board the *Prudent* and the *Bienfaisant* were also contributing factors. As a result the British sailors and marines in the small boats reached their targets completely undetected and had little trouble in clambering on deck. They quickly overpowered the French sailors they encountered and took control of the two warships. The author of an anonymous French journal offered that there were 130 officers and men aboard one ship and 150 on the other, all of whom were "surprised in their sleep." That seems unlikely, though the comment does express the author's frustration that the ships were lost so easily.[96]

Around 1:00 AM, when the drummers of Louisbourg began to beat the *générale*, everyone in town knew instantly that something was amiss; there was some new threat. Cries of "aux armes" echoed up and down the streets, and all available soldiers rushed to the ramparts and the covered way. Governor Drucour hurried to the King's Bastion and Marchant de La Houlière to the Dauphin Demi-Bastion. It was rumored that the British were about to launch a direct assault on the fortifications. Consequently, the French began a continuous musket fire from the covered way, out into the darkness where they believed the British were massing for an attack. Then came word that the enemy had boarded the two remaining warships in the harbor, the *Prudent* and the *Bienfaisant*. The governor and others ran the several hundred meters down the hill to the waterfront, where they found the latest rumor was true. The French fired muskets and grapeshot from the quay wall, killing seven and wounding nine of the British, but it was too little, too late. Boscawen later wrote of those casualties, in light of what had been gained: "Our Loss was inconsiderable."[97]

British sailors aboard the *Bienfaisant* cut its anchor lines while others got into small boats to row the warship to the far end of Louisbourg harbor. It had just become a British warship. No such fate awaited the *Prudent*, for it was hard aground and could not be moved from where it was. Before long it was in flames. It is hard to say whether its British captors burned it or the French from onshore set it alight. Governor Drucour believed the latter. Some French crew from the two ships were taken prisoner; others swam ashore. Drucour was guarded in his comments about

FIGURE 13. *Prudent* Ablaze, *Bienfaisant* Captured, July 26

The dramatic event that brought the siege to its end occurred during the night of
July 25/26, when British boarding crews went aboard the two remaining French warships in Louisbourg harbor. The *Prudent* was burned and sunk, while the *Bienfaisant*
was captured. This is an engraving of a painting by British artist Richard Paton, who
was not on the spot but back in England. *Courtesy of Parks Canada, Fortress of Louisbourg, National Historic Site of Canada, Photo Number: G 69 599.*

the highly embarrassing incident in his journal; Grillot de Poilly was not. He blamed the French naval officers for unforgivable "negligence."[98]

On the morning of July 26, after the nighttime capture of the *Bienfaisant* and the burning of the *Prudent*, Admiral Boscawen came ashore to discuss the next step with Major General Amherst. One imagines they were in a buoyant mood after the most recent developments. The admiral informed his counterpart on land that it was time to send six of his warships past the blocked entrance and into the port, something he foresaw happening the next day, July 27. With no French warships left to oppose them, the British vessels would have the town at their mercy. The French would either surrender or suffer the consequences of a severe bombardment from the water side. If the enemy chose the latter, the onetime stronghold would be reduced to rubble. For his part Amherst offered that there were now breaches in the Louisbourg fortifications large enough for a full infantry assault to take place. While Boscawen and Amherst talked, the British artillery train fired away "with more spirit than ever."[99]

On that same morning of July 26 at first light, Governor Drucour and his senior military, naval, and engineering officers assessed the damage to the bastions and the curtain walls. It was, as Grillot de Poilly put it, a "sad situation." They could see that the British were constructing a second battery on its third parallel—ever closer to the body of the town. At 5:00 AM, immediately following the tour, Drucour convened a war council to which he invited the king's lieutenant of the local garrison and the financial administrator of the colony, Jacques Prévost. The discussion lasted hours and produced a consensus that their ability to defend the town was greatly reduced and that they had held out as long as was reasonable. It was time to "ask the Enemy for a suspension of arms in order to arrive at a capitulation." Each member of the council composed a written statement on the situation in which he explained why he was in favor of ending the conflict. In his document Marchant de La Houlière observed that by surrendering at this point several thousand French soldiers and sailors would retain their arms and their ability to serve Louis XV, once they returned to France. Prévost's primary concern, not surprisingly, was to spare civilian casualties. He worried that the hospital and the storehouses might be hit and burned, and there would be no place for the sick and injured and no food for the inhabitants. The anonymous author of a siege journal stated that those who sat on the war council expected Amherst and Boscawen to offer the same conditions that the victorious French at Port Mahon on Minorca had given to the defeated British back in 1756.[100]

At 10:00 AM on July 26 the defenders of Louisbourg hoisted a white flag in the area of the Dauphin Demi-Bastion. They selected that area because there was a breach in the wall. A drummer beat a signal that let the British know that an envoy was coming out from the battered town. The British ceased firing. The town major, longtime Compagnies franches officer Jean-Chysostome Loppinot, the same man who had gone ashore in July 1749 to discuss the handover of the colony from the British commandant at the time, carried Drucour's letter. If Amherst and Boscawen were pleased that the French governor was finally thinking of surrendering, they did not let that influence their reply. They knew they had Louisbourg at their mercy, and the "precedent" in their mind was not that of Port Mahon in 1756 but the so-called massacre at Fort William Henry in 1757. Amherst and Boscawen were unwilling to discuss or negotiate any terms of the capitulation with Drucour; they were going to dictate them. They wanted their victory at Louisbourg—Britain's first significant gain on land after several years of war—to be as complete as possible.

Drucour opened the British reply, composed in French, in the reassembled war council. The governor read that ships of the Royal Navy would be entering the harbor the following day, July 27, and that an all-out "General Attack" would follow. The only way it could be avoided was if the French surrendered unconditionally with the entire garrison becoming "Prisoners of War." Without such a total capitulation, wrote Amherst and Boscawen, "your Excellency must take upon yourself the fatal consequences of a useless defence." The British commanders concluded their note by informing Drucour he had one hour to reply.

The note stunned the French war council. In an era when respect for rank, title, and position was all-important, they were horrified to think they would be treated so harshly. They had mounted a long and difficult defense against long odds, which they felt entitled them to due consideration from the besiegers. So with the clock ticking on the ultimatum issued by Amherst and Boscawen, the council put together a surrender document they *could* accept. Drucour asked d'Anthonay, lieutenant colonel of the Volontaires Étrangers, to take it back to the waiting enemy. The French version of a capitulation included sixteen articles, one of which stated that their soldiers and sailors would be rendered the "honors of war" and transported to Brest. The civilians were to go to Rochefort along with their movable possessions. The council also requested that the French soldiers be allowed to march out of the fortress with muskets on their shoulders, drums beating, and colors flying. This was a commonly accepted treatment in the eighteenth century. Further, Drucour asked that the French be permitted to fire twenty shots from each of six cannons and two mortars. And the governor also asked for a number of covered small boats that would be off-limits to the British as to who or what was in them.[101]

While d'Anthonay was walking out with the revised surrender proposal, the officers within the town of Louisbourg were scrambling to find a place where their men-at-arms could make a last-ditch stand, if it came to that. The heavily damaged King's, Queen's, and Dauphin Bastions would not do. The bombardment had been heavy on that side of the fortress, and there was insufficient cover. That left only the largely untouched bastions facing the ocean as candidates for a last stand. Chief engineer Louis Franquet proposed the Princess Demi-Bastion, even though some pointed out it had room for only 150 men. There was some talk that the Brouillan Bastion would be the best choice, yet the senior officers found it impossible to examine it closely. A huge crowd of clamoring townspeople surrounded the military leadership, preventing them from moving to the Brouillan Bastion. What exactly the civilian multitude was expressing was not recorded, but one assumes it was their opposition to go through the looming horror of a full-scale British assault.[102]

Confusion and fear were raging within Louisbourg when d'Anthonay returned from the British lines. His news made things worse. Boscawen and Amherst had refused to speak with him at all. Instead, they sent a note to Drucour that they would accept only one answer to their request for a surrender: either "yes or no." There were to be no negotiations, no conditions. They gave the governor a half hour to respond.[103]

Outraged, Drucour immediately reconvened the war council. No one spoke in favor of accepting the humiliation of a total capitulation. Grillot de Poilly, who was not present but was attentive to the rumors that circulated afterward, wrote that the members of the council resolved to defend themselves "rather than submit to the hard and insolent conditions of a vanquisher." Drucour composed a one-sentence reply that he asked Loppinot to take back to Amherst and Boscawen. It read: "I have the honor to reiterate that my stance is the same and that I persist in being willing to suffer the consequences of the general attack you announce to me." French troops were ordered to their posts. Flags were hoisted. Everyone within the walls of the fortified town—soldier and civilian alike—prepared as best he could for the onslaught that was now to come. Would it be that day, or the next, July 27, as Boscawen and Amherst had earlier intimated?[104]

With total devastation looming, not to mention untold loss of life, financial administrator Jacques Prévost made his opinions known. He had previously remained silent as the military officers expressed their preference to die rather than submit to humiliation. After a period of reflection, Prévost felt he had to intervene. At 3:00 PM he presented Drucour with a memorandum that outlined why he thought it best to capitulate as the British requested rather than put up a futile, last-ditch defense. The content and form of the letter suggest that these were ideas Prévost had been mulling over for days if not weeks; it does not read like a hastily prepared document. The financial administrator began by reminding Drucour of the military assessments given at dawn that stated Louisbourg could no longer be defended. Then he wrote of the horror and carnage to which 4,000 civilians and 1,000 to 1,200 sick and injured in tent hospitals would be subjected if there was an all-out British attack. Such a disaster, he contended, would have a long-lasting impact on all French colonies. The tragedy, if it happened, would "become a Barrier of insurmountable terror for all Financiers to whom [the king would] come with the idea of doing commerce in established Colonies, and in new ones." If the civil population could not be protected in overseas settlements, how could the king convince anyone to go to them in the future? Prévost concluded by pointing out that senior military officers were duty bound to speak the way they had. They must think first of "the glory of the arms of the King, their own honor and that of their corps." The governor and financial administrator of a colony, on the other hand, or so Prévost contended, had to take broader factors into consideration. It was their responsibility to govern for the overall good of the king and the state.[105]

Governor Drucour saw the logic of Prévost's arguments. Or perhaps more accurately, he grasped that the financial administrator's letter offered an escape from an otherwise dismal situation. The governor had already declared his personal willingness to endure an all-out assault, thereby demonstrating to his superiors in France that he put honor above everything else. With Prévost's intervention, however, Drucour had a justification to avoid further bloodshed. The governor called yet another war council and ordered the captain of the captured *Bienfaisant*, the chevalier de Courserac, to run after Jean-Chrysostome Loppinot, who was already beyond the covered way en route to deliver Drucour's terse note to Boscawen and Amherst. That note stated Louisbourg would endure an attack rather than surrender without honor; suddenly that might not be necessary.

Drucour and the council went over the issue once more, reviewing the points made by Prévost. One imagines the honor-conscious military men glaring at, maybe even mocking, Prévost during the discussion. The governor stated that for the sake of the civilians and for the sick and the injured, as well as for France's future colonizing ventures, he had changed his mind. He would after all surrender unconditionally, as the conquerors were insisting. He added that he would nonetheless seek more favorable terms for the civil population. Drucour then composed a short capitulation note and dispatched three officers—d'Anthonay of the Volontaires Étrangers and Duvivier and Loppinot of the regular Louisbourg Compagnies franches garrison—to carry it to Amherst and Boscawen.[106]

It is surprising to learn that the British commanders actually listened to Drucour's emissaries this time, because Amherst and Boscawen had insisted on harsh terms all day long. Yet it seems they moderated their stance at the very moment they obtained what they wanted. The two British commanders acknowledged in a note back to Drucour that d'Anthonay had spoken on behalf of the civilian inhabitants. More to the point, the victors added items they called "Demandes Accordées." Those requests were not officially part of the surrender agreement, but they did address how the victors intended to deal with the removal of the French soldiers and civilians. The immediate matter at hand, however, was the capitulation. Amherst and Boscawen asked Governor Drucour to sign two copies of the articles and return them to the British camp.[107]

The surrender terms agreed to on July 26, 1758, were blunt; there were only six points. The first was that the entire Louisbourg garrison would be "Prisoners of War" and sent to England. Second, all artillery, ammunition, arms, and provisions—on both Île Royale and Île Saint-Jean (Prince Edward Island)—were to be turned over to the British. Third, French troops on Île Saint-Jean were to surrender and go aboard British ships, when those ships arrived there. The fourth article was longer as it dealt with details of the handover of Louisbourg. At 8:00 AM on the following day, July 27, the French were to turn over the Dauphin Gate, the town's main landward entrance, to British soldiers. At noon all French soldiers and any civilians who took up arms were to line up on the "Esplanade, where they [should] lay down their Arms, Colours, implements and ornements of War." The French garrison was then to board vessels for the voyage to England, where they were to be prisoners. The fifth article stated that the sick and wounded among the French would receive the "same care" as the British received. The sixth and final term dealt with the noncombatant segment of Louisbourg's civil population. It stated: "[T]he Merchants and their Clerks, that have not carried Arms, shall be sent to France, in such manner as the Admiral shall think proper." Drucour signed both copies of the document, which his officers carried back to the British line.[108]

The siege of Louisbourg was over, even though the British would not actually set foot in the town until the morning of July 27, when the formal handover took place. The ending of the British bombardment and the elimination of a possible all-out assault likely brought relief to most within the walls of the town, civilian inhabitants and soldiers and sailors alike. The officers of the Cambis battalion, however, which had arrived in the colony just as the siege began, wanted no part of the capitulation. A surrender without the honors of war brought anger and shame. Marchant de La Houlière wrote that the Cambis officers were "filled with indignation, tore up their colours, and each soldier, in imitation of them, took his musket by one end and, striking the butt, smashed it to pieces." Some of their counterparts in the Volontaires Étrangers, on the other hand, apparently found a way to profit from the chaos that reigned during the surrender. According to an account that appeared in a Scottish newspaper months later, once the British takeover was certain, the "German" soldiers at Louisbourg "broke open the Military Chest, and took the Money." Thirty or forty of them found enough coins in the Louisbourg treasury, according to the Edinburgh paper, to afford "Servants to dress and wait on them" while detained in Britain before being sent to France. "One of them had as much Gold as it was supposed would fill near half a Peck."[109]

With the formal British takeover only hours away, some inhabitants of Louisbourg engaged in frenzied behavior. According to one contemporary, the last night of the French regime on Cape Breton Island was a time of panic among the civilians. Thomas Pichon wrote that "the priests spent the whole night marrying all the girls of the place to the first that would have them for fear that they should fall into the hands of heretics." If the Récollet priests were still keeping parish records at that point, those records have not been found.[110]

A Change of Empire

On July 27, between 8:00 and 9:00 AM, three companies of British grenadiers came through the Dauphin Gate, known to the British as the West Gate. Their arrival was a little later than specified because the French had difficulty clearing rubble to make the gate passable. The incoming troops immediately posted sentries throughout the town. Brigadier General James Wolfe came into Louisbourg that morning so that he could, as he put it, "pay my devoirs to the ladies, but found them all so pale and thin with long confinement in a casemate, that I made my visit very short." At 11:00 AM the French drummers beat the *générale*, this time not to signal an emergency but to call all soldiers to assemble on the parade square of the King's Bastion. The formal handover took place around noon, between Augustin de Boschenry, chevalier de Drucour, and Brigadier General Edward Whitmore, the eldest of Amherst's three senior officers. The French officers were allowed to keep their swords as a mark of respect, a common courtesy of the period among gentlemen, but the French enlisted men had to turn over their arms. They did so, recorded one French observer, by "throwing them to the ground in a rage and turning away crying." All French units also had to hand over their colors. There were eleven in total since the Cambis officers had burned theirs the day before. The British sent wagons to collect the French munitions and other matériel: 18 mortars, 221 cannons, 7,500 muskets, and 80,000 cartridges. Whitmore inspected the French troops, then went to dinner with Governor Drucour. When word of the victory at Louisbourg reached William Pitt weeks later, he would name Whitmore governor of Cape Breton Island and Saint John's Island (Prince Edward Island).[111]

After the formal surrender ceremony, the vanquished soldiers made their way to makeshift shelters around Louisbourg. Their faces apparently revealed their fatigue and the emotions of defeat. Grillot de Poilly described what he saw and how it affected him: "[O]ur garrison, which was good, valorous, and patient, felt deeply the hardness of this act [the surrender]; in reality it is humiliating, it brought me to tears." Elsewhere in Louisbourg on July 27 there were random incidents of looting by individual British soldiers. The British leadership did not look the other way; they shot three of their own men and hanged another as they established control. Over the next few days additional British troops entered the town. The first warships sailed into the harbor on July 29, followed by more vessels the following day.[112] The pageantry on the water made a lasting impression on Olaudah Equiano, an African slave aboard one of the British ships. Equiano wrote in his diary:

> We had the most beautiful procession on the water I ever saw. All the Admirals and Captains of the men-of-war, full dressed, and in their barges, well ornamented with pendants, came alongside of the *Namur*. The Vice-admiral then went on shore in his barge, followed by the other officers in order of seniority, to take possession . . . of the town and fort. Some time after this, the French governor and his lady, and other persons of note, came on board our ship to dine. On this occasion our ships were dressed with colors of all kinds, from the top-gallant mast head to the deck; and this, with the firing of guns, formed a most grand and magnificent spectacle.[113]

The days and weeks that followed saw the British toiling at repairing the heavily damaged town, making it their own possession. Inside the walls they did what they could to make the place more habitable and more defensible; outside the walls they leveled many of the siege batteries and trenches they had constructed during the preceding two months. Although it is hard to believe, Amherst and Boscawen were so busy overseeing a multitude of projects and tasks in the immediate aftermath of the surrender that they did not get around to sending word of their victory back to Great Britain until July 30. On that day Captain William Amherst, a brother as well as an aide-de-camp of the commander of the land forces at Louisbourg, and Captain Edgecomb, representing the navy, sailed for England aboard the *Shannon*. Besides dispatches, the duo carried with them the colors taken from the French units. Jeffery Amherst sent along a letter in which he informed William Pitt: "[I]f I can go to Quebeck, I will." The commander's most active brigadier, James Wolfe, was certainly urging yet another campaign. Wolfe was convinced that an expedition up the Saint Lawrence River could be successful if they acted quickly. There was still "fine weather enough left for another blow," he thought, "and as our troops are improved by this siege, the sooner we strike the better."[114]

While the British pondered whether they had time to attack Quebec before the onset of colder weather, thousands of French soldiers, sailors, and civilians waited in Louisbourg for their removal. There were 5,637 prisoners of war (3,031 soldiers and 2,606 sailors) to be transported to England and 3,000 to 4,000 civilians to be taken to France.[115] The days after the formal surrender on July 27 brought new miseries to all these people. Homeowners faced the virtual certainty of never seeing their residences, or indeed Louisbourg, ever again. Parents worried about the voyage ahead and whether all family members, especially the young and the old, would survive. Meanwhile, the professional military and naval personnel of all ranks found that the sting of total defeat would not go away. And for those of a reflective turn of mind, there was the poignant realization that the colony of Île Royale—so long an object of attention, expenditure, hope, and fear—had come to a conclusive end. The French initiative, begun forty-five years earlier with the "taking of possession" of Louisbourg in September 1713 and recommenced in July 1749, had run its course. The role and function Louisbourg might have for the British in their empire were as yet unknown.

7

Winner Take All

The last days of July and early days of August 1758 brought little respite for the victors or the vanquished other than that the bombardment stopped. One task confronting both sides was a tabulation of dead and injured. As the attacker of an entrenched fortification, the British expected their casualties to be higher than those of the French, and they were. One count, which did not include the sailors lost during the June 8 landing and afterward, came up with 172 killed and 352 wounded. The only individuals identified by name on that list were officers, the 12 who had been killed and the 23 wounded. The rest—the NCOs, drummers, and privates—were totaled by category but not named individually.[1] A second count, which included seamen, offered that 15 officers and 214 enlisted men were killed during the landing and siege with the wounded totals coming to 32 officers and 339 enlisted.[2]

The French casualty list was more personalized, for it did name all individual combatants, gave the dates of their death or injury, and in a few instances commented on the number of dependents left behind. It was not, however, a complete list of all the people who had been killed or maimed at Louisbourg between early June and July 26. The focus was completely on men-at-arms, whether from regular military units or from the militia raised among the adult male civilians. Conspicuous by their absence from the document were any women and children or Native warriors.³ It was mentioned, however, that there were injured people in the hospital or dead whose names were unknown. The categorized totals for French military losses were officers, 27 injured and 9 dead; enlisted men of all units, 181 injured and 65 killed; and militia, 29 injured and 19 killed. Totaled the French numbers came to 237 injured and 93 killed.⁴ Their fatalities were 40 percent and their injuries 63 percent of the British totals. But again, those figures do not include the many civilian casualties that occurred during the days and nights of bombardment nor the Native warriors who fell in combat. If those numbers were included, the French total may have matched the British losses in both categories.

Following the formal British takeover around noon on July 27, the victors faced the enormous task of cleaning up and rebuilding much of what they had spent weeks knocking down. They had to render the place habitable and defensible in the event a French expedition arrived in the future to attempt to recapture the lost stronghold. Among other things that meant the British had to destroy many of their own siege works so they could not be reused. An urgent undertaking was the cleanup of the harbor, which was described as "a dismal Scene of total Destruction."⁵ Equally important, the incoming British soldiers had to be housed. The destruction of Louisbourg's two major barracks, in the King's and Queen's Bastions, left the town without sufficient quarters for the redcoats, even after they had taken over what roofed accommodation was still livable and forced the defeated French garrison to sleep outdoors in makeshift shelters.

The nearly ten thousand French soldiers, sailors, and civilians made do as best they could until they started to board British transports. The new administration wanted the captured soldiers and sailors sent away first, then the civilians. The first vessel left Louisbourg on August 9, with the rest following over the next several weeks. There were a few exceptions to the general policy of shipping away the French aboard transports. Passage was found for Governor Drucour, Madame Drucour, and Marchant de La Houlière aboard the British warship, the seventy-four-gun *Terrible*. On August 28, a month after the siege ended, Major General Amherst wrote William Pitt: "Admiral Boscawen is shipping off the Inhabitants as fast as possible, I dont know their Numbers exactly; I think

there were on this Island about 3,000." The removal lasted at least another month, for Boscawen wrote on September 13: "I hope to clear the
Inhabitants out of this Town in about fourteen days."[6]

There are no sources to suggest what was said or thought by the French
as they waited to be taken away from the colony. For perhaps a thousand
of them, mostly children and young adults, Louisbourg was their place of
birth; for others it had long been their home, or at least a place to work
and to defend.[7] Scapegoats are common in such situations, and the obvious ones in this instance were the senior naval officers. More than a
few land officers had complained during the siege of the ineffectiveness
of the ships of the line under the overall command of the marquis des
Gouttes, and it is hard to believe that the civilian population did not come
to share those opinions.[8] On the other hand, the officers and crews of the
warships resented bitterly what had happened to their ships and fellow
sailors, and it is easy to imagine that they stood up for their service. The
denunciations from all quarters likely grew once the conflict was over, especially since the land forces felt they had fought valiantly against over-
whelming odds, holding out longer than many expected. It may well be
that French naval officers and sailors were delighted to board the British transports to get away from a mood of recrimination.

As busy as Amherst and Boscawen were overseeing the removal of the
French from Louisbourg, the two commanders had to reach a decision
about whether they were going to attack Quebec before the weather window disappeared. After all, William Pitt's strategy called for taking both
Louisbourg and Quebec in 1758. Boscawen and Amherst finally settled the
matter on August 6, when they agreed that there were not enough weeks
of summer left to carry through with a second—undoubtedly lengthy—
siege. That decision taken, in secret, Amherst tried to give precisely the
opposite impression to all observers. He let it be known openly at Louisbourg that he was hiring French pilots to guide the fleet up the Saint
Lawrence. It was a deliberate ruse, one he hoped the rumor mill might
spread to Canada, compelling the French to keep some of their forces
unnecessarily at Quebec. If they did, then that would in turn help General Abercromby in his attempt to capture Fort Ticonderoga. The capture of Louisbourg was but a piece in the larger puzzle of winning the

vast North American campaign, and Amherst and Boscawen never forgot the larger, multiyear goal.[9]

Once a Quebec campaign was off the table, British attention turned to other French targets within the Atlantic region that they could strike during the late summer and early autumn of 1758. The outlying settlements on Cape Breton Island—it was no longer Île Royale—were the closest. Soldiers rounded up colonists in those outports and brought them to Louisbourg, from which they were transported to France. When the soldiers encountered German-speaking settlers on the Mira River—German Catholics who had come to Île Royale from Halifax back in the 1750s so they could practice their religion—the British administration gave them the option of remaining on the island or being transported to Lunenburg on Nova Scotia's south shore. More or less simultaneously, Amherst dispatched Lord Rollo and a five-hundred-man detachment to take control of Saint John's Island (the former Île Saint-Jean, today's Prince Edward Island). The terms of the Louisbourg capitulation included the surrender of the French garrison there. Once Rollo arrived he implemented a forced removal of about thirty-five hundred Acadian and French inhabitants from the island. Hundreds more fled to the woods, some of whom eventually made their way to Quebec and what is today New Brunswick. Two overcrowded transports from Saint John's Island sank en route to France in 1758; another ran aground. More than sixteen hundred drowned or died from disease, or almost half the deportees, making it not just the largest but also the deadliest of all the removals carried out by the British between 1755 and 1762.[10]

Near the end of August 1758, around the time Jeffery Amherst was setting sail from Louisbourg bound for Boston, Colonel Robert Monckton set off for the Bay of Fundy with a force of about two thousand soldiers. In late September and early October, at the mouth of the Saint John River where Fort Ménagouèche had stood until Boishébert destroyed it in 1755, the British constructed Fort Frederick. With that base established, Monckton and some of his troops proceeded upriver destroying any Acadian settlements they came across. They captured or killed whoever did not flee into the forest or get away upstream, en route for Quebec.[11]

Brigadier General James Wolfe received a similar assignment soon afterward. Throughout September 1758 Wolfe participated in an expedition that traveled along the Atlantic coast of what is now New Brunswick and the Gaspé Peninsula of Quebec. Sir Charles Hardy commanded the naval squadron of seven ships of the line and three frigates that carried Wolfe and the three regiments with him. Wherever they found French inhabitants—at Miramichi, Gaspé, and other settled harbors—soldiers took prisoners and burned buildings. In total the British destroyed over one hundred houses, nearly two hundred fishing boats, and about thirty-six thousand quintals of dried cod. On his return to Louisbourg, Wolfe wrote Amherst: "[W]e have done a great deal of mischief,—spread the terror of His Majesty's arms through the whole gulf; but have added nothing to the reputation of them."[12]

On October 7, 1758, George II issued a proclamation that annexed Cape Breton Island to Nova Scotia. It would remain part of Nova Scotia for over a generation, until large numbers of Loyalists arrived on the island in 1784–85. At that point Cape Breton became a separate British colony with its own government, apart from Nova Scotia. That arrangement lasted until 1820, when the island was once again made part of Nova Scotia.

The victory at Louisbourg prompted widespread rejoicing in Great Britain. Officials and the general public had waited two long years for a conquest to celebrate, and finally they had one. George II gave the considerable sum of five hundred pounds to each of the two messengers, Captains Amherst and Edgecombe, who carried the good news to London. The eleven French regimental colors brought from Louisbourg were taken first to Kensington Palace and then carried in an elaborate procession to Saint Paul's Cathedral, where they were put on what was said to be "permanent" display. (By the late twentieth century no one knew where they might be.) William Pitt found himself the toast of Britain and the recipient of at least fifty formal addresses of congratulation. Amherst and Boscawen would also be treated as conquering heroes when they eventually reached the mother country, but those celebrations lay in the future. Indeed, the months after Britain learned of the capture of Louisbourg would see the production of numerous medals, paintings, and engravings to mark the victory and its most dramatic moments. Understandably, France had no such commemorative enthusiasm to mark what it had lost. Yet some artist, presumably French, did create a huge canvas of the 1758 siege of Louisbourg that hangs today in a museum in Honfleur, Normandy.[13]

The Anglo-American colonies shared the relief expressed in Great Britain in the latter half of 1758. Many colonists had already savored the taste once before, in 1745, when a New England expedition captured Louisbourg for the first time. The second time around the celebration was just as sweet. Boston lit a massive bonfire; Newport offered fireworks and a general illumination; Philadelphia rang bells and fired guns; and New York gave an official dinner and artillery salutes. Small communities offered sermons of thanksgiving for the victory at Louisbourg.[14]

The exhilaration felt by British subjects when they heard news of the conquest of Louisbourg is described by a military officer who was at Annapolis Royal. A sloop from Boston sailed into the basin on September 6, 1758, causing the local garrison and townspeople to run to the water's edge. "What news from Louisbourg?" some yelled. Little guessing that the people had not heard of the capitulation back in late July, the master of the vessel replied, "Nothing strange." His answer put the crowd "into great consternation"; and they "looked at each other without being able to speak." Then one of the Annapolis Royal soldiers cried out: "Damn you, Pumkin,—is not Louisbourg taken yet?" The New Englander answered: "Taken! Ay, above a month ago." The crowd exulted, and the diarist recorded: "Words are insufficient to express our transports of joy at this speech. . . . instantly all hats fell off, and we made the neighbouring woods resound with our cheers and huzzas, for almost half an hour."[15]

Back in Louisbourg the British were making the place their own. Name changes were the easiest, so the designations for streets and features in and around Louisbourg lost their French names and received new ones. The changes included Anse de la Cormorandière, which was renamed Kennington Cove, after the frigate *Kennington*, which led the bombardment of French positions at that cove prior to the landing on June 8. Another change was that Louisbourg lost its second *o* when its captors spelled it and sometimes even appeared as Lewisburg.

Since the town had to be garrisoned for the foreseeable future, the leadership selected contingents from four regiments (Twenty-second, Twenty-eighth, Fortieth, and Forty-fifth) to remain at Louisbourg under the command of Governor Whitmore. The rest of the massive army that had assembled for the campaign was transported elsewhere, with battalions going to Halifax and to Anglo-American ports. They and others were going to be needed for the campaigns of 1759. One new unit was the Louisburg Grenadiers, composed of elite soldiers of the Twenty-second, the Fortieth, and the Forty-fifth Regiments who had shown merit in the Cape Breton campaign. Like the Fraser Highlanders and some other veterans of 1758, the Louisburg Grenadiers would be with Wolfe at Quebec in 1759.[16]

At the same time the British were considering the next stages in their war strategy, the French colonists and Acadian inhabitants from Île Royale and Île Saint-Jean were arriving in France. Most were destitute, and the months and years to follow were to bring more hardships. A large number of former Louisbourg residents looked to Louis XV and his royal officials for pensions or at least for some assistance in the form of rations or minimal payments.[17] As for the military officers who defended Louisbourg in 1758, not many saw further action in North America. Only a few would be at Quebec in 1759 or at Restigouche in 1760. Many more found themselves with new assignments defending France's interests in warmer climes, especially the Caribbean.

By 1760, with Quebec and Montreal both having fallen to the British, William Pitt looked ahead to the official end of the conflict with France. A dozen years earlier, in 1748, the New Englanders' conquest of Louisbourg had been handed back to Louis XV. No one could say for sure that the next treaty might not do the same thing. The need to juggle imperial interests to achieve an overall balance of power meant that such exchanges sometimes occurred. Indeed, soon after Louisbourg was taken, the suggestion arose on the British side that they might give it back to France to reacquire Minorca, lost to them in 1756. Pitt would not hear of it, and George II backed him up: "We must keep Cape Breton, take Canada, drive the French out of America. . . . we must conquer Martinique as a set-off to Minorca."[18]

The French, of course, had their own priorities. In February 1760, writes historian Ian Steele, the duc de Choiseul "made it clear . . . that France was willing to cede all of Canada except Louisbourg." An opening bargaining stance? Most likely, for although Louisbourg had been a key in the French maritime economy for decades and an element in their strategic thinking for nearly as long, the pleas to reacquire Cape Breton Island came almost exclusively from the ports on the west coast of France, where merchants and fishers were used to making profits overseas.[19]

Whether France sincerely wanted to get Louisbourg back, William Pitt was not about to risk the reemergence of Cape Breton Island as a French stronghold. Soon after Choiseul indicated his desire to reacquire Louisbourg, Pitt informed Jeffery Amherst, now the commander in chief of all British forces in North America, that the king wanted "the said Fortress, together with all the works, and Defences of the harbour, be most effectually and most entirely demolished." Amherst, who had sailed from Louisbourg eighteen months earlier, passed the order on to Whitmore. Accordingly, a systematic destruction of the place's fortifications occurred over the summer of 1760. The action had two immediate consequences. It ensured the French would not be able to reuse Louisbourg without massive new expenditures if it were handed back by treaty. It meant equally that the British did not envision using the one-time fortress in the same way the French had for over four decades. Now that the British possessed their own fortified naval base at Halifax, Louisbourg was superfluous to their needs.[20]

By 1763 what had once been developed and defended as Île Royale was off the list of places France was seeking to retain. Indeed, Louis XV's administration had come to see Quebec, Montreal, Louisbourg, and the rest of New France as all expendable, an attitude epitomized by the character in Voltaire's *Candide* who dismissed the Anglo-French war as being over a "few acres of snow." France gladly signed the Treaty of Paris (1763), which ended the Seven Years' War, putting its overseas losses and the devastation of its navy behind it. Article 4 of the peace confirmed that Canada, Cape Breton, and other formerly French-settled regions were to remain British territory. Article 5, on the other hand, articulated that the French were to have rights to a dry fishery along a part of the Newfoundland coast (the so-called French shore, which would shift in the years that followed until 1904, when French claims and access ended completely). Under the same article France obtained sovereignty over two small islands in the Gulf of Saint Lawrence, Saint-Pierre and Miquelon, which have remained a part of France ever since. Former Louisbourg officer Gabriel-François Dangeac was named first governor of the tiny archipelago in 1763. When his term ended ten years later, his successor was his nephew, yet another former Louisbourg officer, Charles-Gabriel Sébastien de l'Espérance.[21]

It was unusual for the veterans of the 1758 defense of Louisbourg to end up so close to the lost colony of Île Royale. With France's imperial interests in the 1760s and 1770s focused on the Caribbean, the destinies of Louisbourg veterans were more likely to unfold in more southern climes. Two assistant engineers who had served at Louisbourg went to Martinique in 1760; two years later three artillery officers went to Saint-Domingue (Haiti), two other artillerists to Louisiana, and another to Cayenne (French Guiana). With the signing of the Treaty of Paris in 1763, finalizing the territories to remain with Louis XV, there followed a great many appointments. Three former Louisbourg officers were named governors of islands much smaller than Île Royale. As mentioned Gabriel-François Dangeac became the first governor of Saint-Pierre and Miquelon; Gabriel Rousseau de Villejouin went to La Désirade (off Guadeloupe); and Joubert to Marie-Galante (also off Guadeloupe). The colony that attracted the greatest number of former Île Royale officers was French Guiana, on the north coast of South America. On May 1, 1764, nearly thirty Compagnies franches officers who had served at Louisbourg in 1758 were named to go there. Louis Le Neuf de La Vallière became the major, and with him went twenty-seven officers who had been at Louisbourg. The next most common destination was Saint-Domingue, where a half-dozen Louisbourg officers ended up. In a few cases some former Compagnies franches officers began to serve in regular infantry regiments.[22]

One child deported from Louisbourg in 1758, six-year-old Pierre Martin, son of a sergeant in the garrison and a woman from Quebec, would later on rise very high. After being sent to France at the end of the siege, the boy grew up to be a sailor, pilot, naval officer, and eventually, under Napoleon, a count of the Empire and vice admiral. He is the only person born in Louisbourg to have his name carved on to the stone of the Arc de Triomphe in Paris.[23]

As for the leading figures in the defense of Louisbourg in 1758, their fates were as varied as their personalities and characters. Augustin de Boschenry, chevalier de Drucour, returned to France deeply in debt, as he had feared would be the case when he reluctantly accepted the governorship of Île Royale in 1754. He had borrowed heavily to maintain a governor's lifestyle at Louisbourg and was unable to pay off all his debts when he returned to France. Drucour's health deteriorated, and he died at Le Havre in 1762. The naval commander who had repeatedly clashed with Drucour, the marquis des Gouttes, was more fortunate. Six years after his involvement on Île Royale, des Gouttes retired with the pension of a rear admiral. Meanwhile, the young and heroic Jean Vauquelin, commander of the frigate *Aréthuse*, served at Quebec in 1759. Two years later he finally received a regular commission in the navy and went on to have an active career in the West Indies and India throughout the 1760s.[24]

Financial administrator Jacques Prévost left Louisbourg to find higher appointments back in France. His career culminated in 1776, when he was named intendant of the major naval port at Toulon. At the time of his death at Bordeaux in 1791, at the age of seventy-six, Jacques Prévost de La Croix could look back on having crossed the Atlantic ten times, surviving one shipwreck, and being twice injured, three times a prisoner, and a participant in several battles on land and sea, including the one at Louisbourg in June and July 1758. The most intriguing post-Louisbourg twist was that of Mathieu-Henri Marchant de La Houlière, commander of the troops throughout the siege. Marchant de La Houlière returned to the Pyrenees region after the Louisbourg campaign, and decades later, in 1789, when he was seventy-two, he became enthusiastic about the revolutionary changes taking place in France, even after they turned violent. Following a military setback in 1793, Marchant de La Houlière took his own life; the former senior officer of the king left a note that explained he was dying a "faithful Republican."[25]

Turning to the British principals in the 1758 siege, we find that they showed a similar range of destinies. Jeffery Amherst took over in November 1758 as commander in chief of the overall British campaign in North America and oversaw the success of those efforts. Back in England in retirement, Amherst lived until he was eighty, dying in 1797. His reputation remained intact for a long time after his passing, but suffered significantly in the late twentieth century when it came to light that during his years in North America he condoned deliberately spreading smallpox-infected materials among the indigenous peoples who opposed the British advance. Edward Boscawen did not have a long life after the Louisbourg expedition. In the European theater in 1759, Boscawen commanded the Western Squadron, which devastated a French fleet under La Clue-Sabran along the Portuguese coast. True to form, the admiral was decisive in the action, not hesitating for a moment to follow a vulnerable enemy into the neutral waters of Portugal to strike a fatal blow. Less than two years later, in January 1761, when he was not even fifty years old, Edward Boscawen took ill, caught a fever, and died.[26]

As for the three brigade commanders at Louisbourg, none lived long after 1758. James Wolfe would be dead in a little over a year, slain on Quebec's Plains of Abraham as the force he commanded defeated the French led by the marquis de Montcalm. Edward Whitmore, named governor of Cape Breton Island and Saint John's Island (Prince Edward Island) in 1758, was serving in that capacity in December 1761, when, on a voyage from Louisbourg for Boston, he was swept overboard and drowned. Charles Lawrence returned to Halifax in the fall of 1758, where as governor of Nova Scotia he finally introduced an elected assembly, the first in the history of what a century later would become the Dominion of Canada. Two years later, still in office in Halifax, he caught a chill and died suddenly. The people who had served under him found it hard to believe that Charles Lawrence, an "enormous, bluff, and competent man," could be gone. Exiled Acadians, the victims of the deportation policy Lawrence oversaw, likely smiled when they heard the news.[27]

Given that New France officially became part of British America at the end of the Seven Years' War, and what had been Canada became Quebec, it is no surprise that many British officers and engineers at Louisbourg in 1758 went on to wield great influence on the subsequent history of the land. Samuel Holland, a junior engineer in the 1758 campaign, went on to become surveyor general of much of British America. While strolling along a beach near Louisbourg after the 1758 capture, Holland had made the acquaintance of James Cook, master of the sixty-gun *Pembroke* and future explorer of much of the Pacific Ocean. Cook's captain aboard the *Pembroke* was John Simcoe, father of the future first lieutenant governor of Upper Canada. A full quarter century later, some participants from the Louisbourg siege were still exerting an influence on the course of events in what is now Atlantic Canada. When the Loyalists migrated northward after the American Revolution, two veterans of the 1758 campaign—John Parr and Joseph Frederick Wallet Des Barres—were named governor of Nova Scotia and Cape Breton Island, respectively.[28]

§

The 1758 siege at Louisbourg brought an immediate end to the French regimes on Cape Breton Island and on Prince Edward Island, and it was the first step in the disappearance of the walled town of Louisbourg itself. The British would maintain a garrison there for ten years after the conquest, yet with each passing year the town looked less and less like the one the French had built and lived in for four decades. In 1762 fire swept through part of Louisbourg, and to contain the flames the British pulled down over a dozen buildings. The final blow was the withdrawal in 1768 of the remaining soldiers. More than half of the five hundred inhabitants living in Louisbourg in 1767 departed when the soldiers left in 1768. What once was a prosperous and strategically significant French stronghold became a "decayed city . . . going to ruin." Before they pulled out, the British erected a monument "made with the Hewen Stones of the Ruinous Fortifications" to commemorate the victory a decade earlier. They polished and inscribed the stones so that those who would come afterward would know what was achieved back in 1758. They believed that "the Injurys of Time [could] make but little impression" on the monument. Yet within a few years all trace and recollection of the inscribed stones had disappeared. The commemoration was likely taken down by those who carried off whatever lumber and building stone they could salvage for use elsewhere.[29]

Fleeting though the British monument was, the impact of what was gained and lost at Louisbourg in 1758 was long lasting. The British victory put a halt to the development of Cape Breton Island for roughly thirty years. While the French had expended much effort and money at Louisbourg and made the port prominent on the North Atlantic stage, the island's population and economy plummeted when the British took over. It was not just a case of a difficult transition from one empire to another. Unlike the French the British deliberately discouraged settlement on Cape Breton Island. British engineer Samuel Holland, a participant in the 1758 siege, commented: "No Part of North America can boast of a more advantageous Situation for Commerce & Fishing, than the Island of Cape Britain. . . . The French were early sensible of this, & improved upon it, grudging no Expence however exorbitant that could in the least conduce to the Felicity of this Colony." How different it was after the British took over. They introduced disincentives to development such as refusing to register any land grants; they denied the people who lived on the island any representation in the elected assembly in Halifax; they established no courts of local justice; and they set aside the coal resources in the Sydney area and the timber reserves in other parts of the island exclusively for military purposes. Interests from the Isle of Jersey and Acadians returning after the years of deportation began new communities on Isle Madame in the 1760s, which totaled a few hundred people. The rest of Cape Breton Island, however, saw little settlement. In the words of historian D. C. Harvey, Cape Breton in 1784 was "practically unencumbered by any title to land and was a *tabula rasa* on which the Imperial Government could write its decrees for the future."[30] Only in the 1780s with the influx of Loyalists to the Sydney area and of Acadians to Chéticamp did the island's population began to show growth.

The advent of British control also had a major, long-lasting impact on the former Île Saint-Jean, today's Prince Edward Island. Following an extensive survey directed by Samuel Holland, which divided the island into sixty-seven large lots and three royalties or townships, the British government held a lottery in 1767 to give away virtually the entire island, mostly to military and naval officers residing in Britain. The system of absentee proprietors that was introduced, with settlers who came to live on the island paying rents as tenants, was to persist for more than a century, until 1875.[31]

One of the places the Loyalists came to on Cape Breton Island was Louisbourg, though not to the old French town site. Their focus was instead on the north shore of the harbor, where there had once been many French fishing properties and a fortification known as the Royal Battery. The setting did not much please the Loyalists, and most moved on to Sydney. Louisbourg would eventually reemerge as an important port, especially in the 1890s and early 1900s as the terminus of a local railroad and a winter export harbor for Cape Breton coal. For two centuries the village was Louisburg, without a second *o*. The municipality reinserted the missing letter in 1951, and the provincial government passed an act in 1966 to formalize the switch back to French spelling.[32] Yet never again, at least not yet, has modern Louisbourg had as many inhabitants as it once did, before the events of 1758.

Conclusion

Historian Ian Steele succinctly observes that the successful British campaigns in 1758 show that "fortune favours the biggest armies." In the case of Louisbourg, one would say "armies and navies." Of course, armies and navies do not appear or prevail at will. The state that wants to overmatch its adversary with military might requires both an ability and a willingness to commit the financial resources that will give it the necessary edge. In the case of Great Britain, its desire to win the Seven Years' War in North America led its government to accumulate "a total war debt of £137 million, with interest payments alone consuming more than 60 percent of the annual peacetime budget."[33] The cost was enormous, though no one objected until after the victories were secured and they were asked to pay for what had been achieved. France too committed many soldiers, sailors, and ships to the North American theater, at a huge cost, yet it was less than what Britain spent, and it was not enough to win the day.

On the North American stage the string of British victories that began at Louisbourg in 1758 led directly to the fall of New France. In a single generation there would be equally dramatic changes within Britain's new overseas empire. Just as the French foreign minister the duc de Choiseul foresaw, the prosperous Anglo-American colonies grew increasingly distant from the mother country once the "menace" of the French colonies was removed. The alienation process accelerated when Parliament introduced taxation measures to help pay the debts incurred in winning the Seven Years' War. Those measures kindled a reaction that eventually culminated in the War of Independence. So the successes of Louisbourg (1758), Quebec and Guadeloupe (1759), Montreal (1760), Dominica (1761), Martinique, Saint Lucia, Grenada, and Saint Vincent (1762) brought unprecedented short-term gain and in so doing sowed the seeds for long-term loss. It is one of the striking ironies of the imperial chess match between Great Britain and France that the British were no sooner victorious than they lost what they had long held, the thirteen Anglo-

American colonies. Sticking with the ironic theme, we should note that much of the territory that ended up remaining with Britain in the aftermath of the American Revolution had started out as French possessions: Acadia, Île Royale, Île Saint-Jean, parts of Newfoundland, and Canada. To be sure, relative Acadien and Canadien attachment to the new British administrations were not the only factors. British troops and ships, along with population movements by New England Planters, Loyalists, and immigrants from the British Isles helped ensure that the connection with Britain was maintained.

For France the end of the Seven Years' War represented a particularly low point in its quest for overseas colonial holdings. Most of its North American territory changed flags, either to Britain or to Spain, which took Louisiana. Yet the surprise two and a half centuries later is that most of what was accorded Louis XV by the Treaty of Paris in 1763 remains with France in the present day. The Caribbean islands of Martinique and Guadeloupe and the North Atlantic archipelago of Saint-Pierre and Miquelon continue to be attached to the fifth French Republic, now as official departments, not colonies.

As for the Native allies of the French, the fall of Louisbourg removed any doubt the Mi'kmaq, the Maliseet, and the Abenaki might have had about which European power they would be dealing with in the years ahead. Those who had already entered into treaties with the British prior to 1758 were proven to have chosen the right side. Those who had allied themselves with the French suddenly had to improvise new strategies. The small turnout of warriors at Louisbourg in 1758, in comparison with 1757, suggests that some Native leaders were already withdrawing from the old ties in preparation to forming new ones. Yet it was not an easy transition. The departure of the French meant there would be no more full-time missionaries dedicated to looking after the spiritual needs of the Mi'kmaq, as had been the case throughout the French period. Also ended were the gift exchange ceremonies by which the Louisbourg administration kept the alliance alive, through the provision of food supplies, blankets, muskets, and gunpowder. Many Mi'kmaq of Unama'ki (Cape Breton Island) moved to other parts of Atlantic Canada, temporarily or permanently. The largest number, between 1763 and 1768, crossed to Newfoundland, where "Jeannot Peguidalouet, the eastern Mi'kmaq chief of Cape Breton . . . sometimes overwintered with a group of as many as 200 followers."[34]

Turning specifically to the Louisbourg campaign, I have several observations. First, the casualties were not negligible. The British suffered over six hundred soldiers and sailors killed and wounded, while the French totals were over three hundred, not including civilian casualties, which appear to have been sizable during the last week of bombardment. The deadly realities of the campaign are more important to retain, it seems to me, than the exchange of pineapples and wine and the ceremonial cannon firings by Madame Drucour.

Second, the inability of the French to get all the intended naval squadrons to Louisbourg in the spring of 1758, before the British blockaded the eastern coast of Île Royale, was decisive. The Royal Navy more than half won the eventual siege by keeping those ships completely out of the equation. Had the French possessed anything like the contingent of warships that were at Louisbourg the previous year, and had Blénac-Courbon been in charge of the defense instead of Drucour, it would have been a different defense, and it might have had a different outcome.

A third observation is that there is no reason to revise the long-held assessment that the British land and sea components showed exemplary cooperation throughout the siege, and that the French leadership revealed bitter divisions between its military and naval components.[35] The contrast between the two sides is no great mystery. Once the British made it ashore on June 8, the outcome of the contest was practically decided given the weight of forces they had on their side. Harmony comes easily when one holds all the advantages, at least over the short term, and the subsequent siege lasted less than two months. In contrast the defenders' choices ranged between bad and worse. Should they sacrifice only the town, or the town and the naval squadron along with it? With such alternatives, how could there not be strife and a profound difference of opinions? Had the roles been reversed, the British would almost certainly have shown the same tension and fractures that surfaced among the French at Louisbourg.

Strictly within the British camp, the events of June and July 1758 provided opportunities for James Wolfe to play a leading role at every crucial stage of the campaign. Clearly, this reflected not only Wolfe's abilities and energies but also the decision-making capacity of Jeffery Amherst. There is no written evidence, but it stands to reason that other senior British officers at Louisbourg were trying to catch Amherst's eye as he was handing out the choice assignments. Like a coach of a winning sports team, however, Amherst repeatedly gave the most critical missions to the individual he thought was most likely to bring success: James Wolfe. Despite having the confidence of his superior, Wolfe, ever impetuous and eager for action, frequently criticized Amherst for his methodical planning and cautious approach to the battlefield. Yet without that caution and discipline, the British would have suffered many more casualties than they did. Thus, I support the assessment that historian C. P. Stacey offered years ago of Jeffery Amherst: "[H]e was an organizer of victory, who left nothing to chance in the fields of supply and transport, and this thoroughness was what the war in America mainly required."[36]

§

The final twist in the story of the aftermath of the 1758 siege at Louisbourg came two centuries later, when the federal Canadian government decided to undertake a partial reconstruction of the onetime French stronghold. In 1960, two hundred years after William Pitt ordered the systematic demolition of Louisbourg's fortifications, a Canadian Royal Commission recommended a "symbolic reconstruction" of the bygone French fortified town to put unemployed coal miners to work on Cape Breton Island, with an eye to it becoming a tourist attraction. The federal government of Prime Minister John Diefenbaker accepted the recommendation in 1961. The cabinet minutes expressed the idea as follows: "The Fortress of Louisbourg is to be restored partially so that future generations can thereby see and understand the role of the Fortress as a hinge of history. The restoration is to be carried out so that the lessons of history can be animated."[37] Interestingly, it was the near total abandonment of the original town site after 1768 that created a virtual time capsule for archaeologists two centuries later.

If the late twentieth-century reconstruction of Louisbourg was undertaken in part to mark the largest, most colorful, and most significant event in Louisbourg's history, the siege of 1758, that is not how it turned out. The decision to reconstruct a portion of the original walled town—it

ended up being about one-fifth of the town and one-quarter of the fortifications—and to put people in period costumes meant that the interpre-
tive emphasis at the fortress of Louisbourg National Historic Site neces-
sarily shifted from a British feat of arms and a valiant French defense to
a focus on daily life during peacetime. The pendulum may be about to
swing in the twenty-first century, for in recent years Parks Canada, the
agency that administers the site, is attempting to refocus its interpretation on the primary reasons why Louisbourg was designated a place of
national importance. In the course of those efforts, the siege of 1758 is
bound to become a priority storyline. When that time comes, many of
the places where the monumental struggle unfolded—landing beaches,
siege camps, and battery locations—will perhaps become attractions for
visitors. For many of those features are still there, silent witnesses to a
time of high promise, great glory, and profound despair.

French Ships to Louisbourg, 1758

Ships	Guns	Crew	Commander	Note
Prudent*	74	680	Marquis Charry des Gouttes	Burned, July 25/26
Entreprenant*	74	680	Beaussier de L'Isle	Burned, July 21
Célèbre*	64	550	Chevalier de Marolles	Burned, July 21
Capricieux*	64	550	Chevalier de Tourville	Burned, July 21
Bienfaisant*	64	550	Courserac	Captured, July 25/26
Comète*	74		Chevalier de Lorgeril	Escaped to France, June 10
Formidable	80		Guichen (with Blénac-Courbon)	Returned to Brest
Dragon	64		Comte du Chaffaut de Besné	To Quebec, then France
Belliqueux	64		Martel	To Quebec, then captured
Sphinx	armé en flûte		Vendes Turgot	To Quebec, then France
Hardi	64		La Touche de Tréville	To Quebec, then France
Zéphyr	frigate		Terny d'Arsac	
Brillant	Cie de Indes		Saint-Médard	To Port Dauphin, then France
Aréthuse*	36	280	Vauquelin	Escaped to France, July 15
Bizarre*	64		Breugnon	To Quebec, June 10
Echo*	32	250		Captured June 10
Apollon*	50	400		Sunk as block ship, June 28/29
Diane*	36	300		Captured April 18
Chèvre*	22	200		Sunk as block ship, June 28/29
Fidèle*	22	200		Sunk as block ship, June 28/29
Biche*	16	150		Sunk as block ship, June 28/29

Note: The asterisk (*) indicates the ships that were in Louisbourg harbor at the beginning of the siege. The combined total for those vessels was 692 cannons and over 5,000 sailors. That was roughly one-third of the sea forces the British were bringing to bear against them.

Sources: LaCour-Gayet, *La Marine militaire de la France*, 532; Caron, *La guerre incomprise*, 319 n2; Boscawen, "Combined Operation against Louisbourg."

British Ships at Louisbourg, 1758

Ships of the line	Guns	Crew	Commander
Namur	90	780	Boscawen/Buckle
Royal William	84	765	Hardy/Evans
Princess Amelia	80	665	Durrell/Bray
Dublin	74	600	Rodney
Terrible	74	600	Collins
Northumberland	70	520	Colville
Orford	70	520	Spry
Somerset	70	520	Hughes
Vanguard	70	520	Swanton
Burford	70	520	Gambier
Lancaster	66	520	Edgecombe
Devonshire	66	520	Gordon
Captain	64	480	Amherst
Bedford	64	480	Fowke
Prince Frederick	64	480	Mann
Defiance	60	400	Baird
Pembroke	60	420	Simcoe
York	60	480	Pigot
Kingston	60	420	Parry
Prince of Orange	60	420	Ferguson
Nottingham	60	420	Marshall
Centurion	50	420	Mantell
Sutherland	50	350	Rous
Arc-en-Ciel	50	350	Captured from French, 1756
SUBTOTAL	1,586	12,170	

Frigates, sloops, fireships, etc.	Guns	Crew	Commander
Diana	32	220	Schomberg
Juno	32	220	Vaughan
Boreas	28	200	Boyle
Trent	28	200	Lindsay
Shannon	28	200	Medows
Hind	24	160	Bond
Portmahon	24	160	Ourry
Nightingale	24	160	Campbell
Scarborough	20	160	Routh
Kennington	20	160	Jacobs
Squirrel	20	160	Wheelock
Gramont	18	125	Stott
Beaver	16	150	Gascoigne
Hunter	14	140	Laforey
Hawke	14	140	Hathorne
Halifax	12	120	Taggart
Aetna	8	80	Balfour
Lightning	8	80	Goostrey
Tayloe	6	40	Pryce
SUBTOTAL	376	2,875	
OVERALL TOTAL	1,962	15,045	

Note: These totals do not include the 127 transports and their crews.

Sources: McLennan, *Louisbourg from Its Foundation*, 261; Boscawen, "Combined Operation against Louisbourg."

French Land Forces at Louisbourg, 1758

Unit	Fit for duty on June 8	Fit for duty on July 27
24 marine companies & 2 artillery companies	1,120	822
Artois Regiment (2nd Battalion)	520	439
Bourgogne Regiment (2nd Battalion)	520	383
Cambis Regiment (2nd Battalion)	680	504
Volontaires Étrangers Regt. (2nd Battalion)	680	440
TOTALS	3,520	2,588

The difference between the two lists of French men-at-arms is 932. As of July 27 there were 443 soldiers listed as sick and injured. The other 489 were either dead, prisoners of the British, or deserters.

	Fit for duty Early July	Fit for duty Late July
French naval officers and sailors come ashore	2,606	1,259

Source: McLennan, *Louisbourg from Its Foundation,* 263, 288.

British Land Forces at Louisbourg, 1758

Regiment	Name	Officers, NCOs, drummers	Rank & file	Total
1	2nd Battalion, Royals (Royal Scots Regiment)	82	854	936
15	Amherst's (East Yorkshire Regiment)	96	763	859
17	Forbes's (Leicestershire Regiment)	81	660	741
22	Whitmore's (Chesire Regiment)	97	910	1,007
28	Bragg's (Gloucester Regiment, 1st battalion)	81	627	708
35	Otway's (Royal Sussex Regiment)	61	566	627
40	Hopson's (Prince of Wales Volunteers– South Lancashire Regiment)	81	550	631
45	Warburton's (Sherwood Foresters– Derbyshire Regiment, 1st battalion)	92	864	956
47	Lascelles' (Loyal North Lancashire Regiment– Wolfe's Own)	92	857	949

Regiment	Name	Officers, NCOs, drummers	Rank & file	Total
48	Webb's (Northhamptonshire Regiment, 1st battalion)	97	932	1,029
58	Anstruther's (Northhamptonshire Regiment, 2nd battalion)	70	615	685
60	Monckton's (King's Royal Rifle Corps)	98	925	1,023
60	Lawrence's (King's Royal Rifle Corps)	87	814	901
78/63	Frazer's (Seaforth Highlanders)	115	1,084	1,199
	Engineers	12		12
	Rangers	50	499	549
	Train of artillery	57	267	324
	New England carpenters		103	103
	TOTALS	1,349	11,890	13,239

Sources: McLennan, *Louisbourg from Its Foundation*, 262; Boscawen, "Combined Operation against Louisbourg."

Notes

Prologue

1. Two excellent, chapter-length summaries that do cover the period are John G. Reid on the 1750s in *Six Crucial Decades*; and Stephen E. Patterson, "1744–1763."

2. This is certainly the case in the much-praised book by Fred Anderson, *Crucible of War*, chap. 25, titled "Amherst at Louisbourg." Anderson's book is a terrific piece of scholarship and writing; yet while it treats the military actions in the Anglo-American colonies in great depth, he summarizes the siege at Louisbourg quickly and with no reference to French sources. In fact, Anderson's treatment of Louisbourg is essentially that of Corbett, *England in the Seven Years' War*; and Gipson, *British Empire*, vol. 7. Anderson makes no reference to the 1918 study of J. S. McLennan (see note 3), who provides by far the greatest amount of information on the siege of 1758. A recent book on the Seven Years' War, Fowler's *Empires at War*, offers an account of the 1758 siege at Louisbourg without presenting much evidence from French sources.

3. McLennan, *Louisbourg*. A recent addition to the literature is Chartrand's well-illustrated *Louisbourg 1758*. Chartrand provides a capsule history of the units that fought in the siege and of the progress of the attack.

4. There is an extensive literature on eighteenth-century Louisbourg. For an introduction to the economy of the town, see Balcom, *Cod Fishery*; and Christopher Moore, "Cape Breton and the North Atlantic World in the Eighteenth Century," in Kenneth Donovan, ed., *The Island: New Perspectives on Cape Breton History, 1713–1900* (Fredericton NB: Acadiensis; Sydney NS: Cape Breton University Press, 1990), 30–48. Donovan has published many articles on Louisbourg, one of which is "Slaves and Their Owners." A recent study is Johnston, *Control and Order*.

5. An example of a recent work on New France that gives proper treatment to the history and role of Louisbourg and Île Royale is Moogk, *La Nouvelle France*.

6. François Caron, *La guerre incomprise*, 195. Dull, *French Navy*, 13, asserts that Île Royale rivaled the sugar-producing colonies in the West Indies in its economic importance to France, whereas the colony along the Saint Lawrence River, known as Canada, was an "economic liability" to the mother country.

7. Johnston, *Life and Religion*.

8. Reed Browning writes of the 1740s that "the hoary assumption that sovereigns

could exchange people and places to suit their own interests reigned with undiminished force," *War of the Austrian Succession*, 366.

9. The seminal study of this aspect is Mahan, *Influence of Sea Power*. Dull points out that "in the early 1690s France had the world's most powerful navy," *French Navy*, 9. By 1715, however, France had "fewer than half the number" of ships of the line that it had possessed twenty years earlier. Another recent study of the French navy is Pritchard, *Louis XV's Navy*.

10. Dr. Johnson, quoted in Rashed, *Peace of Paris*, 7.

11. B. A. Balcom, "Defending Unama'ki: Mi'kmaw Resistance in Cape Breton, 1745," unpublished manuscript, is a fascinating study of Mi'kmaw involvement in the 1745 siege of Louisbourg. A recent, comprehensive study showing the involvement of Native warriors in the American colonies is Anderson, *Crucible of War*; see the many entries for "Indian Peoples" in the index, p. 848. There are numerous works on the subject by others, among them Francis Jennings, Ian Steele, and Peter Macleod.

12. The various books of Naomi Griffiths on the Acadians come to mind, especially *From Migrant to Acadian*. So too does Geoffrey Plank's *Unsettled Conquest* and Wicken's *Mi'kmaq Treaties on Trial*.

13. In *Crucible of War*, Anderson writes that the Seven Years' War was "the most important event to occur in eighteenth-century North America" (xv). The author goes on to explain why he thinks that war was more important than the American Revolution.

14. In the first two chapters of *Frigates and Foremasts*, Gwyn looks at British strategic thinking and naval policies concerning how best to combat the French presence in Atlantic Canada.

15. In *Nova Scotia's Massachusetts* Rawlyk gives the population of Massachusetts in 1750 as 190,000 (xiii).

16. There are several good maps of the French forts, settlements, and posts in Balesi, *Time of the French*.

17. For an in-depth analysis of the work of French missionaries in what is now Atlantic Canada, see Dumont-Johnson, *Apôtres ou agitateurs*. This is not the place to discuss the Mi'kmaq-British relationship, which was marked by both frequent conflict and ongoing attempts at finding treaty solutions. For an introduction to the subject, see Wicken, *Mi'kmaq Treaties on Trial*.

18. Steele, *Warpaths*, 77.

19. In *La pensée et l'action*, Filion states that in 1729 the French cod fisheries for Île Royale, the Gulf of Saint Lawrence, and on the Grand Banks consisted of 296 ships of 26,007 tons employing 7,489 sailors (70). He observes that Louisbourg became a "junction" (*charnière*) and that it was a "new structure" for French colonial possessions (165). Banks offers a detailed examination of three elements in that French overseas world in *Chasing Empire*.

20. Filion, *Maurepas, ministre de Louis XV*, 36; Filion, *La pensée*, 67–68.

21. This particular quote comes from Joseph Bernard, marquis de Chabert de Cogolin, *Voyage fait par ordre du roi en 1750 et 1751 dans l'Amérique septentrionale*, facsimile of 1753 edition (East Ardsley, England: S. R. Publishers, 1966), 103.

22. Louisbourg's population is discussed in chap. 1 of Johnston, *Control and Order*.

23. McNeill provides a summary of the geographical setting and climate on Cape Breton Island, *Atlantic Empires*, 14.

24. Archives nationales, Archives des colonies, c11b, vol. 9, fol. 40, St-Ovide and Mezy, 15 décembre 1727; the British engineer was John Henry Bastide, quoted in Fortier, *Fortress of Louisbourg*, 66. The French writer was Pichon, *Lettres et mémoires*.

25. Laplante, "Pourquoi les Acadiens"; Bernard Pothier, "Acadian Emigration to Île Royale after the Conquest of Acadia," *Histoire sociale / Social History* 3, no. 6 (November 1970): 116–31; A. J. B. Johnston, "Un regard neuf sur les Acadiens de l'Île Royale," *Cahiers de la Société historique acadienne* 32, no. 3 (September 2001): 155–72.

26. Clark contends that Île Royale's lack of self-sufficiency was a sign of the weakness of its economy, "New England's Role," 1–12. Moore argues otherwise in "Cape Breton and the North Atlantic World." See also Anne O'Neill, "The Gardens of 18th-Century Louisbourg," *Journal of Garden History* 3, no. 3:176–78.

27. McLennan, *Louisbourg*, appendix on p. 370 of the first edition; the appendices were not reprinted in any edition after 1918; Giraud, "France and Louisiana"; Lacour-Gayet, *La Marine militaire*, 93–95; Desbarats, "France in North America," 21.

28. McLennan, *Louisbourg*, appendix on p. 370. Government expenditures in the 1720s ranged from 120,000 to 159,000 livres. In the 1730s the figures ranged from 296,000 to 349,000 livres. In the 1740s the expenditures rose again, to 495,468 in 1743 and up to 547,436 livres in 1744.

29. Thorpe, *Remparts lointains*, 28–29n24. Balcom, *Cod Fishery*, table 4, p. 17. There are at least fifteen years missing from the table, yet for the twenty years for which figures are available, the combined value in France of cod and cod liver oil was over 55 million livres. Moore, "Other Louisbourg." Another study by Moore, "Commodity Imports of Louisbourg," Manuscript Report Series 317 (Ottawa: Parks Canada, 1975) provides a picture of the range of commodities that arrived in Louisbourg.

30. Greer, *Soldiers of Isle Royale*. Jean-Éric Labignette in "Louisbourg en L'Isle Royale, 1713–1761," (ca. 1955) ms. on file at Archives of the Fortress of Louisbourg, wrote that Louisbourg had begun "à présenter un aspect de cité forte et offrait quelque ressemblance avec la ville de Saint-Malo" (79). The evolution of the fortifications is the focus in Fry, *"Appearance of Strength."* The development of the urban setting within the fortifications is the subject of an entire chapter in Johnston, *Control and Order*.

31. The minister of the Marine (the comte de Pontchartrain) declared in 1715: "[I]f France would lose this island, it would be irreparable and as a necessary consequence we would have to abandon the rest of northeastern America," Archives nationales, Archives des colonies, B, vol. 37, fol. 28, 10 février 1715. Writing after the loss of

Louisbourg and the rest of New France, Voltaire offered the following: "[T]he island of Louisbourg or of Cape Breton, was then an important island for the French . . . the key to their possessions in North America. The territory had been ceded to France by the peace of Utrecht. The cod fishery carried out in its waters was the object of a useful commerce, employing each year more than 500 small vessels. . . . It was a school of sailors; and of commerce; which joined to that of the cod fishery, kept 10,000 men working and circulated 10 millions [livres]," from his "Précis du siècle de Louis XV," in *Oeuvres historiques* (Bruges: Éditions Gallimard, 1957), 1462.

32. Colonel Samuel Vetch, cited in McLennan, *Louisbourg*, 21.

33. Samuel Holland, in Harvey, *Holland's Description*, 60.

34. Brière's figures are quoted in Dull, *French Navy*, 14.

35. Franklin, quoted in John Fortier, *Fortress of Louisbourg*, 7; Philip Durell, *A Particular Account of the Taking of Cape Breton from the French by Admiral Warren and Sir William Pepperell the 17th of June 1745* (London: W. Bickerton, 1745), pamphlet in the Rare Book Dept. of the Boston Public Library, G.31.63; Jean-Pierre Roma, cited in Fry, *"Appearance of Strength,"* 54. On the subject of exaggeration, one historian writes: "Migration inspired extravagant ideas on every hand of what the migrants were, what they were engaged upon, and what they discovered," in Michael Zuckerman, "Identity in British America: Unease in Eden," in Canny and Pagden, *Colonial Identity in the Atlantic World*, 120.

36. Johnston, *Summer of 1744*; Bernard Pothier, *Course à l'Accadie*.

37. Brebner, *New England's Outpost*; Wrong, *Louisbourg in 1745*, 15; Shirley, quoted in Baker, *Campaign of Amateurs*, 7.

38. Gwyn, *Enterprising Admiral*. Some texts have the surrender occurring on June 17, 1745, because the British and the New Englanders were then following the outdated Julian calendar, eleven days behind the Gregorian calendar. In 1752 Great Britain and its colonies switched to the calendar the French were using, which we still use today. One study of the 1745 siege is Rawlyk, *Yankees at Louisbourg*; another is by Baker, *Campaign of Amateurs*. The unidentified marine's description is in Durell, *Particular Account*. The church he refers to is the Chapelle Saint-Louis within the barracks of the King's Bastion. French accounts of the destruction of civilian houses during the siege are not numerous; one is in Gwyn and Moore, *La chute de Louisbourg*, 85.

39. Gwyn, *Frigates and Foremasts*, 13–14.

40. Filion, *Maurepas, ministre de Louis XV*, 45.

41. There are numerous indications of the French sending on information about Louisbourg in O'Callaghan, *Documents*; the citation comes from "Military and Other Operations in Canada during the Years 1745–46," 47.

42. Pritchard, *Anatomy of a Naval Disaster*. Filion, *Maurepas, ministre de Louis XV*, 44, offers this comparison of the two navies in 1746: the British possessed 161 vessels with 40 or more guns while the French had only 50 vessels with 40 or more guns. Of

those totals, the British had 26 ships with 80 guns, 12 with 90 guns, and 7 with 100 guns. The French navy possessed only a single ship with 80 guns.

43. Sosin, "Louisbourg."

1. Opening Moves, 1749

1. This English translation, along with the original Mi'kmaq version, is published in Whitehead, *Old Man Told Us*, 114. The original French version of the document was published in Olive Patricia Dickason, "Louisbourg et les Indiens: Une étude des relations raciales de la France, 1713–1760," in *Histoire et archéologie* no. 6 (Ottawa: Parks Canada, 1979), 154–55.

2. Steele, *Warpaths*, 67.

3. The 1750s is the subject of a chapter in John G. Reid, *Six Crucial Decades*, and of an article by Stephen E. Patterson, "1744–1763."

4. This material is contained in Archives nationales, Archives des colonies, C11B, vol. 27, and in occasional memoranda in Archives nationales, Archives des colonies, B, vols. 83–89.

5. Archives nationales, Archives des colonies, C11B, vol. 27, fols. 304–5v, Prévost, 20 avril 1748.

6. Archives nationales, Archives des colonies, B, vol. 88, fol. 351, 11 novembre 1748.

7. Archives nationales, Archives des colonies, B, vol. 88, fol. 364, 9 décembre 1748. One of the few groups whose whereabouts are known precisely was the Sisters of the Congregation of Notre-Dame. They passed the 1745–49 period in the Hôpital St-Étienne in La Rochelle; Johnston, *Life and Religion*, 98–99.

8. Johnston, *Life and Religion*, 6–7; and Schmeisser, "Population of Louisbourg."

9. Archives nationales, Archives des colonies, B, vol. 90, p. 57, 24 janvier 1749; p. 92, 6 mars 1749; p. 106, 24 mars 1749.

10. Archives nationales, Archives des colonies, B, vol. 89, p. 324, 28 mars 1749; p. 209, 11 avril 1749.

11. The figures provided are for companies at full strength, a situation rarely achieved.

12. There are various mentions of the Île Royale troops in Archives nationales, Archives des colonies, B, vols. 87 and 88. Authorization for the Compagnies franches of Île Royale to have their own flags while at Quebec is located in Archives nationales, Archives des colonies, B, vol. 87, 7 février 1748; vol. 88, 7 février 1748.

13. Archives nationales, Archives des colonies, C11C, vol. 8, fol. 192, n.d. [1749]; Schmeisser, "Building a Colonial Outpost," 38.

14. Maurepas was removed in April 1749. Maurice Filion offers the following assessment: "On peut affirmer que l'érection de Louisbourg est vraiment l'oeuvre de Maurepas: les sommes affectées à cette construction durant son ministère représentent

plus de 80 percent des dépenses faites pour Louisbourg entre 1714 et 1744 et plus de 71 percent de toutes celles faites entre 1714 et 1756," *La pensée et l'action*, 165.

15. Barbier noted in his journal: "M. de Maurepas avait dit au roi en conversation, peut-être dans le temps de la prise du Cap-Breton sur nous, et des bruits que cela faisait répandre, qu'il avait bien des ennemis, et que si Sa Majesté était mécontente de ses services, il la priait de le lui annoncer elle-même," *Journal historique et anecdotique*, 3:78.

16. Caron, *La guerre incomprise*, 116.

17. Dull, *French Navy*, 11–12.

18. Pritchard, *Louis XV's Navy*, 6–7.

19. The differing perspectives on retaining or returning Louisbourg are explored in Andrew Peter Podolsky, "Site of Imagination: The Fortress at Louisbourg and Stories of Empire" (PhD diss., Northwestern University, 1998). The quote from the Earl of Chesterfield appears on pp. 115–16.

20. Gwyn, *Frigates and Foremasts*, 19.

21. Stephen White, "The True Number of Acadians," in LeBlanc, *Du Grand Dérangement*, 21–56.

22. Gwyn, *Frigates and Foremasts*, 6.

23. The expedition is the subject of Pritchard, *Anatomy of a Naval Disaster*.

24. For the battle of 1747 Grand-Pré, see Charles Morris, 1748, "A Brief Survey of Nova Scotia with an account of the Several Attempts of the French this War to recover it out of the hands of the English," Library and Archives Canada, MG 18, vol. F.4–F.10; Benjamin Goldthwaite's account, *The Boston Post Boy*, March 7, 1747, Nova Scotia Archives and Record Management, MG 100, vol. 198, no. 2; Louis de La Corne's narrative, September 28, 1747, Nova Scotia Archives and Record Management, MG 100, vol. 198, no. 2c; and Daniel-Hyacinthe-Marie Liénard de Beaujeu, "Journal de la Campagne du Détachement de Canada a l'Acadie et aux Mines en 1746–47," in *Le Canada-Français, Collection de documents inédits sur le Canada et l'Amérique*, vol. 2 (Quebec: L.-J. Demers et frère, 1889), 16–75. This episode is the focus of MacMechan, *Red Snow on Grand-Pré*.

25. Letter of the Duke of Bedford to the Duke of Cumberland, October 11, 1748, in Pargellis, *Military Affairs in North America*, 6–7.

26. I discuss this issue in some detail in "Borderland Worries."

27. The importance of "Protestantness" to the British idea is articulated in Colley, *Britons*. In her introduction Colley explains that "as an invented nation" Great Britain was "heavily dependent for its *raison d'être* on a broadly Protestant culture, on the threat and tonic of recurring war, particularly war with France, and on the triumphs, profits and Otherness represented by a massive overseas empire" (6).

28. A 1717 proposal for the settlement of Nova Scotia stipulated that "all Foreigners who shall settle and inhabit there and take the oaths to His Majesty shall enjoy the same Libertys and Immunities within the said Province as any of His Majesty's Subjects"; Bell, *"Foreign Protestants,"* 33–34.

29. Bell, *"Foreign Protestants,"* 17–83.

30. Frégault, *Canada*, 170.

31. Letters and a fortifications proposal by sieur Delabat appear in William Inglis Morse, ed., *Acadiensis Nova (1598–1779)*, vol. 2 (London: Bernard Quaritch, 1935), 1–14.

32. Gwyn, *Frigates and Foremasts*, 23.

33. Manning, *British Colonial Government*, 166–67. The first two quotes are comments by Manning; the citation from Burke comes from the same study.

34. A transcript of the British advertisement appears as an appendix to Akins, "History of Halifax City," 239–41. According to the Gregorian calendar, which had not yet been adopted by the British in 1749, the founding of Halifax was not on June 21, as is traditionally celebrated at Halifax, but on July 2.

35. Brumwell describes how wary the British were in their attitudes toward warfare in the Americas, *Redcoats*, 137–61.

36. Akins provides the names of the ships and how many they carried, as well as the names of the principal inhabitants, "History of Halifax City," 5–6. The quotation comes from the footnote on pp. 6 and 7.

37. Excerpt from the "Instructions to Cornwallis," cited in Douglas, "Halifax as an Element of Sea Power," 22.

38. J. Murray Beck, "Cornwallis, Edward," in *Dictionary of Canadian Biography*, 4:168–71.

39. Fingard, Guildford, and Sutherland, *Halifax*, 15.

40. A lengthy discussion of the North American style of warfare can be found in Brumwell, *Redcoats*, 191–226.

41. The importance of the "sea militia" during the early years of Halifax is discussed in Douglas, "Halifax."

42. Extract from a letter, in Akins, "History of Halifax City," 12–13.

43. Raddall, *Halifax*, 34; Fingard, Guildford, and Sutherland, *Halifax*, 15.

44. Brumwell, *Redcoats*, chap. 6.

45. Stephen E. Patterson, "1744–1763," 129.

46. Olive Dickason, *Canada's First Nations: A History of Founding Peoples from Earliest Times* (Toronto: McClelland and Stewart, 1992), 149.

47. Stephen E. Patterson, "1744–1763," 129; Wicken, *Mi'kmaq Treaties on Trial*, 61–159.

48. Stephen E. Patterson, "Indian-White Relations," 27.

49. A study of French missionary activity is Dumont-Johnson, *Apôtres ou agitateurs*.

50. Abbé Le Loutre to Rouillé, minister of the Marine, July 29, 1749, in *Report concerning Canadian Archives for the Year 1905*, vol. 2 (Ottawa: Queen's Printer, 1906), 283–84.

51. I recently published a book on this topic: *Storied Shores*.

52. Whitehead, *Old Man Told Us*, 114.

53. The letter is dated October 2, 1720, *Collection de Manuscrits rélatifs à la Nouvelle-France*, vol. 3 (Quebec: A. Côté, 1883–85), 46–47.

54. Details are provided in Stephen E. Patterson, "Indian-White Relations," 30–31; Akins, "History of Halifax City"; and other sources.

55. Whitehead, *Old Man Told Us*, 117. Mi'kmaw historian Daniel N. Paul offers his thoughts on this phase of Nova Scotia's history in *We Were Not the Savages*.

56. James Axtell has explored the origins and history of scalping in several publications, including *The European and the Indian*.

57. For examples of scalps being brought for payment, see O'Callaghan, *Documents*, vol. 10. A 1696 Massachusetts broadside that offered bounties for the scalps of Indian men, women, and children is reproduced in Plank, *Unsettled Conquest*, 34.

58. Doughty, *Historical Journal*, 2:197.

59. McLennan, *Louisbourg*, 187; the names of the men-of-war were *Tigre* and *Intrépide*; the frigate *Anémone* followed soon after. Information on de Gannes, Loppinot, and other officers of the Louisbourg garrison up until 1745 can be found in Johnston, "Officers of Isle Royale."

60. Wendy Cameron provides a biography of Hopson (?-1759) in *Dictionary of Canadian Biography*, 3:294–95.

61. The burial records for 1749 are located in Archives de la France d'outre mer, G1, vol. 408, reg. 1.

62. This is the assessment of John Fortier in the brief biography of the governor, in *Dictionary of Canadian Biography*, 3:182–84.

63. There were 1,966 men, women, and children listed in the Louisbourg census for 1749, Archives de la France d'outre mer, G1, vol. 466, pièce 76, plus another 21 people described as "habitans de L'Isle Royalle Residente à Rochefort le 17 aout 1749," Archives Maritimes, Port de Rochefort, série 1R, vol. 47. The names and positions of Desherbiers' servants are provided on the former document.

64. Archives de la France d'outre mer, G1, vol. 466, pièce 75, "Liste des familles qui ont resté a l'isle Royalle depuis 1745 jusqu'au mois septembre 1748." The man's name was Jean-Baptiste Dion.

65. La Galissonière to the minister of the marine, September 3, 1748, letter transcribed in *Report concerning Canadian Archives for the Year 1905*, vol. 2 (Ottawa: Queen's Printer, 1906), 281.

66. McLennan, *Louisbourg*, appendix 9, pp. 409–12. The appendices to McLennan's study were published only in the original 1918 edition.

67. The document that certifies the transfer of Louisbourg from British to French possession is transcribed in *Report concerning Canadian Archives for the Year 1905*, 2:282–83. Incoming governor Desherbiers offers a lengthy description of the French taking possession of Louisbourg in a letter dated July 29, 1749, Boston Public Library, Rare Book Dept, G 41.26. Artillery salutes to mark the *prise de possession* cost 337 livres.

Another 388 livres were spent on cannon salvos on the occasion of the funeral of the duc d'Enville, while an additional 546 and 454 livres were spent on "diverses fournitures" and funeral costs for the reinterment ceremonies, respectively. The sources for the expenditures are Archives nationales, Archives des colonies, c11b, vol. 27, fols. 266–69, 30 septembre 1751; c11c, vol. 13, fols. 73 and 83, 13 septembre 1751.

68. McLennan, *Louisbourg*, 187n3. The original parish record entry is in Archives de la France d'outre mer, g1, vol. 408, reg. 1, baptism on July 27.

69. Information on the 1749 Te Deum is located in Archives nationales, Archives des colonies, B, vol. 89, fol. 305, 28 mars 1749; and c11b, vol. 28, fol. 75v, 9 août 1749.

70. See Pritchard, *Anatomy of a Naval Disaster*, 227, for the removal of the remains to Louisbourg.

71. The sources for the expenditures are Archives nationales, Archives des colonies, c11b, vol. 27, fols. 266–69, 30 septembre 1751; c11c, vol. 13, fols. 73 et 83, 13 septembre 1751. For a comparison the artillery salutes offered to mark the *prise de possession* in late July 1749 cost 337 livres.

72. Chartrand, *Canadian Military Heritage*, 2:15. Chartrand provides the following increases, as of 1750, for these colonies: Louisiana, from 850 to 2,000; Louisbourg, from 700 to 1,200; Canada, from 812 to 1,500.

2. Middle Game, 1750–1755

1. In *Anatomy of a Naval Disaster*, 226, Pritchard dates the clarifying process as beginning with the events of 1745–46, which were then followed up by the initiatives of 1749.

2. Archives nationales, Archives des colonies, c11b, vol. 28, fols. 126–27, 9 août 1749.

3. Archives nationales, Archives des colonies, c11b, vol. 29, fols. 73–73v, 22 juillet 1750.

4. A short summary on Roma (fl. 1715–57), prepared by Margaret Coleman, is in *Dictionary of Canadian Biography*, 3:566–67. Roma's report is in two parts; Archives nationales, Archives des colonies, c11b, vol. 29, fols. 359–84v, and fols. 400–407v, 1750. "Much," in French, is underlined in the original document, fol. 366.

5. F. J. Thorpe, "Franquet, Louis," *Dictionary of Canadian Biography*, 3:228–31.

6. Baker, *Campaign of Amateurs*, 50.

7. Michel Parent and Jacques Verroust, *Vauban* (Paris: Éditions Jacques Fréal, 1971), 95–96, 236.

8. This insight comes from McNeill, *Atlantic Empires*.

9. Fry, *"Appearance of strength,"* 1:164.

10. Archives nationales, Archives des colonies, B, vol. 92, p. 352, 30 janvier 1750; vol. 91, p. 317, 3, février 1750; c11b, vol. 28, fols. 276–276v, 18 février 1750.

11. The increase in the number of baptisms, marriages, and burials at Louisbourg during the 1750s, in comparison with the period before 1745, is depicted on a graph in

Johnston, *Life and Religion*, 137. The corresponding figures from the period 1722–45 are 1,119 baptisms, 233 marriages, and 599 burials.

12. There is a chapter on each of the respective groups in Johnston, *Life and Religion*.

13. This paragraph summarizes material in Johnston, *Control and Order*, chap. 5.

14. Donovan, "Marquis de Chabert."

15. Archives nationales, Archives des colonies, C11B, vol. 29, fols. 209–10v, 9 décembre 1750.

16. Archives nationales, Archives des colonies, C11B, vol. 29, fols. 66–71v, 6 décembre 1750.

17. Archives nationales, Archives des colonies, C11C, vol. 9, fol. 172v, Dénombrement de 1751. A recent book on that part of Île Royale is Johnston, *Storied Shores*, 74–86.

18. Dull, *French Navy*, 15.

19. Frégault, *Canada*, 167; Cornwallis to Robert Napier, adjutant general and secretary for military affairs under the Duke of Cumberland, in Pargellis, *Military Affairs*, 8–9.

20. Frank H. Patterson, *History of Tatamagouche*; Stanley, *New France*, 126; Margaret Coleman, *Acadian History in the Isthmus of Chignecto*, Manuscript Report 29 (Ottawa: Dept. of Indian Affairs and Northern Development, 1968), 70–72; Caron, *La guerre incomprise*, 197–98n, offers a transcription of a February 1755 document that outlines the French perspective on the importance of retaining the Chignecto region.

21. Douglas, "Halifax as an Element of Sea Power," 67.

22. Hand summarizes some of the French moves in *Siege of Fort Beauséjour*, 16–17. For French activity involving the Saint John River in the late 1600s, see John Clarence Webster, ed., *Acadia at the End of the 17th Century: Letters, Journals and Memoirs of Joseph Robineau de Villebon, Commandant in Acadia, 1690–1700 and Other Contemporary Documents* (1934; reprint, Saint John: New Brunswick Museum, 1979). In "Survey for French Military Supply Depots," Leonard summarizes research undertaken by Regis Brun. There is a biography of La Corne, by C. J. Russ, in *Dictionary of Canadian Biography*, 3:331–32. See also Phyllis LeBlanc, "Deschamps de Boishébert et de Raffetot, Charles," in *Dictionary of Canadian Biography*, 4:212–25; Campbell, *Road to Canada*; and Pothier, *Battle for the Chignecto Forts*.

23. Griffiths, *From Migrant to Acadian*, 260–61, 279–80, 370, 386, 403, 412–13, 418, 438–39; Johnston, "Borderland Worries." For the complete text of an ultimatum given to the Acadians by the administration at Quebec, see Brebner, "Canadian Policy." Dunn, *History of Port-Royal*, 196.

24. Dunn, *History of Port-Royal*, 196. Both locations are National Historic Sites of Canada. The original blockhouse put up in 1750 still stands at Fort Edward, Windsor, Nova Scotia.

25. On Lunenburg, see Bell, *"Foreign Protestants."* For a map showing the areas in the Chignecto region and the upper Bay of Fundy where the British wanted to locate Protestants to counterbalance the Acadians, see Gipson, *British Empire*, 6:264.

26. Hand, *Siege of Fort Beauséjour*, 20–21.

27. Archives nationales, Archives des colonies, CIIB, vol. 29, fol. 75v, Prévost, 22 juillet 1750; "A Letter from Louisbourg, 1756," introduced by Ken Donovan, *Acadiensis* 10, no. 1 (Autumn 1980): 127. Thanks to Earle Lockerby for pointing out that the writer previously known only as Monieur de la Varenne was almost certainly René Gaultier de Varennes, an ensign in the Louisbourg Garrison from 1750 to 1757. René and his career are mentioned in S. Dale Standen's biography of Jacques-René Gaultier de Varennes in *Dictionary of Canadian Biography*, 3:245–46.

28. Lord Holdernesse, quoted in Dominick Graham's biography of Charles Lawrence in *Dictionary of Canadian Biography*, 3:364. For more on Fort Beauséjour and Fort Gaspereau, see Schmeisser, "Narrative and Structural History"; and Pothier's and Hand's studies referenced earlier.

29. Johnston, "Desertion, treason"; Du Boscq de Beaumont, *Les derniers jours*, 84; Archives nationales, Archives des colonies, CIIB, vol. 33, 197–201, 16 août 1753.

30. The "between two fires" phrase comes from Parkman's *Half-Century of Conflict*, cited in Griffiths, *Acadian Deportation*, 39; Stephen White, "The True Number of Acadians," in LeBlanc, *Du Grand Dérangement*, 21–56. Bona Arsenault states that six thousand migrated between 1749 and 1752 and thousands more between 1752 and 1755, "Les Acadiens réfugiés à la baie des Chaleurs, en 1758," *Cahiers de la Société historique acadienne* 17, no. 3 (July–September 1986): 89.

31. For Acadians moving to Île Royale, see A. J. B. Johnston, "Before the Loyalists: Acadians in the Sydney Area, 1749–1754," *Cape Breton's Magazine* no. 48 (June 1988); and Johnston, "Un regard neuf sur les Acadiens de l'Île Royale," *Cahiers de la Société historique acadienne* 32, no. 3 (September 2001): 155–72. For the situation on Île Saint-Jean, see D. C. Harvey, *The French Regime in Prince Edward Island* (New Haven CT: Yale University Press, 1926); and Georges Arsenault, *Island Acadians*.

32. Archives nationales, Archives des colonies, série B, vol. 95, fols. 288 (23), 10 juillet 1751. See also A. J. B. Johnston, "French Attitudes toward the Acadians, ca. 1680–1756," in LeBlanc, *Du Grand Dérangement*, 131–66.

33. The bounty on Mi'kmaq scalps is a major focus in Paul, *We Were Not the Savages*. For the broader context of the era, see Stephen E. Patterson, "Indian-White Relations," 23–59. The treaty negotiations of 1725–26 are the focus of Wicken, *Mi'kmaq Treaties on Trial*.

34. Extracts from a letter of Jacques Prévost to the minister of the Marine, Archives nationales, Archives des colonies, CIIB, vol. 33, fol. 159, 12 Mai 1753; translated in Whitehead, *Old Man Told Us*, 136–37.

35. The texts of the 1725, 1726, 1752, and other treaties are published in *The Mi'kmaq Treaty Handbook* (Sydney, NS: Native Communications Society of Nova Scotia, 1987.)

36. A biography of Raymond by Terence Crowley can be found in *Dictionary of Canadian Biography*, 4:655–57.

37. Archives de la France d'outre mer, GI, vol. 408, reg. II, fols. 42–45v, 2 octobre 1752.

38. Webster, *Thomas Pichon*, 5.

39. Archives du Séminaire de Québec, polygraphie 56, no. 64, "Sotises."

40. Christopher Moore, "Street Life and Public Activities in Louisbourg," in Moore, "Miscellaneous Louisbourg Reports," Manuscript Report Series 317 (Ottawa: Parks Canada, ca. 1979), 48–49; Archives nationales, Archives des colonies, CIIB, vol. 32, fols. 169–70v, 30 septembre 1752; Archives nationales, Archives des colonies, F3, vol. 50, fols. 477–78v, mémoire non signée, 28 mai 1752; McLennan, *Louisbourg*, 192–93; Johnston, "In the Name of the King."

41. Lacour-Gayet, *La marine militaire*, 235. The author gives July 30, 1754, as the date Rouillé left the marine ministry and passed to foreign affairs. Dull mentions in *French Navy*, 75, that "as controller general before 1754 he [Machault] had made himself the symbol of high taxes."

42. John Fortier prepared a short biography of Drucour for *Dictionary of Canadian Biography*, 3:71–73.

43. Hopson's and Lawrence's biographies are in *Dictionary of Canadian Biography*, 3:294–95 and 361–66, respectively. In addition to Lawrence, the members of the council in 1755 were Massachusetts-born merchant and officeholder Benjamin Green (1713–72); English-born, retired army officer John Collier (? -1769); William Cotterell; New England naval and privateer captain John Rous (c. 1700–1760); and the Boston-born and Harvard- and Cambridge-educated lawyer and chief justice of Nova Scotia, Jonathan Belcher (1710–76).

44. The latest study of the period is Anderson, *Crucible of War*. The author is thin on details in matters relating to Atlantic Canada yet masterful in retelling the events on the interior of the continent. A collection of documents that reflects the mood of the era is O'Callaghan, *Documents relative to the Colonial History*. A good source for the perspective of an individual French officer who was caught up in changing conditions is Joseph L. Peyser, *On the Eve of the Conquest*.

45. Cited in Frégault, *Canada*, 20.

46. The conflict has been the subject of many books and articles. For a brief overview, see Eccles, *Canadian Frontier*, chap. 8. For more extensive treatments, see Anderson's *Crucible of War*; and Gipson, *British Empire*, vols. 6 and 7.

47. Archives nationales, Archives des colonies, CIIB, vol. 35, fols. 319–20v.

48. Monsieur Lartigue, the king's storekeeper at Louisbourg, wrote on December 24, 1754: "[J]e puis vous assurer que je leur ay souvent entendu dire qu'en nous rendant Louisbourg, ils ne nous avoient fait qu'un prest," Lartigue à Surlaville, in Du Boscq de Beaumont, *Les derniers jours*, 134. Lartigue gives other examples of British boasts and warnings.

49. The official correspondence of 1755 is in Archives nationales, Archives des colonies, CIIB, vol. 35; and B, vol. 102; Eccles, *Canadian Frontier*, 168; Archives

nationales, Archives des colonies, c11B, vol. 35, fols. 216–17, letters of Machault to Drucour and Prévost, 17 mars 1755.

50. Mahan, *Influence of Sea Power*, 74–75. Two detailed studies of the French navy are Pritchard, *Louis XV's Navy*; and Dull, *French Navy*. Caron provides a table comparing French and British warships as of January 1751 in the footnote on p. 119 of *La guerre incomprise*. As of that date, Britain had 137 ships of the line and France only 60.

51. G. F. G. Stanley, *New France*, 166.

52. Cited in McLennan, *Louisbourg*, 175.

53. This point was first brought to my attention in McNeill, *Atlantic Empires*.

54. Details on the squadrons and their escort from Brest are in Dull, *French Navy*, 25; and Caron, *La guerre incomprise*, 140–42.

55. Archives nationales, Archives des colonies, c11B, vol. 35, fols. 216–17, letters of Machault to Drucour and Prévost, 17 mars 1755. The seventy-four-gun ships were the *Défenseur*, the *Dauphin Royal*, and the *Espérance*. Accompanying the large ships was a convoy of smaller vessels.

56. Orders to Boscawen, cited in Stanley, *New France*, 133.

57. Eccles, "Preemptive Conquest," 137.

58. Eccles, "Preemptive Conquest," 137.

59. Caron, *La guerre incomprise*, 159–61; Eccles, *Canadian Frontier*, 168; Stanley, *New France*, 134.

60. Eccles, "Preemptive Conquest," 138.

61. Douglas, "Halifax as an Element of Sea Power," 69; Archives nationales, Archives des colonies, c11B, vol. 35, fols. 281–81v, 31 août 1755.

62. McLennan, *Louisbourg*, 205; Janzen, "Eviction of French Fishermen"; Akins, "History of Halifax City," 48. A French version of Captain John Rous's letter asking the French along the Newfoundland coast to surrender is in Archives nationales, Archives des colonies, c11B, vol. 35, fol. 342, 23 août 1755.

63. Chartrand, *Louis XV's Army (2)*, 35.

64. Caron, *La guerre incomprise*, 156.

65. Rawlyk, *Yankees at Louisbourg*; Johnston, *Summer of 1744*; Baker, *Campaign of Amateurs*.

66. Lawrence to Halifax, August 23, 1754, in Pargellis, *Military Affairs in North America*, 26–29.

67. I. K. Steele, "Robert Monckton," in *Dictionary of Canadian Biography*, 4:540–41.

68. Corbett, *England in the Seven Years' War*, 1:27; Caron, *La guerre incomprise*, 197.

69. Gipson, *British Empire*, 6:230–31, places great stress on the importance of Pichon's spying. For more on Pichon and his betrayal of the French, see Webster, *Thomas Pichon*; Archives nationales, Archives des colonies, B, vol. 101, fol. 205v, 5 septembre 1755.

70. Details on the assault on the fort are found in Pothier, *Battle for the Chignecto Forts*; Hand, *Siege of Fort Beauséjour*; and Schmeisser, "Narrative and Structural History." I. K. Steele offers a short biography on Monckton in *Dictionary of Canadian Biography*, 4:540–42. The commanders of the Massachusetts troops were Lieutenant Colonel John Winslow and Lieutenant Colonel George Scott. The British regulars were from the Fortieth and Forty-fifth Regiments of Foot. Rawlyk states that 87 percent of the soldiers were from Massachusetts, *Nova Scotia's Massachusetts*, 206.

71. Hand, *Siege of Fort Beauséjour*, 45–48.

72. There is a summary of Vergor's career in Johnston, "Officers of Isle Royale," 57–58.

73. There are various eyewitness journals of the events of the siege. See John Clarence Webster, *The Forts of Chignecto: A Study of Eighteenth-Century Conflict between France and Great Britain in Acadia* (privately printed, 1930); and Hand, *Siege of Fort Beauséjour*; Archives nationales, Archives des colonies, CIIB, vol. 35, fol. 80v, Drucour au ministre, 8 juillet 1755.

74. Du Boscq de Beaumont, *Les derniers jours*, 146, Joubert à Surlaville, n.d.

75. Archives nationales, Archives des colonies, CIIB, vol. 35, fols. 233–36, Villeray.

76. Morris, quoted in Phyllis R. Blakeley, "Morris, Charles", in *Dictionary of Canadian Biography*, 4:559–63; Faragher, *Great and Noble Scheme*, 328, see also 288–90.

77. Rawlyk, *Nova Scotia's Massachusetts*; Massachusetts Historical Society, Mascarene Papers, vol. 3, p. 62. Thanks to Sandy Balcom for providing me with this source and reference. Brebner, "Canadian Policy."

78. Dunn, *History of Port-Royal*, 198–99.

79. The summary provided in the next few paragraphs is based on T. B. Akins, ed., "Papers relating to the Forcible Removal of the Acadian French from Nova Scotia, 1755–1768," in *Selections from the Public Documents of the Province of Nova Scotia* (Halifax: Public Archives of Nova Scotia, 1869), 247–357.

80. Marshall, *Georges Island*.

81. John A. Dickinson, "Les réfugiés acadiens au Canada, 1755–1775," *Études canadiennes / Canadian Studies*, no. 37 (1994): 52–53n4. See also Jean Daigle and Robert LeBlanc, "Acadian Deportation and Return," plate 30, in Harris and Matthews, *Historical Atlas of Canada*, vol. 1.

82. Douglas, "Halifax as an Element of Sea Power," 72. The Acadian refuge just beyond Beaubears Island on the Miramichi River is briefly discussed by Phyllis LeBlanc in "Deschamps de Boishébert et de Raffetot, Charles," in *Dictionary of Canadian Biography*, 4:212–25. Dunn, *History of Port-Royal*, 210.

83. Eccles, *Canadian Frontier*, 168–72.

84. The first, and perhaps the only, written comment by Governor Drucour about the first of the deportations appears to be the following note sent to the minister of the Marine: "Nous avons Scû ces Jours passés par des accadiens refugiés a l'isle St

Jean, que les anglois avoient brulé Cobeguy, Tatamigouche et devasté touttes ces parties là, nous Jugeons que c'est dans la crainte qu'ils ont de ne pouvoir garder ce Pays là," Archives nationales, Archives des colonies, CIIB, vol. 35, fol. 97, Drucour, 14 octobre 1755.

85. Archives nationales, Archives des colonies, CIIB, vol. 36, fols. 4–7v, Drucour et Prévost, 6 avril 1756; "A Letter from Louisbourg, 1756," *Acadiensis* 10, no. 1 (Autumn 1980): 126–27. As explained in note 27, earlier in this chapter, the writer identified as "Monsieur de la Varenne" was likely René Gaultier de Varennes.

3. The Match Heightens, 1756–1757

1. The expression *tableau de tristesse* was used by a number of eighteenth-century writers on Louisbourg.

2. McLennan, *Louisbourg*, 205.

3. There is an entire chapter on Jean Lelarge in Moore, *Louisbourg Portraits*. The next few paragraphs are based on Moore's summary.

4. Archives nationales, Archives des colonies, CIIB, vol. 36, fol. 3, 6 avril 1756.

5. The official correspondence for 1756 is found in Archives nationales, Archives des colonies, B, vol. 103; and Archives nationales, Archives des colonies, CIIB, vol. 36. An example of rotten supplies reaching Louisbourg is in Archives nationales, Archives des colonies, CIIB, vol. 36, fols. 105–6v, Prévost, 12 mai 1756. Frégault states that in 1757 insurance rates in France rose 75 percent, *Canada*, 144. For Machault's worries, see Archives nationales, Archives des colonies, B, vol. 104, fol. 375, 24 septembre 1756.

6. Rawlyk, *Nova Scotia's Massachusetts*, 195. Governor Cornwallis estimated in 1751 that no fewer than 150 New England vessels traded at Louisbourg that year; three years later acting governor Charles Lawrence made a similar complaint. Lunn, "Agriculture and War."

7. Du Boscq de Beaumont, *Les derniers jours*, 186, des Bourbes à Surlaville, 18 avril 1756.

8. There are numerous examples of news and sightings being gleaned from arriving ship crews. One example is Archives nationales, Archives des colonies, CIIB, vol. 36, fols. 57–58, Drucour, 19 mai 1756.

9. Harris and Matthews, *Historical Atlas of Canada*, vol. 1, plate 31; and Jean Hamelin and Jacqueline Roy, "François-Pierre de Rigaud de Vaudreuil," in *Dictionary of Canadian Biography*, 4:660–74.

10. Archives nationales, Archives des colonies, CIIB, vol. 37, fols. 102–9, Prévost, 21 septembre 1757; Journal of "Le Formidable," 8; and Journal of "L'Inflexible," 6; Du Boscq de Beaumont, *Les derniers jours*, 219–20, de La Houssaye à Surlaville, 14 octobre 1757. Bernard Pothier's biography of the Joseph-Nicolas Gautier appears in *Dictionary of Canadian Biography*, 3:254–55; Andrew Rodgers's biography of Nicolas Gautier is in *Dictionary of Canadian Biography*, 5: 338–39, and includes information on Pierre. On Louis Mercure, see Campbell, *Road to Canada*, 28 and 42.

11. Archives nationales, Archives des colonies, C11B, vol. 36, fols. 52–54v, Drucour, 10 mai 1756. The interrogation of the Irish deserter was conducted by M. Macarty, an Irish officer in the French service.

12. Archives nationales, Archives des colonies, C11B, vol. 36, fols. 120–23v, Prévost, 13 juillet 1756. A section on military punishments at Louisbourg can be found in Johnston, *Control and Order*.

13. Du Boscq de Beaumont, *Les derniers jours*, 186, des Bourbes à Surlaville, 18 avril 1756. With regard to the drop in the number of marriages, the parish record totals (Archives de la France d'outre mer, G1, vol. 408) are as follows: six months in 1749, 27; 1750, 36; 1751, 37; 1752, 55; 1753, 49; 1754, 42; 1755, 23; 1756, 23.

14. Archives Saint-Sulpice de Montreal, Côte 544, 4.32, Mandement du 9 février 1756.

15. Most of the case is in Archives de la France d'outre mer, G2, vol. 206, dossier 411; the final sentences for Anne Lando and Pierre LeRoy *dit* Larmement are in Archives de la France d'outre mer, G2, vol. 193, reg. III, 31 août 1756, and reg. III, 10 janvier 1757. For a general look at punishments in the town, see Johnston, *Control and Order*.

16. There are several letters on this marriage and its sad ending in Du Boscq de Beaumont, *Les derniers jours*. Although his death was an evident suicide, Montalembert was buried in the parish cemetery on orders from the civil authorities; see Johnston, *Life and Religion*, 146.

17. Greer, "Mutiny at Louisbourg." Greer explores another, much smaller mutiny, one at Port Toulouse in 1750, in "Another Soldiers' Revolt in Île Royale, June 1750," *Acadiensis* 12, no. 2 (Spring 1983): 106–9.

18. This note covers this paragraph and much of the following one. Initially 340 soldiers were to be sent; then the number was increased to 600. For correspondence on the troops, supplies, and fortifications, see Archives nationales, Archives des colonies, B, vol. 104, fol. 82v, 13 janvier 1756; fols. 468–70, 13 janvier 1756; vol. 103, fols. 117–17v, 15 mars 1756; fol. 178, 15 mars 1756.

19. On the cost of the Troupes de Terre serving in the colony, see Du Boscq de Beaumont, *Les derniers jours*, 182, des Bourbes à Surlaville, 8 janvier 1756.

20. Archives nationales, Archives des colonies, B, vol. 103, fols. 187–87v, 19 avril 1756; vol. 105, fol. 234, 22 juin 1757.

21. The figures for royal expenditures and the separate cost of fortifications work are in McLennan, *Louisbourg*, 1918 ed., appendix 2, 370.

22. Lacour-Gayet, *La Marine militaire*, 93–95, 240–41.

23. Giraud, "France and Louisiana," 673–74. The chevalier de Raymond used the term "gateway" to describe Île Royale in his 1754 reflections on the French colonies. See Peyser, *On the Eve of the Conquest*, 60.

24. Library and Archives Canada, MG11, CO217, vol. 28, Knowles and Bastide, "State of the Fortifications," July 8, 1746. The July 1749 statement on the condition of the

fortifications and public buildings at Louisbourg is fully transcribed in appendix 9 of McLennan, *Louisbourg*, 409–21.

25. Some of Franquet's suggestions are in Fry, *"Appearance of Strength,"* 2:77–90. F. J. Thorpe's biography of the engineer is in the *Dictionary of Canadian Biography*, 3:228–31. McLennan, *Louisbourg*, appendix 2, p. 370.

26. The various decisions and their rationale mentioned in this paragraph are discussed in Archives nationales, Archives des colonies, c11b, vol. 36, fols. 279–85, 26 mars 1756; Archives nationales, Archives des colonies, B, vol. 103, fols. 182–84, 26 mars 1756. Archives nationales, Archives des colonies, c11b, vol. 36, fols. 279–85, Franquet, 24 juin 1756; Fry, *"Appearance of Strength,"* 2:145.

27. Fry, *"Appearance of Strength,"* 1:89–90; Archives nationales, Archives des colonies, c11b, vol. 36, fols. 251–52, Franquet, 19 mai 1756.

28. Fry says the hills were eventually lowered seven to eight *pieds*, *"Appearance of Strength,"* 90. Franquet reported in late 1756 that he had three *pieds* taken off the Hill of Justice; Archives nationales, Archives des colonies, c11b, vol. 36, fols. 271–72, Franquet, 20 décembre 1756. More of the hill was removed in 1757.

29. Archives nationales, Archives des colonies, c11b, vol. 36, fols. 249–50, Franquet, avril 1756. See Fry, *"Appearance of Strength,"* 2:117, for a photo of an archaeological excavation of a turf and fascine revetment at the King's Bastion.

30. Rossel, "Journal de ma campagne," 375.

31. Webster, *Thomas Pichon*, esp. 47–48. Lawrence to Pitt, February 14, 1757, in Kimball, *Correspondence of William Pitt*, 1:11.

32. Barnes, *History of the Regiments*, 59–60. Archives nationales, Archives des colonies, c11b, vol. 37, fol. 115, 30 septembre 1757; fol. 58, 4 octobre 1757. The use of *Te Deums* in France to celebrate military victories is explored in Michèle Fogel, *Les cérémonies de l'information dans la France du XVIe au XVIIIe siècle* (Paris: Fayard, 1989).

33. Plumb, *Chatham*, 54. Hughes, *Britain in the Mediterranean*. John Knox Laughton, "Edward Boscawen," in *Dictionary of National Biography*, 2:879.

34. Black, *Rise of the European Powers*, 114–15.

35. Anderson, *Crucible of War*, 167. Stanley describes the victory at Oswego as one "of great significance. It meant the capture of 1,600 prisoners, 121 guns, the whole of the English shipping on Lake Ontario and large quantities of stores and provisions," *Canada's Soldiers*, 73.

36. Stanley makes the point that "[t]he large number of raiding parties dispatched from Fort Duquesne during 1756 and 1757 emphasized the fact that the future of New France in the Ohio region was dependent, almost entirely, upon the support of the Indians," *New France*, 149. Eccles, *Canadian Frontier*, 173; Brumwell, *Redcoats*, 201.

37. Dunn, *History of Port-Royal*, 210.

38. A recent study of the Halifax-based squadron during this period is Gwyn, *Frigates and Foremasts*; see 29–30. Des Bourbes à Surlaville, 31 août 1756, in Du Boscq de

Beaumont, *Les derniers jours*, 190; McLennan, *Louisbourg*, 206; Du Fresne du Motel à Surlaville, 1 décembre 1756, in Du Boscq de Beaumont, *Les derniers jours*, 204–5.

39. Joubert à Surlaville, 30 juillet 1756, in Du Boscq de Beaumont, *Les derniers jours*, 188.

40. Archives nationales, Archives des colonies, C11B, vol. 36, fols. 12–13v, 61–62v, 112–13v, 114–15, 116–17v, dispatches written in June and July 1756.

41. Archives nationales, Archives des colonies, C11B, vol. 36, fols. 63–65, Drucour, 10 juillet 1756.

42. Archives nationales, Archives des colonies, C11B, vol. 36, fols. 130–33v, Prévost, 11 août 1756; fols. 14–15v, Drucour et Prévost, 27 juin 1756; fols. 18–19v, procès-verbal, 22 juin 1756; Frégault, *Canada*, 144.

43. Archives nationales, Archives des colonies, C11B, vol. 36, fol. 254v, Franquet, 14 juillet 1756.

44. Archives nationales, Archives des colonies, C11B, vol. 36, fols. 125–27, Prévost, 18 juillet 1756.

45. McLennan, *Louisbourg*, 199; see W. J. Eccles, biography of Montcalm, in *Dictionary of Canadian Biography*, 3:458–68; Archives nationales, Archives des colonies, C11B, vol. 36, fols. 71–72, Beaussier de l'Isle, 3 juillet 1756. The large ships were the *Héros* (seventy-four guns) and the *Illustre* (sixty-four guns) and the frigates the *Licorne* and the *Sirenne*. Drucour reports on what was in his reply to Beaussier in another letter, Archives nationales, Archives des colonies, C11B, vol. 36, fols. 68–70, 18 juillet 1756.

46. Details on the battle are in Des Bourbes à Surlaville, 10 août 1756, in Du Boscq de Beaumont, *Les derniers jours*, 194. This sea battle off Louisbourg is perhaps the one Julian Gwyn references when he writes: "In July, four French ships inflicted sufficient damage on a British blockading force off Louisbourg in a three-hour battle that it had to return to Halifax for repairs," Gwyn, *Frigates and Foremasts*, 29–30. Douglas, "Halifax as an Element of Sea Power," 88–90; Archives nationales, Archives des colonies, C11B, vol. 36, fols. 130–33v, Prévost, 11 août 1756; Lacour-Gayet, *La Marine militaire*, 382–83; Étienne Taillemite, "Louis-Joseph Beaussier de Lisle," in *Dictionary of Canadian Biography*, vol. 3.

47. Archives nationales, Archives des colonies, C11B, vol. 37, fols. 239–45, Prévost, 30 janvier et février 1757; John Fortier, "Mascle de Saint-Julhien, Jean," in *Dictionary of Canadian Biography*, 3:440.

48. Archives nationales, Archives des colonies, C11B, vol. 36, fols. 145–47v, Prévost, 1 octobre 1756; fols. 35–38v, Rousseau de Villejouin, 3 novembre 1756.

49. Archives nationales, Archives des colonies, C11B, vol. 36, fols. 166v–67, Prévost, 29 novembre 1756.

50. Donovan, "Inflation at Louisbourg"; Archives nationales, Archives des colonies, C11B, vol. 36, fols. 76v–77, 4 décembre 1756. The signatures on the petition were Denis Bonnaventure, Duhaget, Loppinot, Denys, Joubert, Garsement de Fontaine,

Montalembert, and Dufrene. Officers write about the rise in the cost of living at Louisbourg in Du Boscq de Beaumont, *Les derniers jours*, 204–6; Archives nationales, Archives des colonies, B, vol. 107, fol. 369, 18 février 1758.

51. Some individuals at Louisbourg, at least occasionally, could be optimistic about how things looked. An engineer at Louisbourg, M. Portal, closed a letter to Surlaville on August 11, 1756, with the following: "Du monde, des vivres, de l'argent, de la bonne volonté, voilà notre position. Les Canadiens font des merveilles," in Du Boscq de Beaumont, *Les derniers jours*, 195; F. J. Thorpe, "Grillot de Poilly, François Claude-Victor," in *Dictionary of Canadian Biography*, 3:267–68.

52. Quoted in Frégault, *Canada*, 143.

53. Plumb, *Chatham*, 58. For the various upswings and downswings in his popularity, see Peters, *Pitt and Popularity*.

54. George Fisher Russell Barker provides a synopsis of Pitt's life and career in the *Dictionary of National Biography*, 45:354–67; the quote is on p. 358.

55. Barker, "William Pitt," in *Dictionary of National Biography*, 45:358.

56. Rogers, *British Army*, 129, makes the comparison that Ligonier and Anson functioned in similar fashion to the joint chiefs of staff in the Second World War. Biographies of Anson and Ligonier can be found in the *Dictionary of National Biography*.

57. Black, *Rise of the European Powers*, 115.

58. Pargellis, *Military Affairs in North America*, introduction, xii.

59. As original as the secretary of state's conception was in Great Britain, a broad segment of British American colonists had come to the same conclusion years earlier. The idea that the French could be thoroughly defeated across the board in North America grew in strength following the successful intercolonial expedition against Louisbourg in 1745; Andrew Peter Podolsky, "Site of Imagination: The Fortress at Louisbourg and Stories of Empire" (PhD diss., Northwestern University, 1998), 114.

60. Mathieu, *La Nouvelle-France*, 224; Stanley, *New France*, xv.

61. Brumwell, *Redcoats*, 20.

62. The names of the ships in the 1757 squadrons, how many guns they carried, who the captains were, and from which port they had sailed is provided by Rossel in "Journal de ma campagne," 374–75. See also Lacour-Gayet, *La Marine militaire*, appendix 11, p. 530.

63. Dull, *French Navy*, 77; on the change of ministers, see Lacour-Gayet, *La Marine militaire*, 240–41. The author comments: "[O]n a dit qu'il semblait qu'on eût choisi à M. De Machault le successeur le plus inepte, afin de le faire regretter davantage."

64. The first memo from Moras concerning Île Royale is dated February 20, 1757; on March 2, 1757, he wrote to Drucour and Prévost, Archives nationales, Archives des colonies, B, vol. 105, fol. 49, fol. 226. The note to Franquet informing him he would be acting governor is in fol. 231v, 9 avril 1757. For the urgent need for provisions, see fol. 262, 11 mars 1757. The memo on the fleets is in fols. 228–29, 31 mars 1757.

On Saint-Julhien's personality, see John Fortier, "Mascle de Saint-Julhien, Jean," in *Dictionary of Canadian Biography*, 3:440.

65. A British officer tallied 140 pieces of French artillery in the aftermath of the 1758 siege, "Copy of Journal," 152.

66. Caron includes the lengthy letter of instruction to the comte de Bauffrement for this mission in *La guerre incomprise*, 217–18; "Journal of M. De Vaudreuil's Voyage to Canada," in O'Callaghan, *Documents relative to the Colonial History*, 297–99. For the favorable comment, see Dull, *French Navy*, 48. The harsh criticisms occur repeatedly in Caron, *La guerre incomprise*; see p. 183, and for other examples, p. 149 and p. 155.

67. "Journal of 'Le Formidable,'" 4; Rossel, "Journal de ma campagne," 376.

68. Proulx, *Between France and New France*; Rossel, "Journal de ma campagne," 374; Boyce Richardson, "1757," 38. Rossel, "Journal de ma campagne," provides a detailed account of how the disease ravaged the crews of the squadrons. It is worth noting that a year or two earlier the Royal Navy had suffered an outbreak of typhus and scurvy that cost the lives of two thousand men. Dull, *French Navy*, 51; Eccles, *Canadian Frontier*, 176; Archives nationales, Archives des colonies, C11B, vol. 37, fols. 86–88, Prévost, 1 juillet 1757.

69. Lacour-Gayet, *La Marine militaire*, 383–84, 530. The citation comes from "Journal of 'L'Inflexible,'" 5.

70. Doughty, *Historical Journal*, 1:21–22. Knox's journal provides a detailed account of the crossing to North America and all the preparations that went into it; Douglas, "Halifax," 102–4; Gwyn, *Frigates and Foremasts*, 30.

71. McLennan, *Louisbourg*, 202; Corbett, *England in the Seven Years' War*, 1:167–68.

72. Loudoun to Pitt, May 30, 1757, in Kimball, *Correspondence of William Pitt*, 1:71–72.

73. Anderson, *Crucible of War*, 178, 208; Corbett, *England in the Seven Years' War*, 1:168.

74. Doughty, *Historical Journal*, 1:30. See also Richardson, "1757."

75. Doughty, *Historical Journal*, 1:35; McLennan, *Louisbourg*, 203; Captain James Abercrombie to Lord Loudoun, August 8, 1757, cited in Donovan, "'After Midnight We Danced,'" 35.

76. Stanley, *Canada's Soldiers*, 74–75. The latest account of the siege and its infamous aftermath is in Anderson, *Crucible of War*.

77. Archives nationales, Archives des colonies, C11B, vol. 37, fol. 286, 15 mai 1757. The reference to 18 *pouces* of snow falling is in fols. 3–8, 12 mai 1757. A *pouce* was slightly larger than an inch.

78. For talk about spies, see Archives nationales, Archives des colonies, B, vol. 105, fol. 225, and C11B, vol. 37, fols. 48–49.

79. Archives nationales, Archives des colonies, C11B, vol. 37, fols. 3–8, Drucour et Prévost, 12 mai 1757.

80. Archives nationales, Archives des colonies, CI 1B, vol. 37, fols. 50–53, Drucour, 16 juin 1757.

81. Archives nationales, Archives des colonies, B, vol. 105, fol. 249v, Moras, 27 juillet 1757.

82. Archives nationales, Archives des colonies, CI 1B, vol. 37, fols. 285–86, Franquet, 15 mai 1757; fols. 287–88, Franquet, 30 mai 1757.

83. Archives nationales, Archives des colonies, CI 1B, vol. 37, fols. 289–91, Franquet, 18 juin 1757.

84. Rossel, "Journal de ma campagne," 378.

85. Anonymous journal of an officer aboard the *Inflexible*, in "Journal of 'L'Inflexible,'" 5.

86. The anecdote comes from the memoirs of the Scottish Jacobite officer who was serving in the marine troops at Louisbourg, the chevalier James Johnstone; *Memoirs*, note at the bottom of pp. 180–81.

87. Du Boscq de Beaumont, *Les derniers jours*, 216, Joubert à Surlaville, 12 août 1757; Archives nationales, Archives des colonies, CI 1B, vol. 37, Franquet, fols. 289–91, 18 juin 1757. Additional details are in fols. 292–93, Franquet, 27 juin 1757.

88. Rossel, "Journal de ma campagne," 380.

89. Du Boscq de Beaumont, *Les derniers jours*, 222–23, Joubert à Surlaville, 15 octobre 1757; Archives nationales, Archives des colonies, CI 1C, vol. 16, "Recapitulation 1757," no date or folio.

90. The details on the preparations at Grand Lorembec come from a French plan, known as 1757-4 in the Archives of the Fortress of Louisbourg, "Plan de Retranchement fait a l'Anse du grand Lorembec"; Archives nationales, Archives des colonies, CI 1C, vol. 16, description contained in a document that begins with "C-67–lt-24" at the top of a page.

91. Archives nationales, Archives des colonies, CI 1B, vol. 37, fols. 102–9, Prévost, 21 septembre 1757.

92. The details in this paragraph come from the plan known in the Archives of the Fortress of Louisbourg as 1757-5, "Plan des retranchements faits a l'Anse de la Pointe Platte."

93. The details in this paragraph come from the plan in the Archives of the Fortress of Louisbourg known as 1757-2, "Plan des retranchements faits au pourtour des Anses au Ruisseau et du sable comprises dans celle de la grande Cormorandière."

94. Brumwell, *Redcoats*, 182–89. The quote from Wolfe is on p. 183.

95. Archives nationales, Archives des colonies, CI 1C, vol. 14, fols. 67–75 and 111–12v, Bordereaux . . . 1757; Archives de la Marine, B4, vol. 76, no. 3, Mémoire concernant les Sauvages . . . en 1757; Rossel, "Journal de ma campagne," 380.

96. See "Reasons . . . against Going to Louisbourg," by Sir Charles Hardy and following documents, in Pargellis, *Military Affairs in North America*, 387–94; Douglas, "Halifax," 105–7; Corbett, *England in the Seven Years' War*, 1:169–72.

97. Anonymous journal of an officer aboard the *Inflexible*, in "Journal of 'L'Inflexible,'" 5.

98. The plan is known at the Archives of the Fortress of Louisbourg as 1757–7; the original map, "Plan de la ville de Louisbourg en 1757 / Escadre angloise commandee Par lamiral Francois Holburne," is in the Bibliothèque Nationale (Paris), Cartes et plans, Ged 1348.

99. Anonymous journal of an officer aboard the *Inflexible*, in "Journal of 'L'Inflexible,'" 6; Corbett, *England in the Seven Years' War*, 1:172.

100. On celebrations of the *fête de Saint-Louis* at Louisbourg, see Johnston, *Life and Religion*, 15–19; quotation from the anonymous journal of an officer aboard the *Inflexible*, in "Journal of 'L'Inflexible,'" 6.

101. "Journal of 'Le Formidable,'" 8.

102. "Journal of 'Le Formidable,'" 8.

103. Chevalier James Johnstone, quoted in McLennan, *Louisbourg*, 207. Johnstone's biography is in the *Dictionary of Canadian Biography*, 4:400–401.

104. The actual name of the ship was *L'Abénaquise*. "Journal of 'L'Inflexible,'" 6.

105. Holburne to Pitt, September 29, 1757, in Kimball, *Correspondence of William Pitt*, 1:114.

106. Accounts of the storm's impact on the British fleet are in Douglas, "Halifax," 109; "Journal of 'Le Formidable'" and "Journal of 'L'Inflexible'"; McLennan, *Louisbourg*, 207–10, Gwyn, *Frigates and Foremasts*, 30–31; Archives nationales, Archives des colonies, C11B, vol. 37, fol. 59, Drucour, 5 octobre 1757.

107. "Journal of 'Le Formidable,'" 12.

108. Willson, *Life and Letters of James Wolfe*, 319–33; Peters, *Pitt and Popularity*, 91–101. Another who took part in the expedition was Charles Knowles. He served as a vice-admiral under Admiral Edward Hawke and had been governor of Louisbourg in 1746–47. Stuart Reid states that Wolfe made "no mention of his having reconnoitred the fort at Fouras, as is sometimes claimed," *Wolfe*, 139.

109. Wolfe, quoted in Stuart Reid, *Wolfe*, 140–41.

110. Du Boscq de Beaumont, *Les derniers jours*, 218–19, Loppinot à Surlaville, 6 octobre 1757.

111. Archives nationales, Archives des colonies, C11B, vol. 37, fols. 223–26, Prévost, 27 décembre 1757.

112. Pritchard, *Louis XV's Navy*, 83–84; "Journal of 'L'Inflexible,'" 9.

113. Unidentified surgeon, quoted in Mackay, *Admiral Hawke*, 184; Richardson, "1757," 45–46; Lacour-Gayet, *La Marine militaire*, 384–85; Dull, *French Navy*, 81.

114. Douglas, "Halifax," 110–13; McLennan, *Louisbourg*, 205n; Gwyn, *Frigates and Foremasts*, 31.

115. Archives nationales, Archives des colonies, C11B, vol. 37, fols. 39–43, 253–56, 257–59, Drucour et Prévost, 28 décembre 1757; fols. 269–72, Prévost, 30 décembre 1757.

116. Archives nationales, Archives des colonies, c11b, vol. 37, fol. 238, Prévost, 31 décembre 1757. The totals were as follows: Artois Regiment, 507 men; Bourgogne Regiment, 499 men; Marine troops, 1,009 men.

117. Archives nationales, Archives des colonies, c11c, vol. 16, not paginated, list showing all the defenders at Louisbourg in 1757, including one hundred Mi'kmaq in one location and two hundred "Malichites et Cannibas" (Maliseet and Kennebecs) at another.

118. Du Boscq de Beaumont, *Les derniers jours*, 224, Joubert à Surlaville, 15 octobre 1757; ibid., "Pensées diverses sur l'Isle Royale," 268.

119. Archives nationales, Archives des colonies, c11b, vol. 37, fols. 14–17, Drucour et Prévost, 30 septembre 1757; fol. 68, Drucour, 15 octobre 1757; fols. 322–23, Prévost, 20 octobre 1757; c11c, vol. 15, "Isle Royale Troupes," document 272.

120. Archives nationales, Archives des colonies, c11b, vol. 37, fols. 227–36, Prévost, 28 décembre 1757.

121. Archives nationales, Archives des colonies, B, vol. 107, fol. 356, 11 février 1758; c11b, vol. 38, fols. 16–18v, 30 avril 1758; B, vol. 108, fol. 226, 28 avril 1758; B, vol. 107, fol. 389, 30 avril 1758. Letters and announcements relating to Houlière's appointment are in Archives nationales, Archives des colonies, B, vol. 107, fols. 380–81v, 30 et 31 mars 1758.

122. John Fortier, "Mascle de Saint-Julhien, Jean," in *Dictionary of Canadian Biography*, 3:440; Archives nationales, Archives des colonies, c11b, vol. 37, fols. 327–31, 1757. The letter is undated and unsigned, but the contents indicate that it was written late in 1757 by either Saint-Julhien or an admirer.

123. Archives nationales, Archives des colonies, c11b, vol. 37, fols. 294–96, Franquet, 8 octobre 1757; fol. 297, Franquet, 9 octobre 1757; fols. 303–5, Franquet, 16 novembre 1757.

124. Archives nationales, Archives des colonies, c11c, vol. 15, document 281, décembre 1757; Moore, *Louisbourg Portraits*, 201–2.

125. Archives nationales, Archives des colonies, B, vol. 105, fols. 254–54v, Moras, 31 octobre 1757; B, vol. 106, fols. 310–10v, 14 novembre 1757; c11b, vol. 37, fol. 74, Drucour, 22 novembre 1757; B, vol. 106, fols. 320–22, Moras, 19 décembre 1757.

126. Archives nationales, Archives des colonies, c11b, vol. 37, fols. 223–26, Prévost, 27 décembre 1757. See also vol. 38, fols. 324–26, sans date.

127. Archives nationales, Archives des colonies, c11b, vol. 37, fols. 303–5, Franquet, 16 novembre 1757; fols. 72–73, Drucour, 16 novembre 1757; fol. 74, Drucour, 22 novembre 1757; c11c, vol. 15, document 279; vol. 16, "Mémoire sur la situation de l'Isle Royale," 21 décembre 1757.

128. Archives nationales, Archives des colonies, B, vol. 105, fols. 256–59, Moras, 24 décembre 1757; vol. 106, fols. 317–18, Moras, 24 décembre 1757.

129. Peters, *Pitt and Popularity*, 96–101. See also John Knox Laughton's biography of "Edward Hawke (1705–1781)," in the *Dictionary of National Biography*, 25:192–99;

Pitt's letters to Loudoun and Abercromby are in Kimball, *Correspondence of William Pitt*, 1:133–35.

130. Pitt's letters of December 30, 1757, to the American governors and to Abercromby are in Kimball, *Correspondence of William Pitt*, 1:136–51.

4. Beginning of the End, Early 1758

1. F. J. Thorpe provides a biography of François-Claude-Victor Grillot de Poilly (1726–1761) in *Dictionary of Canadian Biography*, 3:267–68. Grillot de Poilly's journal is located in Archives de la Guerre, Archives du Comité technique du Génie, manuscrit 66, "Mémoire des Evenemens qui interesseront cette Colonie Pendant l'année 1758," par Grillot de Poilly (hereafter cited as Grillot de Poilly Journal). For the comments of Madame Bégon (Marie-Élisabeth Rocbert de la Morandière), see *Rapport de l'Archiviste de la Province du Quebec pour 1934–1935* (Quebec: Rédempti Paradis, 1935), 22.

2. Grillot de Poilly Journal, 26 février 1758.

3. The Louisbourg parish records for the first three months of 1758 are located in Archives de la France d'outre mer, G1, vol. 409.

4. Grillot de Poilly Journal, 26 janvier 1758.

5. Grillot de Poilly Journal, entries of 12, 16, 17, 24, and 25 février 1758.

6. Dull, *French Navy*, 84–87.; Choiseul, cited in Mackay, *Admiral Hawke*, 186.

7. Archives nationales, Archives des colonies, C11B, vol. 38, fols. 112–19v, 24 janvier 1758.

8. Archives nationales, Archives des colonies, C11B, vol. 37, fols. 327–31, 1757.

9. Archives nationales, Archives des colonies, B, vol. 107, fols. 366–67, 18 février 1758; fol. 343, 11 janvier 1758. A point by point reply to the various requests of Drucour and Prévost is in vol. 107, fols. 387–88, 28 avril 1758.

10. In November 1758, after the fall of Louisbourg, John Rous toured the rest of Cape Breton Island and reported, "[T]here has been no Fishery carried on in any of them [ports] these two years past"; cited in Douglas, "Halifax," 117.

11. Dull, *French Navy*, 114.

12. Archives nationales, Archives des colonies, B, vol. 107, fol. 344, 11 janvier 1758; vol. 108, fol. 478, 14 janvier 1758; fol. 480, 14 janvier 1758; vol. 108, fol. 499, 10 février 1758; vol. 107, fol. 360, 20 février 1758.

13. Archives nationales, Archives des colonies, B, vol. 107, fol. 362, 14 février 1758; C11B, vol. 38, fols. 324–26, sans date; B, vol. 107, fol. 364, 1 février 1758; B, vol. 107, fol. 361, 14 février 1758; Balesi, *Time of the French*, 225.

14. On foreign troops serving in France, see Chartrand, *Louis XV's Army (3)*, 3. For information on the Karrer Regiment and the 1744 uprising at Louisbourg, see Greer, "Mutiny at Louisbourg."

15. The buttons of the Volontaires Étrangers were pewter, and their tricorn was black with silver hat lace. This was another difference between them and the Artois and

Bourgogne soldiers, whose uniforms had brass buttons and gold lace on their tricorns. Chartrand, *Louis XV's Army (3)*, 7, 20; Chartrand, *Louis XV's Army (2)*, 16–18.

16. The information summarized in this and the next paragraph is based on Michel Wyczynski, "Expedition of the Second Battalion." The officers corps sent to Louisbourg break down as follows: 1 colonel, 1 battalion commander, 1 adjutant, 2 ensigns, 17 captains, 17 lieutenants, and 1 sub-lieutenant of grenadiers. The 685 soldiers of the Second Battalion included 34 sergeants, 51 corporals, 51 lance corporals, and 17 drummers. Additional uniform information on the Cambis Regiment is found in Chartrand, *Louis XV's Army (2)*, 24 and plate E.

17. The date is provided in Archives nationales, Archives des colonies, c11B, vol. 38, fols. 6–9v, Drucour et Prévost, 3 mai 1758.

18. Archives nationales, Archives des colonies, B, vol. 107, fol. 377, 11 mars 1758; Lacour-Gayet, *La Marine militaire*, 385, 532–33. Only one of the ships in this squadron, the *Célèbre*, had been part of the 1757 fleet. Another ship that was also there in 1757 would make it to Louisbourg in 1758, the *Belliqueux*. The captains were not the same for the different crossings.

19. The dates of arrival of the various French ships are provided in Archives nationales, Archives des colonies, c11B, vol. 38, fols. 6–9v, 19–20v, and 122–27, letters of Drucour and Prévost, 3 and 4 mai 1758.

20. Mackay, *Admiral Hawke*, 190–91; entry for Edward Hawke (1705–81) in *Dictionary of National Biography*, 192–99; Archives nationales, Archives des colonies, B, vol. 107, fols. 385–85v, 14 avril 1758.

21. Wyczynski, "Expedition of the Second Battalion," 99; Lacour-Gayet, *La Marine militaire*, 532; Dull, *French Navy*, 107.

22. Dull has La Clue's squadron intending to sail not to Île Royale but to the West Indies (*French Navy*, 115). I have stayed with Lacour-Gayet's interpretation; Archives nationales, Archives des colonies, c11B, vol. 30, fols. 201–1v, 27 juin 1751; he commanded *Le Triton*, which left the colony on September 14, 1751.

23. Lacour-Gayet, *La Marine militaire*, 302–4; Boscawen, "Combined Operation against Louisbourg," appendix 3.

24. Dull, *French Navy*, 106–7, identifies ten separate contingents sent to Louisbourg; Archives nationales, Archives des colonies, c11B, vol. 29, fols. 29–32v, 6 août 1750; fols. 98–99, 1 septembre 1750; Lacour-Gayet, *La Marine militaire*, 385–86; McLennan, *Louisbourg*, 245, 316; Dull, *French Navy*, 107. Letters about and instructions to Blénac-Courbon are located in Archives nationales, Archives des colonies, B, vol. 107, fols. 382–83, 10 avril 1758. I have used Dull's date for Blénac-Courbon's return to Brest; Lacour-Gayet placed it one day later.

25. Webster, *Thomas Pichon*, 56; Anderson, *Crucible of War*, 742.

26. Desbarats, "Cost of Early Canada's Native Alliances," 629; Dickason, "Louisbourg and the Indians"; Archives nationales, Archives des colonies, c11B, vol. 1, fols.

249–56, memoir on the Mi'kmaq, ca. 1739; CIIC, vol. 15, document 280, "Mémoire sur la situation de l'Isle Royale," 21 décembre 1757.

27. Dumont-Johnson, *Apôtres ou agitateurs*. A recent study is Matteo Binasco, "The Role and Activities of the Capuchin, Jesuit and Recollet Missionaries in Acadia/Nova Scotia from 1654 to 1755" (MA thesis, Saint Mary's University, 2004); Micheline Dumont-Johnson, "Pierre Maillard," in *Dictionary of Canadian Biography*, 3:417–18.

28. Johnston, *Summer of 1744*.

29. Letter of 1749, in Whitehead, *Old Man Told Us*, 114.

30. Anonymous orator, in Whitehead, *Old Man Told Us*, 122.

31. Declaration of war, cited in Whitehead, *Old Man Told Us*, 131–32.

32. Letter of Monsieur de La Varenne, in Louisbourg, to a friend at La Rochelle, dated May 8, 1756. The entire selection was reprinted in *Acadiensis* 10, no. 1 (Autumn 1980), with an introduction by Kenneth Donovan. The letter is one of four selections in *An Account of the Customs and Manners of the Micmakis and Maricheets, Savage Nations, Now Dependent on the Government of Cape Breton* (London: Printed for S. Hooper and A. Moreley, 1758).

33. Whitehead, *Old Man Told Us*, 123.

34. Thomas Thorner with Thor Frohn-Nielsen, eds., *"A Few Acres of Snow": Documents in Pre-Confederation Canadian History* (Peterborough ON: Broadview, 2003), 21. Jesuit missionary Paul Le Jeune wrote: "This fury is common to the women as well as the men, and they even surpass the latter in this respect" (21).

35. Unidentified Mi'kmaw woman, cited in Whitehead, *Old Man Told Us*, 148–49, 121.

36. Stokesbury, *Navy and Empire*, 146.

37. Stanley, *New France*, 164. Stanley adds: "Because they differed fundamentally in policy, the French provided less than one-third the number of regular troops sent to America by the British: 6,800 to 32,000."

38. Stokesbury writes: "The great strength, as well as the chief peculiarity, of seapower lies in its potential ubiquity, and overseas territories might be won or lost by a battle that occurred off the coast of France," *Navy and Empire*, 130.

39. There have been many studies of the British campaign, which spread across nearly half the continent. The most recent is Anderson, *Crucible of War*.

40. In an explanatory note on p. 166 of *Historical Journal*, vol. 1, editor Arthur Doughty states that the force organized for the various campaigns in North America were as follows: Louisbourg—14,215 British troops, 600 rangers, and 90 carpenters; Canada—6,884 British troops, 17,480 provincials; defense of Nova Scotia—989 British troops; Fort Duquesne—1,854 British troops, 5,000 provincials.

41. Summaries of the lives and careers of George Anson (1697–1762) and John Ligonier (1680–1770) are in the *Dictionary of National Biography*; Dull, *French Navy*, 88, 100.

42. Pitt's letters to Loudoun and Abercromby are in Kimball, *Correspondence of William Pitt*, 1:133–35.

43. Amherst's ties to Ligonier are discussed in Mayo, *Jeffery Amherst*; J. Hitsman with Bond, "Assault Landing at Louisbourg," 319. Biographical information on Jeffery Amherst is widely available; two sources are the entry in the *Dictionary of National Biography* and Mayo, *Jeffery Amherst*.

44. This aspect of Boscawen's career is mentioned in the *Dictionary of National Biography* entry on George Anson (1697–1762).

45. McLennan, *Louisbourg*, 237.

46. "Copy of Journal," 103; Kimball, *Correspondence of William Pitt*, 1:211–12, Colville to Pitt, March 20, 1758, and Hardy to Pitt, March 22, 1758.

47. McLennan, *Louisbourg*, 236–37; Grillot de Poilly Journal, entries of April 12, 17, 21, 21, and 23, 1758.

48. Douglas, "Halifax," 116, appendix 3, pp. 186–87.

49. Doughty, *Historical Journal*, 1:173.

50. Chartrand, *Louisbourg 1758*, 34; eyewitness account of James Cunningham, on Abercromby's staff, in a May 30, 1758, letter to Lord Sackville, cited in McLennan, *Louisbourg*, 239.

51. C. P. Stacey provides a biography of George Scott in the *Dictionary of Canadian Biography*, 3:589–90.

52. Cunningham, transcribed in McLennan, *Louisbourg*, 237–41.

53. Annand, "Hugh Montgomerie"; Willson, *Life and Letters of James Wolfe*, letter to Lord George Sackville, May 12, 1758, 363. There are many other letters concerning the expedition to Halifax and against Louisbourg on the preceding and following pages.

54. The orders issued by Boscawen can be found in Doughty, *Historical Journal*, 1:177–78, 207, 208, 213.

55. Willson, *Life and Letters of James Wolfe*, letter to Lord George Sackville, May 24, 1758, 366.

56. Major, "Great Pontack Inn," 181; Raddall, *Warden of the North*, 52–54.

57. Kimball, *Correspondence of William Pitt*, 1:260–61, Boscawen to Pitt, May 27, 1758; Akins, "History of Halifax City," 54; McLennan, *Louisbourg*, 242n2.

58. Doughty, *Historical Journal*, 1:166. When the Fifty-eighth Regiment sailed for Cuba in 1762, seventy-one women went along. Brumwell, "Rank and File," 16. Public Record Office, Admiralty 1, vol. 2295, "State . . . of Transports . . . Louisbourg Expedition," June 7, 1755; thanks to B. A. Balcom for providing this reference. Doughty, *Historical Journal*, 1:177.

59. Mayo, *Jeffery Amherst*, 61–65. The captain of the *Dublin* was George Brydges Rodney, who would eventually become a renowned admiral. That Amherst joined the *Namur* off Cape Sable is mentioned in "Copy of Journal," 106.

60. Boscawen, cited in Doughty, *Historical Journal*, 1:173; Wolfe comment in Willson, *Life and Letters of James Wolfe*, 366.

61. The figures for the participants in the 1759 British assault on Quebec come

from W. J. Eccles and Susan L. Laskin, "The Seven Years' War," plate 42, in Harris and Matthews, *Historical Atlas of Canada*, vol. 1.

62. Archives nationales, Archives des colonies, CI IB, vol. 38, "Journal ou Relation sur ce qui se passera des mouvemens pour l'attaque et de la deffense de la Place de Louisbourg pendant la presente année 1758" [hereafter cited as Drucour Journal], fol. 57, 1 avril 1758; vol. 38, fols. 122–27, Prévost, 4 mai 1758; Grillot de Poilly Journal, entry of April 21, 1758.

63. Grillot de Poilly Journal, entries of April 12, 15, and 24, 1758.

64. Grillot de Poilly Journal, entries of April 27 and 28, 1758. The detail attributed to Prévost is in Archives nationales, Archives des colonies, CI IB, vol. 38, fols. 122–27, 4 mai 1758. See also fols. 19–20v, Drucour, 4 mai 1758.

65. Archives nationales, Archives des colonies, CI IB, vol. 38, fols. 172–74, Franquet, 6 mai 1758.

66. Dull, *French Navy*, 117.

67. Archives nationales, Archives des colonies, CI IB, vol. 38, fols. 6–9v, 3 mai 1758.

68. Archives nationales, Archives des colonies, CI IB, vol. 38, fols. 172–74, 6 mai 1758.

69. Phyllis E. LeBlanc offers a biography of Charles Deschamps de Boishébert et de Raffetot in *Dictionary of Canadian Biography*, 4:212–25; Archives nationales, Archives des colonies, CI IB, vol. 38, fols. 6–9v, 19–20v, and 122–27, 3 mai et 4 mai 1758.

70. Archives nationales, Archives des colonies, CI IB, vol. 38, fols. 19–20v, 4 mai 1758.

71. The orders to the three men are in Drucour Journal, fols. 57–58v, 14 mai 1758. Short descriptions of the men and their careers are in McLennan, *Louisbourg*, appendix 1, pp. 316, 327, 329.

72. Grillot de Poilly Journal, entries of April 28, 29, 30, May 1, and 3, 1758.

73. Grillot de Poilly Journal, entries of April 30, May 1, 3, 8, 11, 12, 14, and 15, 1758.

74. Hitsman with Bond, "Assault Landing at Louisbourg," 320.

75. Grillot de Poilly Journal, entries of May 6 to May 18, 1758.

76. Grillot de Poilly Journal, entries of May 10 and May 15, 1758.

77. Grillot de Poilly Journal, entries from May 14 to May 23, 1758.

78. Grillot de Poilly Journal, May 21 and May 29, 1758.

79. Drucour Journal, fol. 59, entry for June 1, 1758.

80. Grillot de Poilly Journal, entry for June 1, 1758.

81. The Corpus Christi (Fête Dieu) procession and its significance are treated in more detail and from a different perspective in Johnston, *Life and Religion*, 109–10. Grillot de Poilly's reference to it occurs in his entry for June 1, 1758.

82. Drucour Journal, fol. 59; Grillot de Poilly Journal, entry for June 1, 1758; Wyczynski, "Expedition of the Second Battalion," 101–2.

83. McLennan, *Louisbourg*, 262.

84. The total number of sailors comes from McLennan, *Louisbourg*, 263.

5. This Time for Real, June 1–7, 1758

1. For a summary of Drucour's career, see John Fortier's biography of Drucour in *Dictionary of Canadian Biography*, 3:71–73.

2. Du Boscq de Beaumont, *Derniers jours*, 175, Joubert à Surlaville, n.d.; John Fortier, "Drucour," in *Dictionary of Canadian Biography*, 3:72.

3. McLennan, *Louisbourg*, 325–26 in appendix 1, 245, including n. 7; Chartrand, *Louisbourg 1758*, 30–31.

4. Lacour-Gayet, *La Marine militaire*, 385, 532n2. McLennan, *Louisbourg*, appendix 1, p. 320.

5. F. J. Thorpe, "Franquet, Louis," in *Dictionary of Canadian Biography*, 3:228–31. The citation from Grillot de Poilly is quoted by Thorpe, 230.

6. T. A. Crowley, entry on Prévost de la Croix in *Dictionary of Canadian Biography*, 4:643–47.

7. Johnstone, *Memoirs*, 180; Huille, "De Louisbourg à Toulon."

8. Phyllis LeBlanc, biography of Boishébert, in *Dictionary of Canadian Biography*, 4:212–25; Chartrand, *Louisbourg 1758*, 38.

9. "Journal de ma campagne de Louisbourg," 48.

10. Some quotes come from the entry on Jeffery Amherst prepared by Henry Morse Stephens, in *Dictionary of National Biography*, 1:357–59. See also Mayo, *Jeffery Amherst*. The last comment was by Sir Nathaniel William Wraxall, cited in C. P. Stacey, "Amherst, Jeffery" in *Dictionary of Canadian Biography*, 4:26.

11. Review by G. M. Wrong of Webster's *Journal of Jeffery Amherst*, *Canadian Historical Review* 13, no. 1 (March 1932): 53–55. There are many instances of implied criticism in the letters published in Willson, *Life and Letters of James Wolfe*.

12. Hart, *Fall of New France*, 158; entry on Edward Boscawen in the *Dictionary of National Biography*, 2:877–81; C. P. Stacey, "British Forces in North America"; Chartrand, *Louisbourg 1758*, 28–29.

13. Julian Gwyn, "Whitmore, Edward," in *Dictionary of Canadian Biography*, 3:662–63. All quotes come from that short article. Whitmore's dates were ca. 1694–1761.

14. Dominick Graham, "Lawrence, Charles," in *Dictionary of Canadian Biography*, 3:361–66.

15. C. P. Stacey, "Wolfe, James," in *Dictionary of Canadian Biography*, 3:666–73; Quebec House Permanent Advisory Committee, *Wolfe, Portraiture and Genealogy* (Westerham, England, 1959).

16. Entry on Jeffery Amherst prepared by Henry Morse Stephens, in *Dictionary of National Biography*, 1:357–59.

17. This story is often cited, including by McLennan, *Louisbourg*, 281.

18. Willson, *Life and Letters of James Wolfe*, 390, letter of July 30, 1758. Venning

mentions this involvement in *Following the Drum*, 113, though her interpretation suggests it was more than "several" women on "one occasion".

19. Quoted in Brumwell, *Redcoats*, 125.

20. Quotation and figure for the Prussian army is from Willerd R. Fann, "On the Infantryman's Age in Eighteenth-Century Prussia," *Military Affairs* 41, no. 4 (December 1977): 167, 165; for the British army, see Sylvia Frey, *The British Soldier in America: A Social History of Military Life in the Revolutionary Period* (Austin: University of Texas Press, 1981), 23; Brumwell, "Rank and File," 11, 13; Johnston, "Men of the Garrison," 47–48.

21. Harper, *Short History*, 12. Brumwell mentions Sergeant Macleod in *Redcoats*, 303.

22. In the early 1750s roughly 5 percent of the one thousand Marine troops at Louisbourg were not from France. The largest minority of foreign-born soldiers at that time were from Spain. Johnston, *Control and Order*, 187; Brumwell, *Redcoats*, 76.

23. See appendix 1 of Boscawen, "Combined Operation against Louisbourg," for a list of the warships before Louisbourg; the 150 transports are named and detailed in Library and Archives of Canada, MG12, Admiralty 1, vol. 2295, "State . . . of Transports . . . Louisbourg Expedition, 7 June 1758."

24. C. P. Stacey credits Amherst with making the switch to the beaches to the west of Louisbourg, in *Dictionary of Canadian Biography*, 4:666–73.

25. Kimball, *Correspondence of William Pitt*, 1:271–75, Amherst to Pitt, June 11, 1758.

26. Speech of Jeffery Amherst, June 3, 1758, LO 5847. This item is reproduced by permission of the Huntington Library, San Marino, California.

27. Knollenberg, "General Amherst and Germ Warfare."

28. Kimball, *Correspondence of William Pitt*, 1:271–75, Amherst to Pitt, June 11, 1758.

29. McLennan, *Louisbourg*, 242–43, 301. The quotes from Grillot de Poilly are on p. 301.

30. Kimball, *Correspondence of William Pitt*, 1:180, Pitt to Boscawen, February 3, 1758.

31. Drucour Journal and Grillot de Poilly Journal, entries for June 2 and 3; and "Copy of Journal" [hereafter cited as Gordon Journal], p. 106.

32. Drucour Journal, entries for June 4 and 5, 1758.

33. Drucour Journal, June 5, 1758; Wyczynski, "Expedition of the Second Battalion," 101–2.

34. Drucour Journal, entry for June 6, 1758; Grillot de Poilly Journal, entries for June 5 and 6, 1758. Drucour recorded that there were ten companies of Cambis soldiers; Poilly wrote there eight and one-half companies.

35. Drucour and Grillot de Poilly Journals, entries for June 6, 1758.

36. Grillot de Poilly Journal, entries for June 5 and 6, 1758.

37. Kimball, *Correspondence of William Pitt*, 1:272, Amherst to Pitt, June 11, 1758.

38. Drucour Journal, June 7, 1758.

39. Each order can be found in Doughty, *Historical Journal*, 1:213–18.

6. Attack and Defend, June 8–July 27, 1758

1. Except where otherwise noted, the events summarized in this and the next several paragraphs comes from Doughty, *Historical Journal*, 1:217–18; Gordon Journal, 112–16; Kimball, *Correspondence of William Pitt*, 1:272, Amherst to Pitt, June 11, 1758.

2. An artist's depiction of what some of the boats may have looked like is found in Chartrand, *Louisbourg 1758*, 46–47. The illustration is based on longboat models in the collection of the National Army Museum in Great Britain. Brumwell, *Redcoats*, 239–240.

3. Brumwell, *Redcoats*, 71.

4. C. P. Stacey provides a biography of Scott, whose birth date is unknown, in the *Dictionary of Canadian Biography*, 3:589–90.

5. Doughty, *Historical Journal*, 1:177. The bread and cheese direction was part of the instructions Admiral Boscawen issued in Halifax on May 21, and Major General Amherst did not rescind the order.

6. Gordon Journal, 100–102.

7. Burke, "Progress of the Archaeological Survey Project," 3; Boscawen's account of the landing on June 8 as well of those of many others are presented in McLennan, *Louisbourg*, 256–60. The quotation relating to Philip Durell comes from W. A. B. Douglas's biography of the naval officer in the *Dictionary of Canadian Biography*, 3:208–10.

8. Grillot de Poilly Journal, entry for June 8, 1758.

9. Kimball, *Correspondence of William Pitt*, 1:273, Amherst to Pitt, June 11, 1758.

10. Thompson account cited at length in Harper, *Fraser Highlanders*, 48–49. The size of the traditional tartan is given in Summers and Chartrand, *Military Uniforms in Canada*, 48.

11. Letter of Murray to his wife, June 13, 1758, transcribed in "Life and Letters of Sandy"; the sergeant is cited in Downey, *Louisbourg*, 157; and McLennan, *Louisbourg*, 252. Equiano, *Interesting Narrative*, 68–69.

12. Cited in McLennan, *Louisbourg*, 257.

13. Harper, *Fraser Highlanders*, 50.

14. Gordon Journal, 115; Willson, *Life and Letters of James Wolfe*, 372–73.

15. Archives nationales, Archives des colonies, C11B, vol. 38, fols. 150–51, Marchant de La Houlière, 10 juin 1758.

16. See various journal extracts in McLennan, *Louisbourg*, 256–60.

17. McLennan, *Louisbourg*, 252n3.

18. McLennan, *Louisbourg*, 259.

19. The account of the landing sent to France aboard the *Comète* on June 10 is located in Archives nationales, Archives des colonies, c11b, vol. 25, fols. 233–35. The so-called anonymous journal is in Archives nationales, Archives des colonies, c11c, vol. 10; the quotation is on fol. 5v.

20. Grillot de Poilly Journal, June 8, 1758, "Journée fatale à la France"; McLennan, *Louisbourg*, 325–26, in appendix 1.

21. Archives nationales, Archives des colonies, c11b, vol. 38, fols. 150–51, Marchant de La Houlière, 10 juin 1758.

22. Archives nationales, Archives des colonies, c11b, vol. 31, fols. 222–22v, Keridisien, 10 juin 1758.

23. McLennan, *Louisbourg*, 258. Gordon Journal, 116.

24. McLennan, *Louisbourg*, 247; Archives nationales, Archives des colonies, c11c, vol. 10, fol. 5, anonymous journal. The French diarist discusses the landing again on June 19 (fol. 8), again emphasizing the unoccupied lookout. The British diarist's observation is from "An Anonymous Journal," quoted in McLennan, *Louisbourg*, 257.

25. Wolfe to Sackville, in McLennan, *Louisbourg*, 253n2.

26. The stories and quotes come from the account of Sergeant Thompson, cited in Harper, *Fraser Highlanders*, 51.

27. McLennan, *Louisbourg*, 252–53.

28. Boscawen's journal cited in McLennan, *Louisbourg*, 256. One of the text sections on a map in the William L. Clements Library, University of Michigan, Ann Arbor, offers the following breakdown of the British casualties on June 8: three land officers, forty-nine privates, and nine sailors killed; five land officers, fifty-three privates, four marine officers, and fifty-three sailors wounded. Kimball, *Correspondence of William Pitt*, 1:274, Amherst to Pitt, June 11, 1758; 283, Amherst to Pitt, June 23, 1758. McLennan, *Louisbourg*, 253nn.

29. Harper, *Fraser Highlanders*, 52.

30. Letter of Murray to his wife, June 13, 1758, transcribed in "Life and Letters of Sandy." John Humphreys provides a biography of Alexander Murray in the *Dictionary of Canadian Biography*, 3:479–80; Equiano, *Interesting Narrative*, 69.

31. The quotes come from Kimball, *Correspondence of William Pitt*, 1:275, Amherst to Pitt, June 11, 1758; 283, Amherst to Pitt, June 23, 1758; and Gordon Journal, 117–18. See also McLennan, *Louisbourg*, 264–65.

32. "Journal de ma campagne de Louisbourg," 48; the note about the quartermaster general is in Pargellis, *Military Affairs*, 417.

33. Grillot de Poilly Journal and Drucour Journal, entries for June 8, 1758.

34. The letter the marquis des Gouttes sent to Drucour is transcribed in Caron, *La guerre incomprise*, 297–98.

35. In *La guerre incomprise*, Caron repeatedly laments the decision that Drucour took to keep the warships in the harbor rather than let them sail away. Caron completely adopts the point of view of the ship captains. Indeed, he goes further, accusing

Drucour of "treason" to France. For examples, see pp. 322 and 411. In attendance at the Conseil de Guerre were Drucour, Franquet, Prévost, Marchant de La Houlière, Mascle de Saint-Julhien, Marin, Danthonay, and Claude-Élisabeth Denys de Bonnaventure, according to Archives nationales, Archives des colonies, c11B, vol. 38, fols. 23–23v, 10 juin 1758.

36. Kimball, *Correspondence of William Pitt*, 1:283, Amherst to Pitt, June 23, 1758.

37. Archives nationales, Archives des colonies, B, vol. 107, p. 346, draft of a letter to Drucour.

38. Archives nationales, Archives des colonies, c11B, vol. 38, fols. 189–90, des Gouttes, 10 juin 1758. Marchant de La Houlière's comment to much the same effect appears at the end of his June 10 letter to the minister, in Archives nationales, Archives des colonies, c11B, vol. 38, fols. 150–51.

39. Grillot de Poilly, who did not participate in the war council, discusses the two points of view at some length in his journal, entry for June 9, 1758; Drucour, who was there and cast the deciding vote, did not mention the debate at all in his, entry for June 9.

40. Drucour and Grillot de Poilly Journals, entries for June 10, 1758. Drucour: "nous nous preparons a faire toutte la resistance possible"; Poilly: "il seroit bon d'embosser une fregate pour prendre nos hauteurs de revers, on espère que cela se fera." McLennan, entry on Jean Vauquelin in the appendices to the first edition of *Louisbourg*, 330–31.

41. Grillot de Poilly Journal, entry for June 22, 1758.

42. Kimball, *Correspondence of William Pitt*, 1:283, Amherst to Pitt, June 23, 1758.

43. Burke, "Progress of the Archaeological Survey Project," 8; Wolfe, cited in Willson, *Life and Letters of James Wolfe*, 376; anonymous officer, cited in Burke, "Progress of the Archaeological Survey Project," 8; Gordon Journal, 129.

44. Amherst links Bastide with Green Hill on several occasions; see Kimball, *Correspondence of William Pitt*, 1:283, Amherst to Pitt, June 23, 1758, and 1:291, Amherst to Pitt, July 6, 1758.

45. Gordon Journal, 118–20.

46. LeGoff, "Artillery at Louisbourg," 83–86, 119.

47. Letters prepared by des Gouttes and other ship captains during this time period are transcribed in Caron, *La guerre incomprise*, 302–3.

48. Willson, *Life and Letters of James Wolfe*, 377, Wolfe to Amherst, June 19, 1758. For a summary of the events leading up to the batteries opening fire, see Gordon Journal, 118–24; Drucour Journal, near the end of the entry for June 19, 1758; Grillot de Poilly Journal for June 19, 1758.

49. Grillot de Poilly Journal, entries for June 13 and 14, 1758.

50. Drucour Journal, entry for June 12, 1758; Grillot de Poilly Journal, entry for June 13, 1758.

51. Doughty, *Historical Journal*, 1:219, orders of June 9, 1758; Drucour Journal, entries from June 11 to 19, 1758. British confidence about victory found its way into a letter written on June 16, sent to a British officer at Annapolis Royal: "when we have reduced this garrison, which now I make no doubt of," quoted in Doughty, *Historical Journal*, 1:184. Archives nationales, Archives des colonies, C11B, vol. 25, fols. 233–35, "Relation de l'Ile Royale," sans date; this is the dispatch sent aboard the *Comète*. Hitsman with Bond, "Assault Landing at Louisbourg," 329, place the British casualties at 62 killed or missing and 112 wounded. The numbers I provide come from the tabulation lists on an original British document in the William L. Clements Library, University of Michigan, Ann Arbor. On that document the breakdown was 3 land officers, 49 privates, and 9 sailors killed; 5 land officers, 53 privates, 4 marine officers, and 53 sailors wounded.

52. Grillot de Poilly Journal, entries for June 18 and 19, 1758. In Boishébert's own account, "Journal de ma campagne de Louisbourg," 48–53, he states that estimates of his force ranged as high as twelve hundred.

53. Gordon Journal, 122; I thank one of the anonymous readers of the manuscript, at the peer review stage for publication by the University of Nebraska Press, for pointing out the symbolism of the pineapples; Drucour Journal, entries for June 14 and 18, 1758.

54. In *La guerre incomprise*, 303–4, Caron gives June 24 as the date for this meeting. The other sources cited in the next few notes place the decision to allow a few ships to leave and others to be sunk as occurring on June 22. Caron provides a lengthy transcription of des Gouttes' account of his meeting with Drucour.

55. Archives nationales, Archives des colonies, C11B, vol. 38, fols. 152–53, 22 juin 1758. The merchant ships were not mentioned by name, but the warships were to be the frigates *Chèvre* and *Fidèle* and the flute *Apollon*.

56. Drucour and Grillot de Poilly Journals, entries of June 20–22, 1758; Archives nationales, Archives des colonies, C11B, vol. 38, fol. 182, Keridisien, 20 juin 1758.

57. Drucour and Grillot de Poilly Journals, entries of June 22 and 23, 1758.

58. Drucour Journal, entry of June 24, 1758; Chartrand, *Louisbourg 1758*, 57.

59. The lengthy lament about Maillard is in Drucour's journal, entry for July 1, 1758. That section, translated into English, is presented in McLennan, *Louisbourg*, 270–71.

60. "Journal de ma campagne de Louisbourg," 49; Aégidius Fauteux, *Les Chevaliers de Saint-Louis en Canada* (Montréal: Les Éditions de Dix, 1940); letter to Boishébert dated June 24, 1758, in Drucour Journal, fols. 71v–74.

61. Kimball, *Correspondence of William Pitt*, 1:291–92, Amherst to Pitt, July 6, 1758.

62. Chartrand, *Louisbourg 1758*, 60.

63. Drucour and Grillot de Poilly Journals, entries from June 25–29, 1758; letter of Murray to his wife, July 2, 1758, in "Life and Letters of Sandy"; Gordon Journal, 128.

64. Willson, *Life and Letters of James Wolfe*, 378, Wolfe to Amherst, June 20, 1758. The citation from the orders comes from Gordon Journal, 123.

65. Letter of Murray to his wife dated July 2, 1758, in "Life and Letters of Sandy"; the estimate of six hundred yards comes from Gordon Journal, 125.

66. Chartrand, *Louisbourg 1758*, 60; McLennan makes reference to the man up the mast in *Louisbourg*, 275n1; Kimball, *Correspondence of William Pitt*, 1:292, Amherst to Pitt, July 6, 1758; Gordon Journal, 127–28.

67. Grillot de Poilly Journal, entries of June 28 and 29, 1758; Gordon Journal, 126.

68. Archives nationales, Archives des colonies, c11b, vol. 25, fols. 233–35, sans date; B, vol. 107, fol. 393, à Drucour et Prévost, 30 juin 1758; fols. 395–98v, à Des Gouttes et al, 30 juin 1758.

69. Kimball, *Correspondence of William Pitt*, 1:293, Amherst to Pitt, July 6, 1758.

70. Letter of Murray to his wife, July 6, 1758, in "Life and Letters of Sandy."

71. Archives nationales, Archives des colonies, c11b, vol. 38, fols. 154–55, Marchant de La Houlière, 7 juillet 1758; Gordon Journal, 128; Amherst quoted in C. P. Stacey, "Jeffery Amherst," *Dictionary of Canadian Biography*, 4:22.

72. The incidents involving the ship captains in early July are discussed in McLennan, *Louisbourg*, 271–74; and the journals of Drucour and Grillot de Poilly, July 1–6, 1758; the citations come from the Drucour Journal entry of July 3 and July 6; and from Prévost's letter in Archives nationales, Archives des colonies, c11b, vol. 38, fol. 37, 7 juillet 1758.

73. Drucour and Grillot de Poilly Journals, entries of July 1–5, 1758; Gordon Journal, 128–30.

74. Gordon Journal, 130; Drucour Journal, entry for July 6, 1758.

75. Amherst cited in Kimball, *Correspondence of William Pitt*, 1:293, letter of July 6, 1758, and 305, letter of July 23, 1758; Grillot de Poilly Journal, entries for July 5, 6, and 7, 1758.

76. Drucour Journal, July 6. The *religieux* would have been Brothers of Charity. Gordon Journal, 130–31; Willson, *Life and Letters of James Wolfe*, 379, Wolfe to Amherst, n.d.

77. Gordon Journal, 136; Steele, *Warpaths*, 204–5; Chartrand, *Quebec 1759*, 14.

78. Drucour Journal, lengthy entry of July 7, 1758; Kimball, *Correspondence of William Pitt*, 1:302, Amherst to Pitt, July 23, 1758. Details on the strolls taken during the lull in the fighting are in Grillot de Poilly Journal, entry for July 7, 1758; in Archives nationales, Archives des colonies, c11c, vol. 10, fol. 12v; and in McLennan, *Louisbourg*, 276.

79. Archives nationales, Archives des colonies, C11B, vol. 38, fols. 154–55, Marchant de La Houlière, 7 juillet 1758.

80. Details on the raid of July 8/9 are found in Drucour and Poilly Journals; McLennan, *Louisbourg*, 277–78; Kimball, *Correspondence of William Pitt*, 1:302–3, Amherst to Pitt, July 23, 1758; Gordon Journal, 133–34.

81. Grillot de Poilly journal, entries from July 8–15, 1758; Kimball, *Correspondence of William Pitt*, 1:303, Amherst to Pitt, July 23, 1758.

82. Kimball, *Correspondence of William Pitt*, 1:303, Amherst to Pitt, July 23, 1758.

83. Archives nationales, Archives des colonies, C11B, vol. 38, fols. 11–11v, Drucour et Prévost, 7 juillet 1758; fols. 36–38v, Prévost, 7 juillet 1758; fols. 154–55, Marchant de La Houlière, 7 juillet 1758; Kimball, *Correspondence of William Pitt*, 1:303, Amherst to Pitt, July 23, 1758. Wolfe is quoted by McLennan in *Louisbourg*, 278; McLennan, *Louisbourg*, appendix 1 of first edition, pp. 330–31.

84. Archives nationales, Archives des colonies, C11B, vol. 38, fols. 31–33v, Drucour, 15 juillet 1758; fols. 34–35, Prévost, 15 juillet 1758. The contrast between British concord and French friction is discussed in McLennan, *Louisbourg*; and Hitsman with Bond, "Assault Landing at Louisbourg."

85. Drucour Journal, entry for July 16, 1758; Archives nationales, Archives des colonies, C11B, vol. 38, fols. 24–26, Drucour, 13 juillet 1758; Gordon Journal, 136–37; "Journal de ma campagne de Louisbourg," 49.

86. The first quote is from Gordon Journal, 137; the second from Kimball, *Correspondence of William Pitt*, 1:304, Amherst to Pitt, July 23, 1758; the third is from Drucour Journal, entry for July 18, 1758.

87. Gordon Journal, 137–38; Grillot de Poilly and Drucour Journals, entries for July 19, 20, and 21, 1758.

88. Drucour and Grillot de Poilly Journals, entry for July 21, 1758; Gordon Journal, 138; McLennan, *Louisbourg*, 280–81. The quote is from Gordon.

89. The thought that the French were sinking their own ships, and the final citation in the paragraph, come from Gordon Journal, 138; Amherst's comment to Pitt is in Kimball, *Correspondence of William Pitt*, 1:304, July 23, 1758; for Drucour, see his journal, entry for July 21, 1758.

90. Grillot de Poilly and Drucour Journals, entries for July 21, 1758.

91. Grillot de Poilly Journal, July 21, 1758; Gordon Journal, 139.

92. Gordon Journal, 139; Drucour and Grillot de Poilly Journals, July 22–July 24, 1758; Kimball, *Correspondence of William Pitt*, 1:305, Amherst to Pitt, July 23, 1758; Archives nationales, Archives des colonies, C11B, vol. 38, fols. 43–46, Prévost, 29 juillet 1758.

93. Archives nationales, Archives des colonies, C11C, vol. 10, fol. 19v, anonymous journal; Gordon Journal, 139–40; Kimball, *Correspondence of William Pitt*, 1:305, Amherst to Pitt, July 23, 1758; Drucour and Grillot de Poilly journals, July 22–24, 1758.

94. Willson, *Life and Letters of James Wolfe*, 381, Wolfe to Amherst, July 25, 1758; 390, Wolfe to Lord Sackville, July 30, 1758.

95. Kimball, *Correspondence of William Pitt*, 1:306, Amherst to Pitt, July 27, 1758.

96. Kimball, *Correspondence of William Pitt*, 1:306, Amherst to Pitt, July 27, 1758; 307–9, Boscawen to Pitt, July 28, 1758; Drucour and Grillot de Poilly Journals, entries for July 25–26, 1758.

97. Kimball, *Correspondence of William Pitt*, 1:306, Amherst to Pitt, July 27, 1758; 307–9, Boscawen to Pitt, July 28, 1758; Drucour and Grillot de Poilly Journals, entries for July 25–26, 1758.

98. Kimball, *Correspondence of William Pitt*, 1:306, Amherst to Pitt, July 27, 1758; 307–9, Boscawen to Pitt, July 28, 1758; Drucour and Grillot de Poilly Journals, entries for July 25–26, 1758.

99. Kimball, *Correspondence of William Pitt*, 1:306, Amherst to Pitt, July 27, 1758; 307–9, Boscawen to Pitt, July 28, 1758; Gordon Journal, 141.

100. Drucour and Grillot de Poilly Journals, July 26, 1758; Archives nationales, Archives des colonies, c11c, vol. 10, fol. 17. Franquet's report on the town's defenses and the opinions of the members of the war council are in Archives nationales, Archives des colonies, c11b, vol. 38, fols. 88–93v.

101. Archives nationales, Archives des colonies, c11b, vol. 38, fols. 94v–97, 26 juillet 1758.

102. Grillot de Poilly Journal, July 26, 1758.

103. Archives nationales, Archives des colonies, c11b, vol. 38, fol. 97, 26 juillet 1758.

104. Grillot de Poilly Journal, July 26, 1758; Archives nationales, Archives des colonies, c11b, vol. 38, fols. 97–97v, 26 juillet 1758.

105. Archives nationales, Archives des colonies, c11b, vol. 38, fols. 97v–99v, 26 juillet 1758.

106. Archives nationales, Archives des colonies, c11b, vol. 38, fols. 99–100, 26 juillet 1758.

107. Archives nationales, Archives des colonies, c11b, vol. 38, fols. 101–1v, 26 juillet 1758. The items granted specified that the soldiers and civilians could take away their personal effects, including what the Cambis battalion had left at Sainte-Anne; the women and children were to go to France; and the male inhabitants to Rochefort.

108. The articles of capitulation can be found in various locations, including in French in Archives nationales, Archives des colonies, c11b, vol. 38, fols. 100v–101, 26 juillet 1758; and in English in the Gordon Journal, 142.

109. Archives nationales, Archives des colonies, c11b, vol. 38, fol. 210v, Marchant de La Houlière, 19 septembre 1758, translated in Wyczynski, "Expedition of the Second Battalion," 108. *Caledonian Mercury* (Edinburgh), no. 5742, October 14, 1758. Thanks to René Chartrand for providing me with this reference.

110. Pichon, *Lettres et mémoires*, 311.

111. Willson, *Life and Letters of James Wolfe*, 382, letter to mother, July 27, 1758; Gordon Journal, 143; on the munitions, see Mayo, *Jeffery Amherst*, 89; Whitmore's appointment is in Kimball, *Correspondence of William Pitt*, 1:347; Archives nationales, Archives des colonies, CI 1C, vol. 10, fol. 19v, anonymous journal.

112. Grillot de Poilly Journal, July 27, 1758; Gordon Journal, 149.

113. Equiano, *Interesting Narrative*, 69.

114. Gordon Journal, 149; Kimball, *Correspondence of William Pitt*, 1:307, Amherst to Pitt, July 27, 1758; Willson, *Life and Letters of James Wolfe*, 384, letter to his father, July 27, 1758.

115. Archives nationales, Archives des colonies, CI 1B, vol. 38, fol. 29, 26 juillet 1758.

7. Winner Take All

1. Gordon Journal, 143.

2. These numbers come from the text sections on a map in the William L. Clements Library, University of Michigan, Ann Arbor.

3. One Mi'kmaw injured at Louisbourg in 1758 is mentioned in Pacifique de Valigny, "Le Pays des Micmacs: Cap Breton," *Bulletin de la Société de Géographie de Québec* 27, no. 1 (January 1933): 34, 48. Thanks to Sandy Balcom.

4. Archives nationales, Archives des colonies, CI 1B, vol. 38, fols. 104–6. There is a problem with the numbers as totaled in the original source. When one adds up all the casualties by category, the totals come to 237 injured and 93 killed. Yet the grand totals presented on the original source states there were 210 injured and 93 killed.

5. The quotation comes from McLennan, *Louisbourg*, 288.

6. Kimball, *Correspondence of William Pitt*, 1:312–15, 332–34, 351, Amherst and Boscawen to Pitt, letters of August 10, 12, 14, and 28 and September 13, 1758.

7. Regarding the estimate of a thousand or more Louisbourgeois who were born in the town, the 1752 census listed 776 children in the town at that time, and between 1750 and 1757 the number of baptisms per year ranged between 90 and 150 per year; Johnston, *Control and Order*, table 3, p. 39; and Johnston, *La religion dans la vie à Louisbourg (1713 à 1758)* (Ottawa: Environnement Canada, 1988), fig. 8, p. 153.

8. For an example of someone blaming the naval officers, see the concluding comments offered by the author of the anonymous journal on July 27 in Archives nationales, Archives des colonies, CI 1C, vol. 10, fols. 19v–20.

9. Kimball, *Correspondence of William Pitt*, 1:312–13, Amherst to Pitt, August 10, 1758.

10. Kimball, *Correspondence of William Pitt*, 1:312–13, Amherst to Pitt, August 10, 1758; Lockerby, "Deportation of the Acadians."

11. Campbell, *Road to Canada*, 29. Thomas Davies' painting of the destruction of one Acadian village is reproduced on p. 30.

12. The campaign to the Gaspé is well covered in appendix 11 of McLennan, *Louisbourg*, 417–23; citation from Wolfe is from Willson, *Life and Letters of James Wolfe*, 397, letter to Amherst of September 30, 1758.

13. For British commemorations, see Mayo, *Jeffrey Amherst*, 90–93; Peters, *Pitt and Popularity*, 125–28; McLennan, *Louisbourg*, appendix 14, pp. 436–39. Regarding the painting at Honfleur, I thank Monsieur Jean-Marie Huille, Commissaire Général de la Marine (C.R.) à Toulon for informing me of this painting and sending along photographs. In 1999 the painting was in the possession of the Musée Eugène Boudin.

14. Mayo, *Jeffrey Amherst*, 91–92.

15. Doughty, *Historical Journal*, 1:204–5.

16. Summers and Chartrand, *Military Uniforms in Canada*, 51–53; Harper, *Fraser Highlanders*, 46–101.

17. A census of these refugees or deportees was drawn up in 1759; see Archives nationales, Archives des colonies, C11B, vol. 38, fols. 265–86v. Among the documents that track these colonists after their arrival in France was a list drawn up at Cherbourg in August 1761 that gives information on which individuals were to continue to receive 6 sols per day and which were to have that allowance canceled; see Archives nationales, Archives des colonies, C11B, vol. 38, fols. 253–64v.

18. Rashed, *Peace of Paris*, 9.

19. Steele, *Warpaths*, 223–24; Desbarats, "France in North America," 27.

20. A much longer extract from Pitt's letter can be found in McLennan, *Louisbourg*, 290. Harvey's opinion was that the demolition of Louisbourg's fortifications were "a sign and symbol of the complete destruction of French power in North America, and as an intimation that British power would henceforth concentrate at Halifax which had been built at such great expense to offset Louisbourg," *Holland's Description*, 7.

21. The complete text of the treaty is in Rashed, *Peace of Paris*, 212–29.

22. McLennan, *Louisbourg*, appendix 1, pp. 331–46.

23. Pichette, *Pour l'honneur de mon prince*, 93–95.

24. John Fortier, "Drucour," in *Dictionary of Canadian Biography*, 3:72; Lacour-Gayet, *La Marine militaire*, 385, 532n2. McLennan, *Louisbourg*, appendices, 320, 330–31.

25. Huille, "De Louisbourg à Toulon"; McLennan, *Louisbourg*, 325–26, in appendix 2.

26. C. P. Stacey provides an account of Amherst's life and career in the *Dictionary of Canadian Biography*, 4:20–26; Knollenberg, "General Amherst and Germ Warfare"; entry on Boscawen in the *Dictionary of National Biography*, 2:877–81; C. P. Stacey, "The British Forces in North America during the Seven Years' War," in *Dictionary of Canadian Biography*, 3:xxiv–xxx; Chartrand, *Louisbourg 1758*, 28–29.

27. Julian Gwyn, "Whitmore, Edward," in *Dictionary of Canadian Biography*, 3:662–63. All quotes come from that short article. Whitmore's dates were ca. 1694–1761; Dominick Graham, "Lawrence, Charles," in *Dictionary of Canadian Biography*, 3:361–66.

28. Richardson, "To Halifax with Captain Cook"; some individuals mentioned

in this section are discussed in Willson, "Wolfe's Men and Nova Scotia." There are articles on all of them in the *Dictionary of Canadian Biography*.

29. Johnston, "Commemorating Louisbourg"; Johnston, "Preserving History."

30. Harvey, ed., *Holland's Description*, 60. Holland offers that at Louisbourg "scarce any Resemblance remains of its former State; the Demolition of its Fortifications, & the little Encouragement it has met with; have concurred in reducing its Buildings, Fisheries, & Trade, to a very low Degree. It is difficult on a slight Inspection to believe that there were 300 Shallops, & as many decked Vessels for the banks, once employed in the Fishery" (80). Harvey's comment is on p. 31.

31. Andrew Hill Clark, *Three Centuries and the Island: A Historical Geography of Settlement and Agriculture in Prince Edward Island* (Toronto: University of Toronto Press, 1959).

32. O'Shea, *Louisburg Brass Bands*.

33. Steele, *Warpaths*, 215. The author notes that while the British "fielded eleven thousand men in 1755, [they] were using forty-four thousand in 1758" (225).

34. Martijn, "Early Mi'kmaq Presence," 80–81. An account of the missionaries who gave their attention to the Mi'kmaq of Cape Breton Island before and after the fall of Louisbourg is found in Johnston, *Storied Shores*, 98–124, 134.

35. Among others, see Hitsman with Bond, "Assault Landing at Louisbourg."

36. C. P. Stacey, "Amherst", in *Dictionary of Canadian Biography*, 4:26.

37. Quoted in MacLean, *Louisbourg Heritage*, 23.

Bibliography

Archival Sources

Archives de la France d'outre mer, Aix-en-Provence, France

G1   Registres de l'état-civil, recensements et documents divers (vols. 408–11, 458–59, 462, 466–67)

G2   Greffes des tribunaux de Louisbourg et du Canada, Conseil supérieur et bailliage de Louisbourg (vols. 189, 193, 200–203, 205, 206, 209–12)

DFC   Dépôt des fortifications des colonies, Amérique septentrionale, n° d'ordre 216

Archives de la Guerre, Vincennes, France

Archives du Service historique de l'Armée

A1   Correspondance générale (vols. 3343, 3393, 3457)

Archives du Comité technique du Génie, Manuscrit 66, Journal de Poilly

Archives de la Marine, Paris, France

A2   Actes du pouvoir souverain (article 24)

B4   Campagnes, 1640–1782 (vol. 76)

C7   Personnel individuel

Archives du Séminaire de Québec, Musée de la Civilisation, Quebec City

Archives Maritimes, Port de Rochefort, Rochefort-sur-Mer, France Série 1R, vol. 47

Archives nationales, Archives des colonies, Paris, France

B   Lettres envoyées (vols. 81–112), 1745–60

C11B   Correspondance générale. Lettres reçues. Île Royale (vols. 27–38), 1745–58

C11C   Amérique du Nord (vols. 7–16)

D2C   Troupes des colonies (vols. 47–48, 53, 57–60)

E   Dossiers personnels

Archives Saint-Sulpice de Montreal, Montreal, Quebec

Bibliothèque nationale, Paris, France

British Museum, London, England

Burney Collection, Burney 463 (*Whitehall Evening Post* or *London Intelligencer*)

Huntington Library, Art Collections, and Botanical Gardens, San Marino, California
   Speech of Jeffrey Amherst, June 3, 1758, LO 5847
Library and Archives Canada, Ottawa, Canada
   MG12, Admiralty 1, vol. 2295, "State . . . of Transports . . . Louisbourg Expedition, 7 June 1758."
   MG18, F12, vol. 1, Tableau de l'État
Massachusetts Historical Society, Boston, Massachusetts
   Mascarene Papers
Nova Scotia Archives and Record Management, Halifax, Nova Scotia
   MG 100, vol. 198, no. 2 and 2c
Public Record Office, London, England
   Admiralty 1, vol. 3817

Books, Articles, and Reports

Akins, Thomas Beamish. "History of Halifax City." *Collections of the Nova Scotia Historical Society* 8 (1892–94): 3–272.

Anderson, Fred. *Crucible of War: The Seven Years' War and the Fate of Empire in British North America, 1754–1766.* New York: Alfred A. Knopf, 2000.

Annand, Major A. McK. "Hugh Montgomerie, 12th Earl of Eglington, K.T." *Journal of Army Historical Research* 39 (1961): 37–40.

Arsenault, Georges. *The Island Acadians, 1720–1980.* Charlottetown PEI: Ragweed Press, 1989.

Axtell, James. *The European and the Indian: Essays in the Ethnohistory of Colonial North America.* New York: Oxford University Press, 1982.

Baker, Raymond F. *A Campaign of Amateurs: The Siege of Louisbourg in 1745.* 1978. Reprint, Ottawa: Parks Canada, 1995.

Balesi, Charles J. *The Time of the French in the Heart of North America, 1673–1818.* Chicago: Alliance Française Chicago, 1992.

Balcom, B. A. *The Cod Fishery of Isle Royale, 1713–1758.* Ottawa: Parks Canada, 1984.

Banks, Kenneth J. *Chasing Empire across the Sea: Communications and the State in the French Atlantic, 1713–1763.* Montreal: McGill–Queen's University Press, 2002.

Barbier, E. J. F. *Journal historique et anecdotique du règne de Louis XV.* 4 vols. 1847–56. Reprint, New York: Johnson Reprint, 1966.

Barnes, Major R. Money. *A History of the Regiments and Uniforms of the British Army.* 1950. Reprint, London: Seeley Service, 1962.

Basque, Maurice. *Des hommes de pouvoir: Histoire d'Otho Robichaud et de sa famille, notables acadiens de Port-Royal et de Néguac.* Néguac NB: Société historique de Néguac, 1996.

Bell, Winthrop Pickard. *The "Foreign Protestants" and the Settlement of Nova Scotia: The History of a Piece of Arrested British Colonial Policy in the Eighteenth Century.* Toronto: University of Toronto Press, 1961.

Bingeman, John M., and Arthur T. Mack. "The Dating of Military Buttons: Second Interim Report based on Artefacts Recovered from the 18th-Century Wreck *Invincible*, between 1979 and 1990." *International Journal of Nautical Archaeology* 26, no. 1 (1997): 39–50.

Black, Jeremy. *The Rise of the European Powers, 1679–1793.* London: Edward Arnold, 1990.

Bodin, Jacques. *L'histoire extraordinaire des Soldats de la Nouvelle-France.* Poitiers: Édition O. C. A. Communication, 1993.

Boscawen, Hugh. "The Combined Operation against Louisbourg, 1758." Undergraduate diss., University of Bristol, 1976. Copy at Archives of the Fortress of Louisbourg.

Bourinot, Sir John. "The Siege of Louisbourg in 1758." *Canadian History,* no. 8:203–6.

Brebner, J. B. "Canadian Policy towards the Acadians in 1751." *Canadian Historical Review* 12, no. 3 (1931): 284–86.

———. *New England's Outpost: Acadia before the Conquest of Canada.* New York: Columbia University Press, 1927.

Browning, Reed. *The War of the Austrian Succession.* New York: St. Martin's, 1993.

Brumwell, Stephen. "Rank and File: A Profile of One of Wolfe's Regiments." *Journal of the Society for Army Historical Research* 79, no. 317 (Spring 2001): 3–24.

———. *Redcoats: The British Soldier and War in the Americas, 1755–1763.* Cambridge: Cambridge University Press, 2002.

Buckner, Philip A., and John G. Reid, eds. *The Atlantic Region to Confederation: A History.* Toronto: University of Toronto Press and Acadiensis Press, 1994.

Burke, Charles A. "Progress of the Archaeological Survey Project, Fortress of Louisbourg National Historic Park, 1987–88," *Research Bulletin* 277 (May 1989). Ottawa: Environment Canada, 1989.

Campbell, W. E. (Gary). *The Road to Canada: The Grand Communications Route from Saint John to Quebec.* New Brunswick Military Heritage Series 5. Fredericton NB: Goose Lane Editions and the New Brunswick Military Heritage Project, 2005.

Canny, Nicholas, and Anthony Pagden, eds. *Colonial Identity in the Atlantic World, 1500–1800.* Princeton NJ: Princeton University Press, 1987.

Caron, François. *La guerre incomprise ou les raisons d'un échec (Capitulation de Louisbourg—1758).* Vincennes: Service historique de la marine, 1983.

Chartrand, René. *Canadian Military Heritage.* Vol. 1, *1000–1754.* Montréal: Art Global, 1993.

———. *Canadian Military Heritage.* Vol. 2, *1755–1871.* Montréal: Art Global, 1995.

———. *Louis XV's Army (2): French Infantry.* Color plates by Eugène Lelièpvre. Men-at-Arms Series 302. London: Osprey, 1996.

———. *Louis XV's Army (3): Foreign Infantry.* Color plates by Eugène Lelièpvre. Men-at-Arms Series 304. London: Osprey, 1997.

———. *Louisbourg 1758: Wolfe's First Siege.* Battle scene plates by Patrice Courcelle. Campaign Series 79. London: Osprey, 2000.

———. *Quebec 1759, The Heights of Abraham 1759, The Armies of Wolfe and Montcalm.* Order of Battle Series 3. Oxford: Osprey, 1999.

"Chronicle of Occurrences." *Magazine of Magazines, or Universal Register,* July 1759, p. 69. (List of ships won and lost in present war—including Louisbourg.)

Clark, Andrew Hill. "New England's Role in the Under-development of Cape Breton Island during the French Regime, 1713–1758." *Canadian Geographer / Le géographe canadien* 9 (1965): 1–12.

Cleare, Geoffrey H. "The Louisbourg Expedition, 1758," from Engineer Adam Williamson's Notebook and Colonel George Williamson's Letter-Books. *Journal of Army Historical Research* 39 (1961): 193–97.

Colley, Linda. *Britons: Forging the Nation, 1707–1837.* New Haven CT: Yale University Press, 1992.

"Copy of Journal kept by ——Gordon, One of the Officers engaged in the Siege of Louisbourg under Boscawen and Amherst, in 1758." *Collections of the Nova Scotia Historical Society,* vol. 5 (1886–87): 97–158.

Corbett, Julian S. *England in the Seven Years' War: A Study in Combined Strategy.* 2 vols. London: Longmans, Green, 1907.

Desbarats, Catherine M. "The Cost of Early Canada's Native Alliances: Reality and Scarcity's Rhetoric." *William and Mary Quarterly,* 3d series, 52, no. 4 (October 1995): 609–30.

———. "France in North America: The Net Burden of Empire during the First Half of the Eighteenth Century." *French History* 11, no. 1 (1997): 1–28.

Dickason, Olive Patricia. "Louisbourg and the Indians: A Study in Imperial Race Relations." In *History and Archaeology / Histoire et Archéologie,* 6:3–236. Ottawa: Parks Canada, 1976.

Dictionary of Canadian Biography. Edited by Francess G. Halpenny and Jean Hamelin. Vols. 3, 4, and 5. Toronto: University of Toronto Press; Quebec: Presses de l'Université, 1974, 1979, 1983.

Dictionary of National Biography. Vols. 1 and 2. Edited by Sir Leslie Stephen and Sir Sydney Lee. Oxford: Oxford University Press, 1959–60. Vol. 25. Edited by Sir Leslie Stephen and Sir Sydney Lee. London: Smith, Elder, 1891. Vol. 45. Edited by Sir Sydney Lee. London: Smith, Elder, 1896.

Donaldson, Gordon. *Battle for a Continent, Quebec 1759*. Toronto: Doubleday Canada, 1973.

Donovan, Kenneth, ed. "'After Midnight We Danced until Daylight': Music, Song and Dance in Cape Breton, 1713–1758." *Acadiensis* 32, no. 1 (Autumn 2002): 3–28.

———. *Cape Breton at 200: Historical Essays in Honour of the Island's Bicentennial, 1785–1985*. Sydney NS: University College of Cape Breton Press, 1985.

———. "Inflation at Louisbourg, 1757." *Canadian Collector* 18, no. 1 (January–February 1983): 20–22.

———. "The Marquis de Chabert and the Louisbourg Observatory in the 1750s." *American Neptune* 44, no. 3 (Summer 1984): 186–97.

———. "A Nominal List of Slaves and Their Owners in Île Royale, 1713–1760." *Nova Scotia Historical Review* 16, no. 1 (1996): 151–62.

———. "Slaves in Île Royale, 1713–1758." *French Colonial History* 5 (2004): 25–42.

———. "Slaves and Their Owners in Île Royale, 1713–1760." *Acadiensis* 25, no. 1 (1995): 3–32.

Doughty, Arthur G., ed. *An Historical Journal of the Campaigns in North America for the Years 1757, 1758, 1759, and 1760 by Captain John Knox*. 3 vols. Toronto: Champlain Society, 1914.

Douglas, W. A. B. "Halifax as an Element of Sea Power, 1749–1766," MA thesis, Dalhousie University, 1962.

Downey, Fairfax. *Louisbourg: Key to a Continent*. Englewood Cliffs NJ: Prentice-Hall, 1965.

Du Boscq de Beaumont, Gaston, ed. *Les derniers jours de l'Acadie (1748–1758): Correspondances et mémoires*. Geneva: Slatkine, 1975.

Dull, Jonathan R. *The French Navy and the Seven Years' War*. Lincoln: University of Nebraska Press, 2005.

Dumont-Johnson, Micheline. *Apôtres ou agitateurs: La France missionnaire en Acadie*. Trois-Rivières QC: Boréal, 1970.

Dunn, Brenda. *A History of Port-Royal / Annapolis Royal, 1605–1800*. Halifax: Nimbus, 2004.

Eccles, W. J. *The Canadian Frontier, 1534–1760*. New York: Holt, Rinehart and Winston, 1969.

———. *France in America*. New York: Harper and Row, 1972.

———. "The Preemptive Conquest, 1749–1763." In *Readings in Canadian History: Pre-Confederation*, edited by R. Douglas Francis and Donald B. Smith, 5th ed., 143–52. Toronto: Nelson Thomson Learning, 1998.

Equiano, Olaudah. *The Interesting Narrative of the Life of Olaudah Equiano, Written by Himself*. Edited with an introduction by Robert J. Allison. Boston: Bedford Books, 1995.

Faragher, John Mack. *A Great and Noble Scheme: The Tragic Story of the Expulsion of the*

French Acadians from Their American Homeland. New York: W. W. Norton, 2005.

Fenn, Elizabeth. "Biological Warfare in Eighteenth-Century North America: Beyond Jeffery Amherst." *Journal of American History* 86, no. 4 (March 2000): 1552–80.

Filion, Maurice. "Maurepas, Minister of the Navy, 1723–1749: A New Portrait." *Cornell Library Journal* 2 (1967): 34–47.

———. *Maurepas, ministre de Louis XV (1715–1749).* Montreal: Les Éditions Leméac, 1967.

———. *La pensée et l'action coloniale de Maurepas, vis-à-vis du Canada, 1723–1749, l'âge d'or de la colonie.* Montreal: Les Éditions Leméac, 1972.

Fingard, Judith, Janet Guildford, and David Sutherland, *Halifax: The First 250 Years.* Halifax: Formac, 1999.

Fortescue, J. W. *A History of the British Army.* 2 vols. London: Macmillan, 1910.

Fortier, John. *Fortress of Louisbourg.* Toronto: Oxford University Press, 1979.

Fowler, William M., Jr. *Empires at War: The Seven Years' War and the Struggle for North America, 1754–1763.* Vancouver: Douglas and McIntyre, 2005.

Frégault, Guy. *Canada: The War of the Conquest.* Translated by Margaret Cameron. Toronto: Oxford University Press, 1969.

Fry, Bruce W. *"An Appearance of Strength": The Fortifications of Louisbourg.* 2 vols. Ottawa: Parks Canada, 1984.

Gagnon, C. O., ed. *Lettre de M. L'abbé Le Guerne Missionaire de l'Acadie.* Québec: Imprimerie générale,1889.

Gibson, Tom. *The Wiltshire Regiment: The 62nd and 99th Regiments of Foot.* London: Leo Cooper, 1969.

Gipson, Lawrence Henry. *The British Empire before the American Revolution.* Vol. 6, *The Great War for the Empire: The Years of Defeat, 1754–1757.* New York: Alfred A. Knopf, 1968.

———. *The British Empire before the American Revolution.* Vol. 7, *The Great War for the Empire: The Victorious Years, 1758–1760.* New York: Alfred A. Knopf, 1967.

Giraud, Marcel. "France and Louisiana in the Early Eighteenth Century." *Mississippi Valley Historical Review* 36, no. 4 (March 1950): 657–74.

Greer, Allan. "Another Soldiers' Revolt in Île Royale, June 1750." *Acadiensis* 12, no. 2 (Spring 1983): 106–9.

———. "Mutiny at Louisbourg, December 1744." *Histoire sociale / Social History* 10, no. 20 (November–December 1977): 305–36.

———. *Soldiers of Isle Royale,1720–45.* History and Archaeology 28. Ottawa: Parks Canada, 1979.

Griffiths, N. E. S. *The Acadian Deportation: Deliberate Perfidy or Cruel Necessity?* Toronto: Copp Clark, 1969.

———. *The Contexts of Acadian History, 1686–1784*. Montreal: McGill–Queen's University Press, 1992.

———. *From Migrant to Acadian: A North American Border People,1604 to 1755*. Montreal: McGill–Queen's University Press, 2004.

———. "The Golden Age: Acadian Life, 1713–1748." *Histoire sociale / Social history* 17, no. 33 (May 1984): 21–34.

———. "Réflexions et commentaires sur la déportation de 1755." *Cahiers de la Société historique acadienne* 36, nos. 2 and 3 (September 2005): 91–101.

Gwyn, Julian, *The Enterprising Admiral: The Personal Fortune of Admiral Sir Peter Warren*. Montreal: McGill–Queen's University Press, 1974.

———. "French and British Naval Power at the Two Sieges of Louisbourg: 1745 and 1758." *Nova Scotia Historical Review* 10, no. 2 (1991): 63–93.

———. *Frigates and Foremasts: The North American Squadron in Nova Scotia Waters, 1745–1815*. Vancouver: University of British Columbia Press, 2003.

Gwyn, Julian, and Christopher Moore, eds. *La chute de Louisbourg: Le journal du per siège de Louisbourg du 25 mars au 17 juillet 1745 par Gilles Lacroix-Girard*. Ottawa: Éditions de l'Université d'Ottawa, 1978.

Hand, Chris M. *The Siege of Fort Beauséjour, 1755*. Fredericton NB: Goose Lane Editions and the New Brunswick Military Heritage Series, 2004.

Hansen, Erik S., and J. Sherman Bleakney. *Underwater Survey of Louisbourg Harbour for Relics of the Siege of 1758*. Wolfville NS: Acadia University Institute, 1962.

Harper, J. R. *The Fraser Highlanders*. Montreal: Society of the Montreal Military and Maritime Museum, 1979.

———. *A Short History of the Old 78th Regiment or Fraser's Highlanders, 1757–1763*. Chomedy QC: Devsco, 1966.

Harris, R. Cole, and Geoffrey J. Matthews, eds. *Historical Atlas of Canada*. Vol. 1, *From the Beginning to 1800*. Toronto: University of Toronto Press, 1987

Hart, Gerald E. *The Fall of New France, 1755–1760*. Montreal: W. Drysdale, 1888.

Harvey, D. C., ed. *Holland's Description of Cape Breton Island and Other Documents*. Halifax: Public Archives of Nova Scotia, 1935.

Hitsman, J. Mackay, with C. C. J. Bond. "The Assault Landing at Louisbourg, 1758." *Canadian Historical Review* 35, no. 4 (December 1954): 314–30.

Hughes, Quentin. *Britain in the Mediterranean and the Defence of Her Naval Stations*. Liverpool: Penpaled Books, 1981.

Huille, Jean-Marie. "De Louisbourg à Toulon: L'aventure canadienne du Commissaire de la Marine Prévost de la Croix, communication à la Section d'Histoire de l'Académie du Var le 29 avril 1992." Copy in Archives of the Fortress of Louisbourg.

Janzen, Olaf U. "The Eviction of French Fishermen from Newfoundland in 1755: Dress Rehearsal for the Acadian Deportation?" Unpublished paper.

343

Jennings, Francis. *Empire of Fortune: Crown, Colonies, and Tribes in the Seven Years' War in America.* New York: Norton: 1988.

Johnston, A. J. B. "Alcohol Consumption at Louisbourg (and the Vain Attempts to Control It)." *French Colonial History* 2 (2002): 61–76.

———. "Avant les loyalistes—les Acadiens dans la région de Sydney, 1749–1754." *Cahiers de la Société historique acadienne* 19, no. 3 (July–September 1988): 105–13.

———. "Borderland Worries: Loyalty Oaths in *Acadie*/Nova Scotia, 1654–1755." *French Colonial History* 4 (2003): 31–48.

———. "Commemorating Louisbourg, c. 1767." *Acadiensis* 13, no. 2 (Spring 1984): 147–49.

———. *Control and Order at French Colonial Louisbourg, 1713–1758.* East Lansing: Michigan State University Press, 2001.

———. "Desertion, Treason and the Concept of Loyalty on the Frontier of New France." In *Proceedings of the Fifteenth Meeting of the French Colonial Historical Society, Martinique and Guadeloupe, May 1989,* edited by Patricia Galloway and Philip P. Boucher, 178–88. Lanham MD: University Press of America, 1992.

———. "The Fishermen of Eighteenth-Century Cape Breton: Numbers and Origins." *Nova Scotia Historical Review* 9, no. 1 (1989): 62–72.

———. "In the Name of the King: The Monarchical Atmosphere of French Colonial Louisbourg, 1713–1758." In *Majesty in Canada: Essays on the Role of Royalty,* edited by Colin Coates, 196–216. Toronto: Dundurn Press, 2006.

———. *Life and Religion at Louisbourg, 1713–1758.* 1984. Reprint, Montreal: Mc-Gill–Queen's University Press, 1996.

———. "The Men of the Garrison: Soldiers and Their Punishments at Louisbourg,1751–53." *Nova Scotia Historical Review* 10, no. 2 (1991): 45–62.

———. "Officers of Isle Royale (1744)—Accommodations and Biographical Summaries." Manuscript Report Series 270. Ottawa: Parks Canada, 1978.

———. "The People of Eighteenth-Century Louisbourg." *Nova Scotia Historical Review* 11, no. 2 (1991): 75–86.

———. "Preserving History: The Commemoration of 18th-Century Louisbourg, 1895–1940." *Acadiensis* 12, no. 2 (Spring 1983): 53–80.

———. *Storied Shores: St. Peter's, Isle Madame, and Chapel Island in the 17th and 18th Centuries.* Sydney NS: Cape Breton University Press, 2004.

———. *The Summer of 1744: A Portrait of Life in 18th-Century Louisbourg.* 1983. Reprint, Ottawa: Parks Canada, 1991.

Johnstone, James. *Memoirs of the Chevalier de Johnstone.* Translated by Charles Winchester. Aberdeen: D. Wyllie and Son, 1870.

"Journal de ma campagne de Louisbourg." *Bulletin des recherches historiques* 27, no. 2 (February 1921): 48–53. (Journal of Boishébert, 1758.)

"Journal of 'Le Formidable,' in 1757." In *Report concerning Canadian Archives for the Year 1905*, vol. 1, pt. 7, 3–12. Ottawa: Queen's Printer, 1906.

"Journal of 'L'Inflexible,' in 1757." In *Report concerning Canadian Archives for the Year 1905*, vol. 1, pt. 8, 1–4. Ottawa: Queen's Printer, 1906.

Kimball, Gertrude Selwyn, ed. *Correspondence of William Pitt when Secretary of State with Colonial Governors and Military and Naval Commissioners in America*. 2 vols. London: Macmillan, 1906.

Knollenberg, Bernhard. "General Amherst and Germ Warfare." *Mississippi Valley Historical Review* 16 (1954–55): 489–94.

Krause, Eric, Carol Corbin, and William O'Shea, eds. *Aspects of Louisbourg: Essays on the History of an Eighteenth-Century French Community in North America*. Sydney NS: Cape Breton University Press, 1995.

Lacour-Gayet, G. *La Marine militaire de la France sous le règne de Louis XV*. Paris: Honoré Champion, 1910.

Landry, Nicolas, and Nicole Lang. *Histoire de l'Acadie*. Sillery QC: Septentrion, ca. 2001.

Laplante, Soeur Corinne. "Pourquoi les Acadiens sont-ils demeurés en Acadie? (1713–1720)." *Cahiers de la Société historique acadienne*, 21ste Cahier, 3, no. 1 (October–December 1968): 4–17.

La Roque de Roquebrune, Roger. "Uniformes et drapeaux des régiments au Canada sous Louis XIV et Louis XV." *Revue de l'Université d'Ottawa* 20, no. 3 (July–September 1950): 327–42.

LeBlanc, Ronnie-Gilles, ed. *Du Grand Dérangement à la Déportation, nouvelles perspectives historiques*. Moncton NB: Chaire d'études acadiennes, Université de Moncton, 2005.

LeGoff, Tim. "Artillery at Louisbourg." Unpublished report. Archives of the Fortress of Louisbourg (1967).

Leonard, Kevin. "A Survey for French Military Supply Depots Built in 1749–50 at the Port of Shediac and on the Shediac River." Archaeological report for Shediac Bay Watershed Association, 2001.

"The Life and Letters of Sandy (Lt-Colonel Alexander Murray of Cringletie) 1719–1762." Unpublished typescript. Parks Canada, Halifax NS.

Lockerby, Earle. "The Deportation of the Acadians from Île St.-Jean, 1758." *Acadiensis* 27, no. 2 (Spring 1998): 45–94.

Lunn, Jean Elizabeth. "Agriculture and War in Canada, 1740–1760." *Canadian Historical Review* 16, no. 2 (June 1935): 127–36.

Macdonald, C. Ochiltree. *The Last Siege of Louisburg*. London: Cassell, ca. 1908.

Mackay, Ruddock F. *Admiral Hawke*. Oxford: Clarendon Press, 1965.

MacLean, Terry. *Louisbourg Heritage: From Ruins to Reconstruction*. Sydney NB: Cape Breton University Press, 1995.

MacLeod, Malcolm. "Letter from Another World, 1757." *Nova Scotia Historical Quarterly* 3, no. 3 (September 1973): 197–213.

MacMechan, Archibald. *Red Snow on Grand-Pré.* Toronto: McClelland and Stewart, 1931.

Mahan, A. J. *The Influence of Sea Power upon History, 1660–1783.* London: Sampson Low, Marston, Searle, and Rivington, 1890.

Major, Marjorie. "The Great Pontack Inn." *Nova Scotia Historical Quarterly* 3, no. 3 (September 1973): 171–90.

Manning, Helen Taft. *British Colonial Government after the American Revolution, 1782–1820.* Hamden CT: Archon Books, 1966.

Marshall, Dianne. *Georges Island: The Keep of Halifax Harbour.* Halifax: Nimbus, 2003.

Martijn, Charles A. "Early Mi'kmaq Presence in Southern Newfoundland: An Ethnohistorical Perspective, c. 1500–1763." *Newfoundland Studies* 19, no. 1 (Spring 2003): 44–102.

Mathieu, Jacques. *La Nouvelle-France: Les Français en Amérique du Nord, XVIe–XVIIIe siècle.* Quebec: Presses de l'Université Laval, 1991.

Mayo, Lawrence Shaw. *Jeffery Amherst, A Biography.* New York: Longmans, Green, 1916.

McLennan, J. S. *Louisbourg from Its Foundation to Its Fall.* 1918. Reprint, Halifax: Book Room, 1983. (Original edition has appendices.)

McNeill, John Robert. *Atlantic Empires of France and Spain: Louisbourg and Havana, 1700–1763.* Chapel Hill: University of North Carolina Press, 1985.

Miquelon, Dale. *The First Canada: To 1791.* Toronto: McGraw-Hill Ryerson, 1994.

———. *New France, 1701–1744: "A Supplement to Europe."* Toronto: McClelland and Stewart, 1987.

Moogk, Peter. *La Nouvelle France: The Making of French Canada—A Cultural History.* East Lansing: Michigan State University Press, 2000.

Moore, Christopher. "Colonization and Conflict: New France and Its Rivals (1600–1760)." In *The Illustrated History of Canada,* edited by Craig Brown, 105–88. Toronto: Lester and Orpen Dennys, 1987.

———. *Louisbourg Portraits.* Toronto: Macmillan, 1982.

———. "The Other Louisbourg: Merchant Enterprise in Île Royale, 1713–1758." *Histoire sociale / Social History* 12 (1979): 79–96.

Newbigging, William James. "The Cession of Canada and French Public Opinion." In *France in the New World: Proceedings of the 22nd Annual Meeting of the French Colonial Historical Society,* edited by David Buisseret, 163–76. East Lansing: Michigan State University Press, 1998.

O'Callaghan, E. B., ed. *Documents relative to the Colonial History of the State of New-York; Procured in Holland, England and France.* Vol. 10. 1858. Reprint, New York: AMS Press, 1969.

O'Shea, William. *Louisburg Brass Bands*. Louisbourg, Nova Scotia: Louisbourg Heritage Society, 1991.

Pargellis, Stanley, ed. *Military Affairs in North America, 1748–1765: Selected Documents from the Cumberland Papers in Windsor Castle*. N.p.: Archon Books, 1969.

Patterson, Frank H. *A History of Tatamagouche, Nova Scotia*. 1917. Reprint, Belleville ON: Mika, 1973.

Patterson, Stephen E. "1744–1763: Colonial Wars and Aboriginal Peoples." In Buckner and Reid, *Atlantic Region to Confederation*, 125–55, 413–19.

———. "Indian-White Relations in Nova Scotia, 1749–61: A Study in Political Interaction." *Acadiensis* 23, no. 1 (Autumn 1993): 23–59.

Paul, Daniel N. *We Were Not the Savages: A Micmac Perspective on the Collision of European and Aboriginal*. Halifax: Nimbus, 1993.

Peters, Marie. *Pitt and Popularity: The Patriot Minister and London Opinion during the Seven Years' War*. Oxford: Oxford University Press, 1980.

Peyser, Joseph L., trans. and ed. *On the Eve of the Conquest: The Chevalier de Raymond's Critique of New France in 1754*. East Lansing: Michigan State University Press; Mackinac Island: Mackinac State Historic Parks, 1997.

Pichette, Robert. *Pour l'honneur de mon prince*. Moncton NB: Michel Henry, 1989.

Pichon, Thomas. *Lettres et mémoires pour servir à l'histoire naturelle, civile et politique du Cap Breton, depuis son établissement jusqu'à la reprise de cette isle par les Anglois en 1758*. La Haye: P. Gosse, 1760.

Piers, Harry. *The Evolution of the Halifax Fortress, 1749–1928*. Halifax: Public Archives of Nova Scotia, 1947.

Plank, Geoffrey. "New England Soldiers in the St. John River Valley, 1758–1760." In *New England and the Maritime Provinces: Connections and Comparisons*, edited by Stephen Hornsby and John G. Reid, 59–73. Montreal: McGill–Queen's University Press, 2005.

———. *An Unsettled Conquest. The British Campaign against the Peoples of Acadia*. Philadelphia: University of Pennsylvania Press, 2000.

Plumb, J. H. *Chatham*. 1953. Reprint, London: Collins, 1965.

Pothier, Bernard. *Battle for the Chignecto Forts, 1755*. Canadian War Museum Canadian Battle Series 12. Toronto: Balmuir Books, 1995.

———. *Course à l'Accadie: Journal de campagne de François du Pont Duvivier*. Moncton NB: Éditions d'Acadie, 1982.

Pritchard, James. *Anatomy of a Naval Disaster: The 1746 French Expedition to North America*. Montreal: McGill–Queen's University Press, 1995.

———. *In Search of Empire: The French in the Americas, 1670–1730*. Cambridge: Cambridge University Press, 2004.

———. *Louis XV's Navy, 1748–1762: A Study of Organization and Administration*. Montreal: McGill–Queen's University Press, 1987.

Proulx, Gilles. *Between France and New France: Life aboard the Tall Sailing Ships.* Toronto: Dundurn, 1984.

Quebec House Permanent Advisory Committee. *Wolfe, Portraiture and Genealogy.* Westerham, England, 1959.

Raddall, Thomas H. *Halifax, Warden of the North.* Toronto: McClelland and Stewart, 1977.

Rashed, Zenab Esmat. *The Peace of Paris, 1763.* Liverpool: University Press of Liverpool, 1951.

Rawlyk, George A. *Nova Scotia's Massachusetts: A Study of Massachusetts–Nova Scotia Relations, 1630 to 1784.* Montreal: McGill–Queen's University Press, 1973.

———. *Yankees at Louisbourg.* Orono: University of Maine, 1967.

Reid, John G. "*Pax Britannica* or *Pax Indigena*? Planter Nova Scotia (1760–1782) and Competing Strategies of Pacification." *Canadian Historical Review* 85, no. 4 (December 2004): 669–92.

———. *Six Crucial Decades: Times of Change in the History of the Maritimes.* Halifax: Nimbus, 1987.

Reid, Stuart. *Wolfe: The Career of General James Wolfe from Culloden to Quebec.* New York NY: Sarpedon, 2000.

Richardson, Boyce. "1757—Year of Failure and Tragedy." *The Beaver* 66, no. 2 (April/May 1986): 36–46.

———. "To Halifax with Captain Cook." *The Beaver* 66, no. 5 (October/November 1986): 27–32.

Rogers, Col. H. C. B. *The British Army of the Eighteenth Century.* New York: Hippocrene Books, 1977.

Rossel, Louis-Auguste. "Journal de ma campagne à l'Île Royale (1757)." RAPQ *RAPQ pour 1931–1932.* Québec: Imprimeur de Sa Majesté le Roi, 1932.

Roy, Régis. "Au siège de Louisbourg en 1758." *Bulletin de la revue historique* 4, no. 1 (January 1935): 55–57.

Schama, Simon. *Dead Certainties: Unwarranted Speculations.* New York: Vintage Books, 1992.

Schmeisser, Barbara. "Building a Colonial Outpost on Île St. Jean, Port La Joye, 1720–1758" (2000). Unpublished manuscript. Halifax, Parks Canada.

———. "A Narrative and Structural History of Fort de Beauséjour, 1751–1755" (1980). Unpublished manuscript. Halifax, Parks Canada.

———. "The Population of Louisbourg, 1713–1758." Manuscript Report Series 303. Ottawa: Parks Canada, 1975.

Sobey, Douglas. "The Department of the Marine and the Search for Masts on Île Saint-Jean." *The Northern Mariner / Le marin du nord* 13, no. 1 (January 2003): 1–18.

Sosin, Jack M. "Louisbourg and the Peace of Aix-La-Chapelle, 1748." *William and Mary Quarterly*, 3rd series, 14 (October 1957): 516–35.

Stacey, C. P. "The British Forces in North America during the Seven Years' War." In *Dictionary of Canadian Biography*, vol. 3, xxiv–xxx.

Stanley, George F. G. *Canada's Soldiers: The Military History of an Unmilitary People.* 1954. Reprint, Toronto: Macmillan, 1974.

———. *New France: The Last Phase, 1744–1760.* Toronto: McClelland and Stewart, 1968.

Steele, Ian K. *Warpaths: Invasions of North America.* New York: Oxford University Press, 1994.

Stokesbury, James L. *Navy and Empire.* New York: William Morrow, 1983.

Summers, Jack L., and René Chartrand. *Military Uniforms in Canada, 1665–1970.* Ottawa: National Museums of Canada, 1981.

Taillemite, Étienne. *L'Histoire ignorée de la marine française.* Paris: Librairie Académique Perrin, 1988.

Thorpe, Frederick J. *Remparts lointains: La politique française des travaux publics à Terre-Neuve et à l'île Royale, 1695–1758.* Ottawa: Éditions de l'Université d'Ottawa, 1980.

Venning, Annabel. *Following the Drum: The Lives of Army Wives and Daughters, Past and Present.* London: Headline, 2005.

Webster, John Clarence, ed. *Thomas Pichon, 'The Spy of Beauséjour': An Account of His Career in Europe and North America.* Translated by Alice Webster. Sackville NB: Public Archives of Nova Scotia, 1937.

Whitehead, Ruth Holmes. *The Old Man Told Us: Excerpts from Micmac History, 1500–1950.* Halifax: Nimbus, 1991.

Wicken, William C. *Mi'kmaq Treaties on Trial: History, Land and Donald Marshall Junior.* Toronto: University of Toronto Press, 2002.

Willson, Beckles. *The Life and Letters of James Wolfe.* London: William Heinemann, 1909.

———. "Wolfe's Men and Nova Scotia." Paper presented at the meeting of the Nova Scotia Historical Society on February 6, 1914.

Wrong, G. M., ed. *Louisbourg in 1745: The Anonymous "Lettre d'un Habitant de Louisbourg" (Cape Breton), Containing a Narrative by an Eye-witness of the Siege in 1745.* Toronto: Warwick and Rutter, 1897.

———. Review of *The Journal of Jeffery Amherst recording the Military Career of General Amherst in America from 1758 to 1763.* Edited and introduced by J. Clarence Webster. *Canadian Historical Review* 13, no. 1 (March 1932): 53–55.

Wyczynski, Michel. "The Expedition of the Second Battalion of the Cambis Regiment to Louisbourg, 1758." *Nova Scotia Historical Review* 10, no. 2 (1991): 94–110.

———. "The Fortress of Louisbourg in 1758." *The Archivist* 17, no. 2 (March–April 1990): 6–8.

Index

*Italicized page numbers indicate illustrations
and maps.*

Abenaki Indians, 12, 23, 287; at Louisbourg
  in 1757, 126, 142
Abercromby, Major General James, 146,
  147; made commander-in-chief for
  North America, 165, 275
Aboriginal warriors and nations, 8, 9, 35–
  36, 85, 121; European attitudes toward
  and vice versa, 24, 33, 37, 40, 63, 67,
  104, 130, 162–63, 197–98, 222–23, 282;
  French expenditures on, 130–31, 159–60;
  importance and effectiveness of, 7, 11,
  24, 102, 104. *See also* Abenaki Indians;
  Fox Indians; Huron Indians; Indians
  (of North America); Mi'kmaq; Native
  alliances and warriors; Passamaquoddy;
  Wolastoqiyik (Maliseet)
Acadia (Acadie), 13, 19, 25, 30, 56, 185,
  188, 287. *See also* Nova Scotia
Acadians, 9, 12, 15, 19, 20, 23, 29, 31, 36,
  39, 46, 48, 54, 55, 56, 57, 59, 60, 61, 69,
  72, 75, 287; coming to Cape Breton in
  1780s, 285; defending Louisbourg in
  1757 and 1758, 125, 126, 177, 179, 183,
  189, 204, 223, 225, 228; at the fall of Fort
  Beauséjour, 76–79; forcible removals of,
  10, 79–86, 91, 92, 96, 104, 191, 210, 276,
  279, 283, 310n84; places of refuge and
  plight of refugees, 109, 122, 146
Admiralty Court: at Halifax, 168; at
  Louisbourg, 106, 141
Africa, 4, 8, 16, 40, 195, 271. *See also*
  Equiano, Olaudah

Aix-la-Chapelle, Treaty of, 21, 22, 23, 25,
  26, 31, 42, 55, 68, 87; unclear boundaries
  of, 74
Algonquin Indians, 12
Allegheny Mountains, 104
American Revolution (War of
  Independence), 94, 194, 284, 286, 287
Amherst, Capt. William, 272, 277, 292
Amherst, Jeffery, 192, 193; address to the
  troops in 1758, 196–98; aftermath of
  victory, 272, 274, 275–76, 277, 280;
  directs careful advance, 229–37, 240, 242,
  243, 246, 248, 250, 251, 252, 253, 254,
  255, 256, 258, 259, 260, 261, 264, 289;
  on the eve of 1758 siege, 179, 195–96,
  198–201, 205–6; and gift exchanges
  with French, 237, 240–41; joins 1758
  expedition, 172–73; and the June 8
  landing and soon after, 207, 210, 212,
  215, 218, 219, 222, 223; later life, 282;
  named to lead army for 1758 assault
  on Louisbourg, 166–67, 170, 171;
  negotiation of surrender, 265–70; profile
  of, 189–90
Anderson, Fred, 103, 159, 297n2
Angélique, 44
Anglo-American colonies and colonists, 11,
  12, 13, 18, 21, 30, 40, 43, 50, 52–53, 66,
  67, 68, 75, 83, 85, 103, 104, 113, 127,
  141, 147, 159, 162, 164, 165, 169, 195,
  210, 279, 286; rejoicing by in 1758, 278;
  thoughts about Louisbourg, 28–29
Anglo-French rivalry in North America,
  6–9, 24–25, 66–87
Angoulême, 64

Annapolis Royal, 13, 19, 29, 30, 37, 38, 40,
54, 55, 56, 59, 63, 73, 80, 81, 84, 85, 104,
161; news of 1758 victory reaches, 278.
See also Port-Royal

Anse à Gautier, 127, 180, 201, 206, 209,
229, 235

Anse au Foulon, 79

Anse de la Cormorandière (Kennington
Cove): French defenses at, 128, 178, 180,
181, 182, 201, 202, 204; June 8 British
landing at, 196, 207–24, 233, 261; later in
siege, 243; maps of, *129, 203, 208, 231*;
renaming of, 278

Anson, First Lord of the Admiralty George,
112, 147, 165, 166

Argenson, comte d' (Pierre-Marc de Voyer
de Paulmy), 114

artillery: British use of at Louisbourg, 211,
222, 223, 230, 238, 240, 242, 244–45,
247, 248, 249, 250, 252, 253–54, 256–57,
259–60, 261–62, 264, 296; French loss
of and handover, 221, 271; French use
of at Louisbourg, 212–13, 215, 250, 251,
254, 260, 294, 304n67, 305n71; impact of
on town of Louisbourg, 259–60; view of
British battery, *248*

Artois Regiment: activities, disputes, and
problems of, 96, 97, 108–9, 110, 142,
143, 149; defending Louisbourg and
coast, 128, 130, 178, 213, 217, 294; sent
to Louisbourg in 1755, 70, 72–73, 92,
116, 154

Atlantic Canada, 5, 12, 13, 21, 22, 25, 48,
63, 66, 85, 87, 104, 134; British naval
presence in, 30; strategic importance of,
9, 11, 31, 284–86

Aubert de Courserac, Marie-Anne
(Madame Drucour), 66, 185–86, 274;
firing cannons during siege, 193; and gift
exchanges with Amherst, 237, 240, 252,
288

Baie des Espagnols (Sydney), 202

Baie Verte, 20, 57, 58, 77

Bailliage, 141

Baleine, 53, 171

Balfour, Captain George, 261, 293

Barachois at Louisbourg, 225, 244

Basque Roads (Charente estuary), 137

Bastide, Colonel John Henry, 98, 230

Bauffremont, Joseph de, prince de
Listenois, 116, 119, 316n66

Bay of Fundy, 19, 59, 84

Bayonne, 51, 255

Beaubassin, 56, 57, 58; burning of, 60–61;
erection of Fort Lawrence at, 61, 192

Beauséjour, 58, 61, 74

Beaussier de l'Isle, Louis-Joseph de: at
Louisbourg in 1758, 174, 176, 291; naval
battle in 1756, 107–8, 314nn45–46; sent
to Louisbourg in 1758, 155–56, 157

Bégon, Madame, 148

Bengal, 112

Bigot, François, 31, 79, 188

Black Rock. *See* Cap Noir (Black Rock)

Blacks. *See* Africa; Equiano, Olaudah

Blakeney, General, 102

Blénac-Courbon, Charles de: and attempt
to sail to Louisbourg in 1758, 158, 185,
288, 291

Bloody Creek, 85

Board of Trade, 32, 66, 74

Boishébert et de Raffetot, Charles
Deschamps de, 58, 79, 276; establishes
refuge for Acadians, 85; expedition
toward Louisbourg, 177, 183, 236–37,
241, 255–56; profile of, 189

Bordeaux, 26, 51, 106, 144, 282

Boscawen, Admiral Edward, 103, 292;
actions as 1758 siege develops, 229, 240,
242, 251, 252, 255; in the aftermath of
1758 victory, 272, 274, 275–76, 277;
during June 8 landing, 211, 212, 214,
219, 222, 223; on the eve of 1758 siege,
179, 195, 198–201, 206; implements plan
to end 1758 siege, 261–64; intercepting
French ships in 1755, 71–72, 92,
105; later life of, 283; negotiation of
surrender, 265–70; preparations for
1758 attack on Louisbourg, 94, 166–67,

170–73; profile of, 189, 190–91, 193; role in 1755 Acadian Deportation, 83, 191

Boston, 37, 70, 73, 74, 79, 92, 140, 276, 278, 283

Bourgogne, duc de: birth of, 65

Bourgogne Regiment: activities, disputes, and problems of at Louisbourg, 96, 97, 108–9, 110, 142, 143, 149; defending Louisbourg and nearby coast, 128, 130, 176, 178, 217, 252–53, 294; sent to Louisbourg in 1755, 70, 72, 73, 92, 116, 154

Bourtz, Marin Michel de, 178

Braddock, Edward, 2, 85, 194

Bras d'Or Lake, 106, 161

Brest, 28, 69, 70, 113, 115, 116, 117, 144, 154, 155, 156, 157, 158, 167, 185, 186, 188, 233, 266, 291; death toll at in 1757, 139–40, 146, 174

Breugnon, 291

Brière, Jean-François, 18

British Isles, 287

Brittany, 26, 51, 139, 154, 166, 191, 245

Brothers of Charity of St. John of God at Louisbourg, 51, 152

Brouillan Bastion at Louisbourg, 99, 266

Brown, Lieutenant, 215, 216

Burke, Edmund, 33

Byng, Admiral John, 102–3, 111, 132, 146, 171

Calcutta, 103

Cambis Regiment: arrive on Île Royale, 182–83; chosen to go to Louisbourg, 153, 154–57, 176, 320n15, 321n16; destroy weapons and colors, 269, 271; during 1758 siege, 202, 225, 294

Canada, Dominion of, 283

Canada, French colony of, 7, 13, 20, 21, 32, 45, 48, 49, 50, 53, 58, 60, 67, 71, 78, 85, 86, 99, 103, 104, 106, 109, 110, 117, 121, 141, 142, 148, 176, 187, 188, 204, 279, 287, 315n51; impact of harvest failures, 91

Candide, 103, 280

Canoniers-bombardiers: defending Louisbourg, 146; return to Louisbourg, 27

Canot, P., 234

Canso, 19, 29, 30, 37, 39, 76

Canso Strait. *See* Fronsac (Canso Strait)

Cape Breton Island, 3, 7, 8, 9, 12, 15, 18, 20, 21, 22, 23, 24, 25, 31, 54, 73, 91, 164, 167, 171, 172, 198, 279, 283; annexed to Nova Scotia, 277; British, French, and Anglo-American views on, 28–29, 279–80; end of French regime and introduction of British regime on, 269–70, 271, 276, 284–85; impact on Mi'kmaq of regime change, 287–88. *See also* Île Royale; Louisbourg

Cape North, 107

Cape Sambro, 172

Cap Finistère, 166, 188, 191

Cap Noir (Black Rock), 100, 123, 132, 178, 204, 252, 254, 259

Caribbean, 135, 169, 279, 281, 287

Carolina, 104

Caron, François, 3

Cartagena, 158

Carthage, 5

casualties: of British, 273, 288, 328n28, 330n51, 334n4; of French, 273–74, 288

Cayenne (French Guiana), 281

Chabert de Cogolin, Joseph-Bernard, 52

Champlain, Samuel de, 58

Chapel Island. *See* Île de la Sainte-Famille

Chapelle Saint-Louis at Louisbourg, 44, 51

Charente River, 137, 156, 157

Chassin de Thierry, Marie-Charlotte, 96

Chesterfield, Earl of, 29

Chéticamp, 285

Chibouquetou. *See* Halifax

Chickasaw Indians, 11

Chignecto isthmus, 37, 38, 39, 47, 49; contested zone of, 55–62, 67; military expedition of 1755 into, 73–79, 104, 192; removal of Acadians from, 79–84, 91

Choiseul, Étienne-François duc de, 55, 151, 279

Citadel Hill at Halifax, 35
Clinton's army, 194
Clive, Robert, 112
Cobequid, 60, 81, 311n84
Colville, Commodore Alexander, 140, 292
Compagnies des Indes ships, 20
Compagnies franches de la Marine, 27, 73, 94, 126, 127, 128, 153, 188, 194, 195, 204, 228, 241, 265, 294; careers after Louisbourg, 281; compared with Troupes de Terre, 142–43
Congregation of Notre Dame, Sisters of, 5, 141, 301n7
Constantinople, 185
Cook, Captain James, 283
Cope, Jean-Baptiste, 63
Cork (Ireland), 118
Corne, Louis de la, 58, 59
Cornwall, 191
Cornwallis, Edward, 33, 35, 37, 39, 40, 41, 55, 60, 74, 81
Corpus Christi (Fête Dieu), 181–82, 324n81
Courserac, chevalier de, 268, 291
Culloden, 33, 191
Cumberland, Duke of, 78, 103, 112, 190
Cumberland Basin, 105
Cuthbert, Lieutenant, 213

Dakar, 113
Dangeac, Gabriel-François, 280, 281
Danks, Benomi, 168
D'Anthonay, Henry Valentin, 178, 212, 249, 266, 268
Dartmouth, 39, 59
Dauphin Demi-Bastion, 99, 123, 242, 245, 258, 259, 260, 262, 265, 266
Dauphin Gate (Porte Dauphine and West Gate), 49, 125, 178, 225, 242, 244, 245, 248, 256, 257, 269, 270
Davies, Thomas, 247
Desbarats, Catherine, 16, 159
Des Barres, Governor Joseph Frederick Wallet, 284

desertion as problem and opportunity, 61, 94, 122, 124, 236, 256, 259, 260, 294
des Gouttes, marquis (Jean-Antoine Charry): actions and conflicts during 1758 siege, 225–26, 227, 233, 238, 240, 244, 245, 248, 249, 255, 258, 291; at Louisbourg, 174, 183; on the eve of 1758 siege, 199, 200, 201; later life, 282; profile of, 187; en route to Louisbourg, 156, 275
Desherbiers de la Ralière, Charles: as governor at Louisbourg, 42, 64; view of Acadian refugees, 62
Des Rochers, chevalier, 255
Dettingen, 189, 192
Dickason, Olive, 37
Diefenbaker, Prime Minister John, 289
Dieskau, Jean-Armand, baron de, 70, 107
Dominica, 169, 286
Dorset, Duke of, 189
Drucour, chevalier de (Augustin de Boschenry): actions and comments as governor, 72, 75, 77, 78, 86, 90, 92, 107, 110, 115, 116, 122–23, 125, 126, 139, 142–43, 144, 146, 149, 151, 152, 188; actions and comments June 8 to June 10, 195, 200–202, 204, 206, 220, 224–29; comments and actions while leading the defense, 233–37, 238, 240–41, 243, 245, 246, 248, 249, 250, 251, 252, 254, 255, 256, 258, 262, 263, 288; defense on the eve of 1758 siege, 158, 173–83; disagreement with Des Gouttes and ship captains, 233; later life, 281–82; named governor of Île Royale, 66; profile of, 185–86; surrender discussions and aftermath, 264–71, 274, 328n35
Drucourt, 66
Du Bois de la Motte, comte Emmanuel-Auguste de Cahideuc: and impact at Louisbourg in 1757, 123–31, 132, 133, 134, 139, 143, 152; impact of hurricane on his ships, 135–37; squadron to Louisbourg in 1757, 116–18, 119, 120,

141, 157, 194, 219; squadron to Quebec, 70, 73; worries about Louisbourg, 142
Du Chaffault de Besné, comte (Louis-Charles), 157, 176, 182, 291
Dull, Jonathan, 115, 140, 175
Dundonald, Earl of, 253
Dunkirk, 90
Duquesne, marquis de, 157, 159
Duquesnel, Jean-Baptiste-Louis Le Prévost: as governor at Louisbourg, 44
Durell, Commodore Philip, 211–12, 214
Durrell, Thomas, 32
Duvivier, Compagnies franches officer, 268

East Indies, 190
Eccles, W. J., 104
Edgecombe, Captain, 272, 277, 292
Edinburgh, 270
England 7, 8, 31, 66, 68, 85, 110, 111, 112, 119, 120, 122, 158, 166, 167, 173, 189, 221, 233, 263, 269, 272, 282
Enville, duc d': re-burial at Louisbourg, 44, 304–5n67; 1746 expedition of, 21, 32, 73
Equinao, Olaudah, 223, 271. *See also* Africa
Espérance, 149

Falkland, battle of, 191
Faragher, John Mack, 79
Five Nations, 7
Flanders, 33, 191
Flat Point. *See* Pointe Platte (Flat Point)
Fletcher, Colonel, 210
Florida, 32
Fontenoy, 189
Forant, Isaac-Louis de: as governor at Louisbourg, 44
Fort Beauséjour, 61, 65, 74, 80, 84, 92, 96, 101, 105, 120, 169; campaign against in 1755, 75–79, 164, 210. *See also* Beaubassin; Beauséjour; Chignecto isthmus; Fort Cumberland (formerly Fort Beauséjour)
Fort Bull, 103
Fort Carillon (later Fort Ticonderoga) 2, 6, 164, 275

Fort Cumberland (formerly Fort Beauséjour), 78, 84, 105
Fort de Chartres, 155
Fort Duquesne, 58, 85, 164, 165, 313n36
Fort Edward, 59, 210
Fort Frederick, 276
Fort Gaspereau, 58, 61, 74, 77, 78, 79
Fort George, 67
Fort Lawrence, 61, 74, 75, 76, 192
Fort Ménagouèche, 276
Fort Necessity, 67, 85
Fort Niagara, 58
Fort Rouillé, 58
Fort Saint Philip, 102
Fort Ticonderoga. *See* Fort Carillon (later Fort Ticonderoga)
Fort William Henry, 2, 121, 146; influence on siege of Louisbourg, 251, 265
Fox Indians, 11
France, 7, 8, 9, 14, 20, 21, 25, 26, 27, 28, 37, 42, 47, 49, 50, 52, 54, 55, 57, 64, 67, 68, 70, 73, 82, 83, 86, 87, 88, 89, 90, 98, 100, 102, 109, 112, 113, 117, 125, 135, 137, 139, 142, 144, 150, 152, 153, 158, 174, 177, 182, 186, 187, 194, 200, 227, 264, 270, 277, 279, 280, 281, 282, 286, 291, 298n9; comments on impact of Louisbourg's capture on future colonizing initiatives of, 267–68
Franklin, Benjamin, 18
Franquet, Louis, 121, 125; actions and comments during 1758 siege, 251, 266; actions and comments on the eve of the siege, 175, 176; actions and comments prior to 1758, 106, 110, 116, 123–24, 125, 126, 144; arrival at Louisbourg and initial assessment, 49–50; opinion of Raymond, 65; profile of, 187–88; proposals for Louisbourg fortifications, 99–101
Fraser, Colonel, 221
Frederick I, 137
Frégault, Guy, 55
French Guiana, 281

French Inhabitants or French Neutrals, 80.
  See Acadians
Freshwater Brook and Cove, *203, 231*
Fronsac (Canso Strait), 107

Gabarus and Gabarus Bay, 124, 125, 131,
  132, 170, 178, 186, 195, 196, 199, 200,
  204, *205*, 206, 207, *208*, 220, 227
Gannes de Falaise, Michel de, 41
Gaspé Peninsula, 105, 277
Gaspereau, 61
Gaultier de Varennes, René, 60, 86, 307n27
Gautier, Nicolas, 92
Gautier, Pierre: providing information on
  British, 92, 94
Gautier *dit* Bellair, Joseph-Nicolas, 92
Gédaïque (present-day Shediac), 58
George II, 19, 30, 69, 78, 82, 101, 111, 166,
  277, 279
Georges Island at Halifax, 44, 82, 83
Georgia, 30, 32, 84
Germany, 31, 61, 137, 154, 189, 195, 270,
  276
Gibraltar, 3, 29, 102, 157
Gordon (British officer), 219
Gorée, 113
Gorham, John, 35, 168
Grand Lorembec (Big Lorraine): French
  defenses at, 127, 317n90
Grand-Pré, 30, 39, 59, 79, 80, 84
Grant, Ensign, 215, 216
Great Britain, 7, 8, 9, 13, 14, 43, 54, 55, 57,
  67, 69, 71, 81, 90, 120, 137, 151, 163,
  173, 194, 272, 286, 287; rejoicing in 1758
  in, 277
Great Pontack House: party at, 171
Green Hill, 230, 242, 244
Gregorian calendar, x, 33, 300n38, 303n34
Grenada, 286
Grenadiers Redoubt, 230
Grillot de Poilly, François-Claude-Victor:
  arrives at Louisbourg, 99, 100; diary
  comments, 148–49, 150, 168, 174, 178,
  179, 180, 182, 187–88, 199, 200, 201,
  202, 204, 212, 218, 225, 229, 235, 240,
  243, 250, 253, 257, 258, 259, 260, 264,
  267, 271; tour of Île Royale, 110
Guadeloupe, 113, 194, 281, 286, 287
Guichen, 291
Gulf of Saint Lawrence, 4, 18, 280

Halifax, 21, *34, 93*, 285; base for 1757
  expedition against Louisbourg, 124, 191;
  base for 1758 expedition to Louisbourg,
  140, 165, 167, 168–73, 177, 195, 196,
  202, 206, 210, 216, 229; as British centre
  and naval port, 60, 61, 62, 63, 69, 72, 73,
  74, 79, 80, 81, 82, 85, 92, 94, 101, 104,
  105, 122, 134, 137, 145, 150, 161, 279,
  280, 283; British ships at, 118, 119, 120,
  134, 137, 145, 155; founding of, 10, 23,
  24, 31–37, 38, 39, 40, 42, 44, 46, 48, 57,
  59; known as Kjipuktuk, 32
Halifax, Earl of (George Montague Dunk),
  32, 74
Halley, Edmond, 150
Hanover, 111, 112, 195
Hardy, Rear Admiral Sir Charles, 119, 120,
  140, 167, 168, 173, 180, 181, 191, 199,
  200, 252, 254, 277, 292
Harvey, D. C., 285
Hawke, Vice Admiral Edward, 137,
  318n108; action against French ships,
  156–57, 164, 166, 176
Hawley, General, 170
Hill of Justice, lowering of, 99, 256, 257,
  313n28
Holburne, Admiral Francis: 1757 naval
  force led by, 118–21, 131–38; ships
  damaged by hurricane, 135–37, 140
Holland, 8
Holland, Samuel, 17, 284; roles as engineer
  and surveyor, 261, 283, 285
Holmes, Commodore Charles: naval battle
  with Beaussier de l'Isle, 108
Holy Roman Empire, 102
Honfleur, Normandy, 278
Hopkins, Lieutenant, 215, 216
Hopson, Peregrine Thomas, 41, 43, 63,
  66, 74

Hudson River, 31
Huguenot, 112
Huron Indians, 12

Île d'Aix, 137
Île de la Sainte-Famille, 160
Île de Ré, 27
Île Royale, xi, 32, 54; as administration
centre, stronghold, and busy port, 58, 63,
64, 65, 66, 68, 70, 71, 72, 83, 87, 92, 152,
154, 174; affected by British blockades,
105–10, 152–53, 155; as British objective
in 1758, 167; British view of, 17, 18, 165,
166; as destination for migrations and
flights of Acadians, 57, 62, 85, 86; on
the eve of 1758 siege, 173–83, 195–206;
French expenditures at, 15–16, 97–98,
299n28; French measures to protect in
1758, 143–47; French squadrons to, and
at, in 1757, 115–18, 123–31, 139; French
squadrons to, in 1758, 155–58, 164, 288;
impact of 1745 siege and 1749 return of
French on, 20, 23–29, 37, 41–45, 46–55;
importance of, 9, 10, 12, 13, 14, 21, 22,
299–300n31; navigation and ship traffic,
52–53; as nursery of seamen, 17–18;
possibility of distinctive identity, 47;
provisioning problems of, 88–92, 122–23,
152; removal of French population in
1758, 274–76, 279; and 1758 siege, 227,
256; situation with Native allies, 159–63;
surrendered by French to British, 3, 269–
70, 271, 272, 280, 281, 287; threatened
by expedition in 1757, 115, 118, 131–39,
315n62; troops needed for, 142–43, 153.
See also Cape Breton Island; Louisbourg
Île Saint-Jean (Prince Edward Island), 13,
14, 20, 32, 37, 42, 43, 48, 49, 52, 54,
58, 76, 83, 87; destination for Acadian
refugees, 57, 62, 83, 86, 94; French
defensive measures and suggestions
for in 1758, 146, 153, 177, 179; impact
of transition to British rule, 285, 287;
problems of Acadian refugees and
implications for Louisbourg food supply,

91, 109, 122; removal of Acadians and
French in 1758, 276, 279; return of
French soldiers and administration in
1749, 27; surrendered by French to
British in 1758, 269, 271; *See also* Port-
la-Joye
Illinois country, 153
Ince, Captain Charles, 234
India, 8, 16, 103, 112, 282
Indians (of North America), 21, 36, 38,
85, 159, 197, 222, 223, 241. *See also*
Abenaki Indians; Aboriginal warriors
and nations; Kennebec Indians; Maliseet;
Mi'kmaq; Native alliances and warriors;
Passamaquoddy; Penobscot Indians
Ireland, 61, 94, 118, 154, 195, 236, 312n11
Iroquois Indians, 11
Island Battery at Louisbourg, 127, 173, 204,
224–25, 232, 234, 240, 242, 244, 248, 252
Isle Madame, 285
Isle of Jersey, 285
Italy, 154

Jacobites, Scottish, 29, 135, 170, 188, 191,
221
Johnson, Samuel, 8
Johnstone, chevalier James, 135, 317n86
Joubert, 281
Julian calendar, x, 33, 300n38

Karrer Regiment, 27, 154
Kennebec Indians, 126, 159, 161, 163
Kennington Cove, 278. *See also* Anse de la
Cormorandière (Kennington Cove)
Kensington Palace, 277
Kent, England, 189, 192
Keppel, Augustus, 145
King George's War. *See* War of the Austrian
Succession (King George's War)
King's Bastion at Louisbourg, 44, 51, 99,
123, 124, 144, 176, 235, 245, 258, 259,
260, 262, 266, 270, 274
King's Hospital, 51, 109, 117, 180, 250
Kjipuktuk. *See* Halifax
Knowles, Charles, 29, 41, 70, 98, 318n108

Knox, Captain John, 120

La Clue-Sabran, Jean-Franêois Bertet de, 157–58, 174, 283, 321n22
La Corne, Louis de, 58, 59, 60
La Désirade, 281
Laforey, Captain John, 261, 293
La Galissionière, marquis de, 27, 42–43, 102
La Jonquière, marquis de, 58, 166
Lake Champlain, 85, 103
Lake George, 121
Lake Ontario, 58, 103
Lando, Anne, 95
La Rochelle, 27
Lartigue, Monsieur, 308n48
La Sarre Regiment, 107
La Touche de Tréville, 291
La Tour du Chemin, 173
Laurenbec. *See* Lorembec (Lorraine)
Lawrence, Charles, 101, 104, 191; collaboration with William Shirley to capture Chignecto isthmus, 73–79; death of, 283; on the eve of 1758 siege, 195–96; expedition to Beaubassin, 60; during landing on June 8, 207, 209; named acting governor of Nova Scotia, 66; profile of, 192; role in removal of Acadians, 73, 79–84, 192
Lawrencetown, 59
Le Havre, 282
Lelarge, Jean: life and naval career of, 89–90, 92, 145
Lelarge, Jean Aimable, 89
Le Loutre, Abbé Jean-Louis, 37–38, 58, 60, 78, 159, 160
Le Neuf de la Vallière, Louis, 281
Lenormant de Mézy, Sébastien-François-Ange, 176
LeRoy, Pierre *dit* Larmement, 95
L'Espérance, Charles-Gabriel Sébastien de, 281
Levant, 20
Library and Archives Canada, 92, 93
Lighthouse Point at Louisbourg, 127, 132,

173, 174; during 1758 siege, 224, 229, 230–35, 238, 242; sketch of and from, *234*
Ligonier, John, Commander-in-Chief of British Army, 112, 147, 165, 166, 189, 190, 192, 193
Lime Kiln Hill, 257
London, x, 8, 9, 23, 66, 71, 82, 111, 277
London *Gazette*, 33, 35
Loppinot, Jean Chrysostome, 41, 138–39, 265, 268
Loppinot *fils*, 67–68
Lorembec (Lorraine), 53, 124, 171, 180, 196, 206, 209, 229, 232, 243
Lorgeril, chevalier de, 291
Loudoun, Earl of (John Campbell): controlling British army in North America, 103; leading land force against Louisbourg in 1757, 118–21, 131–38, 146; replaced as commander in chief, 165
Louis XI, 154
Louis XIV, 8, 11, 32, 159
Louis XV, 8, 11, 17, 19, 21, 22, 26, 28, 29, 42, 45, 59, 69, 70, 71, 87, 89, 94, 98, 101, 103, 113, 115, 134, 151, 153, 159, 160, 175, 195, 264, 279, 286, 287
Louisbourg, *xii, xiii, 54, 129, 133, 203, 205, 208, 231, 234, 239, 247*; as administrative centre and/or port, 55, 57, 60, 61, 63, 64, 65, 66, 67, 68, 70, 71, 72, 73, 74, 75, 76, 77, 78, 82, 86, 87, 92, 151, 152, 192, 194; affected by British blockades, 105–10, 156–57; British ships and troops offshore in 1758, 168, 292–93, 295–96; civil and military society of in 1749 and early 1750s, 46–53, 94; climate and weather of, 14–15, 47, 121, 148, 150, 180, 202, 206, 223–24, 232; demolition of fortifications in 1760, 5, 280, 335n20, 336n30; early part of siege, 229–37; events and attitudes of June 9 and 10, 224–29; on the eve of 1758 siege, 173–83, 195–206; final days of 1758 siege and surrender discussions at, 261–70, 333n107; France's expenditures on, 15–16, 97–98, 159–60,

299nn28–29; French plans to defend in 1758, 143–47; French squadrons to and at in 1757, 115–18, 123–31, 139, 316n68; French squadrons to and at in 1758, 155–58, 164, 288, 291; garrison and fortifications of, 16–17, 47–48, 49–50, 96–97, 98–101, 110, 141, 142–43, 204, 294, 299n30; growth of settlement and colony, 5; landing and defense of June 8, 207–24; late stage of 1758 siege, 245–60; as major focus of William Pitt, 113; middle part of 1758 siege, 238–45; parish record totals, 4, 51, 94, 149, 305n11; partial reconstruction of in 20th century, 289–90; place in historiography, 2–4; population of, 48, 304n63, 305n11, 334n7, 335n17; possibility of identity as Louisbourgeois, 47; provisioning worries and other problems, 88–92, 122–23, 147, 152; re-founding of by French in 1749, 23–29, 39, 41–45, 46, 58; religious and social life of and samples of crimes, 51–52, 95–96, 148–50, 181–82; siege of 1745, 8, 18–20, 179, 232; significance of siege of 1758, 1–2, 284, 286–90; situation of Native allies in 1758, 159–63; strategic importance of, 5; summary history of to 1748, 12–22; threatened by British expedition in 1757, 115, 118, 131–39, 140, 165; transition from French to British regime, 271–81, 283; use of chess metaphor and imperial context of, 6–12, 298n19; withdrawal of British forces, 284. *See also* Cape Breton Island; Île Royale

Louisbourg, Fortress of: as reconstructed historic site, 289–90

Louisiana, 32, 45, 66, 84, 281, 287

Low Countries, 30

Loyalists, 277, 283–84, 285, 287

Lunenburg, 39, 59, 69, 192, 276

Machault d'Arnouville, Jean-Baptiste: named minister of the marine, 65, 68; 75; replaced as minister, 97, 115, 185,

315n63; on shipping to colonies and other problems, 90, 109–10, 114

Macleod, Sergeant Donald, 194

MacNemara, Jean-Baptsite, 70

Maillard, Abbé Pierre, 37–38, 131, 160, 162, 163, 179, 241

Maine, 19, 37,

Maliseet, 39, 40, 54, 63, 77, 78, 159, 161, 163; impact of 1758 siege on, 287; at Louisbourg in 1757, 126, 130, 142. *See also* Wolastoqiyik (Maliseet)

Marchant de la Houlière, Mathieu-Henri: at Louisbourg, 186–87, 216, 218, 227, 236, 238, 245, 246, 251, 252, 254, 262, 264, 269, 274; named to go to Louisbourg, 143

Marie-Galante, 281

Marin, Lieutenant-Colonel, 252–53

Maritimes, 38. *See also* Île Royale; Île Saint-Jean (Prince Edward Island); New Brunswick; Nova Scotia

Marlborough, 112

Marolles, chevalier de, 291

Marseilles, 20

Martel, 291

Martin, Pierre, 281

Martinique, 113, 185, 279, 281, 286, 287

Maryland, 84

Mascle de Saint-Julhien, Jean: personality and disputes, 109, 116, 142, 143, 144; role in defense of Louisbourg, 201, 213, 217, 219–20

Massachusetts, 10, 19, 30, 67, 73, 74, 75, 84, 91

Massiac, marquis de (Claude-Louis d'Espinal): as minister of Marine, 175, 176, 185, 245

Massif Central, 187

Mathieu, Jacques, 114

Maurepas, comte de (Jean-Frédéric Phélypeaux), 8, 13–14, 17, 26, 27, 301n14, 302n15; replacement of, 28

Maurpeas Gate, 235

McFee, Duncan, 220–21

McKenzie, Sergeant, 213

McLennan, J. S., 3, 199
Mediterranean Sea, 3, 16, 52, 102, 103, 116,
    157, 164, 174, 190
Membertou, 161
Memramcook River, 57
Menadou (Main-à-Dieu), 107
Ménagouèche, fort at, 58
Mercure, Louis, 94
Mi'kma'ki, 30
Mi'kmaq, x, 9, 12, 19, 29, 30, 31, 34, 46,
    48, 54, 55, 59, 69, 76, 78, 94, 104, 105,
    124; Amherst's attitude toward, 197–98;
    attitude of Mi'kmaq women to war, 163;
    French missionaries to, 37–38; impact
    of fall of Louisbourg on, 287–88; letter
    to British in 1720, 38; at Louisbourg in
    reduced numbers in 1758, 159–63, 177,
    179, 241; at Louisbourg in 1757, 126,
    130–31, 136, 141, 319n117; perspective
    on the founding of Halifax, 22–23, 33,
    35, 37–40; relations with French, British,
    and Acadians, 62–64, 85; treaties with
    British, 63–64
Minas, 36, 40
Mines, Les, 81, 82
Ministry of the Marine, 4, 25, 73, 97,
    98, 114, 115, 119, 122, 255. *See also*
    Machault d'Arnouville, Jean-Baptiste;
    Massiac, marquis de (Claude-Louis
    d'Espinal); Maurepas, comte de (Jean-
    Frédéric Phélypeaux); Peyrenc de Moras,
    François-Marie; Pontchartrain, comte de;
    Rouillé, Antoine-Louis (comte de Jouy)
Minorca: capture of by French, 102, 111,
    118, 137, 157, 265, 279
Miramichi River, Acadian refuge at, 85;
    warriors and Acadians from, 128, 177,
    189, 277
Mira River, 95, 170–71, 179, 181, 196, 202,
    215, 219, 225, 241, 255, 276
Missaguash River, 60, 61, 76
Mississippi River, 11, 153
Mohawk River, 121
Mohawks, 35
Monckton, Colonel Robert: expedition
    against Acadians in late 1758, 276;
    expedition to Chignecto isthmus, 74–79;
    role in 1755 Acadian Deportation, 80, 84
Monongahela, 85
Mons, sieur de, 58
Montagne du Diable near Louisbourg, 204,
    225
Montalemebert de Cers, Pierre, 96, 312n16
Montcalm, marquis de, 2, 103, 107, 121,
    251
Montreal, 3, 9, 164, 280, 286
Mordaunt, Lt. Gen. Sir John, 137, 146
Morris, Charles: and role in removal of
    Acadians, 79, 80
Mostyn, Vice-Admiral Savage, 72, 83
Moulins, 187
Murray, Major Alexander, 210, 214, 244,
    246

Nantes, 51
Napoleon I, 89, 289
Native alliances and warriors, 11, 12,
    57, 59, 60, 79, 85, 103, 112, 113, 125,
    126, 128, 130, 142, 146, 159–63, 177,
    183, 189, 251; Amherst's view of,
    197–98; impact on 1758 siege of, 287; at
    Louisbourg in 1758, 195, 202, 204, 210,
    214, 217, 220, 222–23, 242, 256, 287; not
    listed among casualties, 273–74. *See also*
    Aboriginal warriors and nations; Indians
    (of North America)
New Brunswick, 37, 47, 54, 55, 56, 63, 85,
    94, 128, 189, 276, 277
Newcastle, Duke of, 111
New England, 7, 13, 19, 20, 21, 25, 29,
    36, 46, 48, 49, 53, 59, 63, 68, 72, 75, 76,
    78, 79, 80, 87, 91, 99, 126, 128, 132,
    168, 179, 259, 279; celebrations in, 278;
    Planters of, 287
Newfoundland, 18, 30, 71, 72, 75, 89, 92,
    116, 120, 280, 287; French shore of, 280;
    Mi'kmaq relocating to, 287–88
New France, 3, 12, 42, 58, 67, 70, 71, 73,
    79, 91, 103, 121, 157, 164, 187, 204; end
    of, 280, 283, 286

New Orleans, 175
Newport, 278
New York, 30, 31, 104, 136, 194, 278; as a base of operations in 1757, 118–19, 120, 121, 132; role in 1758 campaign, 167
Niganiche, 53
Noble du Revest, Jean-François de, 116, 140
Normandy, 66, 185
North Carolina, 84
Northumberland Strait, 58
Northwest Arm at Halifax, 35
Nova Scotia, 13, 15, 19, 21, 24, 30, 31, 33, 35, 36, 37, 39, 47, 52, 55, 61, 63, 66, 68, 69, 72, 73, 79, 82, 83, 85, 86, 104, 134, 159, 167, 283–84, 302n28; British expedition to in 1757, 118–21, 277; British naval presence in, 30; vulnerability of from the British perspective, 29. *See also* Acadia (Acadie)
Nova Scotia Council, 63, 66, 75, 80, 81, 82, 83, 84, 103, 120, 308n43

Ohio River, 11
Ohio Valley, 66, 67
Order of Saint-Louis, 241
Osborne, Vice-Admiral Henry: actions against French ships, 157–58, 164, 166
Oswego, 2, 68, 103, 313n35

Pacific Ocean, 283
Paris, x, 192, 281
Parkman, Francis, 61
Parks Canada, 290
Parliament of Great Britain, expenditures on Halifax and in Seven Years' War, 32–33, 286
Parr, Governor John, 284
Passamaquoddy, 37, 159, 161, 163
Paton, Richard, 263
Peguidalouet, Jeannot, 287–88
Penobscot Indians, 63, 159, 163
Pepperrell, William, 19
Périer de Salvert, Antoine-Alexis, xii, 70, 73, 99, 117

Perpignan, 186
Petitcodiac River, 57, 58
Petit-de-Grat, 53
Petit Lorembec (Little Lorraine), 127
Peyrenc de Moras, François-Marie: as minister of the Marine, 97, 115, 116, 123, 142, 143, 144, 146, 151, 152, 153, 158, 164, 175, 185
Philadelphia, 104, 278
Philipps, Richard, 38; oath of Acadians accepted by, 81
Pichon, Thomas, 64, 65, 74, 77, 101, 122, 169, 210, 270
Pisiquid (Windsor, Nova Scotia), 39, 56, 59, 81, 82, 84, 210
Pitt, William, 2, 189, 192, 193, 277, 289; campaign priorities, 113–14, 119, 136, 137, 279, 280; hopes for 1757 campaign, 118; informed about Louisbourg's condition and advance of siege, 101, 244, 246, 250, 253, 258, 271, 272, 274, 275; joins British government, 111–13; regarding importance of taking Louisbourg in 1758, 140, 146–47, 155, 163–66, 171, 179, 200, 315n59; on Rochefort campaign, 1757, 138
Pittsburgh, 58
Plains of Abraham, 2, 79, 194, 283
Plaisance (Placentia), 13, 89
Plassey, battle of, 112
Plumb, J. H., 111
Pointe Blanche (White Point), 168, 178, 179, 180, 196, 202, 203, 204, 209, 212, 221, 224, 225, 229, 231
Pointe Platte (Flat Point), 128, 168, 178, 180, 196, 201, 202, 203, 204, 206, 209, 212, 221, 224, 228, 230, 231
Pompadour, Madame de, 28, 115
Pontbriand, Henri-Marie Dubriel de: pastoral letter of, 95
Pontchartrain, comte de, 8, 299n31
Pontleroy, Nicolas Sarrebource de, 99, 100
Port-aux-Basques, 72
Port Dauphin (Englishtown), 106, 108, 125, 175, 177, 180, 182, 183, 202, 204, 227, 291

Port-la-Joye, 27. *See also* Île Saint-Jean
(Prince Edward Island)
Port-Louis, 245
Port Mahon, 118, 265
Port-Royal, 13, 38, 41, 56, 161. *See also*
Annapolis Royal
Portsmouth, 103, 167, 190
Port Toulouse (St. Peter's) 27, 38, 53, 94,
161, 177, 179, 204, 237, 241, 256
Portugal, 8, 145, 283
Potlotek, 28
Prévost, Jacques, 47, 52, 90, 117, 139,
146, 149, 150, 152, 174, 175; actions
and comments during 1758 siege, 245,
248–49, 254, 255, 264; attitude toward
Acadians, 52, 86; disputes with Artois
and Bourgogne battalions, 108–9;
friction with Du Bois de la Motte, 125;
intervention during 1758 surrender
process, 267–68; later life of, 282;
measures by relating to food supply, 91,
109–10, 122–23, 145; profile of, 188;
suggestions and comments to France,
142–43, 144, 151–52, 176
Prince Edward Island, 13, 42, 54, 271, 276,
283, 284, 285. *See also* Île Saint-Jean
(Prince Edward Island); Port-la-Joye
Princess Demi-Bastion: at Louisbourg, 99,
100, 123, 178, 182, 201, 266
Pritchard, James, 139
Protestant religion, 15, 18, 39, 59, 81,
154, 195, 302n27, 306n25; proposal to
send foreign Protestants to Nova Scotia,
30–31, 192, 306n25
Prussia, 102, 146, 194
Pyrenees, 282

Quebec, 3, 9, 10, 21, 27, 42, 48, 55, 57,
58, 59, 70, 71, 76, 78, 95, 99, 107, 110,
113, 114, 116, 117, 118, 119, 120, 131,
141, 152, 153, 164, 165, 175, 177, 188,
189, 191, 194, 200, 226, 241, 251, 272,
275, 276, 277, 279, 280, 283, 286, 291;
comparison between its siege of 1759 and
Louisbourg's in 1758, 173

Queen's Bastion at Louisbourg, 99, 245,
252, 259, 260, 266, 274
Queen's Gate at Louisbourg, 49, 123, 253
Queue, chevalier de, 255

Raddall, Thomas, 36
rangers, warfare of, 165, 169, 216, 296
Raymond, comte de (Jean-Louis de
Raymond): as commander of Île Royale,
64–65, 74
Récollets of Brittany, 51
regiments, British: assigned to garrison
Louisbourg in 1758 and later withdrawn,
278–79; attacked near Annapolis Royal,
104; committed to North America,
163–66, 322n40; contrast with French
approach and resources, 164, 288,
336n33; details on enlisted men, 193–95;
on the eve of 1758 siege, 178–79, 189,
190, 191, 192, 206; Fraser Highlanders,
194, 213, 214, 220–21, 279; in Halifax,
35; Louisburg Grenadiers, 279; qualities
Amherst wanted to see in soldiers of, 197;
sent to Louisbourg, Halifax, and New
York in 1758, 152, 167, 168–71, 295–96,
322n37, 322n40; sent to Louisbourg in
1757, 118–19, 121; and siege of 1758,
209–11, 243, 259
regiments, French: numbers sent to New
France compared with British sent to
North America, 322n37; not sent to
North America or sent to places other
than Louisbourg, Béarn, 70; Berry, 117;
Cent-Suisses, 154; Clare, 94; Foreign
Legion, 154; Gardes Marines, 187;
Guyenne, 70; Languedoc, 70; La Reine,
70; La Sarre, 107; Royal Rousillon, 107;
Vexin, 64. For those sent to Louisbourg,
see also Artois Regiment; Bourgogne
Regiment; Cambis Regiment; Karrer
Regiment; Troupes de Terre (French
infantry regiments); Volontaires
Étrangers regiment
Restigouche, 279
Richelieu, duc de, 102, 113

Rochefort, 26, 27, 28, 51, 69, 88, 90, 106, 115, 123, 145, 152, 153, 154, 155, 156, 157, 164, 174, 176, 184, 266; 1757 British expedition near in 1757, 137, 138, 146, 165, 192, 198
Rochefort Point, 73, 99, 201, 204, 225, 232, 255
Rogers, James, 168
Rollo, Lord Andrew, 276
Roma, Jean-Pierre, thoughts regarding Louisbourg, 48–49
Roman Catholic religion, 18, 31, 41, 47, 57, 59, 61, 81, 131, 134, 181–82, 195, 276, 287
Rossel, Louis-Auguste, 131
Roucoux, 189
Rouillé, Antoine-Louis (comte de Jouy): making changes at Louisbourg, 64, 65; reaction to fortification proposals, 50; taking over Marine portfolio, 28; view of Acadian migration, 62
Rous, Captain John, 72, 75, 120, 131, 292, 309n62
Royal American Regiment, 259
Royal Battery at Louisbourg, 134, 224, 285
Royal Navy, 20, 31, 113, 133, 135, 146; actions in 1758 against naval ports of France, 156–58, 164; blockade of Louisbourg in 1758, 155, 168, 180–81, 183, 229, 247, 265, 292–93; contrast with French navy, 28, 69–70, 151, 300n42; squadrons intercepting French ships, 71–72, 81, 89–91, 104–8; squadrons to Halifax and Louisbourg in 1758, 163–73, 199–201; squadrons to Louisbourg in 1757, 118; strength of, 11; vital role played by, 288
Russia, 102

Sackville, 39, 59
Saint Anne's Bay, 182
Saint-Domingue (Haiti), 116, 153, 185, 281
Saint-Esprit, 53, 136
Saint-Jean-de-Luz, 26, 47
Saint John River, 54, 57, 58, 76, 79, 276

Saint John's Island: given name, 271; removal of Acadians and French, 276, 283
Saint Lawrence River, 3, 70, 91, 96, 98, 110, 272, 275
Saint Lucia, 286
Saint-Malo, 26, 51, 152, 176, 180
Saint-Médard, 291
Saint Paul's cathedral, 277
Saint Pierre and Miquelon, 280, 281, 287
Saint Vincent, 286
Salces, 186
Samson, Louise, 89
scalps: bounties for, 63, 104, 177, 304n57; taken by British at Louisbourg, 223, 243
Scatarie, 53, 105
Scotland, 30, 33, 152, 154, 170, 188, 191, 192, 193, 194, 195, 212, 213, 220, 221, 223
Scott, George Colonel: role in attack on Beauséjour, 75; role in attack on Louisbourg, 168–69, 200, 211, 215–16, 232, 233
Senegal, 113
Seven Years War (French and Indian War), 2, change of British focus under William Pitt, 113, 163–66; contrasts between Britain and France, 114–21, 164, 286; end of, 280, 283, 287 foreigners in French army during, 154; importance of, 9; officially declared and begun, 101–4; view from Quebec in 1756, 110–11
Shediac. *See* Gédïaque (present-day Shediac)
Shediac River, 58
Shepody River, 57
ships, British: *Aetna*, 293; *Arc-en-Ciel*, 292; *Beaver*, 293; *Bedford*, 292; *Boreas*, 293; *Burford*, 292; *Captain*, 292; *Centurion*, 292; *Defiance*, 140, 292; *Devonshire*, 292; *Diana*, 208, 212, 293; *Dublin*, 167, 170, 172, 292, 323n59; *Gloucester*, 174; *Grafton*, 108; *Gramont*, 209, 212, 293; *Halifax*, 210, 212, 293; *Hawke*, 140, 293; *Hind*, 293; *Hunter*, 293; *Juno*, 293;

ships, British (*continued*)

Kennington, 201, 202, 210, 212, 278, 293; *Kingston*, 140, 292; *Lancaster*, 292; *Lightning*, 293; *Namur*, 166, 172, 195, 196, 214, 218, 271, 292; *Neptune*, 207, 210; *Nightingale*, 293; *Northumberland*, 140, 292; *Nottingham*, 108, 292; *Orford*, 140, 292; *Pembroke*, 283, 292; *Portmahon*, 140, 293; *Prince Frederick*, 292; *Prince of Orange*, 292; *Princess Amelia*, 292; *Royal William*, 292; *Scarborough*, 293; *Shannon*, 209, 212, 272, 293; *Somerset*, 140, 292; *Squirrel*, 212, 293; *Sutherland*, 136, 140, 212, 292; *Tayloe*, 293; *Terrible*, 140, 274, 292; *Tilbury*, 136; *Tor Bay*, 145; *Trent*, 293; *Vanguard*, 292; *York*, 292

ships, French: *Alcide*, 71, 92; *Apollon*, 156, 174, 177, 240, 243, 291; *Arc-en-Ciel*, 105–6, 140; *Aréthuse*, 155, 180, 228–29, 244–45, 248, 249, 254–55, 282, 291; *Belliqueux*, 157, 291, 321n18; *Biche*, 243, 291; *Bienfaisant*, 155, 174, 244, 257, 291; capture of, 261–64, 268; *Bizarre*, 180, 186, 291; *Brillant*, 157, 291; *Capricieux*, 155, 174, 243, 244, 247, 257, 258, 291; capture of, 261–64; *Célèbre*, 155, 174, 238, 240, 244, 247, 257, 258, 291, 321n18; *Chariot Royal*, 145; *Charmante*, 107; *Chèvre*, 156, 174, 240, 243, 291; *Comête*, 155, 174, 226, 245, 291; *Concorde*, 105–6, 107, 108; *Dauphin Royal*, 71; *Dianne*, 176, 291; *Dragon*, 157, 291; *Echo*, 155, 180, 291, 226, 227; *Entreprenant*, 155, 174, 238, 240, 244, 247, 257, 258, 291; *Fidèle* (*Fidelle*), 174, 243, 291; *Formidable*, 158, 291; *Hardi*, 157, 291; *Héros*, 108, 314n45; *Illustre*, 108, 314n45; *Inflexible*, 118, 124; *Juste*, 155; La *Bénaquise* (*L'Abénaquaise*), 136; Le *Grand Saint-Esprit*, 44; *Licorne*, 108, 314n45; *Lys*, 71; *Parfaitte Union*, 106, 107; *Prudent*, 156, 174, 218, 233, 244, 248, 249, 257, 291; *Rhinocéros*, 88–90; *Saint-George*, 207; *Sirenne*, 314n45; *Sphinx*, 33, 35, 157; *Ville de Saint-Malo*, 240, 243; *Violet*, 207; *Zéphyr*, 157, 291

Shirley, William, 19, 67; actions as governor of Massachusetts, 73; collaboration with Charles Lawrence to attack Chignecto isthmus, 73–79; role in deportation of Acadians, 79; steps down as head of British forces in North America, 103

Shubenacadie, 38

Simcoe, John, 283, 292

South Carolina, 30, 32

Spain, 8, 84, 102, 153, 158, 287

Stacey, C. P., 289

Stanley, George, 69, 114

Stark, John, 168

Steele, Ian, 11, 279, 286

St. Michael's Day, 38

Stockholm, 185

St. Peter's, 38. *See also* Port Toulouse (St. Peter's)

Strait of Belle Isle, 116

Supreme Court of Canada, 64

Surlaville, Michel Le Courtois de, 65, 142

Sydney, Cape Breton, 285

Tatamagouche, 57, 311n84

Te Deums, 44, 65, 102

Terny d'Arsac, 291

Thane, John, 136

Thompson, Sergeant James, 213

Thorpe, Fred, 16

Tor Bay, 134

Toulon, 28, 69, 102, 113, 115, 116, 117, 156, 157, 158, 174, 175, 185, 282

Tourville, chevalier de, 291

Treaty of 1725–26, 37

Treaty of 1752, 63–64, 159

Trois Rivières, 92

Troupes de Terre (French infantry regiments), 71, 73, 107, 114, 116, 117, 130, 142, 143, 194, 228; cost of, 97, 143, 155. *See also* Artois Regiment; Bourgogne Regiment; Cambis Regiment; Volontaires Étrangers Regiment

Unama'ki (Cape Breton Island), 287

Upper Canada, 283

Utrecht, Treaty of (1713), 7, 32, 89; leaving unclear boundaries, 57, 74

Vauban, Sébastien Le Prestre de, 49, 50
Vaudreuil, François-Pierre de Rigaud de: directs campaign on interior of North America, 121; as prisoner in Halifax, 92, 93
Vauquelin, Jean: as commander of *Aréthuse*, 228–29, 244, 245, 248, 249, 254–55, 282, 291
Vendes Turgot, 291
Vergor, Louis du Pont du Chambon de: commander at Beauséjour, 76–79, 80; at Quebec, 79, 80
Versailles, 3, 9, 11, 28, 49, 96, 145, 151, 152, 182, 227, 245, 255
Villejouin, Gabriel Rousseau de, 153, 179, 281
Villeray, 78
Virginia, 25, 30, 35, 84, 85
Volontaires Étrangers Regiment, 153–54, 155, 156, 157, 174, 175, 176, 178, 194, 212, 225, 227, 249, 250, 266, 294, 320n15; stealing money, 269–70
Voltaire, 17, 103, 280, 300n31

Waldo, Samuel, 179
War Office, 192
War of Jenkins Ear, 19
War of the Austrian Succession (King George's War), 5, 19, 20, 21, 29
War of the Spanish Succession, 13
Warren, Admiral Peter, 20, 29, 32, 136
Washington, George, 67
West Indies, 13, 16, 53, 66, 89, 151, 153, 190, 191, 192, 282
White Point. *See* Pointe Blanche (White Point)

Whitmore, Brigadier General Edward, 195, 196, 207, 209, 270, 271, 278, 280, 283; profile of 191–92
Williamson, Lieutenant Colonel George, 230, 248, 259
Wilmot, Montague, 192
Winslow, Lieutenant Colonel John, 74, 75, 310n70
Wolastoqiyik (Maliseet), 12, 19, 23, 37, 40, 54
Wolfe, Brigadier General James, 2, 79, 130, 181, 190, 191, 203, 288–89; comments at Halifax in 1758, 169–71, 172, 173; during landing of June 8, 214, 215–16, 220, 297–311; establishes battery at Lighthouse Point, 232, 233, 234, 235, 242; on the eve of 1758 siege, 195–96; frustration with Rochefort expedition, 1757, 138; at Green Hill and later batteries, 242, 245, 246, 250, 251, 255, 256, 261; profile of, 192–93; sentiments and opinions as siege advances, 229, 230, 243; after the victory of 1758, 272, 276–77, 279, 283; visiting town at end of siege, 270
women: attitude of Mi'kmaw and other Aboriginal women toward war, 163, 322n34; French women finding shelter during 1758 siege, 235; lady touring siege positions, 252; mentioned by Amherst as victims, 197; not listed among casualties, 273–74; participating in British expeditions, 172, 193, 323n58; Wolfe's comments about at end of siege, 270. *See also* Aubert de Courserac, Marie-Anne (Madame Drucour); Bégon, Madame; Congregation of Notre Dame, Sisters of
Wrong, G. M., 190

In the France Overseas series

The French Navy and the Seven Years' War
Jonathan R. Dull

French Colonialism Unmasked
The Vichy Years in French West Africa
Ruth Ginio

Endgame 1758
The Promise, the Glory, and the Despair
of Louisbourg's Last Decade
A. J. B. Johnston

Making the Voyageur World
Travelers and Traders in the
North American Fur Trade
Carolyn Podruchny

A Workman Is Worthy of His Meat
Food and Colonialism in Gabon
Jeremy Rich

Silence Is Death
The Life and Work of Tahar Djaout
Julija Šukys

Beyond Papillon
The French Overseas Penal Colonies, 1854–1952
Stephen A. Toth

Madah-Sartre
The Kidnapping, Trial, and Conver(sat/s)ion
of Jean-Paul Sartre and Simone de Beauvoir
Written and translated by Alek Baylee Toumi
With an introduction by James D. Le Sueur